RESIDENTIAL REAL ESTATE APPRAISAL

Second Edition

Residential Real Estate Appraisal, Second Edition

Published by Anthony Schools® Corporation
San Leandro, California 94578

© 1990, 1987 by Anthony Schools® Corporation

ISBN 0-941833-30-5

Anthony Schools®

Anthony Schools
Real Estate
College Level Courses

Escrows Principles and Procedures
Legal Aspects of Real Estate
Real Estate Appraisal
Real Estate Economics
Real Estate Finance
Real Estate Office Administration
Real Estate Practice
Real Estate Principles
Real Estate Property Management

EDITORIAL AND
EXECUTIVE OFFICES
Anthony Schools Corporation
15942 Foothill Blvd., Suite 100
San Leandro, CA 94578

CONTINUING EDUCATION
INDEPENDENT STUDY OFFICES
Anthony Schools Corporation
15942 Foothill Blvd., Suite 200
San Leandro, CA 94578

COLLEGE-LEVEL
INDEPENDENT STUDY OFFICES
Anthony Schools Corporation
POB 18827
Irvine, CA 92713-8827

Residential Real Estate Appraisal, Second Edition

Published by Anthony Schools® Corporation
San Leandro, California 94578

© 1990, 1987 by Anthony Schools® Corporation

ISBN 0-941833-30-5

ACKNOWLEDGMENT

The publisher wishes to acknowledge the following who have greatly contributed to this book:
Arlen C. Mills, MAI, and Dorothy Mills; American Realty Forms, Inc.; Forms and Worms, Inc.; and Fannie Mae's
"Focus: Appraisal Guide"

DISCLAIMER

This material is for educational purposes only. In no way should any statements or summaries be used as a
substitute for legal or tax advice.

10 9 8 7 6 5 4 3 2

Printed in Hong Kong

Contents

APPENDICES

LIST OF EXHIBITS

WHAT IS AN APPRAISAL?

An appraisal is a supportable or defensible *estimate* of value as of a particular point in time. Appraisers do not make or determine value; they form well-supported estimates of value which are substantiated by the appraiser's research. Since appraising is not an exact science, competent appraisers may differ in their opinions of value but, in most instances, the variance will not be too large.

Variance. Variance exists because value is not intrinsic in real property and appraising is not an exact science. Value is dependent on the expectations of both buyers and sellers and is not always easily measured. Conforming tract homes in active markets will have a smaller potential variance ($\pm 5\%$) than unique properties.

Objectivity. An estimate of value is only as reliable as the ability and objectivity of the appraiser. Uninformed opinions are subjective and of relatively little value. Nonobjective opinions are unethical and are dangerous in a free market. Buyers of appraisal services must be able to assume that the appraiser is a disinterested third party.

Purposes of Appraisals

All appraisals have the same purpose—to estimate the defined value of a property interest in real estate. Typical questions asked of the appraiser include: What is the market value of the property? What is the highest and best use of the land as vacant or improved? What is the value of the portion taken in condemnation?

Lending. Government regulatory agencies which supervise the lending activities of banks, savings and loan associations, insurance companies, credit unions, pension funds, and other lending entities, usually require a professional appraisal. For single-family residences, a form report is usually satisfactory. The government makes stringent requirements as to form and support in appraisals for loans where government insurance or guarantees are involved.

Underwriting Decisions. Lenders look at appraisal data not only for the value, but for the value trends which affect loan security. Lending institutions make underwriting decisions based on the data, analyses, and conclusions set forth in the appraisal. These underwriting decisions include:

☐ The loan-to-value ratio or the amount to be loaned as a percentage of value.

☐ The appropriate number of years over which to amortize the principal of the loan based on value trends in the area and the age and condition of the property.

☐ The appropriate interest rate considering the lender's cost of money and the relative risk of loss through foreclosure of the loan.

Insurance. Lending institutions insist that property be insured against fire loss at a level sufficient to replace the improvements. Failure to insure at replacement value will be interpreted as co-insurance by the property owner.

Example

If replacement value is $100,000 and there is only $60,000 of insurance coverage, the property owner is presumed to be self-insuring for 40% of any loss. A $10,000 partial loss would result in only a $6,000 claim settlement.

Tax Assessment. County assessors employ staff appraisers to appraise real property in their counties. Property taxes in California are not to exceed 1% of the full cash value, to be collected by the counties and apportioned according to law.

☐ Proposition 13, a state constitutional amendment passed in 1978, established "full cash value" as the value shown in the 1975-76 tax bill, or the appraisal value of real property when purchased, newly constructed, or when a change in ownership occurs.

☐ The value base may reflect an inflation rate not to exceed 2% for any given year, or reductions as shown in the consumer price index.

Separate values are required for land and improvements since certain types of improvement bonds are assessed only against land. Assessed value is usually based on a form report setting forth physical data: age, size, features, etc. Many assessors in larger counties use a statistical technique called multiple regression to appraise all conforming single-family residences. When contesting their assessments, property owners frequently engage an independent appraiser to appraise their property and present the appraisal at a tax appeal hearing.

Eminent Domain (Condemnation). "Eminent domain" refers to the right of government to acquire private property for public purposes upon payment of just compensation. City, county, state, and federal governments, school districts, public utilities, redevelopment agencies, flood control districts, and other special districts can all acquire property through eminent domain. Public agencies employ staff or independent fee appraisers to appraise the property being acquired.

If a property owner contests the valuation by a public agency, an independent appraiser may be engaged by owner. If the property owner's appraiser is of the opinion that the property is worth more than the public agency's appraiser's opinion, a trial may be necessary. The court weighs the evidence and testimony of the appraisers and gives final opinion of just compensation.

Disputes Over Division of Property. Dissolution of a business partnership or marriage frequently requires a division of assets. Parties to a dispute may disagree on the value of the real property portion of their assets. The parties may jointly agree to engage an appraiser, or each party may separately engage an appraiser.

Employee Transfers. Many corporations have a policy of buying the homes of employee transferred from one location to another. One or more fee appraisers may be engaged to prepare a report on the employee's house. The employee is immediately paid, and the company arranges for sale of the employee's house through a local broker.

Inheritance Tax. The State of California engages inheritance tax referees to appraise property subject to state inheritance tax. Likewise, the Internal Revenue Service has staff appraisers called "valuation engineers" to value property for federal inheritance taxes. Heirs may engage their own appraiser, and if the conclusions vary, they may contest the state or federal taxes assessed.

Setting Listing Price. Most often, the seller of a property is assisted by the listing real estate broker or salesperson, who reviews recent sales in the neighborhood and recommends a listing price. The listing price should not be so high as to discourage buyers or so low that the property owner suffers a loss from a sale at less than market value. Occasionally, and usually with more complex properties, the seller may engage a professional appraiser.

Setting Offer Price. For single-family homes, buyers usually make their own "appraisal" after shopping the property and comparing it with others available. Buyers of larger properties (e.g., shopping centers, office buildings, and industrial parks) frequently engage a professional appraiser.

Other Uses. Occasionally a property owner will need a current appraisal for secondary financing or a home equity loan, for use in a financial statement, to substantiate casualty losses for tax purposes, to substantiate depreciable basis for investment properties, or to determine the tax basis for a charitable deduction.

Contents of Appraisal Reports

Written reports set forth all the relevant data and the reasoning of the appraiser which leads to a conclusion of value. The major items which should be included are:

Purpose of the Report. Basically, an appraisal is an answer to a question. The question may be simple or complex. Usually it is to estimate market value.

Property Rights Appraised. Usually a fee interest is being appraised, but it may be a leasehold or a fractional interest in ownership. It may be air rights over a specific area, or it may be designated subsurface rights. The appraiser cannot define the problem precisely without knowing exactly what property rights are involved.

Date of Value Opinion. The date of value opinion is not synonymous with date of preparation of the report. It is usually the last day the property was inspected. The specific date is important because the factors that affect value are always changing. Any date in the past may be used if required for legal proceedings, but use of a future date of value is usually considered improper.

Limiting Conditions. Assumptions and premises of the report should be set forth.

Definition of Market Value. The report should include the definition of market value the appraiser is working under.

Description of the Property. The report should include a clear and complete description of the property, including:

- ☐ Full address, legal description, owner of record.

- ☐ The neighborhood should be described including all features which affect value.

- ☐ The site should be described as to its size, dimensions, shape, topography, view, utilities and sewers, streets and access, easements, etc.

- ☐ A plot plan showing the dimension of the lot, width of fronting street, any alleys, and the distance to the nearest corner, is usually required.

- ☐ A complete physical description of the improvements, including size, construction, age, features, quality, condition, and functional utility is normally required.

- ☐ Property taxes, assessed value, and tax rates are usually included.

Statement of "Highest and Best Use."

Value Estimates. Data and analyses for the appropriate approaches to value and an indicated value from each approach to value.

Reconciliation. The report should include a reconciliation of the various indications into a final conclusion of value.

Signature and Certification. The report should include a signed statement that the:

☐ Appraiser has inspected the property.

☐ Appraiser has no past, present, or contemplated interest in the property or the outcome of the report.

☐ Fee is not contingent upon the value reported.

Exhibits and Photographs. As an addendum to the report, where appropriate.

Appraiser's Qualifications. A statement of the appraiser's training and experience.

Types of Appraisal Reports

The appraisal report may be oral or written. Written reports include letter reports, narrative reports and form reports. The client usually specifies the type and content of report.

Oral Reports. Where a close, continuing relationship exists between appraiser and client, an appraiser may give only an oral summary of investigation, analysis, and conclusion. Most clients will still want or need a letter or memorandum summarizing and documenting the oral report. Buyers of single-family residences normally make their own informal appraisal by simply inspecting the property and comparing it to others.

Letter Reports. A letter report communicates an estimate of value and typically includes a brief summary description of the property, the investigation undertaken, and the conclusion, without setting forth all the data and calculations. The appraiser must still have supporting market data and analyses on file. An intuitive guess set down in writing is not a letter appraisal; it is merely an intuitive guess.

Narrative Reports. A narrative report is the most comprehensive and complete discussion of the appraisal problem, the property, the market data, and how the analysis of that data leads to a given conclusion of value. The narrative appraisal report frequently consists of forty to sixty typewritten pages or more, following a style and outline discussed later in the text. Some lenders, attorneys, governmental agencies, and corporations (for employee transfers) will accept only a full narrative appraisal report.

Form Reports. The form report is a structured form of one to four pages, with checklists, questions, and blanks for brief remarks or comments. It typically includes most items contained in a narrative report but in a briefer, standardized format. An advantage is that it allows lenders and governmental agencies to quickly review a large volume of appraisals. Since the form report is relatively easy to complete after the field work is done, lending institutions using form reports usually expect each staff appraiser to prepare two or three reports per day, depending on the complexity of the properties and the location of the assignments.

Standard Forms. By far the most widely used form report for residential appraisals is the *Uniform Residential Appraisal Report (URAR)* form, which is required by HUD/FHA, the USDVA, the Farmers Home Administration (FmHA), FNMA and FHLMC. Additional forms used by governmental agencies include the *Individual Condominium or PUD Unit Appraisal Report* and the *Small Residential Income Property Appraisal Report*. In addition, the Employee Relocation Council (ERC), a private organization which assists in the transfer of corporate employees, has developed its own form for use by members, the *Employee Relocation Council (ERC) Residential Appraisal Report*. These forms are reproduced in the Appendix.

THE PROFESSIONAL APPRAISER

Anyone can offer an opinion of value. A professional appraiser is one whose training and experience constitute preparation for full-time, specialized occupation in the field.

Characteristics of a Profession The classical definition of a profession includes such characteristics as:

- ☐ Required specialized educational program.

- ☐ Supervised training and experience to qualify for professional status.

- ☐ Continuing education through seminars, advanced courses, and professional journals.

- ☐ Standards of professional conduct, with a code of ethics governing conduct.

- ☐ Means of recognizing professional competence.

- ☐ Self policing of members through an ethics committee.

Professional Organizations A number of professional organizations for appraisers exist. Those active in the United States, and the professional designations they grant, include the following.

Appraisal Institute. This is the leading appraisal organization, a newly created body resulting from the unification of the American Institute of Real Estate Appraisers and the Society of Real Estate Appraisers. The AIREA was formerly a member group of the National Association of Realtors®, and the SREA grew out of lending institutions and has been an important publisher of comparable sales data. The Appraisal Institute will offer two professional designations, the MAI and the SRA.

MAI Member of the Appraisal Institute, the most prestigious of all appraisal designations, conferred upon appraisers who are considered competent to perform all forms of real estate appraisals. All current SREAs (Senior Real Estate Analyst, the equivalent designation of the Society of Real Estate Appraisers) will be offered the MAI designation. Appraisers holding the Society's SRPA (Senior Real Property Appraiser) designation will have the opportunity to obtain the MAI by fulfilling certain requirements.

SRA Senior Residential Appraiser, the designation for appraisers principally specializing in the valuation of residential property. All current RMs (Residential Member, of the AIREA) will be offered the SRA designation.

American Society of Appraisers. This group represents both real estate appraisers and appraisers of personal property, from works of art to equipment of all types.

ASA American Society of Appraisers, the designation conferred on members whose activity is principally in the valuation of real property.

FASA Fellow of the American Society of Appraisers, designed for members with some designated specialization in personal property appraisal, such as jewelry, equipment, or livestock.

National Association of Real Estate Appraisers. In conjunction with real estate schools around the country, this group offers the designation:

CREA Certified Real Estate Appraiser, the designation for appraisers specializing in the valuation of residential property.

National Association of Review Appraisers and Mortgage Underwriters. This group is devoted to improving appraisal quality and the level of professionalism in real estate loan underwriting.

CRA Certified Review Appraiser, the designation conferred on those who specialize in the review appraisal process.

RMU Registered Mortgage Underwriter, the designation given to those who specialize in business decisions relative to extension of credit using real estate as security.

Requirements for Designations Although each professional association has developed its own set of requirements for professional designations, common to many of them are:

A college degree or equivalent.

Beginning, intermediate, and advanced appraisal courses.

Special examinations.

□ Two to five years full-time professional experience (depending on designation).

□ Evaluation of previous appraisal work (for some designations).

□ Preparation of special demonstration appraisal reports (some designations).

□ Interviews and oral examinations by admissions committee.

Codes Of Ethics Although each professional association, as well as the Appraisal Foundation (see page 10), has adopted its own specific code of ethics or standards of professional conduct, the following provisions are typical:

□ Advocacy and bias are prohibited; the appraisal must be objective.

□ The appraiser must disclose any past, present or future personal interest in the property being appraised.

□ Appraisal findings must be kept confidential with the client.

□ An appraiser should not accept assignments for which he or she is not qualified unless outside assistance from a qualified professional is obtained and such assistance is revealed to the client.

□ The appraiser should perform in a professional and competent manner and conform to professional methods of appraisal.

□ Making appraisal fees contingent on specific findings is unethical.

□ Paying referral fees to others is considered unethical.

California Commissioner's Regulations (a) Unlawful Conduct in Sale, Lease and Exchange Transactions. Licensees when performing acts within the meaning of Section 10131 (a) of the Business and Professions Code shall not engage in conduct which would subject the licensee to adverse action, penalty or discipline under Sections 10176 and 10177 of the Business and Professions Code including, but not limited to, the following acts and omissions:

□ *Commissioner's Regulation 2785(a)(1)*. Knowingly making a substantial misrepresentation of the likely value of real property to: (A) Its owner either for the purpose of securing a listing or for the purpose of acquiring an interest in the property for the licensee's own account. (B) A prospective buyer for the purpose of inducing the buyer to make an offer to purchase the real property.

□ *Commissioner's Regulation 2785(a)(8)*. Making an addition to or modification of the terms of an instrument previously signed or initialed by a party to a transaction without the knowledge and consent of the party.

To promote ethical business practices of real estate licensees, the Real Estate Commissioner has issued Suggestions for Professional Conduct as a companion to the Code of Professional Conduct (Section 2785, Title 10, California Code of Regulations) including the following:

☐ *Suggestions for Professional Conduct (a)(9) and (b)(4).*
  - Advertise or claim to be an expert in an area of specialization in real estate brokerage activity, e.g., appraisal, property management, industrial siting, mortgage loan, etc., only if the licensee has had special training, preparation, or experience.

☐ *Suggestions for Professional Conduct (a)(11) and (b)(6).* Base opinions of value, whether for the purpose of advertising or promoting real estate brokerage business (or mortgage loan brokerage business) upon documented objective data.

APPRAISER LICENSING AND CERTIFICATION

The Financial Institutions Reform, Recovery and Enforcement Act (FIRREA), the "FSLIC Bailout Bill," was passed by Congress in 1989. Title XI of this Act, known as the Real Estate Appraisal Reform Amendment, requires the use of state-licensed or state-certified appraisers in federally related transactions and outlines procedures for monitoring the state appraisal regulatory agencies and for establishing the requirements for appraisers and standards for appraisals.

Federally Related Transaction This is defined as any real estate related financial transaction, such as the sale, purchase, lease, investment in or exchange of real property, including interests in property or the financing or refinancing or use as security for a loan or investment, which a federal financial institutions regulatory agency or the Resolution Trust Corporation (RTC) engages in, contracts for, or regulates and which requires the services of an appraiser.

Agencies **Federal Financial Institutions Regulatory Agencies.** These five agencies are the Comptroller of the Currency, Federal Deposit Insurance Corporation, Federal Reserve Bank, National Credit Union Administration, and Office of Thrift Supervision.

Federal Financial Institutions Examination Council. The FFIEC is the federal agency which appointed the members of the Appraisal Subcommittee (see below). FFIEC consists of representatives of the five federal regulatory agencies listed above.

Office of Management and Budget. The OMB is the executive branch's agency which controls the policies of the FHA, the USDVA, the Farmers Home Administration, and others.

The Appraisal Subcommittee. Established under FFIEC, the Subcommittee is responsible for the approval and monitoring of state appraisal regulatory systems; maintaining a national registry of licensed and certified appraisers; and monitoring activities of the Appraisal

Foundation, the federal financial institutions regulatory agencies and the Resolution Trust Corporation (RTC) relative to appraisal regulation.

Appraisal Foundation. This is a nonprofit corporation organized by a number of appraisal trade organizations. Under Title XI, the Foundation is authorized to develop qualification criteria for licensed and certified appraisers and standards of practice for those appraisers involved in federally related transactions.

Appraiser Qualifications Board. The AQB of the Foundation develops the qualification criteria for licensed and certified appraisers. It is also responsible for the development and approval of certification examinations.

Appraisal Standards Board. The ASB of the Foundation develops the minimum standards for use by appraisers involved in federally related transactions.

Federal Regulations

The RTC and the five federal financial institutions regulatory agencies listed above have issued *Appraisal Standards for Federally Related Transactions*. State certified or licensed appraisers, as appropriate, must be used for federally related transactions by July 1, 1991, unless this deadline is extended by the Appraisal Subcommittee for a given state. Appraisals must comply with the standards by August 9, 1990.

Appraisals Not Required. For any transaction in which: the transaction value is $100,000 or less; a lien on real property has been taken as collateral solely through an abundance of caution and where the terms of the transaction as a consequence have not been made more favorable than they would have been in the absence of a lien; a lease of real estate is entered into, unless the lease is the economic equivalent of a purchase or sale of the leased real estate; there is a subsequent transaction resulting from a maturing extension of credit, with certain provisions; a regulated institution purchases a loan or interest in a loan, pooled loans, or interest in real property, including mortgage-backed securities, provided that the appraisal prepared for each pooled loan or real property interest met the requirements of this regulation, if applicable.

Transactions Requiring a State Certified Appraiser. All transactions of $1,000,000 or more; nonresidential transactions of $250,000 or more; and complex residential transactions of $250,000 or more.

Transactions Requiring a State Certified or Licensed Appraiser. All appraisals for federally related transactions not requiring the services of a State certified appraiser shall be prepared by either a State certified appraiser or a State licensed appraiser.

Standards. The federal regulations also establish standards by which appraisals must be performed in federally related transactions. Generally these regulations require all appraisals, at a minimum, to conform to the Uniform Standards of Professional Practice adopted by the ASB of the Appraisal Foundation.

AQB Qualifications Criteria

The Appraiser Qualifications Board has adopted qualifications for two levels of appraiser classifications: residential and general.

Residential Appraiser. The residential appraiser classification applies primarily for one to four units, and the qualifications include:

☐ Successful completion of a written exam that tests various items, including ethics and conduct.

☐ A four year college degree, or successful completion of 75 classroom hours of courses in subjects related to real estate appraisal including 15 classroom hours related to the Standards of Professional Practice and provisions of the state act.

☐ Equivalent of two years experience within the previous five years. The experience must be supported by adequate written reports or file memoranda. A detailed listing of the reports or file memoranda shall be furnished for each year's experience claimed. The materials substantiating experience may need to be submitted.

☐ The certification shall be not less than two, nor more than four years.

General Appraiser. The qualifications for the general appraiser are:

☐ Successful completion of a written exam that tests various items, including ethics and conduct.

☐ A four year college degree, or successful completion of 165 classroom hours of courses in subjects related to real estate appraisal including 15 classroom hours related to the Standards of Professional Practice and provisions of the state act.

☐ Equivalent of two years experience within the previous five years. The experience must be supported by adequate written reports or file memoranda. A detailed listing of the reports or file memoranda shall be furnished for each year's experience claimed. Supporting materials may need to be submitted.

☐ The certification shall be not less than two, nor more than four years.

Continuing Education. The AQB has adopted mandatory continuing education as a renewal requirement for both levels of appraiser classifications—the equivalent of 10 classroom hours per year.

California Legislation

California AB527 has enacted the Real Estate Appraisers' Licensing and Certification Law commencing with Section 11300 of the B&P Code. This bill, passed by the legislature in July, 1990:

☐ Requires that on or after July 1, 1991, any person who engages in or proposes to engage in federally related real estate appraisal activity to be licensed or certified.

□ Repeals the Lancaster-Montoya Appraisal Act as of July 1, 1991.

"Appraisal" is defined as a written statement independently and impartially prepared by a qualified appraiser setting forth an opinion in a federally related transaction as to the market value of an adequately described property as of a specific date, supported by the presentation and analysis of relevant market information. The term *"appraisal"* does not include an opinion given by a real estate licensee, engineer, or land surveyor in the ordinary course of his or her business in connection with a function for which [his or her] license is required. It also does not include an opinion rendered to the court by a probate referee.

"Federally related transaction" is defined as any real estate-related financial transaction which a federal financial institutions regulatory agency engages in, contracts for or regulates and which requires the services of a real estate appraiser or state certified real estate appraiser regulated by this part. This term also includes any transaction identified as such by a federal financial institutions regulatory agency.

□ Allows a state certified real estate appraiser to use the abbreviation SCREA in his or her real property appraisal business and designate any appraisal which he or she performed, prepared, made, or approved and signed as a "certified real estate appraisal."

□ Creates the Office of Real Estate Appraisers to administer and enforce this law, and a Real Estate Appraisers' Advisory Committee to assist the director of the Office of Real Estate Appraisers.

□ Requires the director to adopt regulations governing the process of applying for certification as a state certified real estate appraiser which shall meet, at a minimum, the requirements and standards established by the Appraisal Foundation, RTC, and the federal financial institutions regulatory agencies acting in pursuant of FIRREA.

□ Allows the director to recognize on a temporary basis the certification or license of an appraiser issued by another state provided the appraiser registers with California, and the certification or licensing standards of the appraiser's state meet or exceed the standards required by California law.

□ Requires continuing education in compliance with the requirements of the Appraisal Foundation and the Appraisal Subcommittee.

□ Establishes examination and license/certification fees.

□ Creates a Real Estate Appraisers Regulation Fund consisting of an Administration Account and a Recovery Account.

FANNIE MAE/FREDDIE MAC

Fannie Mae is a uniquely structured company operating in the secondary mortgage market. Created by Congress as the Federal National Mortgage Association, FNMA or Fannie Mae helps ensure the vitality of American home financing by providing liquidity to the market for single-family and multifamily residential mortgage loans. Fannie Mae is the nation's largest investor in American home mortgages. Its assets of approximately $100 billion make Fannie Mae the third largest corporation in the United States, with its stock publicly traded on the New York and other major stock exchanges. Congress later enacted the Federal Home Loan Mortgage Corporation (Freddie Mac) to provide a similar secondary mortgage money market for the savings and loan industry.

Locations Fannie Mae is headquartered in Washington, DC, and has regional offices in Atlanta, Chicago, Dallas, Los Angeles, and Philadelphia. Fannie Mae Software Systems, a division based in Norcross, Georgia, develops mortgage-related software products.

Role As a federally chartered company, Fannie Mae fulfills the unique role it has been asked to play since 1968—a tax-paying private company serving a public purpose of providing liquidity to the mortgage market. By purchasing mortgage loans from banks, savings and loans, mortgage bankers, and other lenders, the corporation provides mortgage lenders with new capital to lend to home buyers. Fannie Mae also provides liquidity to the mortgage marketplace through its mortgage-backed security (MBS) guaranty activities.

Servicing The servicing of Fannie Mae-owned mortgages—collection on monthly payments and other dealings with homeowners—is retained by the lenders that originate the loans and sell them to Fannie Mae. This retained servicing permits lending institutions to maintain customer contact and community identity, while homeowners continue their relationship with their local lenders. Lenders receive a fee from Fannie Mae for performing this service.

Importance of the Appraisal The appraisal is a critical part of the mortgage underwriting process. The value of the property represents the ultimate security for the mortgage loan. As a mortgage investor and guarantor of mortgage-backed securities, Fannie Mae establishes standards for quality mortgages. Because the property value is such a critical part of the mortgage underwriting decision, it is important for the appraiser to provide the underwriter with all of the information needed to establish appropriate loan terms.

Responsibility for Appraisal Fannie Mae has no direct role in the processing, underwriting, approval, and closing of mortgages. It also does not approve appraisers or underwriters. The mortgage lender handles the total origination process, including appraiser selection. When delivering a mortgage to Fannie Mae, the lender certifies that it meets Fannie Mae's standards for a quality mortgage. This certification includes an assurance that the appraisal was prepared in accordance with the guidelines contained in the *Selling Guide*.

FNMA Standards Fannie Mae's standards are intended to inform underwriters and appraisers about the type of information needed to make a prudent underwriting decision. They provide what might be called minimum acceptable appraisal standards, recognizing that the appraiser's analysis may not comply with their specific guidelines for every appraisal assignment. The standards allow appraisers discretion in properly developing value estimates, but they must provide sound reasons in their appraisal reports for working outside of these standards, and are always required to provide complete and accurate reports. The estimate of market value must represent the appraiser's professional conclusion, based on market data, logical analysis, and judgment.

Time Limits The property must have been appraised within the 12 months that precede the date of the note and mortgage. When the appraisal report will be more than four months old on the date of the note and mortgage—regardless of whether the property was appraised as proposed or existing construction—the appraiser must inspect the exterior of the property and review current market data to determine that the property has not declined in value since the date of the original appraisal. Fannie Mae requires that the appraiser provide a certification to that effect, based on exterior inspection of the property and knowledge of current market conditions. The inspection and the certification must occur within the four months that precede the date of the note and mortgage. If the appraiser cannot make the required certification, Fannie Mae will require a new appraisal.

Proposed Construction For proposed construction, the appraisal may be based on plans and specifications if the lender obtains a certification of completion before it delivers the mortgage to Fannie Mae. This certification should be completed by the appraiser and must be accompanied by photographs of the complete improvements. The appraiser must certify that the improvements were completed in accordance with the requirements and conditions stated in the original appraisal report. Minor items that do not affect livability may be incomplete as long as the lender has arranged for an adequate escrow to guarantee their completion. Fannie Mae considers funds equal to at least one and one-half times the cost to complete the items as a reasonable amount to escrow.

Existing Construction For existing construction, the improvements must be complete when the mortgage is sold to Fannie Mae. The appraisal may be based on the condition of the property "as is" if minor conditions that do not affect the livability of the property exist—e.g., peeling paint or minor deferred maintenance—as long as the appraiser's estimate of value reflects the existence of these conditions. The lender does not need to require minor repairs to be completed before it sells the mortgage. The lender must review carefully the the appraisal for a property "as is" to assure that there are no deficiencies or conditions that affect livability.

Repairs and Certifications When there are incomplete items or conditions that do affect livability—such as a partially completed addition or renovation or physical deficiencies that could affect the soundness or structural integrity of the improvements—the property must be appraised subject to completion of the alternations or repairs. In such cases, the lender must obtain a certificate of completion from an appraiser before it delivers the mortgage to Fannie Mae. The certification does not need to include photographs unless those that accompanied the original appraisal report are no longer representative of the completed property.

Second Appraiser. Generally, the original appraiser should complete the certification of completion or value; however, the lender may use a substitute appraiser as long as it explains why the original appraiser was not used. The substitute appraiser must review the original appraisal and certify that the appraiser's estimate of market value was reasonable on the date of the original appraisal report.

Appraiser Qualifications Fannie Mae does not approve appraisers. Since lenders are responsible for the selection of appraisers and will be solely accountable for their performance, they ensure that an appraiser is qualified to appraise the particular types of property involved. If a lender chooses to rely on a specific appraiser or appraisal service to review qualifications or select an appraiser for the lender, the lender should at least establish qualifications. When the lender relies on an appraiser or appraisal service to make these selections, Fannie Mae will recommend that it require the appraiser or appraisal service to assume full responsibility for the quality of the appraisal. However, this will in no way relieve the lender of its warranties related to the appraisal or the condition of the property.

Appraisal Reviews. Sometimes a lender will approve an appraiser subject to the appraiser's work being reviewed and signed by a review appraiser. Typically, the review appraiser is the appraiser's employer or supervisor, who is also assuming full responsibility for the quality of the appraisal. The lender or its representative should review the qualifications of both the appraiser and the review appraiser, and should not rely solely on the qualifications of the review appraiser. Fannie Mae considers the appraiser to be the individual who personally inspected the subject property, inspected the exterior of the comparables, performed the analysis, and prepared, certified, and signed the report as the appraiser; therefore, Fannie Mae does not require review appraisers to sign appraisal reports. However, when a review appraiser does sign the appraisal, that individual is indicating concurrence with the contents of the appraisal report, and must indicate on the appraisal report form whether he or she personally inspected both the inside and the outside of the subject property.

Rejection of Appraisers. Fannie Mae has the right, at any time, to refuse to accept appraisals prepared by specific appraisers or to notify a lender that they will no longer accept appraisals prepared by a given appraiser. When this happens, the lender has a certain amount of time to clear its mortgage pipeline—after that, it must not submit mortgages secured by any properties that were appraised by that individual.

Review of Qualifications. When evaluating an appraiser's qualifications, a lender should review the appraiser's education and experience, sample appraisals, professional affiliations, and references from prior clients and employers. The appraiser must be experienced in appraising the types of properties that the lender intends to use his or her services for, and should be currently active in appraisal work. Before using an appraiser's services, the lender should be satisfied that the appraiser had demonstrated the ability to perform quality appraisals.

Professional Designations. Fannie Mae does not require professional appraisal designations, although they can be helpful to lenders in evaluating an appraiser's qualifications, particularly when the designation is from a nationally recognized organization that has formal experience, education, and ethics requirements that are strongly administered. If the lender considers an appraisal designation in its evaluation, it should be familiar with the appraisal organization's specific requirements to assure that the designation is evaluated appropriately.

Ongoing Review. Lenders must continually evaluate the quality of the appraiser's work through the normal underwriting review of all appraisal reports, as well as through the spot-check field review of appraisals as part of its quality control system. Lenders must be satisfied that any appraisers they use for spot-check field reviews are well qualified.

Reviewing the Appraisal Report Fannie Mae holds the lender responsible for the quality of the appraisal it uses to support the market value of a security property. Therefore, the lender must make sure that it not only provides the appraiser with appropriate information about the financing and sales data, but also that it has sufficient knowledge of Fannie Mae's appraisal requirements to enable it to determine that the appraiser has properly addressed their specific criteria and that the appraiser has not engaged in any unacceptable appraisal practices.

Lender-Supplied Information. The lender must tell the appraiser about all financing data and sales concessions for the property that will be, or have been, granted by anyone associated with the transaction. Generally, this can be accomplished by providing the appraiser a copy of the complete, ratified sales contract. If the lender is aware of additional pertinent information that is not included in the sales contract, it should inform the appraiser. Information that must be disclosed includes:

□ Settlement charges

□ Loan fees or charges

□ Discounts to the sales price

□ Payment of condominium/PUD fees

□ Interest rate buydowns or other below-market-rate financing

□ Credits or refunds of the borrower's expenses

□ Absorption of monthly payments

□ Assignment of rent payments

□ Non-realty items that were included in the transaction.

Unacceptable Practices The following are examples of appraisal practices that Fannie Mae considers unacceptable:

□ Inclusion of inaccurate factual data about the subject neighborhood, site, improvements, or comparable sales.

□ Failure to comment on negative factors with respect to the subject neighborhood, subject property, or proximity of the subject property to adverse influences.

□ Use of comparables which the appraiser has not personally inspected by at least driving by them.

□ Selection and use of inappropriate comparable sales or the failure to use comparables that are locationally and physically the most similar to the subject property.

□ Use of data—particularly comparable sales data—that was provided by parties who have a financial interest in the sale or financing of the subject property without verifying the information from a disinterested source. For example, it would be inappropriate to use comparable sales provided by the broker who is handling the sale of the subject property, unless the appraiser verifies the accuracy of the data with another source and makes an independent investigation to determine that the comparables provided were the best ones available.

□ Use of adjustments to the comparable sales that do not reflect the market's reaction to the differences between the subject property and the comparables, or failure to make adjustments when they are clearly indicated.

□ Valuation that is based—either partially or completely—on the race, color, or national origin of either the prospective owners or occupants of the property or of the present owners or occupants in the vicinity of the subject property.

□ Development of a valuation conclusion that is not supported by available market data.

Chapter 1 Quiz

1. Which statement is not true?

    (A) Value of property depends on the expectations of buyers and sellers
    (B) An appraisal is a supportable estimate of value as of a particular time
    (C) It is not necessary to analyze market data for a letter report
    (D) It is unethical for an appraiser to make a fee contingent upon specific findings

2. An appraisal is:

    (A) A mathematically precise forecast of value
    (B) A prediction of sales price
    (C) An estimate of sales price
    (D) An estimate of value

3. An appraiser may never obtain outside assistance on a property type with which he or she has no previous experience and is unfamiliar:

    (A) True
    (B) False

4. An appraisal may be necessary to establish a value for:

    (A) Condemnation
    (B) Inheritance taxes
    (C) Lending purposes
    (D) All of the above

5. Which of the following is recommended in the Real Estate Commissioner's Suggestions for Professional Conduct?

    (A) Exaggerating market value to secure a listing
    (B) Claiming to be an expert in appraisal without having special training or experience
    (C) Calling any real property evaluation an "appraisal," even if it is very informal
    (D) None of the above

6. Knowledge of appraisal is particularly useful to real estate licensees because it:

    (A) Is necessary to provide another source of income
    (B) Is required for the state real estate licensing examination
    (C) Enables them to assist clients in setting listing prices
    (D) All of the above

7. The appraisal report which sets forth a full discussion of the appraisal problem, the property, the market data, and how the analysis of that data leads to the conclusion of value is called a:

    (A) Long form report
    (B) Letter form report
    (C) Narrative report
    (D) Short form report

8. An appraiser:

    (A) Determines value
    (B) Determines price
    (C) Estimates value
    (D) Estimates price

9. Federal regulations require appraisers to be state licensed or state certified for appraisals of:

    (A) Certain properties in federally-related transactions
    (B) All properties within a given state
    (C) One- to four-family properties only
    (D) All properties other than one- to four-family homes

10. The organization that is responsible for the development and approval of appraisal certification examinations is the:

    (A) RTC
    (B) AQB
    (C) ASD
    (D) FFIEC

Chapter 2
Characteristics
of Real Property

PREVIEW

The Nature of Real Property

The Nature of Value

Market Value

Principles of Value

THE NATURE OF REAL PROPERTY

The legal concept of *real estate* includes not only the ground or soil, but everything which is attached to the earth. It includes not only the surface of the earth, but everything under it and over it. *Real property* includes land and all improvements both on and to the land. The terms "real estate" and "real property" are used synonymously in California. In most other states, real estate denotes the physical entity while real property refers to the bundle of legal rights inherent in the real estate. To avoid misunderstanding about the meaning of these terms, they are often further defined as follows:

Definitions **Real Estate**. Refers to the physical land and appurtenances, including structures, affixed to or resting on the land.

☐ *Land*. Includes the surface of the earth plus the areas above and below the surface.

☐ *Improvements*. Are constructions such as buildings, fences, etc.

Real Property. Refers to the interests, benefits, and rights inherent in the ownership of the physical real estate. It is the bundle of rights with which the ownership of real estate is endowed.

Distinguishing Characteristics of Real Property
The three most common characteristics of real property which distinguish it from personal property are:

Fixed Location. The physical entity cannot be transferred; only the rights in the property are transferable.

Durability. Land is virtually indestructible.

Uniqueness. Parcels may be similar, but each is unique due to its fixed location.

Legal Aspects: "Bundle of Rights" Certain rights are inherent in ownership of real property and guaranteed by law, but subject to certain limitations and restrictions. They include the right to:

☐ Possession

☐ Control

☐ Enjoyment

☐ Disposition

☐ Use

☐ Exclusion

☐ Right not to exercise any of the above rights.

Limitations on Ownership Three kinds of limitations affect real property ownership: public limitations, involuntary private limitations, and voluntary private limitations.

Public Limitations. These are based on four specific powers of government:

☐ *Taxes*. Property taxes constitute a lien on the real estate until paid. Failure to pay may result in a forced sale.

☐ *Eminent Domain*. Government has the right to take private property for the public good, with compensation for the market value of the property. This right has been extended to quasi-public bodies such as housing authorities and public utilities.

☐ *Police Power*. The state may limit the exercise of private rights in real property to serve the public health, safety, morals, and general welfare. The limitation is made without compensation. Zoning ordinances, building codes, and traffic regulations are based on the police power of government.

☐ *Escheat*. Ownership of property may return to the state if the owner dies leaving no will and no known heirs.

Involuntary Private Limitations. Placed by others on the real estate, these limitations "go with the land." They are usually due to an action or inaction by the owner which resulted in damages to the others.

☐ *Liens*. Charges against property whereby the property is used to secure a debt.

☐ *Encroachments*. Unauthorized uses of owner's property. In general, they are not legally enforceable, but may become "clouds" on the owner's title.

□ *Prescriptive Easements*. Continuous open and unauthorized use of property which may place limitations on the owner's title.

Voluntary Private Limitations. These are placed voluntarily by owners or others.

□ *Deed Restrictions*. These limitations "go with the land," regardless of owner. Most commonly they limit the type of use and intensity of use of the real estate.

□ *Easements*. An easement is a nonownership interest they held by one person in the land of another, allowing the first person partial use of land for a specific purpose.

□ *Leases*. Leases are contracts by which the rights of use and occupancy of real estate are transferred by the owner to another person for a specified period of time for a stated consideration.

□ *Mortgages and Deeds of Trust*. These are conveyances of interests in real property given as security for the payment of debts.

Implications for Appraisal

Immobility. Land cannot be moved to a better market. Thus market and neighborhood analyses are important in appraisal.

Highly Differentiated. Uniqueness of each parcel necessitates a special research study for each valuation problem.

Durability. Real property represents a long-term asset. It is an expensive asset due to its long-term earning expectations. Real property is used or transferred in large economic units. Debt financing is usually necessary and almost always desirable. Thus lenders have a long-term interest in an accurate valuation of each security property.

THE NATURE OF VALUE

"Value" is defined as a measure of the worth or desirability of a thing, usually expressed in monetary terms at a certain time. "Worth" is sometimes described as that for which a thing can be exchanged (substituted).

Determining Value

Objective. The most reliable method of valuation looks at the price at which a willing seller will sell and a willing buyer will buy when neither is under any abnormal pressure to act. This establishes the "market value" (reasonable value at a given price).

Subjective. A personal view of worth usually comes into play along with any objective analysis of the property.

Characteristics of Value	**Depends on Purchaser.** Value pertains to the relationship between a thing desired and a potential purchaser. Value is not inherent in an object. It is created, destroyed, or altered by the factors in this relationship.

Types of Value. There are many types of value applicable to real estate. Some examples are market value, mortgage loan value, and assessed value. In appraisal, market value is almost invariably the value being estimated. |
| **Creating Value** | The following four characteristics are the most important in the creation of value:

Utility. The item must be useful in satisfying human wants and needs.

Scarcity. Supply must be limited and difficult to replace.

Demand. Purchasers must be willing to acquire the goods. "Effective demand" is the *ability* to acquire the goods.

Transferability. The item must be capable of being exchanged. |

MARKET VALUE

The definitions given below are representative of the various views of market value. The current trend is to define market value in probabilistic terms rather than as the highest selling price.

	General Definition. Market value is the most probable selling price for a property, given a willing and able buyer and a willing seller.

Supreme Court. As defined by the California Supreme Court, market value is "the highest price, estimated in terms of money, that a property will bring if exposed for sale in the open market allowing a reasonable length of time to find a buyer who buys with full knowledge of all the uses to which the property is adapted and for which it is capable of being used, neither buyer nor seller being compelled to act."

Market Conditions. Alternatively, market value may be defined as the highest price in terms of money which a property will bring in a competitive and open market under all conditions requisite to a fair sale, the buyer and seller each acting prudently, knowledgeably, and assuming the price is not affected by undue stimulus. |
| **Price vs. Value** | There is a distinction between market value and market price. The price asked for the property and the price at which a property sold are historical facts and may or may not bear any specific relationship to market value. There are many factors that can cause price to deviate from value. |

The Buyer-Seller Relationship

Buyer-Seller Subjective Value Concept. At any given time, the great majority of properties are not available for sale at a price at which many buyers will purchase. This underlines the fact that price and value are not necessarily the same. Where the value of the buyer and seller coincide, neither gains from a transfer. Their valuations are the same. The market actually exists in the shaded area. Here the buyer and seller can adjust their estimates to agree on a market price. This is the area of negotiation. The seller must be convinced to go lower or the buyer to go higher.

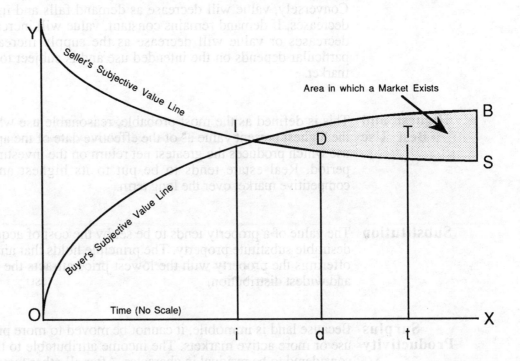

Source: Thurston H. Ross, *Some Economic Aspects of Urban Land Valuation* (Los Angeles: University of Southern California, 1933).

Factors Influencing Value. Many factors may influence either the buyer or seller. For example, there may be several competitive properties that could be purchased and the prospective buyer may consider them in comparison with the subject offering. The effective cost of money may influence the price a property can demand. The seller may be influenced by personal factors including the specific profit, capital gains or other taxes, and the selling cost. All of these considerations on the part of the prospective buyer and seller are subjective. The function of the appraiser is to analyze all such factors objectively and resolve them into a market value.

PRINCIPLES OF VALUE

The principles of land valuation are founded in economics. A comprehension of these concepts is essential to understanding the procedures of estimating value.

Supply and Demand Market value is determined by the interaction of the forces of supply and demand in the appropriate market as of the date of the appraisal. Value will increase as demand rises and decrease as supply expands. Conversely, value will decrease as demand falls and increase as supply decreases. If demand remains constant, value will increase as the supply decreases or value will decrease as the supply increases. Demand in particular depends on the intended use and is subject to change with the market.

Highest and Best Use This is defined as the most probable, reasonable use which will support the highest present value as of the effective date of the appraisal. It is that use which produces the greatest net return on the investment over a given period. Real estate tends to be put to its highest and best use in a competitive market over the long term.

Substitution The value of a property tends to be set by the cost of acquiring an equally desirable substitute property. The principle holds that among comparable offerings the property with the lowest price attracts the greatest demand and widest distribution.

Surplus Productivity Because land is immobile, it cannot be moved to more profitable areas of use or more active markets. The income attributable to the land or site is considered to be residual in character. After all other factors of production have been paid a competitive market return, the remaining income is available to the land. For all but marginal land for any use, the residual income will be in excess of the amount necessary to keep it in production or in the use in question. The surplus income is known as *economic rent* in economic analysis.

Balance The point of maximum productivity and maximum value is achieved when all factors of production (land, labor, capital, and coordination) are in balance with one another. In economic analysis, the point of maximum productivity or balance is known as the point of diminishing returns.

Contribution The value of a component depends upon how much its presence adds to or its absence detracts from the value of the whole. This principle is fundamental to any consideration of the feasibility of remodeling or modernization. (Known also as marginal productivity.)

Increasing and Decreasing Returns When successive amounts of one or more factors are added to fixed amounts of other factors, the resulting benefits, in dollars or amenities, first increase at an increasing rate (the law of increasing returns). When the maximum value has been developed (the point of decreasing returns), any additional expenditures do not produce a return commensurate with these additional investments (the law of decreasing returns).

Anticipation The value of real property is a function of the expected benefits of ownership. The future, not the past, is important in deriving opinions of value.

Change A fundamental characteristic of the real estate market is its continual shifts in supply and demand. Accordingly, a value estimate is valid only as of a specific point in time. Each property has a life cycle, determined by the market. Age is not the major consideration in determining where in the cycle a property lies. Economic and social influences, as well as physical condition, are the indicators the appraiser looks for to place the property in its life cycle.

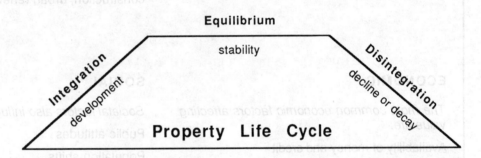

Conformity A reasonable degree of conformance tends to maximize value. The standards of conformity are subject to the principle of change.

Progression. Property tends to increase in value when surrounded by properties of greater value.

Regression. Property tends to decrease in value when surrounded by properties of lesser value.

Competition Moderate profits or benefits attract healthy competition. Excess profits or benefits bring ruinous competition, eventually reducing profits. Profit as applied to real property implies that when net income exceeds the requirements of labor, capital, coordination, and land the excess constitutes profit and encourages competition.

FACTORS INFLUENCING VALUE

PHYSICAL

Common physical factors influencing value are:

Size and shape: odd-sized, irregular-shaped parcels are more difficult to develop.

Accessibility, proximity to good transportation and service facilities.

Homogeneity of surrounding land uses.

Freedom from physical hazards.

Adequacy of utilities, availability of water, power, etc.

Soil composition and drainage.

Climatic conditions.

POLITICAL/GOVERNMENTAL

Political and governmental factors affecting value include:

Federal financing guarantees.

Federal housing and rent subsidies.

Zoning laws.

Building codes.

Environmental impact statements, required for all private and public projects having a significant impact on environmental quality.

Environmental protection policies, for example, the California Coastal Protection Act.

Public works projects, For example, freeway construction, urban renewal, etc.

ECONOMIC

The most common economic factors affecting value are:

Availability of money and credit

Interest rates

Taxation levels

Basic industry production

Private employment

Expansion or contraction

Wage levels

Local government activity

SOCIAL

Societal factors also influence value:

Public attitudes

Population shifts

Changes in family size

Rate of household formation or dissolution, for example, the number of marriages and divorces per year.

Pride of ownership

Chapter 2 Quiz

1. Market value is:

   (A) The most probable selling price
   (B) Equal to the cost of production
   (C) Determined by the appraiser
   (D) What the purchaser is willing to pay

2. The taking of real property to create a public park illustrates the government's right of:

   (A) Police power
   (B) Escheat
   (C) Encroachment
   (D) Eminent domain

3. The four elements which create value are:

   (A) Scarcity, demand, utility, transferability
   (B) Utility, scarcity, supply, transferability
   (C) Effective demand, immobility, durability, exclusivity
   (D) Supply, utility, desire, fixed location

4. The public limitations on free exercise of private property rights are:

   (A) Taxation, eminent domain, police power, liens
   (B) Taxation, police power, easements, escheat.
   (C) Taxation, eminent domain, police power, escheat.
   (D) Taxation, police power, escheat, liens.

5. If the demand for homes remains constant and the supply:

   (A) Decreases, the value will increase
   (B) Remains constant, the value will decrease
   (C) Remains constant, the value will increase
   (D) Increases, the value will increase

6. The Petersons found a home they liked very much but decided not to buy it after learning the price. Their reasoning was probably based on the principle of:

   (A) Anticipation
   (B) Highest and best use
   (C) Change
   (D) Substitution

7. A home which cost $75,000 is surrounded by homes priced substantially higher. Which principle would be most applicable to the $75,000 home in a current appraisal?

   (A) Substitution
   (B) Contribution
   (C) Progression
   (D) Regression

8. Which of the following is not one of the four factors in the production of income?

   (A) Depreciation
   (B) Capital
   (C) Land
   (D) Coordination

9. The integration of a much more expensive home into a neighborhood of smaller, modest homes will most likely:

   (A) Increase the value of the smaller homes
   (B) Decrease the value of the more expensive home
   (C) Increase the value of the more expensive home
   (D) Not exert any influence on housing values in the neighborhood

10. The value of a property tends to be set by the cost of acquiring an equally desirable property. This is a statement of the principle of:

    (A) Substitution
    (B) Balance
    (C) Competition
    (D) Appraisal

PREVIEW

The Nature of a Market

Real Estate Markets

Determinants of Supply and Demand for Residential Properties

Money Markets and Mortgage Markets

THE NATURE OF A MARKET

Definition A market is a system or activity which brings buyers and sellers together through the price mechanism.

☐ There may or may not be a physical marketplace where exchanges occur.

☐ Money, rights, tangible goods, or services may be exchanged. Markets exist for virtually all goods and services which have value and are transferable.

☐ Separate markets exist for all types of goods and services, and are interrelated by their susceptibility to general economic trends.

Purposes The four main purposes of markets are:

☐ Bringing buyers and sellers together.

☐ Setting prices based on the interaction of supply and demand. Markets determine prices; they do not determine value. *Supply* is the quantity of goods or services which sellers offer or will offer to sell at a corresponding series of prices. *Demand* is the quantity of goods or services that are or will be bought by purchasers at a corresponding series of prices.

☐ Allocating goods and services among buyers according to the price that they are willing to pay.

☐ Adjusting supply to demand.

A "Perfect Market" A true competitive market in economic theory is characterized by:

Interchangeable Products. The products offered for sale in a particular market are essentially the same and one unit can be substituted for another. Decisions to buy or sell are based solely on price.

Many Informed Participants. There are large numbers of buyers and sellers, each of whom is well informed about the market and the products.

Rational Behavior. All participants are assumed to behave rationally so as to maximize their own economic well-being.

Absence of Regulation. There is little or no government intervention in the market.

Price Mechanism. The market operates systematically to bring buyers and sellers together. The price mechanism is a balancing agent, always moving the market towards equilibrium.

Competition. Competition exists openly and freely among units of the product (e.g., among various residences of the same type) and among participants in the market.

REAL ESTATE MARKETS

Real estate markets bring buyers and sellers together to exchange rights in realty at mutually advantageous prices. The markets adjust supply to demand and allocate urban space among competing uses.

Various Markets. Various types of real estate markets exist, including sale markets and rental markets. Markets may also be classified by property type, use, price level, location, or by the rights being transferred. Only those products which are perceived as competitive by potential buyers are included in a given market.

An Imperfect Market **Few and Unique Products.** Each product in a real estate market is unique because of its location and immobility. While acceptable substitutes may exist for a given property, there are no perfect substitutes. Thus, the effective market for a specific property or property type is often limited by locational considerations to a small geographical area.

Few Participants, Little Information. There are relatively few buyers and sellers for each particular segment of a market. Since most market information regarding individual transactions is considered confidential, the participants are relatively uninformed.

Subjectivity. Buyers and sellers sometimes fail to behave in a rational manner because their decisions are based on limited knowledge and subjective (emotional) judgments.

Regulation. The extent of government regulation and restriction of real estate market activities is evidenced by zoning and land use controls, regulation of financial institutions dealing in real estate, and the large body of law regarding the transfer of rights in real estate.

Limited Competition. There are numerous submarkets within each real estate market. The pertinent submarket includes only those properties which potential buyers and sellers perceive as competitive with the subject property.

Demand   **Supply and Demand**. Supply of residential properties is relatively slow to respond to change in demand. Construction of additions to the supply may take several months. Legal, financial, and physical factors also slow the supply response.

Basic Demand. Basic demand in residential real estate is a measure of the total need for shelter. It is a function of population size and characteristics, representing the number of households needing homes.

☐ The number of persons seeking to acquire housing may be a deceptive figure. The number of households represented in the market is a more meaningful measure of demand, although a household may consist of only one person. A family of four will purchase one house, not four.

☐ Doubling is another consideration, as when several college students rent one apartment jointly to save money.

☐ Basic demand alone is often misleading. The appraiser must apply analytical skills to determine how many purchasers are truly willing and able to buy; i.e., effective demand.

Effective Demand. Effective demand is an element of the total basic demand. It is distinguished from basic demand by the purchaser's ability to participate in the market, coupled with a need or desire to do so. Effective demand is limited to those purchasers who are both willing and able to buy.

☐ Alternative investment outlets such as stocks and bonds must be taken into consideration.

☐ Funds may also be directed to other competitive uses such as consumer goods and services.

Types of Real Estate Markets
The various submarkets within a real estate market may be categorized in several ways:

Rights. Fee simple ownership, leasehold, life estate, mineral rights.

Price. Under $75,000; over $100,000; between $140,000 and $150,000; $250 per month; $800 per month.

Location. Downtown, suburban, rural, hillside, ocean view.

Use. Single-family, multifamily, resort area, second homes, commercial property, agricultural land.

Occupancy. Owner occupied, renter occupied.

Purpose. Owner occupancy, rental income, gain on speculative purchase.

Supply and Demand Factors
The interaction of supply and demand creates value and sets price. Division of each real estate market into many submarkets necessitates identification of the pertinent submarket at the outset of any analysis. Since the market is defined as those properties which buyers and sellers perceive to be competitive, supply and demand forces must be interpreted through the eyes of typically informed purchasers in the applicable submarket. Analysis of the supply and demand factors must be directed towards the future because real estate is a long-term capital asset.

DETERMINANTS OF SUPPLY AND DEMAND FOR RESIDENTIAL PROPERTIES

Demand Factors
Population. The number of persons and households and their rates of increase or decrease affect the demand for housing.

□ *Population Changes*. Natural increases may indicate a need for different types of housing. If there are more people moving into an area than out of it, an immediate need for additional housing units is usually indicated. A highly mobile population will generally require more rental units than a stable population of similar size.

- [ ] *Age Distribution*. The number of persons in each age category and any trends away from the current distribution influence the demand for various housing types. The housing needs and preferences of growing families differ from those of childless couples or singles.

- [ ] *Household Size and Distribution*. Households represent the basic unit seeking housing. The number of persons per household has decreased in recent years due to the trend toward smaller families and an increase in the number of persons living alone. A household is defined as the person or persons who occupy a dwelling unit.

- [ ] *Buyer Preferences and Tastes*. Architectural styles and housing sizes gain or lose popularity depending on fashion and on their adaptability to various life styles.

Employment Characteristics. The major considerations are the sources of employment and their stability.

- [ ] Employment in numerous, diverse industries tends to minimize the risk of widespread unemployment during periods of economic stagnation or recession.

- [ ] Rates of employment and unemployment are useful as general guides to the stability of employment in an area.

Income Characteristics. Of primary concern are the sources of income, the stability of incomes, and income levels.

- [ ] An investigation of the sources of income will provide an indication of the stability of incomes in the area.

- [ ] Current and expected income levels will determine the affordability of housing.

- [ ] The distribution of income will indicate potential demand for different types of housing.

Housing Acquisition Costs. Rental rates and sales prices will influence the decision to rent or to buy and the type of housing selected. The availability and cost of funds for real estate loans is an essential element of demand. Effective demand depends on the ability of purchasers to participate in the market. Because of the costs of real estate, few would be able to buy without the use of debt financing. Rising construction costs tend to increase the attractiveness of existing housing. Recent income tax law changes have reduced tax incentives to investment in income-producing properties by limiting some previous tax-sheltering provisions. Local rent control laws diminish the supply of housing by making investment in new residential income property less attractive to investors.

Supply Factors

Existing Housing. The appraiser must have a general knowledge of the total existing housing supply. However, the effective supply is limited to those properties which are likely to be put on the market in a given period of time. Properties presently on the market constitute the bulk of the effective supply.

New Construction. The volume of new construction, analyzed by housing type, will provide insight into changes in the housing inventory in the near future.

□ Costs of new construction influence both the number and type of housing units which will be added to the supply. A reasonable expectation of profit must exist as an incentive for builders to proceed with new construction.

□ Conversions represent changes in the types of housing available.

□ Turnover and vacancy rates are indicative of the need for additions to the housing supply.

□ Availability of construction and long-term financing affects the likelihood of new construction and sales of existing units.

□ Individual property prices are largely determined by the prices for competitive units.

MONEY MARKETS AND MORTGAGE MARKETS

Since most real estate transactions require the use of borrowed funds, the appraiser must understand the operations of the money and mortgage markets. These markets determine the cost and availability of loan funds, which in turn influence the price of real estate.

Money Markets

Characteristics of Money. Money is a generally accepted medium of exchange, consisting of all currency and all deposits in private checking accounts, plus "near money," which includes time and savings deposits, S&L shares, mutual savings bank deposits, and short-term U.S. securities. Money has complete liquidity and may be readily converted into other assets. The U.S. dollar market operates on a quasi-open market basis. Official controls are enforced but the market tends to revolve around the traditional laws of supply and demand.

Price of Money. The interest rate is the charge for borrowing money. The value of money is its purchasing power in terms of other currencies or goods and services.

Competition for Money. The uses of money are virtually unlimited and each use must compete for available funds.

The Money Supply. The supply of money is regulated by the actions of the Federal Reserve System and the U.S. Treasury. The function of the Treasury is different from the Federal Reserve System, in that it is obligated to conduct and manage the fiscal policy of the U.S. government. The function of the Federal Reserve system, on the other hand, is to regulate the flow of credit and money to facilitate orderly economic growth. Commercial banks hold the bulk of the money supply in demand deposits. The amount of this supply that must be held in reserve is regulated by the Federal Reserve. Thus, a change in the reserve requirements results in a change in the supply of available funds.

Mortgage Markets

Definition. Mortgage markets are markets for real estate loan funds. As such they perform the following functions:

☐ Bring borrowers and lenders together.

☐ Allocate available funds among competing uses.

☐ Set prices through the interaction of supply and demand forces.

☐ Adjust the supply of funds to demand.

Major Sources of Residential Loan Funds. There are a number of sources for residential loans. The major sources are:

☐ Commercial banks

☐ Mortgage companies and mortgage brokers

☐ Credit unions

☐ Savings and loan associations

☐ Life insurance companies

☐ Mutual savings banks (found primarily in the northeastern states)

☐ Individuals, government agencies, foreign investors, and others.

Mortgage Instruments

A mortgage is a legal document which conveys an interest in real property pledged as security for the payment of a debt. The lender is the mortgagee and the borrower is the mortgagor. Because long-term financing arrangements are necessary in most cases when a home is purchased, the mortgage instrument has been developed to fit these needs. It is a legal document comprised of two parts: the mortgage and the note. Other types of financing include deeds of trust, privately-insured and guaranteed loans, second mortgages, and contract purchases.

Trust Deeds. In California and some other states the deed of trust is used in lieu of the mortgage. There are three parties to a trust deed: the trustor (borrower), the beneficiary (lender) and the trustee (a third party) to whom legal title to the property is conveyed. The trustee holds it in trust for the beneficiary and has the power to sell the property if the trustor does not fulfill the obligations set forth in the agreement. *In this text the terms mortgage and trust deed are usually used synonymously.*

Effect on Mortgage Market. Legal restrictions and requirements applying to mortgage vary from state to state. A state having foreclosure legislation favorable to the borrower may attract few funds. Those states which give the most protection to the lender tend to attract more funds.

Types of Mortgages

A variety of mortgages or trust deeds are used in California:

Purchase Money Mortgage. A purchase money trust deed or mortgage is a trust deed or mortgage given as all or part of the purchase price of the property. The loan can be made by a seller who extends credit to the buyer or by a third party lender that makes a hard money loan to the buyer of real property.

Construction Loan. This is a short-term interim loan to finance the costs of construction.

Open-End Mortgage. An open-end mortgage provides for increases in the outstanding loan amount upon mutual agreement of the lender and the borrower.

Participation Loan. This is a mortgage made by more than one lender or a loan made by one lender in which other lenders have an interest.

Blanket Mortgage. Several properties are covered under one mortgage.

Package Loan. This mortgage includes some personal property as well as the realty as security for the loan.

Discounted Loan. The amount advanced by the lender is less than the amount the borrower has contracted to repay. The discounted amount is expressed as a percentage of the nominal or contract amount, called points. One point is one percent of the loan amount.

Assumed Mortgage. The purchaser takes over primary liability for payment of an existing mortgage. The seller remains secondarily liable for repayment until specifically released by the lender.

Other Classifications of Mortgages

Priority of Lien. A first mortgage has priority over all junior liens. The junior liens are ranked by their labels as second mortgages, etc. In default, the first mortgage is completely paid off before the second mortgage and so on.

Conventional and Insured. On FHA or VA loans, the lender may be insured or guaranteed against loss of a specified amount of the loan principal. This reduces the risk of making some loans and increases their attractiveness to lenders. Conventional mortgages may also be insured by private mortgage insurance.

Loan Amortization. The three basic types of amortization are:

☐ *Straight or Non-Amortized Loans*. Only interest is paid over the term of the loan, with the full principal due in a lump sum at the end of the term. Very few real estate loans of this type have been made on first trust deeds since the 1930s.

☐ *Amortized Loans*. A portion of the principal is repaid with the periodic interest payments. If the entire principal is repaid over the loan term, the loan is said to be fully amortized. Partially amortized loans require a "balloon payment" at the end of the term.

☐ *Adjustable Rate Mortgages (ARMs)*. Interest rates are adjustable periodically, based on some index rate, to reflect changing money market and capital market rates. These instruments have become favored by institutional lenders since interest rates became volatile and unpredictable in the first half of the 1980s. The ARM transfers most of the risks of future higher interest rates from the lender to the borrower.

Interest Rate. The rate of interest represents the charge for the use of borrowed funds. The rate is based on the lender's evaluation of the risks of making the loan, including the current value of the property and its probable future value, the borrower's present and expected income levels and alternative uses for the funds.

Maturity Period. The loan must be repaid in full by the end of this period. The longer the maturity, the smaller the periodic payments, but the larger the total amount repaid.

Example

A $100,000 loan at 10% interest per annum would have quite different monthly payments and quite different total payments if written with different amortization periods.

Amortization Period	Monthly Payment	Total of Payments
10 years	$1,321.50	$158,580.00
15 years	1,074.60	193,429.00
20 years	965.02	231,605.00
25 years	908.70	272,610.00
30 years	877.57	315,726.00
40 years	849.15	407,590.00
50 years	839.10	503,463.00

Note: After about 25 years, additional time added to the maturity period reduces the monthly payment only slightly, but adds significantly to the total of all payments. Loan amortization periods in excess of 30 years become unreasonable.

Mortgage Market Characteristics The primary mortgage market originates loans. Existing loans are bought and sold in the secondary mortgage market. Mortgage markets are relatively unorganized and lack physical concentration. Yet these markets are highly stratified by loan types and sizes. The mortgage market does not operate independently of the total money market or of the economy. Demand is generated by purchases and refinancing of real estate. Supply is a function of the attractiveness of real estate as a use for funds and the volume of savings held by financial institutions.

Effect of Mortgage Market Activities on Real Estate Prices and Value. The availability of funds for real estate loans and the cost of borrowing those funds are determined by the mortgage market.

☐ *Money Supply*. When loan funds are readily available, interest rates drop and real estate sales activity increases. Conversely, interest rates rise and sales decrease in volume as the money supply tightens.

☐ *Terms*. Financing terms are always present in the market as variables and affect decisions of buyers and sellers. There is some tangible relationship between financing and price. The question is how much effect special and unusual financing conditions have on price, cost, and value.

Chapter 3 Quiz

1. The interaction of supply and demand factors in real estate markets:

   (A) Adjusts demand to supply
   (B) Creates value and sets price
   (C) Causes demand to decrease as the supply dwindles
   (D) Is highly predictable, allowing the appraiser to predict future housing needs with near certainty

2. Which of the following are major determinants of housing demand?

   (A) Population changes, age distribution
   (B) Household income, employment
   (C) Housing acquisition costs, income
   (D) All of the above

3. Effective demand is implemented by:

   (A) A strong desire to buy
   (B) Purchasing power
   (C) An increase in population
   (D) High prices

4. Which of the following is *not* a function of a market?

   (A) Bring buyers and sellers together
   (B) Set prices based on the interaction of the forces of supply and demand
   (C) Allocate goods and services among buyers
   (D) Adjust demand to supply

5. Major sources of real estate loan funds include:

   (A) Mortgage companies
   (B) Savings and loan associations
   (C) Commercial banks
   (D) All of the above

6. An amortized mortgage is defined as one that is paid in:

   (A) Interest-only payments
   (B) Arrears
   (C) Monthly installments
   (D) Periodic installments of principal and interest

7. A purchase money mortgage or trust deed is created by:

   (A) Refinancing an existing loan
   (B) Extension of credit by the seller as part of the purchase price
   (C) Pledging notes and other goods as collateral
   (D) Obtaining funds secured by personal property

8. The mortgage market is the market for:

   (A) Real estate loan funds
   (B) Foreclosed properties
   (C) Second and third mortgages
   (D) Construction loans

9. A point is:

   (A) One percent of the loan amount
   (B) Ten percent of the loan amount
   (C) One-tenth of the loan amount
   (D) One hundred dollars

10. A real estate market does *not*:

   (A) Facilitate exchanges
   (B) Set price
   (C) Set value
   (D) Adjust supply to demand

Chapter 4
Overview
of the Appraisal Process

PREVIEW

Step 1: Define the Appraisal Problem

Step 2: Conduct a Preliminary Survey and Appraisal Plan

Step 3: Gather Data

Step 4: Analyze Data

Step 5: Apply the Data

Step 6: Estimate the Value

Step 7: Write the Appraisal Report

STEP 1: DEFINE THE APPRAISAL PROBLEM

The appraisal process is a systematic analysis of the factors which influence the value of real property. There are seven basic steps in the appraisal process, beginning with a definition of the problem to be solved.

Purpose The first step in the appraisal process is to define the type of value to be estimated. Generally this will be the market value, but it may be another type of value.

Property Description Identify and describe the real estate. This could include the street address or a legal description or both—whatever provides a complete, unequivocal identification.

Property Interests Identify the property rights and interests involved. Who holds title? What portion of the "bundle of rights" is being considered? Specify other interests, if any.

Function Determine the objective of the appraisal. Why the appraisal is being made? For whom is the appraisal being made?

Effective Date Determine the effective date of the appraisal. Evaluate changing market conditions as of a specific date. The effective date generally coincides with the date of the appraiser's last inspection of the property. Future dates are rarely appropriate as they represent predictions rather than estimates.

Assignment Review the assignment with the client. This review should include estimated time to completion, and an agreement as to fee.

STEP 2: CONDUCT A PRELIMINARY SURVEY AND APPRAISAL PLAN

Market Factors Identify supply and demand factors relative to the appraisal objective, the effective date of the appraisal, the rights involved, the nature of the property, and the character of the local real estate market.

Data Requirements Determine what data are required, as determined by the nature of the appraisal problem. Identify and develop data sources that are well informed and reliable.

Three Approaches Determine which approaches to value estimation are most appropriate for the problem: market data, cost, and/or income.

Work Plan Develop a detailed work plan. The appraiser should include both general data (locational and economic) and specific data (subject property and comparables).

Report Outline Prepare an appraisal report outline, usually including all three approaches to value estimation: the market data approach, the cost approach, and the income approach.

Completion Schedule Set a schedule for project completion. Assign priorities to assure orderly work flow, and establish time frame for each step.

STEP 3: GATHER DATA

Data gathering sequence should correspond with priority listing of data requirements.

Sources Select and use data sources efficiently. Some sources will consistently provide better data than others. It is not usually necessary to utilize every potential data source.

Verification Verify the data as it is collected. Verification is required by professional standards and public authorities; it should be made with one or more of the principals to the transaction. The data sources must be recorded in the appraisal file for reference purposes.

STEP 4: ANALYZE DATA

Thoroughness and accuracy of the analysis are critical in appraisal. The order of analysis is directly related to the sequence of steps in the appraisal process.

Highest and Best Use Determine highest and best use of the property as a vacant site and as an improved property. That which is legally permitted, physically permitted, economically feasible, and most profitable is the highest and best use.

Neighborhood Influences Evaluate supply and demand factors in the competitive market area and neighborhood and their relationship to the value of the subject property.

Property Characteristics Identify the value-determining characteristics of the subject property. Since all approaches to value estimation are based upon comparison of the subject property with other properties, the appraiser must have a clear understanding of which features are pertinent to the comparison.

Relationships of Data Analyze the interrelationship of data on the property and market influences. Each factor should be considered in relation to the whole.

STEP 5: APPLY THE DATA

Apply the data and the analysis to the approaches to value estimation. The alternative approaches to consider are sales comparison (market data), cost, and income approaches. Although experience and subsequent analysis may indicate that one or more of the approaches is inappropriate for the problem at hand, the appraiser should initially give consideration to all three approaches in residential appraisal.

Sales Comparison Approach This is also called the market data approach. It is particularly applicable to amenity properties (homes) in an active market.

□ Identify the relevant characteristics which determine the value of the subject property.

□ Locate competitive and comparable properties which have sold recently.

- ☐ Gather verified data on the sale of each such property including price, terms and conditions, and date of sale.

- ☐ Compare the pertinent features of the comparable properties to those of the subject, possibly using the "matched pairs" technique (below).

- ☐ Adjust the comparable sales for the market difference of each feature on which the comparables differ from the subject property.

- ☐ Estimate the adjusted sales price at which each comparable would have sold if its features had been the same as those of the subject.

- ☐ Reconcile the adjusted sales prices of the comparables to an indicated market value for the subject property.

Income Approach This is also called gross rent multiplier analysis. While most applicable to income producing properties, it is useful in estimating the market value of residential properties where an active rental market exists.

- ☐ Locate similar rental properties, preferably unfurnished, which were recently sold in the same market area.

- ☐ Using the adjustment analysis, reconcile the monthly unfurnished rentals for the comparable properties to obtain an indicated monthly unfurnished rental for the subject property.

- ☐ Calculate the gross rent multiplier (GRM) for each comparable property by dividing sales price by monthly unfurnished rental.

- ☐ Reconcile the gross rent multiplier for the comparable properties into an indicated GRM for the subject property.

- ☐ To obtain an estimated market value for the subject property, multiply the indicated monthly unfurnished market rental by the indicated gross rent multiplier.

Cost Approach This method is especially applicable to new or proposed construction representing the highest and best use of the site. It is also useful in estimating the market value of unique properties where information on similar properties is unavailable.

- ☐ Estimate the value of the site assuming it is vacant and available to be put to its highest and best use. This is usually accomplished by the direct sales comparison approach.

- ☐ Estimate the cost of reproducing the major buildings.

- ☐ Estimate the accrued depreciation for the major buildings as of the date of the appraisal.

- ☐ Subtract the accrued depreciation from the reproduction cost for the major buildings to obtain their present worth.

□ Estimate the depreciated reproduction cost figures for all components to obtain the estimated total present value of the improvements.

□ Add the depreciated reproduction cost figures for all components to obtain the estimated total present value of the improvements.

□ The indicated market value of the subject property is the sum of the estimated present value of the site and the estimated present value of all improvements.

Matched Pairs Technique

Good appraisal practice requires that adjustments be supported with data from the market. One technique is to extract the amount of adjustment from the market by using "matched pairs."

Comparable 1	Comparable 2
10-Acre Parcel	10-Acre Parcel
3 Bedrooms	3 Bedrooms
2 Baths	1 Baths
Fireplace	Fireplace
Sold Recently for $250,000	Sold Recently for $248,000

It appears from these data that a second bath is worth $2,000 more in the market. This is one indication of an appropriate value adjustment. The above is an example of an adjustment based on only one difference between the matched pairs. Using larger numbers of properties in "pairs," adjustment figures can be obtained for any number of features, and then used to extrapolate a market value for the subject property.

STEP 6: ESTIMATE THE VALUE

Reconciliation

The estimations of market value obtained from the various approaches to value are reconciled to a final estimate. The final estimate is not an average of the indicated values. It is based on an evaluation of the reliability of the data used, the quality and comprehensiveness of the analyses made, and the applicability of each of the approaches to value.

Rounding

The appraiser is usually required to indicate a single market value figure, although it is occasionally more appropriate to indicate a range of values within which the market value falls. The estimate of value should be rounded to an appropriate level. Unrounded numbers imply a degree of precision that is not claimed with an estimate.

STEP 7: WRITE THE APPRAISAL REPORT

The contents, form and length of the written appraisal report may vary depending upon the requirements of the client, the nature of the assignment and the type of property. The report should present in a logical and convincing manner the procedures used by the appraiser. The three kinds of written appraisal reports are the letter report, the form report, and the narrative report.

Letter Report   Any form of report gives the appraiser's opinion of value. Usually a letter report only states the appraiser's opinion of value without inclusion of supporting data or the analysis and interpretation leading to the conclusion. Thus a certificate or letter has limited uses.

Form Report   Standardized forms insure that appraisals are comparable to one another, and help the reviewer find particular categories or items and check that no required items have been overlooked. Form reports are usually preferred by institutions and governmental agencies which handle many appraisals each year; they are considered more efficient and convenient for such purposes.

Narrative Report   Certificates or letters and standard forms are abbreviated reports. A narrative report is more detailed. It allows appraisers to support their opinions and conclusions. The reader of a narrative report is apt to be more convinced of the soundness of the appraiser's estimate.

1. A legal description is likely to be used to identify the property because:

    (A) It is important to include every known fact about the property in an appraisal

    (B) It provides a complete, unequivocal description of the property

    (C) Courts requires every appraisal to include a legal description

    (D) It results in a more professional looking report

2. The primary reason for specifying an effective date on an appraisal is:

    (A) The effective date is the basis for computing the appraiser's fee

    (B) Changing market conditions can be specified only as of a given point in time

    (C) To specify the date as of which all data was verified

    (D) The appraisal is valid for only six months from this date

3. The first step in appraising is to:

    (A) Gather the data
    (B) Inspect the property
    (C) Decide which approach to use
    (D) Define the appraisal problem

4. Reconciliation of the value indications obtained using the three approaches is best accomplished by:

    (A) Computing an average of the three values

    (B) Evaluation of the applicability of each of the approaches to value

    (C) Evaluating the quality and reliability of the data and analyses

    (D) Both B and C

5. Data requirements are determined by the:

    (A) Nature of the appraisal problem
    (B) Client's instructions
    (C) Department of Real Estate
    (D) Society of Real Estate Appraisers

6. The final estimate of value should always be:

    (A) Absolutely precise
    (B) Rounded to the nearest hundred dollars
    (C) Rounded so as not to imply a degree of precision which does not exist
    (D) Rounded to the nearest one thousand dollars

7. Data should be verified:

    (A) If it is obtained from someone who is not an appraiser

    (B) Just before the final report is written to assure that it is up to date

    (C) By the appropriate government agency or department

    (D) By at least one of the principals to the transaction

8. The conclusion as to the highest and best use is part of which step?

    (A) Defining the appraisal problem
    (B) Preliminary survey
    (C) Analyzing the data
    (D) Making the final estimate of value

9. Which approaches are most applicable to the appraisal of a new home?

    (A) Gross rent multiplier analysis, cost approach

    (B) Sales comparison data approach, income approach

    (C) Cost approach, income approach

    (D) Direct sales comparison approach, cost approach

10. In the sales comparison (market data) approach, differences between the properties are accounted for by adjusting the comparables to the subject property.

    (A) True
    (B) False

Chapter 5
Area and Neighborhood Analysis

PREVIEW

The Nature of Market Analysis

Five Levels of Influence

Sources of Data

The URAR Subject and Neighborhood Sections

THE NATURE OF MARKET ANALYSIS

Market analysis is a study of conditions in the market which influence the supply, demand and prices for competitive properties. Market analysis has several objectives:

☐ Identify the competitive market for the subject property.

☐ Examine and evaluate current conditions in the market.

☐ Study past market conditions to gain perspective on the market over a period of time.

☐ Forecast the impact of future market conditions as they relate to current value.

☐ Provide market data and forecasts for use in the approaches to value.

Choice of Market Area   The pertinent market area is that area within which other similar properties are perceived as competitive with the subject by the most probable potential purchasers of the subject property. The boundaries are marked by shifts in land uses, price ranges, types of inhabitants, etc. For analytical purposes, the market area is frequently delineated by political or geographical boundaries such as census tracts, city limits, rivers or hills.

Application to Appraisal   The three major applications of neighborhood analysis in appraisal are:

Measure Impact. Identify and measure the impact of market forces and trends on real estate values.

Set Limits. Set an upper limit on the value of the subject property. Its value will rarely exceed the value of other properties in the neighborhood.

Define Value. Identify the defined value of the subject property.

FIVE LEVELS OF INFLUENCE

Five levels of influence operate simultaneously on the value of any given property: the international, national, regional, community, and neighborhood levels. Changes on the more general levels have less direct and less immediate effects on the subject property. Market analysis begins with the general levels and proceeds systematically to the more specific levels.

International Level   Market forces at this level affect general market conditions, including real estate values and prices.

> **Economic Factors**. Factors such as the balance of payments and gold flows influence price levels and interest rates.

> **Tariffs**. Trade barriers affect competition between foreign and domestic industries. This in turn affects employment and income levels.

> **Demand for Limited Resources**. Scarcity influences the cost of resources. For example, the scarcity of oil in the 1970s increased the cost of home heating fuels and thus the cost of home ownership.

National Level   Government policies at the federal level have substantial impact upon real estate market conditions.

> **Money Supply**. Policies set by the federal reserve and treasury strongly influence the cost and availability of funds for real estate. Federal regulations influence the ability of savings institutions to attract funds available for loans by determining the interest rate which may be paid on savings deposits.

> **Federal Spending**. Federal budgetary policies can increase or decrease inflation which affects construction costs and housing prices.

> **Taxes**. Federal taxing policy is revised periodically in order to bring about economic changes.

> **Federal Housing Regulations**. Construction costs are influenced by FHA standards for housing quality and quantity.

> **Employment Policies**. National employment and income levels affect price levels and the demand for housing.

Regional Level   Population and economic factors have the greatest impact at this level. Regional economic trends may differ from national trends.

> **Population Growth**. This is an important element of the demand for housing within a region. Major shifts in population from one region to another, such as the movement to the Southern states during the last decade, can precipitate a housing boom in the growth areas.

Employment and Income Level. Employment affects the effective demand for housing. This is especially critical where employment is concentrated in a few related industries, since a downturn in these industries will adversely affect the entire regional economy.

Community Level

Market forces at the community and neighborhood levels affect the value of the subject property much more directly than those at the international, national, and regional levels.

Community or Local Market. The market is defined in terms of properties considered by potential purchasers to be competitive with the subject property. In practice, the market area is usually delineated by political boundaries such as city limits or by census tracts.

Four Major Factors. Analysis of the community can be considered under the following headings:

☐ *Economic*. The property tax burden, employment levels, availability of financing, construction costs.

☐ *Political-Governmental*. Cost and quality of community services, local government's reputation, zoning laws and land use regulations and their enforcement.

☐ *Sociological*. Benefits of living in the area as perceived by residents and potential purchasers.

☐ *Physical*. Climate, topography, soil and subsoil conditions.

Economic Base Analysis. This is a useful method for evaluating the current economic structure and forecasting economic trends in a specific market area, providing a look at the economic health of the area and its ability to bring in income from outside. The community that is the most desirable in which to live, has the greatest growth potential, and has the greatest protection against unfavorable economic developments will have the most favorable future. To measure the economic potential of a given community, one must compare it with similar competitive communities.

Definitions. The economic base of a community is the group of industries in that community which are primarily engaged in exporting goods or services to other communities.

☐ *Basic Industries*. Those which produce and sell more goods or services than are consumed locally. They are net exporters, e.g.,manufacturing companies, fabrication and assembly plants, major bank headquarters, and insurance companies.

☐ *Nonbasic Industries*. Those which produce goods or services for local consumption only, e.g., local government service, education, recreation, medicine, law, brokerage. There is no standard, consistent ratio of basic to nonbasic industries for communities.

Data Sources. Recent data on employment, population, and income are generally available from the U.S. Census, the Bureau of Labor Statistics, state and local tax authorities, and other sources.

Data Analysis. Historical as well as a current figures on basic employment are collected and divided into three major categories: industry, specialty, and trade. They are rated according to predicted employment trends, diversification, and cyclical fluctuation. The three major categories are examined using the following criteria:

☐ *Industrial Category*. Heavy and light manufacturing, construction.

Types of employees (e.g., sex, skills, age)

The nature of the goods being manufactured (e.g., heavy steel or light plastic, consumer goods or durable goods, luxury items or necessities)

The diversity and future of employment

Domination by one company or industry

Depletion of natural resources related to the industry

Possible loss of competitive advantage

Cyclical nature of the product or industry.

☐ *Specialty Category*. Education, government, and recreation.

Educational institutions with basic employees, such as state universities, private colleges, technical colleges, parochial high schools, middle schools, nursery schools.

Government entities with basic employees, such as fire department, FBI, sheriff's department, IRS, armed services.

Recreation property, including both public resources and private facilities.

☐ *Trade Category*. Trade, finance, and transportation.

Number and percentage of employees who are basic.

Advantages and Disadvantages of Economic Base Analysis. It is based on readily available data and uses simple calculations. Careful identification of basic industries is required. The assumption of static relationships between population, employment, and income over the forecasting period may not be realistic. The appraiser must still rely on personal judgment in reaching conclusions on the relationship between changes in the community's economic base and real estate values.

Neighborhood Level The character of the immediate neighborhood of the subject property has a direct influence on its value, and to some degree the character of one property affects the character of all other properties.

Definition and Delineation of a Neighborhood. A neighborhood is a geographically circumscribed, named area (usually part of a larger community) which has a distinctive character. Those who live in a neighborhood often feel a sense of belonging to that place and a sense of being part of a group. While some neighborhoods are composed of a narrow range of income levels and social groupings, other neighborhoods exhibit a wide range of diversity. The boundaries of a neighborhood may be determined by:

☐ Changes in land use patterns (the best indication)

☐ Natural barriers such as hills, ravines, rivers, etc.

☐ Man-made barriers such as streets and highways, railroads, different land uses, major utility rights-of-way, etc.

☐ Political boundaries such as census tracts, city limits, school districts.

Neighborhood Life Cycles. The future, not the past, is of primary importance in appraising. Change is occurring constantly. In real estate it affects individual properties, neighborhoods, and cities. Change can be so slow that it is almost indiscernible. Individual properties, districts, neighborhoods, and entire communities often follow a four-phase life cycle.

☐ *Growth (Integration)*. A period of public favor and acceptance.

☐ *Stability*. A period of equilibrium.

☐ *Decline (Disintegration)*. A period of diminishing demand and acceptance.

☐ *Renewal*. Rejuvenation of market demand.

Elements of Neighborhood Analysis. Analysis requires identification and evaluation of the factors and trends affecting property values in a neighborhood. No list of factors can be totally comprehensive and not all of the factors listed will be relevant in every situation. It is insufficient to merely list those factors which affect the value of the subject property. The appraiser must determine which factors are pertinent to the appraisal problem and discuss those in the analysis and value estimation.

PHYSICAL FACTORS

Area

Location in the path of community growth

Commuting time and distance

Topography

Feasibility and cost of construction

Density of development

Privacy

Views

Soil and Subsoil Conditions

Bearing qualities

Construction types and costs

Proximity to earthquake faults

Drainage

Flood hazards, mudslides, etc.

Suitability for septic systems (in rural areas)

Foundation dampness

Climate

Temperatures - extreme heat or cold

Precipitation - heavy rain or snowfall, drought conditions

Prevailing winds

Air quality

Utilities

Public or private

Availability

Cost

Quality, dependability

Type

Capacity

Relationship to Rest of City

In the path of future expansion

Stable area

Declining older section

Convenience to Supporting Facilities in Miles and Minutes

Good schools

Employment centers

Shopping

Health and medical facilities

Recreation

Transportation

Public and private

Access to various means of transportation

Availability of public systems (bus, subway, train, etc.)

Frequency of service

Cost of service

Quality of service

Character and Condition of Surrounding Structures

Compatibility of architectural styles

Maintenance levels (Excessive deferred maintenance lowers property values.)

Similar usage, e.g., single family homes vs. large apartment buildings

Freedom From Hazards and Nuisances

Traffic

Noise

Smoke

Smog

Odors

Airports or industries

ECONOMIC FACTORS

Population

Total population

Rate of increase by subgroups

Age distribution by categories

Number and size of households and families

Educational levels

Sex distribution

In and out migration rates

Employment

Total number employed

Employment by industry

Unemployment rates

Stability of employment

Stability and growth of employing industries

Mix of industries

Wage rates (current and probably future levels)

Skill levels

Labor relations record

Financing

Local availability of mortgage funds (A high rate of personal savings increases availability of mortgage funds.)

Interest rates

General price levels

Insurance rates (Exposure to fewer risks leads to lower rates.)

Rental Market

Availability of good quality units

Rental rates

Vacancy levels

Percent vacant

Cause of vacancy

Length of vacancy (turnover rate)

Amenities offered

Income

Income levels

Disposable income (income after taxes)

Income patterns, e.g., two income families

Nonsalary income, e.g., pensions, investments

Consumer spending patterns

Public and Private Debt Loads

Amount of debt relative to income

Trends

Real Estate Taxes.

Compare the tax burden with those of competitive properties. Also consider the relationship between taxes levied and services provided by the community.

Tax Rate (expressed as a percentage of the assessment)

Tax Burden (or the total tax bill, determined by multiplying the tax rate times the assessed value)

Other taxes and their effect on disposable income

Occupancy

Owner occupied

Tenant occupied

Existing Housing Supply (standing stock)

Number of housing units available

Volume of new construction

Price and availability of vacant land suitable for development

Impact of building codes and zoning ordinances on construction

Cost of construction, labor and materials

POLITICAL-GOVERNMENTAL FACTORS

Planning and Zoning Ordinances

Developed with careful thought and planning

Able and consistent administration

Enforcement and adaptability to changing needs

Building Codes

Electrical

Plumbing

Sanitary

Tax Burden

Level of taxation

Assessed values

Special assessments

Extra fees, e.g., refuse collection, etc.

Equitable adjustment and appeal procedures

Relative to community services provided

Police and Fire Protection

Homeowners will enjoy somewhat lower fire insurance rates if fire protection services in the community are above average.

Maintenance of Roads and Public Facilities

Overall Quality of Local Government

Community reputation

Business "environment"

Community Policies on Growth

Receptiveness to new industries

Urban renewal programs

Public housing

Subdivision regulations

Schools

Quality of system and individual schools

Number of schools at each level

SOCIOLOGICAL FACTORS

Social considerations are necessarily subjective, and difficult to quantify or list. However, the appraiser must make an unbiased attempt to identify and measure the sociological opinions and preferences of participants in the given market as they relate to value. The social characteristics of a neighborhood are significant only to the extent that they are considered by potential purchasers and can be objectively and accurately analyzed by the appraiser.

Compatibility of Residents

While many neighborhoods exhibit a fair degree of social and economic homogeneity, there is a growing preference by some for heterogeneity within neighborhoods.

Stability

If a change of prevailing use or occupancy in the neighborhood is imminent or probable, the impact of the change will be reflected in value. Stability comes from a long-range interest in the character of the community.

Property Maintenance

Well maintained homes increase the attractiveness of the neighborhood and support property values.

Discrimination

Only those elements which have a demonstrable impact on market value should be included in the analysis and value estimation. In particular, the appraiser must avoid unlawful discrimination. The URAR specifies that "race or the racial composition of the neighborhood are not considered reliable appraisal factors."

CHARACTERISTICS OF A GOOD NEIGHBORHOOD

The characteristics more frequently considered by appraisers are:

- ☐ Located in the path of community growth
- ☐ Protected from inharmonious uses, hazards, and nuisances
- ☐ Convenient to supporting facilities such as schools and shopping
- ☐ Adequate utilities available at reasonable cost
- ☐ Relatively new and growing neighborhood
- ☐ Stable population, incomes, land uses, and property taxes

- ☐ Compatible residents, land uses, and zoning
- ☐ Rising sales prices
- ☐ Financing is easily obtained
- ☐ Financing is easily obtained
- ☐ Good local government
- ☐ Fair tax assessments
- ☐ Good community reputation
- ☐ High quality schools.

SOURCES OF DATA

The appraiser must be familiar with numerous published and unpublished data sources. It is necessary to keep informed about new studies which may be useful for future assignments and to establish contacts for less frequently used types of information.

Appraiser's Files These contain information which the appraiser has gathered over time from various sources. When these files are well organized and current, the time and effort required to complete specific assignments can be substantially reduced.

Public Records Information on the following is available from the appropriate departments of city and county governments.

- ☐ Building permits
- ☐ Planning and subdivision regulations, tract maps
- ☐ Building, housing, electrical, plumbing and fire codes
- ☐ Zoning ordinances, variances, exceptions, proposed changes
- ☐ Deed recordings and foreclosures
- ☐ Mortgage recordings
- ☐ Tax assessments, rates
- ☐ Public housing units.

Publications In addition to government agencies, a wide variety of associations, institutions and private firms publish periodic reports on all aspects of real estate. Additional sources are listed in the Appendix.

- □ *Census of Population and Housing,* Bureau of the Census, U.S. Department of Commerce
- □ *City and County Data Book,* Bureau of the Census, U.S. Department of Commerce
- □ *Economic Development,* Economic Development Administration, U.S. Department of Commerce
- □ *Real Estate Market,* National Association of Realtors®
- □ *Neighborhood Standards,* Federal Housing Administration
- □ *Regional and Local Surveys of Vacancies ,* U.S. Postal Service
- □ *Regional and Local Housing Market Analysis,* Federal Housing Administration.

Private Sources Unpublished data and private studies often yield a wealth of information and are generally available upon request. Sources include:

- □ Banks and savings institutions
- □ Area colleges and universities
- □ Title companies and title insurers
- □ Other appraisers and real estate brokers
- □ Chamber of Commerce (data only, not public relations materials)
- □ Private consulting firms
- □ Utility companies
- □ Local and national contractors' associations.

Field Interviews Participants in the real estate market are excellent information sources.

- □ Other appraisers
- □ Buyers and sellers
- □ Lending institutions
- □ Real estate brokers
- □ Property owners and tenants.

The Uniform Residential Appraisal Report includes a neighborhood analysis as the first element of the appraisal, immediately following the identification of the property. This chapter concludes with a detailed look at this section of the form, with guidelines for completion. Subsequent chapters treat the other sections of the URAR in the same manner.

Property Description & Analysis **UNIFORM RESIDENTIAL APPRAISAL REPORT** File No.

SUBJECT						
Property Address				Census Tract	LENDER DISCRETIONARY USE	
City	County		State	Zip Code	Sale Price $	
Legal Description					Date	
Owner/Occupant			Map Reference		Mortgage Amount $	
Sale Price $	Date of Sale			PROPERTY RIGHTS APPRAISED	Mortgage Type	
Loan charges/concessions to be paid by seller $				☐ Fee Simple	Discount Points and Other Concessions	
R.E. Taxes $	Tax Year		HOA $/Mo.	☐ Leasehold	Paid by Seller $	
Lender/Client				☐ Condominium (HUD/VA)		
				☐ De Minimis PUD	Source	

NEIGHBORHOOD									Good	Avg.	Fair	Poor
LOCATION	☐ Urban		☐ Suburban		☐ Rural		NEIGHBORHOOD ANALYSIS					
BUILT UP	☐ Over 75%		☐ 25-75%		☐ Under 25%		Employment Stability		☐	☐	☐	☐
GROWTH RATE	☐ Rapid		☐ Stable		☐ Slow		Convenience to Employment		☐	☐	☐	☐
PROPERTY VALUES	☐ Increasing		☐ Stable		☐ Declining		Convenience to Shopping		☐	☐	☐	☐
DEMAND/SUPPLY	☐ Shortage		☐ In Balance		☐ Over Supply		Convenience to Schools		☐	☐	☐	☐
MARKETING TIME	☐ Under 3 Mos.		☐ 3-6 Mos.		☐ Over 6 Mos.		Adequacy of Public Transportation		☐	☐	☐	☐

PRESENT LAND USE %	LAND USE CHANGE		PREDOMINANT	SINGLE FAMILY HOUSING		Recreation Facilities	☐	☐	☐	☐
Single Family ___	Not Likely		OCCUPANCY	PRICE $ (000)	AGE (yrs)	Adequacy of Utilities	☐	☐	☐	☐
2-4 Family ___	Likely	☐	Owner ☐			Property Compatibility	☐	☐	☐	☐
Multi-family ___	In process	☐	Tenant ☐	Low		Protection from Detrimental Cond.	☐	☐	☐	☐
Commercial ___	To: ___		Vacant (0-5%) ☐	High		Police & Fire Protection	☐	☐	☐	☐
Industrial ___			Vacant (over 5%) ☐	Predominant		General Appearance of Properties	☐	☐	☐	☐
Vacant ___				—		Appeal to Market	☐	☐	☐	☐

Note: Race or the racial composition of the neighborhood are not considered reliable appraisal factors.
COMMENTS: _____

Subject Section—Property Identification

Prior to the URAR, in earlier Freddie Mac/Fannie Mae forms this section was designated "To Be Completed By Lender" and provided the appraiser with the necessary information to begin the appraisal. It is now common practice for the appraiser to complete most of this section with certain data provided by the lender or seller. This section is used to identify the subject property, to describe the property rights to be appraised, and to summarize financing data and sales concessions.

Property Address. The appraiser must identify the subject property by its complete property address and legal description; a post office box number is not acceptable. The appraiser should indicate the nearest intersection if a house number is not available. When the legal description is lengthy, the appraiser may attach the full description as an addendum to the appraisal report, or may refer simply to its location in the public records.

Owner/Occupant. The appraiser should list "Owner," "Tenant," or "Vacant," giving information necessary to gain access to inspect the property.

Map Reference. The appraiser should include in this entry the source of the map referred to and its identification number. Examples of map references include those used by the local tax assessors and government census maps.

Sale Price. In the event of a transfer, the total acquisition price should be entered. If the appraiser knows that the appraisal will be used for a refinance transaction, he or she should indicate that on the form.

Date of Sale. In the event of a transfer, the exact date of sale and the source of verification should be entered.

Loan Charges/Concessions To Be Paid by Seller. The appraiser must state the total dollar amount of the loan charges and/or concessions that will be paid by the seller (or any other party who has a financial interest in the sale or financing of the subject property) and provide a brief description of the items on the appraisal report form.

Real Estate Taxes/Tax Year. The annual property taxes assessed against the property for the most recent year should be entered in this section.

HOA $/Mo. The monthly homeowner's association fee is entered here, if the property is a condominium, cooperative project, PUD or *de minimis* PUD.

Lender/Client. The appraiser should enter the complete name (usually the lender) and mailing address of the lender or the client.

Property Rights Appraised. The appraiser must identify the property rights to be appraised as "fee simple" or "leasehold." In addition, the appraiser must indicate whether the subject property is located in a PUD, *de minimis* PUD, condominium, or cooperative project.

Lender Discretionary Use. This section is not completed by the appraiser. It is included to encourage lenders to provide closing information to comparable sales reporting services.

Neighborhood Section

The purpose of a neighborhood analysis is to identify the area—based on common characteristics or trends—that is subject to the same influences as the subject property. The sales prices of comparable properties in the identified area should reflect the positive and negative influences of the neighborhood. A neighborhood analysis should consider the influence of social, economic, government, and environmental forces on property values in the subject neighborhood.

Note on Discrimination. Neither the racial composition nor the age of a neighborhood is a reliable appraisal factor. A property located in an older neighborhood can be as sound an investment as a property located in a new neighborhood, and a property inhabited primarily by members of one race can be as sound an investment as one located in a racially mixed neighborhood or in a neighborhood inhabited primarily by a different race. The appraiser must be impartial and specific in describing favorable or unfavorable factors in a neighborhood, and should avoid the use of subjective terms or phrases such as "pride of ownership," etc. Fannie Mae does not designate certain areas as being acceptable or unacceptable—in other words, Fannie Mae does not "red-line."

Location. The appraiser must check one of three boxes:

☐ *Urban*. Signifies a well established neighborhood typically found within a city's limits.

☐ *Suburban*. Signifies a neighborhood typically less populated than that found within a city.

☐ *Rural*. Signifies those areas with typically less than 25% development and relatively slow growth rates. Rural includes such properties as farms and ranches.

Built Up. The appraiser must check one of three boxes indicating the percentage of improvement of all property within the neighborhood.

Growth Rate. The appraiser must make a judgment call and check one of three boxes pertaining to the residential growth rate within the subject neighborhood.

Property Values. Again the appraiser checks one of three boxes indicating an opinion of the current trends in the market place. Maximum financing is acceptable when property values are stable or increasing. If values are declining, the appraiser should comment on the reason for the decline and its effect on the property's marketability. Properties in such areas must be reviewed with great care. The reasons for a decline in values and the probability of its continuance are key considerations in the property's acceptability.

Demand/Supply. Of the three possible entries, a shortage of properties or a balance situation is preferred. An over-supply of housing is not desirable, since it indicates that properties are selling slowly with a lot of competition.

Marketing Time. Marketing time is the average time that it takes for a reasonably priced property to sell in the subject neighborhood. When marketing time for a particular area is greater than six months, the appraiser must comment on the reason for the extended marketing period and its effect on the property's value.

Present Land Use. Typically, dwellings best maintain their value when they are situated in neighborhoods that consists of other similar dwellings. Therefore, a single-family property in a neighborhood with apartments and commercial or industrial development may not have the stability required to sustain value over a long period of time. In this section, the appraiser should provide the relative percentages of developed single-family sites, developed two- to four-family sites, etc. The total of the types of land uses must equal 100%. Undeveloped land should be reported as vacant. In addition, if there is a significant amount of vacant or undeveloped land in the neighborhood, the appraiser should include comments to the effect in the "Neighborhood Comments" section of the report to assure that he or she adequately describes the neighborhood.

Land Use Change. In this section the appraiser records his or her opinion of the probability of a significant change in land use. If the opinion is "likely" or "in process" the appraiser should complete the "To" section. Fannie Mae relies on the present land use, the predominant occupancy composition, and the likelihood that either will change to determine whether a neighborhood is undergoing transition. If such is the case, it could have a negative effect on residential values.

Predominant Occupancy. In this section the appraiser indicates the predominant type of occupancy—owner or tenant—and estimates the vacancy percentage. Owner-occupancy generally contributes greatly to the likelihood of long-term sustained value, since owners generally find it in their best interests to maintain their property. A high vacancy rate in the neighborhood must also be considered in terms of its long-range effect.

Single Family Housing—Price and Age. Here the appraiser indicates the price range and predominant price of properties in the subject neighborhood. The price range must reflect high and low prevailing prices of single-family homes—however, isolated high and low extremes should be excluded from the range. The predominant price is that which is the most common or most frequently found in the neighborhood (i.e., the mode, not the mean or median). The appraiser should comment if the subject property's sales price exceeds the upper price range ("over-improvement") or is below the lower price range ("under-improvement"). The age range should reflect the oldest and newest single-family residential properties. The predominant age is the one most common or most frequently found in the neighborhood.

Neighborhood Analysis. This section of the report had been designed to summarize twelve principal items in a neighborhood that generally are considered important by purchasers when they select a home. The appraiser must use the following ratings: "Good" to indicate that the characteristics of the subject neighborhood are outstanding and superior to those found in competing neighborhoods; "Average" to indicate characteristics representing the norm and acceptable for the market area; "Fair" to indicate characteristics that are inferior to those considered acceptable; and "Poor" to indicate substantially inferior characteristics which may adversely affect residential property values. The last two items in the analysis section are of particular importance:

□ *General Appearance*. This is a key factor in determining whether a neighborhood will support an active market. The appraiser must consider the extent to which the properties are receiving proper maintenance. Signs of maintenance usually reflect a strong neighborhood with stable or increasing values.

□ *Appeal to Market*. This is a summary rating of the extent to which all aspects of the neighborhood will appeal to the typical buyer in the market. An individual property by itself cannot overcome a generally prevailing reluctance of the market to invest in a neighborhood. On the other hand, a relatively weak property in a strong, viable neighborhood is likely to sustain its value, although it still must be carefully analyzed.

Comments. This section provides the appraiser with an opportunity for further explanation of earlier described characteristics and any other factors that may impact property values. Note the statement that "race or the racial composition of the neighborhood are not considered reliable appraisal."

Chapter 5 Quiz

1. The pertinent market area for the subject property is best defined as:

    (A) The census tract in which the subject is located
    (B) Only those properties which are acceptable substitutes for the subject
    (C) Delineated by major physical barriers surrounding the subject
    √(D) That area within which other similar properties are perceived as competitive with the subject

2. Which of the following conditions lowers property values?

    (A) Conformity within the neighborhood
    √(B) Excessive deferred maintenance
    (C) High degree of utility
    (D) Excessive demand

3. The scarcity of oil in the 1970s _____ the cost of home ownership.

    (A) Reduced
    (B) Increased
    (C) Stabilized
    (D) Had no effect on

4. The economic base of a community is best measured by:

    (A) Total employment in the community
    (B) Population growth
    √(C) Employment in exporting industries
    (D) Employment in local service industries

5. A property was assessed for property taxes at $100,000. If the local property tax rate was 1.25%, the annual tax bill would most likely be:

    (A) $125.00
    (B) $312.50
    (C) $1,250.00
    (D) $12,500.00

6. A neighborhood is best defined as:

    (A) An area created by zoning regulations
    (B) An area in which there are no undesirable elements
    √(C) An area in which the residents have shared social and economic goals and a sense of belonging
    (D) Set physical boundaries determined solely by location

7. In economic base analysis of a community, real estate brokerage is usually a nonbasic industry.

    (A) True
    (B) False

8. Deferred maintenance of one property can affect the values of other properties in the community.

    (A) True
    (B) False

9. The Uniform Residential Appraisal Report neighborhood section asks about all of the following except the neighborhood's:

    (A) Present land use mix
    (B) Police and fire protection
    (C) Racial composition
    (D) General appearance

10. The URAR requires the appraiser to evaluate the neighborhood's:

    (A) Growth rate
    (B) Public transportation
    (C) Employment stability
    (D) All of the above

Chapter 6
Site and Improvement Analysis

THE NATURE OF PROPERTY ANALYSIS

Site and improvement analysis is the process of identifying and evaluating the characteristics of the subject property. This includes both land and improvements.

Site. A site is a parcel of land (the surface of the earth plus subsurface and suprasurface areas) which is improved to the extent that it is ready for its intended use. A site is land with man-made improvements *on* and *to* the land. These improvements include clearing, grading, utility connections, and means of public access. *Sites* can be created and destroyed, but *land* is fixed in amount.

Improvements. Improvements generally consist of buildings or other permanent structures on a site. Improvements *to* land are site improvements which have been added to the land to make it useful: streets, drains, curbs, gutters, etc. Improvements *on* land are the permanent structures erected for use on a site, such as buildings, fences, and walls.

Objectives Property analysis has three objectives:

☐ Physical and legal identification of the subject property.

☐ Identification of the significant characteristics of the property. These characteristics indicate what data must be collected on other properties and determines what makes them competitive with and comparable to the subject property.

☐ Determination of the highest and best use of the subject property as of the valuation date. Estimations of value are based on the highest and best use. This may or may not be the same as the existing or proposed use. Highest and best use is determined separately for the site and for the improved property as the two uses may differ.

Procedures The following procedures are typically used by an appraiser when conducting a site and improvement analysis:

☐ Inspect the property. The use of a checklist insures that all necessary information will be gathered during the inspection.

☐ Observe the siting and environment of the property.

☐ Note the age, condition, and quality of the subject improvements.

☐ Identify the significant characteristics of the subject property.

☐ Review the legal and public records which pertain to the subject, e.g., deeds, liens, zoning regulations.

☐ Evaluate the physical, legal, economic, and amenity characteristics of the property in terms of acceptability in the market.

SITE ANALYSIS

Analysis of the site includes the identification and evaluation of the characteristics which create, add to or detract from the desirability, utility, and marketability of the site as of the valuation date. The objectives are twofold: to establish the basis of comparison with other sites in order to estimate the market value of the site, and to determine the degree of suitability for the existing or proposed use.

Separate Valuation of the Site The site is always valued as if vacant and available to be put to its highest and best use. The site is valued separately from the improvements although the site and improvements constitute an integral economic unit. The reasons for this include:

☐ Vacant sites have value on their own.

☐ Separate site values are used in the cost approach and in certain income capitalization techniques.

☐ Property tax assessments are based on separate valuations of site and buildings.

☐ Independent values are used to determine the depreciation schedule for improvements and the basis for capital gains calculations for income tax purposes.

□ The courts often require distinct values for sites and improvements, especially in condemnation cases.

□ It may be necessary to estimate the value remaining when the improvements have been destroyed.

□ Separate valuations assist the property owner in determining whether the site should be cleared and put to a new use.

Elements of Site Analysis The market forces which influence site value must be identified and evaluated in terms of what is desirable and acceptable in the market. Careful analysis of market standards is required to determine which factors are truly significant.

Physical Factors The following physical factors are usually considered by the appraiser when conducting a site analysis:

Total Area. The total site area, measured in square feet, square meters, acres, square miles, etc.

Effective Area. The actual buildable area as determined by public or private setback requirements, e.g., zoning regulations and deed restrictions.

Width. The distance between the property side lines, generally measured at building line. The width may vary, as in the case of a triangular parcel.

Depth. The distance between front and rear property lines.

Frontage. The length of boundary along the public thoroughfare that the property abuts. The amount of frontage is an indication of the visibility and accessibility (and often the desirability) of the site. A property may have "frontage" on several streets.

Front Foot. The length of boundary along the main thoroughfare that the property faces. Used as a way of expressing value, e.g., "$600 per front foot," applying only to the front boundary.

Excess Land. The amount by which a parcel exceeds the standard size in the market. In an area where residential lots are typically 50 feet wide, a lot 75 feet wide may not have proportionately greater utility or value. The greater width may even be detrimental due to the increased maintenance costs and higher taxes. Conversely, a 40-foot-wide lot may suffer a disproportionate loss in value because the buildable area is sharply reduced.

Shape. Coupled with size, the configuration of the parcel determines what may be built on the lot within physical and legal constraints. Irregularity of shape often presents serious drawbacks.

Topography. The surface features of a site such as hills, rivers, lakes, ravines, etc. Sites above or below the street grade often require costly leveling or filling to improve accessibility or drainage. Advantages such as privacy or view sometimes offset the additional site improvement costs.

☐ The slope of the land influences the feasibility and costs of construction.

☐ Drainage also influences construction costs, methods, and materials. Inadequate drainage on level sites may result in foundation dampness or flooding; steeply sloping land may be subject to slippage or washouts.

Soil and Subsoil Conditions. Important determinants of construction feasibility. Modification of existing conditions may increase costs substantially.

☐ Soil-bearing qualities determine what type of structure may be built on the site.

☐ Drainage is important to prevent flooding, washouts, and foundation dampness. The percolation and permeability of subsoils is critical for septic tanks and private sewage disposal systems.

☐ Landscaping possibilities vary from site to site. It is often necessary to add another layer of topsoil.

Site Improvements. These are improvements on and to the site which increase its usefulness. They include sidewalks, driveways, fences, walls, and landscaping.

Utilities. The availability, adequacy, and cost of utilities may limit the use of the site and its marketability. Another consideration is whether the utilities are publicly or privately owned. Utilities include:

☐ Water (municipal system or private well)

☐ Electricity

☐ Gas (natural or propane)

☐ Sewage disposal (private septic or community system)

☐ Storm surface water disposal.

Streets and Related Improvements. Includes alleys, curbs, gutters, sidewalks, and street lights; may be dedicated or private.

Orientation to Sun, Wind, and Other Structures. Buildings should be sited to maximize the enjoyment and utility of the property.

Economic Factors   Potentially significant economic characteristics include:

Tax Burden. The cost of ownership is influenced by assessment levels, special assessments, and the tax rate. Tax assessments should be comparable to those of competitive properties.

Prices of Comparable Sites. The value of the subject generally lies within the range of prices of competitive sites.

Cost of Utilities and Community Services. Costs must be considered in absolute and relative terms.

Legal and Governmental Factors   A thorough site analysis will also consider such legal and governmental characteristics as:

Title Data. Information gathered from public records regarding the title of the subject property is used to determine specifically what rights are being appraised. An examination of deeds and other legal records of the appropriate county or municipality will usually yield the desired information.

☐ *Interest Held.* The appraiser must determine the nature and extent of the owner's rights in the property and which of these rights are being appraised.

☐ *History of Ownership.* A summary of the transfers of ownership should include the names of the grantors and grantees, transaction dates, and references to the appropriate volumes and pages of the deed records. This history generally spans at least five years.

☐ *Deed Restrictions and Easements.* The appraiser should carefully identify all such private restrictions and evaluate the limitations they place on the use of the property. Any conflict with public restrictions or regulations should be noted. Easements which go across other land and benefit the subject site should be noted and analyzed.

☐ *Liens and Claims.* Any unsatisfied liens or claims against the property should be noted. The appraiser must determine if they are clouds on the title which affect the marketability or transferability of interests in the property and how they may be extinguished (satisfied).

Zoning Regulations Applicable to the Site. While these regulations restrict potential uses of the site, they also serve to protect it from hazards and inharmonious uses. These regulations include permitted and prohibited uses, setback requirements, and nonconforming uses and violations. It is important to note the existence of any violations. Some communities restrict the length of time nonconforming uses may exist, while others allow them to remain indefinitely.

Taxes and Assessments. The utility of a site is influenced by the way sites are assessed and special assessments are levied.

Community Services. The availability, cost, quality, frequency, and dependability of services should be considered.

Locational Factors

The location of a site is especially significant due to the immobility of real estate.

Relation of Site to the Land Use Pattern. The surrounding land uses provide the setting for the site. The physical characteristics of the site should be similar to those of nearby competitive sites.

Access to Supporting Facilities. The ideal residential site is conveniently close to schools, shopping, transportation, employment centers, and recreational facilities.

Hazards and Nuisances. The proximity of inharmonious uses should be noted and an estimate made of their impact on the use and enjoyment of the site.

Judgments by Appraiser

In addition to estimating highest and best use, site analysis includes identification of locational obsolescence and noncontributory costs and concludes with the estimation of marketability and acceptability.

Locational Obsolescence. This is loss in value resulting from negative environmental forces external to the property. It is sometimes referred to as economic obsolescence. A property suffers from locational obsolescence to the degree that it does not conform to those properties it competes with in the market.

Noncontributory Costs. Excessive expenditures made to prepare the site for its intended use are called "noncontributory." Since cost does not create value, these expenditures may not be recovered through sale of the site on the market. Similarly, excessive costs for utilities and community services may detract from the value of the site.

Estimation of Marketability and Acceptability. The site analysis concludes with the appraiser's estimate of its marketability and acceptability, i.e., how the typically informed purchaser in the local market would react to the subject site on the valuation date. Several analytical tools are available to help the appraiser formulate an estimate. The Federal Housing Administration suggests consideration of the following factors:

☐ Physical and social attractiveness

☐ Level of taxes and special assessments

☐ Sufficiency of utilities and services

☐ Protection against hazards, nuisances, and inharmonious uses.

IMPROVEMENTS ANALYSIS

Analysis of the improvements on land (building analysis) begins with a careful inspection of the structures and detailed identification of their pertinent features. This is the basis for the description and evaluation of the improvements used in all three approaches to value. The market acceptability of the property is largely determined by the physical features of the property, their character, and their condition.

Market Standards   Acceptability must be measured within current standards in the local market, as the standards vary among submarkets and over time. These standards are determined by three groups:

Purchasers. The property must satisfy the standards of buyers active in the current market if it is to be sold.

Lenders. This group is interested in the marketability of the property since it is collateral for the mortgage loan. Lenders seek quick disposition of the property in the event of default and foreclosure on a loan. To be acceptable to lenders, a property must be in good physical condition and should generally conform both to the neighborhood and to the expectations of potential purchasers. The FHA standards of property acceptability are often used as guidelines even when the loan will not be insured by the FHA. The FHA standards basically seek to determine whether the building performs the function for which it was designed. The determination is based on ratings in the following categories.

- ☐ Livability

- ☐ Structural quality

- ☐ Suitability of mechanical equipment

- ☐ Resistance to elements and use

- ☐ Natural ventilation and light

- ☐ Visual appeal.

Community Standards. Zoning regulations, building codes, housing codes, and other local regulations are expressions of the community's standards. They influence marketability by limiting the legal uses of a property.

Functional Utility   Once the appraiser has identified the physical characteristics of the property, it is necessary to evaluate how well the structure performs the function for which it was designed. The ability of the property to perform the function for which it is intended, within current market standards and tastes is called functional utility. It is the sum of the attractiveness and usefulness of the property.

Test of Functional Utility. Marketability is the ultimate test of functional utility. If the property is sufficiently useful and desirable to attract purchasers, and if it can be sold and resold without a substantial discount in price, it has the necessary degree of functional utility to sustain marketability and value. The degree of functional utility is measured in terms of the ability of the property to satisfy the needs and desires of typically informed purchasers in the local market.

Functional Obsolescence. This is defined as the *inability* of a structure to efficiently perform the function for which it was intended. The measure of functional utility provides the basis for estimating functional obsolescence in the cost approach to value.

Function of a Residential Structure. The function of a residence is to provide shelter and the amenities of living as efficiently and economically as possible.

☐ The functional utility of a residence is estimated by comparing it with competitive properties currently in the local market and with typical modern residences.

☐ The highest and best use of an improved property is based on the maximum functional utility of the existing improvements. The function of the improvements dictates their use; the market dictates the feasibility and profitability of that function.

Amenities. Amenities are the tangible and intangible benefits of home ownership, including pride of ownership and sense of accomplishment, responsibility, and belonging. These satisfactions arise from such things as a social environment, architectural excellence, scenic views, etc.

☐ The influence of amenities on value must be inferred from the actions of participants in the market; it is not subject to direct measurement.

☐ Amenities are somewhat dependent upon functional utility, since utility enhances the amenities of occupancy.

Elements of Functional Utility

Analysis of these elements will determine whether they add to or detract from the use and enjoyment of the residence, and hence its marketability. This is the ultimate test of functional utility.

Architecture. The style and design should relate the structure to its site and setting and provide a pleasing appearance inside and out. The elements of good architecture are:

☐ Appropriate relationship to setting

☐ Good proportions and scale

☐ Natural, uncontrived use of quality materials

☐ Expert combination of materials, mass, openings, and detail

☐ Good planning, layout, and room design

□ Lasting appeal to create and sustain value.

Design and Layout. Good design provides maximum utilization of the available space. Design is dictated in part by local codes, local conditions, and public acceptance. Design and layout considerations include:

□ Amount of usable space

□ Range of materials and features

□ Placement of equipment, facilities, and fixtures

□ Relationship of room size and type to function. Rooms should be large enough to meet the requirements of typical buyers. The best combination of room types is determined by the market. In some markets, a three bedroom home with one bath is acceptable, while in others, two baths would be the standard.

□ Natural light and ventilation

□ Traffic pattern. Rooms, doors, and equipment should be placed for efficient circulation with minimal competition for space.

Poor design and layout may be indicated by:

□ Lack of privacy due to poor access and traffic patterns

□ Inadequate storage space

□ Rooms too small or too large

□ Excessive cost for the amount and utility of space provided

□ Poor placement of doors and windows.

Performance Standards. The level of service provided by fixtures and equipment must be evaluated in terms of what is required by market standards. Items to be considered:

□ Heating and cooling equipment

□ Ventilation

□ Insulation

□ Natural light

□ Electrical service, wiring, fixtures, and switches

□ Water heater

□ Kitchen fixtures

□ Bathroom fixtures

□ Piping

□ Laundry facilities.

Elements of Improvement Analysis
The physical condition, effective age, and functional adequacy of the improvements must be evaluated in terms of the standards set by typical purchasers, lenders, and communities. A detailed description of the physical condition of the structural components is made in conjunction with the property inspection to be used in the valuation analysis.

Physical Condition
The physical condition of fixtures, equipment, and structural components determines their usefulness and probable remaining economic life. Marketability is influenced by the cost to bring substandard items up to the standard of acceptability in the market. Physical condition is determined by:

Age and Adequacy of Equipment and Fixtures. The adequacy of service provided, age, and condition of equipment and fixtures must be evaluated, as these elements frequently need replacement during the economic life of the entire structure. This analysis is the basis for estimating charges for physical deterioration in the cost approach.

Deferred Maintenance. Items which are in need of immediate repair or replacement are elements of deferred maintenance.

Previous Repairs. Items which have been previously repaired should be evaluated for both type and quality.

Components and Equipment. The physical condition of these items must be noted, including their quality and cost.

Evidence of Structural Damage or Deterioration. Conditions such as settling, cracks, moisture, or water damage may not be economically feasible to correct.

Effective Age
Economic Life. The economic life of improvements to real estate is the period over which they contribute to the value of the property. The economic life of a residence is the length of time that it provides the services and amenities for residential occupancy at costs competitive with those of other residences. The remaining economic life is the appraiser's estimate of the probable number of useful years remaining in the improvements as of the date of the appraisal. The estimate is based on the physical condition of the property and on the attitudes and responses of purchasers in the market.

Calculating Effective Age. The effective age of a structure or a structural component is the difference between its normal economic life and its remaining economic life; it may be more or less than the actual age. The effective age is dependent upon the degree of use or abuse and the quality of maintenance. It may be determined by observation of the physical condition and utility of the structure.

Functional Adequacy The character of the structure and the performance standards of the market together determine the level of functional adequacy. Functional inadequacy may be the result of either superadequacies or deficiencies in the structure.

Superadequacies. These are elements which, in terms of cost, quality or capacity, are in excess of that necessary to perform the intended function. For example:

☐ Overimprovement of the site as compared to typical improvements in the neighborhood; e.g., a 3,000 square foot home in a neighborhood of homes ranging from 1,200 to 1,500 square feet.

☐ Unusually high quality or oversized structural components.

☐ Excessive capacity or cost in equipment or fixtures.

☐ High operating or maintenance costs due to excessively high ceilings, unusually large rooms, etc.

Deficiencies. These are elements which, in terms of cost, quality or capacity, are deficient or inadequate to perform the intended function.

☐ Underimprovement of the site as compared to typical improvements in the neighborhood, such as a 1,500 square foot residence in a neighborhood of 3,000 square foot homes.

☐ Lack of facilities which are considered necessary or desirable in the market. A three bedroom home with one bath is inadequate where the market standard dictates two baths in three bedroom homes.

☐ Insufficient storage, mechanical systems, utilities, etc.

☐ Inadequate or outmoded equipment.

☐ Too small rooms.

☐ Poor traffic pattern.

DATA COLLECTION AND PROPERTY ANALYSIS

Reporting requirements provide the best indication of the type of data that must be gathered. Professional standards are set forth in the publications of the various appraisal organizations. Requirements set by FNMA-FHLMC are included in Exhibit 2.

Data Sources **Field Inspections.** Site visits can provide much of the necessary data. Conditions which are not readily apparent are often disclosed in interviews with the occupants.

Public Records. City and county records provide legal data and confirm observations made during the field inspection. They may also reveal physical characteristics which would not otherwise be apparent.

☐ Deeds give the legal description of the property and property rights.

- [ ] Assessor's records provide property tax information, site and structural dimensions, actual age of the improvements, the construction type and quality, and the number and types of rooms.

- [ ] Zoning maps indicate the zoning classification of the subject and nearby properties.

- [ ] Building inspectors' or engineers' records indicate the type, age, and dimensions of the improvements.

Maps, Plot Plans, Blueprints, and Floor Plans. These illustrate characteristics of the property which are often difficult to express in narrative form. They assist the appraiser in analysis of the subject property and may also be used effectively as visual aids in the appraisal report.

Field Inspection An on-site inspection is necessary to obtain the required data on the physical characteristics of the subject property. In addition, most appraisals require certification that the appraiser has personally inspected the property.

Preparation. Prepare a detailed checklist of items to be inspected. Numerous checklists may be found in appraisal publications and adapted to the task at hand. The blank form can be completed as the inspection proceeds.

Equipment and Tools. The items generally used include a checklist form and clipboard, camera for property and neighborhood photographs, and measuring tape or wheel to determine size of the improvements.

Measurement Precise, accurate measurement is absolutely essential. Since residential properties are often valued on a per-unit basis, the number of units (e.g., square feet, rooms) has a significant impact on the final value estimate. In addition, the size and number of units determine the standards of comparability for other properties.

Site Measurement. Width, depth, frontage, and area are usually obtained from maps, surveys, and deeds. Engineering scales allow the appraiser to measure dimensions and calculate area from maps and plans.

Building Area. The standard measurement for residences is the total number of square feet of living area. Measurements are taken above the basement or foundation line on the outside dimensions.

- [ ] Total living area equals width times length times number of stories.

- [ ] Rooms are measured by interior dimensions between finished wall surfaces.

- [ ] Porches are usually described as part of the improvement rather than a site improvement. Open porches are generally counted at one-third and enclosed porches at one-half of their total area.

- [ ] Garages are not included in the calculation of living area.

Building Volume. In some sections of the nation, volume is the standard form of measurement rather than area. (See page 81.)

☐ *Standard Cubage*. Height is measured from six inches below the first (or basement) floor to the top of the upper ceiling joists. This is then multiplied by the width and length of the structure.

☐ *Attic Cubage*. Formulas must be employed to determine the cubage of attic areas and upper stories which are not full stories. The formulas vary by the type of roof, from a simple triangular gable to more complex forms

Building Inspection
The appraiser's inspection must be thorough, accurate, and objective since the results of this analysis are basic to the final value estimate.

Procedures. When conducting a thorough building inspection, a competent appraiser will:

☐ Note physical appearance and condition of structure.

☐ Estimate the general deterioration of the structure and the extent of deferred maintenance.

☐ Inspect any major recent repairs and obtain detailed information.

☐ Note items of functional inadequacy.

☐ Estimate the remaining economic life of the structure and of replaceable items.

☐ Photograph the subject site and the interior and exterior of the building(s). Front and street elevation photographs are required for almost all appraisal reports, and additional photos are often necessary to provide a realistic impression of the property and its setting.

☐ Interview owner and/or occupants and brokers to obtain information not revealed by the inspection and to confirm or correct impressions acquired from the visual inspection.

Elements. A competent appraiser will consider the following basic elements when inspecting a building:

☐ Visual appeal of the improvements

☐ Condition and age of the structure

☐ Size of the structure and rooms

☐ Number and type of rooms

☐ Floor plan and traffic routes

☐ Construction quality

☐ Equipment and fixtures

☐ Functional utility.

Building Structure Basic knowledge of construction materials and methods is prerequisite to this portion of the analysis. The appraiser must know what to look for and how to estimate the quality and condition of the structural components.

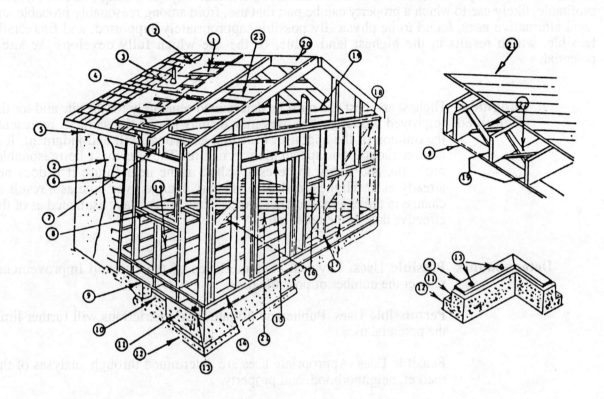

1. **Spaced (or Open) Sheathing**—boards nailed to rafters as base for roof.
2. **Building Paper**—used between sheathing and roof or siding.
3. **Flashing**—metal used to protect against water seepage.
4. **Rafters**—sloping members of roof to support sheathing.
5. **Eaves**—protruding underpart of roof overhanging the wall.
6. **Solid Sheathing**—boards nailed to studs as base for wall.
7. **Cripple**—stud above or below a window or door opening.
8. **Sill**—bottom of a door or window frame.
9. **Mud Sill**—treated member bolted to foundation.
10. **Crawl Space**—unexcavated area under house. FHA minimum: 18".
11. **Foundation**—concrete base of house.
12. **Footing**—expanded portion of concrete foundation.

13. **Anchor Bolt**—used for fastening mud sill to the foundation
14. **Sole Plate**—support on which the studs rest.
15. **Header**—beam over door or window; also called a lintel.
16. **Fire Stop**—used to block flames from spreading to the attic.
17. **Studs**—vertical 2"x4" framework of walls; spaced 16" on center.
18. **Bracing**—diagonal boards on wall to prevent sway.
19. **Joists**—members supporting floor or ceiling loads.
20. **Ridge Board**—top beam for support of rafters.
21. **Subflooring**—rough boards laid on joists to support flooring.
22. **Bridging**—wooden pieces between joists to stiffen and hold them.
23. **Purlin**—a horizontal member which braces and stabilizes the rafters.

ANALYSIS AND ESTIMATE OF HIGHEST AND BEST USE

Highest and best use is defined as that reasonable and probable use of the property which will support the highest present value, as of the valuation date. Other ways of stating this are: the most profitable, likely use to which a property can be put; that use, from among reasonably probable and legal alternative uses, found to be physically possible, appropriately supported, and financially feasible, which results in the highest land value; or the use which fully develops the site's potential.

Judgment Required Highest and best use must be determined separately for the site and for the improved property. The uses may or may not be the same. It represents the opinion of the appraiser based on analytical skill and judgment. It is neither factual nor speculative in nature. The use must be reasonable, probable, and likely to be established in the near future if it does not already exist. Highest and best use may change over time as a result of change in the external market forces. Thus, it is always estimated as of the effective date of the appraisal.

Determinants **Possible Uses.** Physical characteristics of the site and improvements restrict the number of possible uses.

Permissible Uses. Public and private legal restrictions will further limit the potential uses.

Feasible Uses. Appropriate uses are determined through analyses of the market, neighborhood, and property.

Highest and Best Use. Given the preceding constraints, the appraiser must determine which use or uses will provide the highest present value.

Site In the estimation of market value, the site is always valued as if vacant and available to be put to its highest and best use. The suitability of the site for its existing or proposed use as well as suitability for alternative uses must be analyzed. The appraiser should identify the development program for the site which will produce the greatest future benefits for the owner, specifying the form of the benefits to be received and the time period over which they will be received.

Improved Property Estimation of the highest and best use of improved property is an estimation of the highest and best use of the entire property including any existing improvements. Where there are existing improvements this estimate may differ from the highest and best use of the site. It is assumed that the existing use will continue until the value of the site in its highest and best use exceeds the total value of the property in its existing use.

SITE

Dimensions		Topography	
Site Area	Corner Lot	Size	
Zoning Classification	Zoning Compliance	Shape	
HIGHEST & BEST USE: Present Use	Other Use	Drainage	

UTILITIES	Public	Other	SITE IMPROVEMENTS	Type	Public	Private	View	
Electricity	☐		Street		☐	☐	Landscaping	
Gas	☐		Curb/Gutter		☐	☐	Driveway	
Water	☐		Sidewalk		☐	☐	Apparent Easements	
Sanitary Sewer	☐		Street Lights		☐	☐	FEMA Flood Hazard	Yes* ___ No ___
Storm Sewer	☐		Alley		☐	☐	FEMA* Map/Zone	

COMMENTS (Apparent adverse easements, encroachments, special assessments, slide areas, etc.):

IMPROVEMENTS

GENERAL DESCRIPTION	EXTERIOR DESCRIPTION	FOUNDATION	BASEMENT	INSULATION
Units	Foundation	Slab	Area Sq. Ft.	Roof ☐
Stories	Exterior Walls	Crawl Space	% Finished	Ceiling ☐
Type (Det./Att.)	Roof Surface	Basement	Ceiling	Walls ☐
Design (Style)	Gutters & Dwnspts.	Sump Pump	Walls	Floor ☐
Existing	Window Type	Dampness	Floor	None ☐
Proposed	Storm Sash	Settlement	Outside Entry	Adequacy ☐
Under Construction	Screens	Infestation		Energy Efficient Items:
Age (Yrs.)	Manufactured House			
Effective Age (Yrs.)				

ROOM LIST

ROOMS	Foyer	Living	Dining	Kitchen	Den	Family Rm.	Rec. Rm.	Bedrooms	# Baths	Laundry	Other	Area Sq. Ft.
Basement												
Level 1												
Level 2												

Finished area **above** grade contains: _____ Rooms; _____ Bedroom(s); _____ Bath(s); _____ Square Feet of Gross Living Area

INTERIOR

SURFACES	Materials/Condition	HEATING		KITCHEN EQUIP.		ATTIC		IMPROVEMENT ANALYSIS	Good	Avg.	Fair	Poor
Floors		Type		Refrigerator	☐	None	☐	Quality of Construction	☐	☐	☐	☐
Walls		Fuel		Range/Oven	☐	Stairs	☐	Condition of Improvements	☐	☐	☐	☐
Trim/Finish		Condition		Disposal	☐	Drop Stair	☐	Room Sizes/Layout	☐	☐	☐	☐
Bath Floor		Adequacy		Dishwasher	☐	Scuttle	☐	Closets and Storage	☐	☐	☐	☐
Bath Wainscot		COOLING		Fan/Hood	☐	Floor	☐	Energy Efficiency	☐	☐	☐	☐
Doors		Central		Compactor	☐	Heated	☐	Plumbing-Adequacy & Condition	☐	☐	☐	☐
		Other		Washer/Dryer	☐	Finished	☐	Electrical-Adequacy & Condition	☐	☐	☐	☐
		Condition		Microwave	☐			Kitchen Cabinets-Adequacy & Cond.	☐	☐	☐	☐
Fireplace(s)	#	Adequacy		Intercom	☐			Compatibility to Neighborhood	☐	☐	☐	☐

AUTOS

CAR STORAGE:								Appeal & Marketability	☐	☐	☐	☐
	Garage	☐	Attached	☐	Adequate	☐	House Entry	☐	Estimated Remaining Economic Life			Yrs.
No. Cars	Carport	☐	Detached	☐	Inadequate	☐	Outside Entry	☐	Estimated Remaining Physical Life			Yrs.
Condition	None		Built-In	☐	Electric Door	☐	Basement Entry	☐				

Additional features:

COMMENTS

Depreciation (Physical, functional and external inadequacies, repairs needed, modernization, etc.):

General market conditions and prevalence and impact in subject/market area regarding loan discounts, interest buydowns and concessions:

Site In order for a property to qualify for maximum financing, the site should be of a size, shape, and topography that is generally conforming and acceptable in the market area. It must also have competitive utilities, street improvements, and other amenities. Since amenities, easements, and encroachments may either detract from or enhance the site's marketability, the appraiser must comment on them if the site is not typical for the neighborhood.

Dimensions. The subject property's dimensions must be listed (width x length).

Site Area. The total land area must be listed and expressed in terms of square footage or acreage.

Corner Lot. The appraiser should enter a "yes" or "no" and additional information if applicable.

Zoning Classification. The zoning category and major permitted uses must be entered using local zoning code classifications (e.g., "R-1 Residential—Single Family").

Zoning Compliance. The appraiser should enter a "yes" or "no" and a full explanation of non-conforming use.

Highest and Best Use. The highest and best use of a site is that reasonable and probable use that supports the highest present value on the effective date of the appraisal. Usually, the appraiser will indicate "Present Use." However, if the current improvements clearly do not represent the highest and best use of the site as an improved site, the appraiser must so indicate this on the appraisal report in the "Other Use" section.

Utilities. In this section the appraiser identifies five categories (electricity, gas, water, sanitary sewer, and storm sewer) of public or private utility services. In the case of private utilities, the appraiser must explain their adequacy and acceptability. Generally, a property's utilities must meet community standards and be accepted by area residents.

Site Improvements. In this section the appraiser describes five categories (street, curb/gutter, sidewalk, street lights, and alley) and indicates the type of maintenance (public or private).

Physical Characteristics. In this section the appraiser briefly describes ten characteristics of the subject property (topography, size, shape, drainage, view, landscaping, driveway, apparent easements, FEMA Flood Hazard and FEMA Map/Zone.

Comments. This section is provided for the appraiser to comment on any adverse conditions and to address their effect on the subject property's marketability and value.

Improvements   The appraiser must provide a clear, detailed, and accurate description of the improvements. The appraiser should be as specific as possible, and should provide supporting addenda if necessary. Generally, improvements should conform to the neighborhood in terms of age, type, design, and materials used for their construction.

General Description. In this section the appraiser describes the subject property in terms of: Units, Stories, Type (Detached/Attached), Design (Style), Existing, Proposed, Under Construction, Age (Years), Effective Age (Years). The relationship between the actual and effective ages of the property is a good indication of its condition. A property that has been well maintained will generally have an effective age somewhat lower than its actual age. Conversely, a property that has an effective age higher than its actual age probably has not been well maintained or may have a particular physical problem.

Exterior Description. In this section the appraiser describes the subject property in terms of: Foundation, Exterior Walls, Roof Surface, Gutters and Downspouts, Window Type, Storm Sash, Screens, and Manufactured House. The appraiser should be as specific as possible, indicating the method of construction, materials used, etc.

Foundation. In this section the appraiser enters a "yes" or "no" for six categories: Slab, Crawl Space, Basement, Sump Pump, Dampness, Settlement, and Infestation. In the event of a "yes" in any of the last three categories, the appraiser should comment on the location and extent of the condition.

Basement. The basement is considered separately from the room count and square feet of gross living area. The appraiser must describe the basement in terms of: Area in Square Feet, Percent Finished, Ceiling, Walls, Floor, and Outside Entry. Any finished area in the basement should be completely described in the Comments section.

Insulation. This section requires the appraiser to state the "R" value for insulation if he or she is aware of it and to comment on the adequacy of the insulation of Roof, Ceiling, Walls, and Floor. The appraiser should also list the energy efficient items to reflect the overall contribution of these items to the market value of the subject property. The nature of these items and their contribution to value will vary throughout the country because of climatic conditions and differences in utility costs.

Room List   This section of the URAR requires a description of all the rooms in the subject property. In addition, it provides a column for the gross living area per level, as well as space for a summary of the total above-grade room count and the above-grade gross living area. The appraiser should become familiar with and use the local methods of determining room count. Likewise, the appraiser must be consistent when he or she calculates and reports the finished above-grade room count and the square feet of gross living area that is above-grade.

Interior   This section of the URAR provides for a further description of the subject property and for an analysis of the improvements.

Surfaces. In this section, the appraiser enters a description of the type, quality, and condition of the following finished surfaces: Floors, Walls, Trim/Finish, Bath Floor, Bath Wainscot, Doors, and Fireplace(s). Condition is indicated by "Good," "Average," "Fair," and "Poor" ratings using the same criteria as in the Neighborhood section discussed earlier.

Heating and Cooling. In this section, the appraiser enters a brief description, or a simple "yes" or "no," for the type, quality, and condition of the: Heating (Type, Fuel, Condition, Adequacy) and the Cooling (Central, Other, Condition, Adequacy). Opinions regarding the condition and adequacy should based on inspection and research and reflect current market conditions and the purchaser's requirements.

Kitchen Equipment. The appraiser checks the appropriate box to indicate whether the following kitchen items are in place and operating: Refrigerator, Range/Oven, Disposal, Dishwasher, Fan/Hood, Compactor, Washer/Dryer, Microwave, Intercom. If the items are removable and considered personal property, the appraiser should enter a "P" in the box and not consider these in the valuation process.

Attic. If the subject property has an attic (e.g., the space located between the ceiling joists and rafters), the appraiser checks the appropriate box to specify the type of access: None, Stairs, Drop Stair, or Scuttle. In addition, the appraiser checks the appropriate box to further describe the attic in terms of Floor, Heated, Finished.

Improvement Analysis. This section provides a summary of the principal factors about the improvements that have a bearing on the value and marketability of the subject property. The factors are rated to indicate how the subject property compares to competing properties in the general market area. The same ratings that were used in the Neighborhood analysis—Good, Average, Fair, and Poor—are used to summarize the following items: Quality of Construction, Condition of Improvements, Room Sizes/Layout, Closets and Storage, Energy Efficiency, Plumbing–Adequacy & Condition, Compatibility to Neighborhood, Appeal and Marketability. The appraiser must then indicate the Estimated Remaining Economic Life—the estimated period over which the improvements will continue to contribute to the value of the property, or the estimated period in which the improvements increase the value of the property above that for the vacant site. The last entry the appraiser makes in this section is the Estimated Remaining Physical Life—the estimated period over which the improvements will physically last if they receive normal maintenance.

Autos In this section the appraiser describes the type and adequacy of the subject property's car storage facilities: Number of Cars, Condition, Garage, Carport, or None. The condition should be rated using the same ratings that were used in the neighborhood analysis—Good, Average, Fair, and Poor.

Comments The appraiser must address any needed repairs or any physical, functional, or external inadequacies in this section. In addition, the appraiser should also include comments related to general market conditions in the subject market area in the spaces provided in this section.

BUILDING CALCULATIONS

Real property consists of land and structures which have physical dimensions of length, width, area, and volume. Appraisers, lenders, and investors require analysis and comparison of building content. For this purpose, exterior dimensions are used. The square foot system is probably the most popular and can be applied to residential, commercial and industrial structures. Gross floor area is computed excluding porches, garages and basements—which are treated separately. The cubic foot system is used to calculate total volume. It includes attics, basements, and dormer projections which the square foot system does not include. Basic formulas include:

$A = L \times W$ Area of a rectangle equals Length times Width

$V = L \times W \times H$ Volume equals Length times Width times Height

$V = \dfrac{ba}{2} \times L$ Area of a triangle equals Base times Altitude quantity divided by 2 times Length

$D = \dfrac{\text{square units}}{\text{width}}$ Depth equals square units divided by width

$W = \dfrac{\text{square units}}{\text{depth}}$ Width equals square units divided by depth

To Find Area of a Rectangle
Calculate the area of this house.

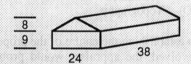

$A = L \times W$
$A = 24 \times 38$
$A = 912 \text{ square feet}$

To Find Cubic Content of a Rectangle
Calculate the volume of the lower part of the house.

$V = L \times W \times H$
$V = 24 \times 38 \times 9$
$V = 8,208 \text{ cubic feet}$

To Find Cubic Content of a Triangle
Calculate the volume of the attic.

$V = \dfrac{ba}{2} \times L$

$V = \dfrac{24 \times 8}{2} \times 38$

$V = 3,648 \text{ cubic feet}$

Volume Calculations Result: 8,208 + 3,648 = 11,856 cubic feet

To Find Depth
Two-story row houses in a certain area have 18'6" fronts. These homes are sold for $16,650, which is equivalent to $12.50 a square foot. How deep are these houses?

$16,650	÷	$12.50	=	1,322 sq. ft.
1,322 sq.ft.	÷	2 floors	=	666 sq. ft. per floor
666 sq. ft. per floor	÷	18,5'	=	36 feet

Chapter 6 Quiz

1. Highest and best use can be best defined as that use:

    (A) Producing the highest gross income
    (B) Complying with zoning and deed restrictions
    (C) Contributing to the best interest of the community
    (D) Which fully develops the site's potential

2. Site analysis includes evaluation of:

    (A) Physical and legal characteristics of the subject property
    (B) Physical, legal and economic characteristics of the subject property
    (C) Physical and legal characteristics of the subject property and the neighborhood
    (D) Physical, legal, economic and locational factors

3. Property analysis evaluates the:

    (A) Unimproved land only
    (B) Site and improvements
    (C) Improvements only
    (D) Value of the subject property

4. The sum of the usefulness and attractiveness of a property is its:

    (A) Highest and best use
    (B) Value
    (C) Functional utility
    (D) Location

5. Which of the following conditions lowers property values?

    (A) Neighborhood conformity
    (B) Deferred maintenance
    (C) Excessive demand
    (D) Highest degree of utility

6. The construction date of an older structure indicates its:

    (A) Effective age
    (B) Economic life
    (C) Remaining economic life
    (D) None of the above

7. To establish the total square footage of a residence, the appraiser would normally measure the:

    (A) Interior of each room
    (B) Interior of each room plus garage
    (C) Exterior dimensions of the dwelling
    (D) Exterior dimensions of the dwelling plus the garage

8. The way in which a structure is placed on a lot in relation to sun, wind, and other structures is called:

    (A) Evaluation
    (B) Conformity
    (C) Orientation
    (D) Topography

9. In establishing the nature of the property rights involved, the appraiser would probably rely mainly on:

    (A) Interviews
    (B) Public records
    (C) On-site inspection
    (D) Zoning maps

10. Which of the following is not an improvement *to* the land?

    (A) Garage
    (B) Landscaping
    (C) Curb and gutter
    (D) Drains

FUNDAMENTALS OF SITE VALUATION

Site valuation is essentially the same as the valuation of improved properties. However, there are several points which merit particular emphasis.

Site vs. Land   Residential sites, not land, are valued. A site is land which has been improved to the point of readiness for its intended use. The only exception to this is raw land which is suitable for or planned for development as residential sites.

Valuation   A site is always valued as if vacant and available to be put to its highest and best use, regardless of whether it is actually vacant or improved. This is the basis for determining whether the present use of the site actually represents its highest and best use.

Effect on Valuation of Improvements. Valuation of the site in terms of its highest and best use means that all physical deterioration and functional obsolescence are appropriately charged to the improvements.

Purpose of   With the exception of raw acreage to be developed for residential use, the
Separate Valuation   site rather than the land is valued in residential property valuation.

Vacant Land. The appraisal assignment may be to estimate the value of a vacant site or of vacant land to be developed as sites.

Cost Approach. The cost approach requires separate valuation of the site.

Income Approach. Some applications of the income approach require independent valuation of the site.

Remainder Value. For insurance purposes, it may be necessary to estimate the remainder value of the site in the event that the improvements are destroyed.

Taxation. Separate valuations for the site and the improvements must often be established for property tax and income tax purposes.

Eminent Domain. Condemnation courts may require separate value estimates.

Land Leases. The site must be valued separately when the land is leased in order to determine the interests of the lessor

SITE VALUATION METHODS

The methods of site valuation are essentially the sales comparison approach and the income capitalization approach, or a variation of one of these.

The sales comparison approach is generally the most applicable method of site valuation. Variations of this approach include:

- ☐ Direct sales comparisons
- ☐ Abstraction, and
- ☐ Ideal neighborhood and site comparison.

Variations of the income capitalization technique include:

- ☐ Direct capitalization of ground rents
- ☐ The land residual technique, and
- ☐ The cost of development method.

Sales Comparison Analysis The sales comparison method is the preferred method whenever adequate quantities of verified sales data of sufficient quality are available. It is presumed that recent sales of comparable sites, competitive with the subject on the local market, are the best indication of the behavior of informed purchasers in the current market.

Requirements. The elements of comparison required for a site valuation are:

- ☐ Detailed site description in terms of the pertinent elements of comparison for each competitive site.
- ☐ Transaction data on the sale of each competitive site; all data must be verified with one of the principals to the transaction.
- ☐ An active market.

☐ At least eight to ten comparable site sales should be analyzed and at least three should be included in the report.

Sources. Data sources are the same as those used in the comparison process for improved properties.

Elements of Comparison. The elements of comparison in site valuation are essentially the same as those used in the comparison process for improved properties.

☐ Location—the most important element

☐ Time

☐ Condition of sale

☐ Terms of financing

☐ Physical characteristics, consisting of both attributes and variable characteristics:

PHYSICAL CHARACTERISTICS

Attributes	**Variable Characteristics**
Municipal services (fire, police protection, etc.)	Area (square feet or acres)
	Dimensions of the lot
Utilities	Width
Topography	Depth
Drainage	Frontage
Soil and subsoil conditions	
Shape of lot	
Access	

Units of Comparison. Use of standard units makes it possible to directly compare sites which vary in shape or size. Minor variations in size may be accounted for by reducing the valuation analysis to a unit basis. However, the appraiser must exercise care to avoid comparing sites which are really in different markets, because the differences in their shape or size affect the use to which they can appropriately be put. The key considerations are the standards of acceptance in the market in which the subject site is located. The appropriate unit may be the:

☐ Acre

☐ Square foot

☐ Front foot, or

☐ Lot. In some areas, minor variations in lot size do not significantly influence value. There may be a fairly standard lot size, perhaps the minimum size specified by zoning regulations.

The Adjustment Process. Again, this process is essentially the same as in the direct sales comparison analysis for improved properties.

☐ Sales prices of comparable sites are adjusted from the comparable to the subject site.

☐ The possible methods of adjustment are:

Plus and minus dollar adjustments

Plus and minus percentage adjustments

Whole property adjustments.

☐ The sequence of adjustments should logically begin with any necessary adjustment for time.

☐ The amount and direction of adjustments are determined from the behavior of typically informed purchasers in the market.

☐ To be an effective indicator of value, the net adjustment for the comparable sales transaction should not exceed 15% to 20% of the actual sales price.

Reconciliation. Adjusted sales prices should point to an estimate of site value, after application of the appropriate adjustments to each comparable sales price. Assuming that these sites are truly comparable and competitive with the subject, the adjusted sales prices should fall within a relatively narrow range. The market value of the subject site should lie within this range. The appraiser must then select the most appropriate indicated market value, based upon an estimate of the reliability of the data used and the justification for each adjustment. As a general rule, the greatest reliance can be placed on those comparable sales which have required the least adjustments.

☐ If a per unit (acre, lot, square foot, front foot) value is estimated, the value must be multiplied by the appropriate number of units to obtain the final estimate.

☐ The final value estimate should always be rounded to an appropriate level. Unrounded numbers imply a greater degree of accuracy than is possible in an estimate.

Abstraction   The abstraction technique involves subtracting the estimated value of the improvements from the sales prices of improved properties. The remainder is the indicated value of the site for that comparable sale. This technique is also referred to as the allocation technique, the distribution technique or the ratio of lot to building costs.

Uses and Limitation. Although considered an acceptable technique, abstraction is limited in its application and use:

☐ Application of the abstraction technique may be necessary where the subject site is located in a built-up area with no recent sales of lots.

☐ The technique is limited in that it is often difficult to justify a division of sales price or value between a given site and its improvements.

☐ It is rarely considered sufficient to rely on abstraction alone in estimating site value.

Ratio of Site Value to Total Property Value. This variation of the technique requires the appraiser to attempt to determine the proportion of the total sales price that is typically attributable to the site.

Illustration

Suppose that a comparable residential property recently sold for $100,000. The house is a typical improvement and is estimated to have a depreciated present worth of $80,000. This is 80% of the sales price, thus the site is said to contribute 20% of the total property value. The building to site ratio is therefore 4:1.

☐ This technique is limited because it assumes that:

The subject site is a typical site developed in a typical fashion.

The conditions of sale and terms of financing for the subject and each of the comparable sales are "normal."

Each of the comparable properties is in the same neighborhood as the subject and is influenced by the same market conditions.

There exists a typical ratio of building to site value which is equally applicable to the subject and each of the comparable sales.

☐ It is often difficult to estimate the depreciated value of the building separately and directly.

☐ The technique cannot be used if the percentages vary or if the subject property is not typical of properties in its market.

Ratio of Site Value to Building Costs. Where it is appropriate to assume that a new residence in a new development represents the highest and best use of a site, the cost of the building may be subtracted from the sales price of the improved property to arrive at the portion of total value attributable to the site. Limitations of this technique arise from the assumptions that appropriate adjustments can be made to allow for the builder/developer's overhead and profit in the building cost, and that the properties included in the analysis are truly comparable to, and highly competitive with, the subject site.

Ideal Neighborhood and Site Comparison Method

This technique is a variation of the direct sales comparison approach in that an ideal neighborhood is used as the base for comparison rather than the subject property. A standard is developed for the "ideal" neighborhood and then the subject and the comparable sales are compared to this standard.

Limitation. The weights assigned in this technique are essentially arbitrary.

Illustration	
Features	**Percent Rating**
Location—access, transportation to employment centers, schools, shopping	15
Surroundings—age, upkeep, price range, percent developed	10
Amenities—appeal, prestige, competitiveness	25
Zoning—compatibility of land uses, protection	15
Services and street improvements—police and fire protection, utilities, street lighting, refuse collection	10
Lot features—appeal, size, shape, topography, landscaping	15
Traffic—access, parking, safety	10
Total Rating	**100**

Site Valuation Rating Table					
				Comparable	Sale
Rating Features	Ideal	Subject	1	2	3
Location	15	10	12	9	15
Surroundings	10	8	6	9	8
Amenities	25	15	18	12	10
Zoning	15	10	8	11	5
Services	10	6	4	5	8
Lot features	15	10	8	7	9
Traffic	10	4	5	5	5
Total Rating	100	63	61	58	60

An adjustment percentage ratio is then established by comparing the subject property with each comparable sale as illustrated in the following table:

Site Valuation Adjustment Table				
Subject Property Rating	Comparable Sale Rating	Adjustment Ratio	Price of Sale Property	Adjusted Price
Comparable Sale 1				
63	− 61	= 1.033	x $74,000	= $76,442
Comparable Sale 2				
63	− 58	= 1.086	x $70,000	= $76,020
Comparable Sale 2				
63	− 60	= 1.050	x $72,500	= $76,125

Direct Capitalization of Ground Rental Where residential sites are rented on long-term ground leases, annual or monthly rentals can be capitalized to develop an estimate of site value. The derivation of net income and an appropriate discount rate will be discussed in Chapter 11.

Illustration. Suppose that a residential site is on a long-term net lease with a ground rent of $1,500 per year. Assuming that the appropriate discount rate is 10%, the estimated site value by direct capitalization is: $1,500 ÷ .10 = $15,000.

Land Residual Technique Because it is based on a forecast of net operating income, this technique is used primarily for income producing properties and is rarely applicable to residential site valuation. Essentially, it is assumed that the site is improved with a building which represents the highest and best use of the site. The reproduction cost new (discussed in Chapter 8) of that building is estimated. Next, the annual income necessary to cover the investment in the building (return on and return of investment) is deducted from the forecast annual net operating income for the property. The remainder or residual net income is then available to support the investment in the land. This residual is capitalized at the appropriate discount rate to obtain an indicated present value for the site.

Cost of Development Method This technique may be used in the valuation of raw acreage, either proposed or designed for residential development. Since it begins with an assumption regarding the sales prices for the completed sites, it cannot be used in the valuation of individual sites. The cost of development method is generally used to determine how much a developer would be justified in paying for the raw acreage for development. For example, assume that market studies have shown that all 100 lots in a particular subdivision can be sold over a one-year period at the following prices:

Cost of Development Illustration

75 lots x $10,000 each	=	$750,000
15 lots x $15,000 each	=	225,000
10 lots x $20,000 each	=	200,000
Total Value of Anticipated Lot Sales		$1,175,000
Less development costs:		
Water mains at $600 per lot	=	$60,000
Storm and sanitary sewers at $500 per lot	=	50,000
Street grading and paving at $600 per lot	=	60,000
Curbs and gutters at $300 per lot	=	30,000
Other indirect costs, including legal and accounting fees, overhead, brokerage commissions, property taxes, etc.	=	50,000
Developer's profit at 10% of gross sales	=	117,500
Total development costs (and profit)	=	$ 367,500
Residual Value of Raw Land	=	$ 807,500

VALUATION OF IMPROVEMENTS TO LAND

Site improvements are generally valued at their depreciated cost new in place. The key consideration in estimating their value is what they contribute to the value of the site and to the value of the improved property. The preferred method for estimating the value of site improvements is to treat them as one factor in the adjustment process in the direct sales comparison approach. Thus, the judgment of the market indicates what a potential purchaser would pay for these improvements as of the date of the appraisal.

EXAMPLES OF LAND SALES ANALYSIS

Per-Unit Approach These parcels of land were all sold recently. There were no significant differences *except for size*.

Sale	Acres	Price Per Acre
1	350	$4,500
2	480	4,000
3	2,700	2,200
4	1,000	3,500
5	5,600	2,000
6	900	3,700
7	5,400	2,200
8	1,475	3,000
9	841	4,000

When data like the above are graphed, the relationship between size and unit price is often illuminated. If a strong relationship is revealed, inferences about similar parcels can be made, with adjustments for size differences.

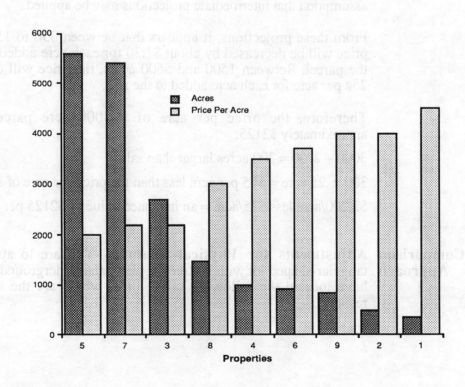

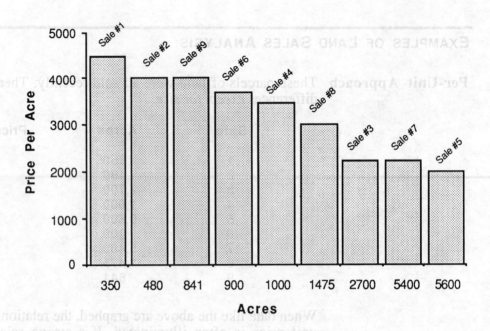

The charts show that as the size of the parcel increases, the cost per acre decreases at a fairly predictable rate. Sale 1, the smallest parcel, sold at a price of $4,500 per acre. Sale 5, the largest, sold at $2,000 per acre. The other sales, at intermediate steps, sold at prices which support the assumption that intermediate projections may be applied.

From these projections, it appears that between 350 to 1500 acres, the price will be decreased by about $1.30 for each acre added to the size of the parcel. Between 1500 and 5600 acres, the price will drop by about 25¢ per acre for each acre added to the size.

Therefore, the price per acre of a 3000 acre parcel should be approximately $2125:

3000 – 2700 = 300 acres larger than sale 3

300 x .25/acre = $75 per acre less than the price per acre of sale 3

$2,200/acre less $75/acre = an indicated value of $2125 per acre.

Sales Comparison Approach   **Adjustments for Physical Features**. You are to appraise a rectangular-shaped lot with no trees, a view, and underground utilities. You have located the following sales, all of which are the same in other respects.

Sale 1 Irregular shape Above-ground utilities Trees No view Sales price - $112,000	**Sale 2** Rectangular shape Underground utilities Trees Good view Sales price - $118,500
Sale 3 Irregular shape Underground utilities No trees Good view Sales price - $115,500	**Sale 4** Rectangular shape Above-ground utilities No trees Good view Sales price - $114,500
Sale 5 Irregular shape Above-ground utilities No trees No view Sales price - $111,000	

The matched pairs technique makes it possible to derive the indicated adjustment for:

Trees   + $1000 for trees (using Sales 1 and 3)

Shape   + $2000 for rectangular

Utilities   + $3000 for underground

View   + $1500 for good view

What is the indicated value of the subject site? The subject is most similar to Sale #2. Subtracting $1000 for no trees, the indicated value is $117,500. This checks with the other sales as well.

Other Adjustments. You are to appraise a vacant lot in the Fig Garden subdivision. There has been a lot of sales activity in this subdivision and you were able to collect four comparable sales. You will adjust for location, condition of sale, and physical characteristics. All other conditions are considered equal to the subject. What will your dollar adjustments be for each of the elements?

Sale 1	**Sale 2**
Condition:	Condition:
10% cash down	10% cash down
Location:	Location:
near the college	away from the college
Physical Characteristics:	Physical Characteristics:
average view lot	average view lot
Sales Price: $145,000	Sales Price: $147,000
Sale 3	**Sale 4**
Condition:	Condition:
20% cash down	20% cash down
Location:	Location:
near the college	away from the college
Physical Characteristics:	Physical Characteristics:
average view lot	excellent view lot
Sales Price: $142,000	Sales Price: $152,000

Location: – $2000 near the college (Sales 1 and 2)

Condition: – $3000 for 20% down (Sales 1 and 3)

Physical Characteristics: + $8000 for excellent view (Sale 4 and the foregoing adjustments)

1. Which of the following is not a method of appraising unimproved real property?

    (A) Reproduction technique
    (B) Direct sales comparison approach
    (C) Cost of development method
    (D) Abstraction

2. Adjustments to the sales prices of comparable sites may be based on:

    (A) Size
    (B) Time of sale
    (C) Financing
    (D) All of the above

3. How many comparable site sales should be analyzed when using the direct sales comparison method?

    (A) Three
    (B) Five to ten
    (C) Eight to ten
    (D) Ten to fifteen

4. In the adjustment process, the sale prices of comparable sites are:

    (A) Adjusted from the subject site to each of the comparable sites
    (B) Adjusted to reflect the attributes of the other comparables; the results are then averaged to obtain an estimated value for the subject
    (C) Simply averaged to obtain an indicated market value for the subject site
    (D) Adjusted from the comparable to the subject site

5. The most important element of comparison in site valuation is:

    (A) Location
    (B) Size
    (C) Conditions of sale
    (D) Date of sale

6. A new home sold for $75,000. Direct construction costs were $48,000 and indirect costs were 10% of direct costs. The builder's overhead and profit were 20% of total costs. Using the abstraction technique, the estimated site value is:

    (A) $ 4,500   52800.
    (B) $ 7,200   63360 —
    (C) $ 9,900
    (D) $11,600

7. A virtually identical comparable site sold two months ago for $25,000. The time adjustment is 12% per year. Determine the adjusted sales price of the comparable site.

    (A) $22,000
    (B) $24,500
    (C) $25,500
    (D) $28,000

8. Separate valuations of sites are often needed for:

    (A) Cost approach appraisals
    (B) Insurance purposes
    (C) Income tax purposes
    (D) All of the above

9. A residential property recently sold for $100,000. The house is estimated to have a depreciated present worth of $80,000. The building-to-site ratio is:

    (A) 4:1
    (B) 4:5
    (C) 1:4
    (D) 1:5

10. In sales comparison analysis, comparable sales are adjusted to:

    (A) An ideal property
    (B) The standards set by the market
    (C) All other comparable sales
    (D) The subject property

Chapter 8
The Cost Approach:
Nature and Use

PREVIEW

PREVIEW

Nature and Use of the Cost Approach to Value Estimation

Types and Use of New Cost Estimates

Data Program

Cost Estimation

Estimation of Total Reproduction Cost New

NATURE AND USE OF THE COST APPROACH TO VALUE ESTIMATION

The cost approach is based on the premise that an informed purchaser would pay no more for a particular property than the cost of producing a substitute property of equal utility.

Principles of Value Involved

Substitution. A rational, informed purchaser will not pay more for a property than the cost of acquiring or producing a substitute property with the same utility as the subject property.

Contribution. The value of a component part of a property is the amount that it contributes to the value of the whole, or how much its absence detracts from the value of the entire property.

Balance. If the improvements on and to the site do not represent the highest and best use of that site, they may detract from the value of the whole property. They may be either underimprovements or overimprovements.

Highest and Best Use. Real estate tends to be put to its highest and best use in a competitive market over the long term. A site is always valued as if vacant and available to be put to its highest and best use. Functional obsolescence results from overimprovement or underimprovement of the property, based on a comparison of the existing improvements with the highest and best use of the site.

Steps in the Cost Approach

Site Value. Estimate the value of the site as if vacant and available to be put to its highest and best use.

Improvement Value. Estimate the reproduction or replacement cost new of the improvements. Then:

☐ Estimate all the elements of accrued depreciation: physical deterioration, functional obsolescence, and economic obsolescence.

☐ Deduct the total amount of accrued depreciation from cost to replace new to derive the present depreciated cost of the basic improvements. This results in the measure of the present worth or contribution of the improvements to the total value of the property.

☐ Add the estimated depreciated present worth of any site improvements excluded from consideration with the major improvements. This gives the present worth of all improvements.

Combined Value. Add the total present worth of all improvements to the established site value.

Value Estimate. Round this figure to an appropriate level. This represents the estimated value of the subject property by the cost approach.

Special Considerations

Cost is not the same as value, nor does it create value. However, cost may be an indication of value under certain circumstances.

Cost new tends to indicate the upper limit of value when the site is improved with new buildings which represent the highest and best use of that site. However, the estimate of value made by the cost approach does not necessarily represent the upper limit of value.

The cost approach, like all other approaches to value estimation, is market-oriented. It reflects market data and the market behavior of purchasers.

Uses and Applications

The nature of the cost approach makes it particularly applicable under certain circumstances.

New or Proposed Construction. The cost approach can be very effective where new or proposed construction represents the highest and best use of the site. Under these conditions, the cost to produce improvements with the same utility as the subject can be estimated with relative ease as there is little or no accrued depreciation.

Unique Properties. The value of special purpose properties or properties for which there are no effectively comparable properties often can be estimated only by the cost approach.

No Market Comparables. Occasionally, there may be a period of no market activity for certain property types, particularly in small communities in which there is necessarily a low level of general market activity. The lack of comparable sales data makes it impossible to use the direct sales comparison approach or the gross rent multiplier method. The cost approach is the only alternative method for estimating value in such situations.

Property Insurance Purposes. The cost approach is normally the basis for determining compensation for fire and casualty losses.

Limitations

Depreciation. Proper use of the cost approach relies heavily on an accurate, defensible estimate of accrued depreciation. As a rule, the greater the amount of accrued depreciation observed in an existing structure, and the more the estimate of value depends on an accurate estimate of that accrued depreciation, the less the reliance that can be placed on the value estimate.

Unrealistic. The typical buyer may not actually consider producing a new structure on a vacant site as a viable alternative to acquiring an existing property.

Complexity. Depending on the method employed, estimation of cost new may be extremely time-consuming and may necessitate assistance from a professional cost estimator.

Upper Limits. The cost approach does not set the upper limit to value. Accrued depreciation can be overestimated or underestimated.   .

Residential Appraisal. Current thinking in the appraisal profession considers the cost approach an unsatisfactory substitute for direct sales comparison, particularly in residential appraisal.

TYPES AND USES OF NEW COST ESTIMATES

Reproduction Cost New

Reproduction cost new is the cost to construct, at current prices, an exact replica of the improvement, using the same materials, construction standards, quality of workmanship, design, and layout, and embodying all the deficiencies, superadequacies, and obsolescence of the subject improvement. It is, therefore, the estimated cost of a structure which has all the functional and locational obsolescence of the existing building, if any, but none of the physical deterioration.

Usage. Reproduction cost new is the starting point for estimating the depreciation which has accrued to the subject building, if any, but none of the physical deterioration. It is used as a basis for analyzing the highest and best use of the site.

Replacement Cost New Replacement cost new is the cost to construct, at current prices, a building having the same utility as the subject building, but built with current materials, standards, design, and layout. This presumably eliminates all functional obsolescence and, therefore, the only depreciation to be measured is physical deterioration and economic obsolescence.

Usage. Replacement cost new may be used when it is impossible to obtain materials used in the subject structure or when the use of new construction techniques and materials make it possible to build a structure with equal utility at less cost.

☐ While reproduction cost new estimates the cost of a duplicate structure, replacement cost new estimates the cost of a structure with the same utility.

☐ Replacement cost new would seem to be more logical in terms of typical market behavior because a purchaser would probably take advantage of technological advancements to produce a modern structure. However, reproduction cost new tends to be used in most appraisals because of the difficulty of measuring utility directly.

Uses **Depreciation.** Cost new estimates are the starting points for estimating accrued depreciation.

Principle of Substitution. Cost new estimates indicate the most probable cost to the purchaser to produce a substitute structure.

Upper Limits. They may indicate an upper limit to value if the new or proposed construction represents the highest and best use of the site and if the cost estimate includes a cost for the time the purchaser must wait from the time construction begins to the time he can put the structure to its intended use.

Separate Valuations. In some situations, the value of the improvements must be estimated separately.

☐ *Highest and Best Use.* When estimating the highest and best use of a site or vacant land, it may be necessary to assume hypothetical new structures which are feasible uses of the site.

☐ *Change.* The feasibility of a change to a different type of use may require an analysis of what costs will be incurred to make the change.

☐ *Tax Assessments.* Property tax assessment procedures in many areas require separate valuation of site and improvements.

☐ *Courts.* The courts often require a separate valuation of the improvements for eminent domain proceedings.

DATA PROGRAM

Data Requirements

Current Standard Costs. All cost data used in formulating an estimate should reflect the current standard costs in the local market. The estimated cost includes all the costs that would be incurred by the typical purchaser in the market in producing a similar structure. The cost data are specific figures representing the most probable cost to the typical purchaser, not general averages. Therefore, it is necessary to specify the:

- ☐ Current conditions in the local market, as of the appraisal date
- ☐ Type of structure
- ☐ Type of construction
- ☐ Quality of construction
- ☐ Materials and equipment necessary for construction.

Direct and Indirect Costs. The elements of cost may be categorized into direct costs and indirect costs.

- ☐ *Direct Costs.* Costs directly associated with the construction of improvements include labor (type and amount of labor, prevailing wage rates in the building trades, practices), materials (type and amount of materials, applicable unit costs), equipment (type of building equipment, installation charges), and subcontractors' fees and charges.

- ☐ *Indirect Costs.* Costs classified as not directly related to construction include surveyor's fees, architect's fees, permit and license fees, legal expenses, accounting fees, financing charges, contractor's or builder's overhead and profit, insurance premiums, taxes, selling costs (brokerage commissions, advertising), and opportunity costs (expenses incurred while construction is in progress).

  The estimate of indirect costs cannot always be made with the same precision as direct cost because there is no exact basis for some of them. They may be affected by conditions of delay, judgment, and circumstances which are rarely identical even in the development of two similar properties.

Data Sources

Based on the nature of the appraisal problem, the appraiser must determine how detailed the cost data must be, what type of information is required, and the level of accuracy required. In any case, the cost data must represent current costs in the local market.

Cost Estimators. The services of a cost estimator may be retained when a great degree of detail and a high level of accuracy are required to complete an appraisal assignment. Cost estimation is a very specialized, technical skill. Most residential appraisals do not require such technical cost estimates.

Local Builders and Contractors. Contractors and builders can provide reliable current data because of their constant involvement in the local market.

☐ *Estimates and Bids*. If an appraisal will rely heavily on the value estimated by the cost approach, the appraiser may request that contractors provide estimates or bids. However, this a time-consuming and costly undertaking, rarely necessary for residential appraisals.

☐ *Contractor's Files*. Specific information on particular properties can often be obtained from the contractor's or builder's records.

Cost Surveys and Studies. Studies are often made of construction costs in local markets by FHA regional offices, builders' associations, university research groups and local appraisal organizations. These studies often provide data on typical structures in different categories. The appraiser must exercise great care in identifying cost differentials and making the appropriate adjustments.

Cost Manuals. Cost manuals provide data for benchmark structures (those having definite identifiable characteristics, familiar to the appraiser) of various types as of a particular date and location. The appraiser adjusts these data for differences in construction between the subject structure and the benchmark structure. The cost service includes a series of index numbers which are used for area and time adjustments. In addition, segregated cost figures are given for individual structural components, features, and equipment plus data on site improvement costs.

☐ *Sources*. Generally, cost services are published in manual form with periodic updates of the cost figures. The appraiser may choose from several national, regional, or local cost services.

☐ *Caution*. The appraiser must exercise great care in identifying differences between the benchmark and subject structures and making the appropriate adjustments.

COST ESTIMATION

An accurate and complete analysis of the improvements is essential for proper cost estimation. The building description should at least include descriptions of the building components, their condition, the appropriate units of comparison and their quantities.

Special Considerations

Amount of Detail Required. The nature of the appraisal problem and the type of depreciation analysis to be made will determine the amount of detail required. The greater the level of accuracy and amount of detail required, the greater the likelihood that the appraiser will need the assistance of a professional cost estimator or a contractor. Generally, the amount of detail provided will depend upon professional standards, local market standards, and the requirements of the client.

Use of Cost Services or Manuals. The success of this method is directly related to the appraiser's understanding of the particular cost service used and the care exercised in the application of cost service data. The appraiser must understand the specifications of the benchmark structure and carefully identify differences between it and the subject structure. It is important to understand what is included in the unit costs and what is not included. Items which have been omitted from the cost service data must be added by the appraiser.

Methods of Cost Estimation

The selection of a method of cost estimation depends upon the type of depreciation analysis to be made. The more detailed methods of depreciation analysis require detailed estimates of cost. Several of the most widely used methods are presented below in increasing order of complexity and costliness.

Comparable Unit Method (Square Foot Method). With this method, cost estimates are made by grouping all the components together on a unit basis such as the cost per square foot of building area or the cost per cubic foot of building volume. This is the easiest method of cost estimation.

☐ Unit costs are obtained from an analysis of benchmark structures and then divided by the appropriate number of units in the benchmark structure.

☐ The unit costs are completed construction costs, including all installation expenses. The builder's profit and overhead are also included. The appraiser must exercise care in determining specifically which costs are included; adjustments are necessary for any omissions.

☐ Time and area adjustments may be necessary, depending on the source of the cost data.

☐ The comparative unit method is acceptable and widely used in practice. However, it is the least accurate method available to the appraiser.

☐ Because incurable physical deterioration can only be estimated on a lump-sum basis when this method is used, it cannot be used where a breakdown of the accrued depreciation estimate is required.

Unit-in-Place. This method involves estimating the installed unit cost of materials or component sections of the structure. Thus, it accounts for the cost of both materials and the labor to put them in place, on a per unit basis.

□ An installed unit cost is developed for each major functional component of the structure such as the foundation, frame, roof, walls, plumbing and electrical systems. This unit cost is then multiplied by the appropriate number of units.

□ Lump-sum additions for equipment, fixtures and indirect costs such as builder's overhead and profit are then made to the sum of the unit-in-place costs for the various structural components to arrive at the final value estimate.

□ This method can be applied using the segregated cost data found in most cost manuals, with appropriate adjustments for time and location.

□ Because it simulates the procedures used by builders in preparing bids and estimates and is readily understandable, the unit-in-place method is widely used and accepted.

Quantity Survey Method. This is the most complex, detailed, costly and time-consuming method of cost estimation. It should be attempted only by an expert. Due to the complexity of the method, its use is rarely justified in residential appraisal.

□ The quantity survey method is a computation of the quantity and quality of all materials used and of all categories of labor hours required, to which unit cost figures are applied to arrive at a total cost estimate for materials and labor. To this are added estimates for other contractor's costs such as permits, insurance, equipment rental, field office expenses, supervision, other overhead and a margin for profit.

□ Use of the quantity survey method is limited as it requires a detailed knowledge of hundreds of prices and wage rates, complete familiarity with local market standards and practices, and a thorough working knowledge of residential construction.

Site Improvements The value of individual site improvements may be estimated in one of three ways.

□ The appraiser may estimate the installed cost new of the site improvements and then subtract the estimated depreciation in the same way as for the major improvements. Cost data may be obtained from cost services, contractors, or cost estimators.

□ Site improvements and minor buildings are frequently valued directly on a depreciated cost basis (as is). If the site improvements constitute a significant part of the total property value, expert advice should be sought.

□ The preferred method is to use comparable sales data for otherwise similar properties with and without the specific site improvement. Thus, the market difference for the site improvement may be measured directly.

ESTIMATION OF TOTAL REPRODUCTION COST NEW

The three steps involved are:

Step 1 Multiply each unit cost by the appropriate number of units. Add the sum total of these products.

Step 2 Add lump sum amounts for any specific items of equipment not included in the above calculation.

Step 3 Add any indirect costs not included in Steps 1 and 2. The result is the most probable reproduction cost new of the structure(s) to the purchaser in the current local market.

Cost Estimation Example

Comparative Unit Method

		Quantity	Cost	Extension
Basic Residence Cost		1,400	$ 26.25	$ 36,750
Adjustments:				
Roofing	Wood Shake	1,400	+ 0.45	+ 630
Flooring	Wood Sub-floor (Base)	—	—	—
Floor Covering	Carpeting	1,000	+ 1.60	+ 1,600
Heating	Forced Air Electric	1,400	− 0.10	− 140
Plumbing	11 Fixtures (Base = 9)	2	+ 350.00	+ 700
Fireplaces	1 Single Story	1	1,500.00	+ 1,500
Built-in Appliances	Gas Range & Oven	1	500.00	+ 500
Sub-total Residence Cost				$ 41,540
Garage	Attached	400	+ 10.40	+ 4,160
Deduct for Common Wall		25	− 22.80	− 570
Sub-total Building Improvement Cost				$ 45,130
Current Cost Multiplier	1.07			x 1.07
Local Cost Multiplier	1.10			x 1.10
Total Building Improvement Cost				$ 53,118
Landscaping		6,600	1.50	9,900
Land Value				50,000
Total Indicated Value				$ 113,018
			SAY	$ 113,000

Unit-In-Place Method

		Units	Quality	Quantity	Unit Cost	Extension
Foundation	Concrete, Frame Residence	Sq.Ft.	Average	1,400	$ .95	$ 1,330
Basement	None	Sq.Ft.	—	—	—	—
Floor Structure	Concrete Slab on Grade	Sq.Ft.	Average	1,400	1.20	1,680
Floor Covering	Carpeting	Sq.Ft.	Good	1,000	1.45	1,450
	Vinyl Asb. Tile	Sq.Ft.	Good	400	.75	300
Exterior Wall	Stucco	Ln.Ft.	Average	156	36.00	5,616
Ceiling	Painted Drywall	Sq.Ft.	Average	1,400	.65	910
Roof	Wood Shake	Sq.Ft.	Average	1,400	3.30	4,620
Interior Construction	One Story	Sq.Ft.	Average	1,400	5.75	8,050
Heating & Cooling	Forced Air Electric	Sq.Ft.	Average	1,400	1.15	1,610
Electrical	Romex	Sq.Ft.	Average	1,400	1.10	1,540
Plumbing	Eleven Fixtures	Each	Average	11	400.00	4,400
Built-In Appliances	Gas Range & Oven	Each	Good	1	575.00	575
Fireplace	One Single Story	Each	Good	1	1,300.00	1,300
Garage—						
Foundation	Frame	Sq.Ft.	Average	400	3.50	1,400
Exterior Wall	Stucco	Ln.Ft.	Average	57	36.00	2,052
Roof/Floor	Wood Shake/Con.	Sq.Ft.	Average	400	4.00	1,600

Subtotal, Building Improvement Cost		$ 38,433
Current Cost Multiplier 1.07		x 1.07
Local Cost Multiplier 1.10		x 1.10
Total Building Improvement Cost		$ 45,236
Landscaping		9,900
Land Value		50,000
Total Indicated Value		$ 105,136
	SAY	$ 105,000

Sample Problems: Developing Cost Factors

You are asked to appraise a single-family residence. Several builders in this area who build homes with similar construction qualities are consulted to assist you in your appraisals.

The subject is a 3-bedroom, $2\frac{1}{2}$-bath, Tudor-style home, with 2500 square feet of living area and a 3-car attached garage.

In your analysis you have developed the following information:

1. Builder Walters sells a 2,000-square-foot house, on a lot worth $49,000, for $210,000.

2. Builder Flynn sells a 2,400-square-foot house, on a lot worth $52,000, for $235,000.

3. Builder Hansen sells a 2,500-square-foot house, on a lot worth $55,000, for $235,000. This model has a two-car garage and the builder will add a third garage for $5,000.

Problems to solve:

1. What is likely to be the approximate reproduction cost of the subject?

2. What is the unit relationship between cost and size?

Cost Approach

You are appraising a five-year-old, one-story, 2,100-square-foot home. Attached to the house is a two-car garage. The land is typical for the area.

In developing cost information, you have found three homes that were just built and sold by a contractor.

Sale 1	Sale 2	Sale 3
Bedrooms: 4	Bedrooms: 2	Bedrooms: 3
Baths: 2	Baths: 2	Baths: 2
Living Area: 2,400 sq. ft.	Living Area: 2,000 sq. ft.	Living Area: 2,200 sq. ft.
Sales Price: $158,400	Sales Price: $154,000	Sales Price: $157,000

Based on the above, what do you estimate the cost per square foot of the subject to be?

1. Which approach would be most appropriate to appraise a uniquely designed library?

    (A) Direct sales comparison
    (B) Cost
    (C) Income
    (D) Building residual

2. Replacement cost new:

    (A) Is the cost to construct, at current prices, a building having the same utility
    (B) Assumes using current materials, standards, design and layout
    (C) Eliminates functional obsolescence
    (D) All of the above

3. Sources of information on building costs include:

    (A) Local builders
    (B) Professional estimators
    (C) Cost manuals
    (D) All of the above

4. Reproduction cost new may be defined as the present cost:

    (A) Of replacing the improvement with one having the same utility
    (B) Of a desirable substitute property
    (C) Of reproducing a replica of the improvement using identical or highly similar materials
    (D) Any of the above

5. The use of replacement cost new in cost estimating eliminates all functional obsolescence.

    (A) True
    (B) False

6. Which is the easiest method of cost estimation to understand and apply?

    (A) Segregated costs
    (B) Quantity survey
    (C) Unit-in-place
    (D) Square foot

7. A residence contains 800 square feet of living space on each of two stories, plus an attached garage measuring 30' x 20'. The estimated reproduction cost new per square foot is $40 for living area and $20 for garage area. What is the total reproduction cost new of the house and garage?

    (A) $44,000
    (B) $56,000
    (C) $76,000
    (D) $88,000

8. The most detailed method of estimating cost new is the:

    (A) Quantity survey method
    (B) Unit-in-place method
    (C) Segregated cost method
    (D) Square foot method

9. Which of the following statements is correct?

    (A) A quantity survey estimate requires a separate calculation of building materials and labor.
    (B) Square foot or cubic foot building costs are obtained from local contractors, or cost manuals
    (C) Unit-in-place costs refer to the combined cost of material and labor to install a unit of material
    (D) All of the above

10. A two story commercial building measures 46' x 80' at its base. The height of the first story is 16' and the height of the second story is 14'. Replacement cost of the first story is calculated to be $0.80 per cubic foot; the second story cost is $0.60 per cubic foot. What is the replacement cost of the building?

    (A) $51,520
    (B) $77,280
    (C) $78,016
    (D) $98,624

Chapter 9
The Cost Approach:
Accrued Depreciation

PREVIEW

Nature of Accrued Depreciation

Types and Sources of Accrued Depreciation

Measuring Accrued Depreciation

Derivation of Value Estimate by the Cost Approach

The URAR Cost Approach Analysis Section

NATURE OF ACCRUED DEPRECIATION

Accrued depreciation is defined as the difference between the reproduction cost new or replacement cost new of the improvements and their present worth, both measured as of the date of the appraisal.

Diminished Utility   Accrued depreciation is also referred to as diminished utility, because it represents the loss in utility resulting from deterioration and obsolescence. The degree of diminished utility is measured by a comparison of the utility of the improvements in their present condition and the utility possessed by hypothetical new improvements representing the highest and best use of the site.

Time. Accrued depreciation occurs continuously over time. However, there is not a proportional relationship between the passage of time and accrued depreciation.

Accounting. Accrued depreciation in appraisal is not the same as depreciation in accounting. It is neither a historical fact nor a loss from he historical cost.

Applicable to Improvements Only. While land may decrease or increase in value, it does not depreciate. Accrued depreciation is applicable only to specific improvements on a specific site.

Objectives **Estimate Present Worth of Improvements.** Use of the cost Approach requires the appraiser to make separate estimates of the present worth of the site and the improvements. In order to estimate the present worth of the improvements, the appraiser must estimate the accrued depreciation and deduct this amount from the reproduction cost new.

Estimate Contribution of Improvements. The contribution of the improvements to total property value is the total property value less the value of the site, as if vacant and available to be put to its highest and best use. The role of the improvements in total property value provides a guide to future use of the property.

Estimate Diminished Utility of the Improvements. The cost approach seeks to determine the remaining utility of the improvements, but utility cannot be measured directly and must be inferred from price and cost data. Consequently, the remaining utility is determined by subtracting the diminished utility (accrued depreciation) from the total utility (represented by the reproduction cost new of the improvements).

Simulate Market Behavior. The appraiser's formal estimate of accrued depreciation parallels the informal estimate made by the typical informed purchaser in arriving at the price to pay for the subject property "as is" on the valuation date.

TYPES AND SOURCES OF ACCRUED DEPRECIATION

The three major types of accrued depreciation are physical deterioration, functional obsolescence and locational obsolescence.

Physical Deterioration Physical deterioration is the actual wearing out of a building through age and use, resulting in a loss of utility. It may be curable or incurable.

Sources. Physical deterioration arises from wear and tear, use, weathering, damage, breakage, deferred maintenance, and pest infestation. It is evidenced by disintegration, decay, dry rot, encrustation, cracks, and structural defects.

Curable Physical Deterioration. This is deterioration which the prudent buyer would anticipate correcting upon purchase of the property. It involves components of the building which are normally replaced during the life of the structure and items which must be repaired to prevent further damage or to make the property saleable. The measure of curable physical deterioration is the cost to cure or repair such things as an old furnace, broken windows, or peeling paint.

Incurable Physical Deterioration. Deterioration of any of the building components which are not normally replaced during the life of the structure is classified as incurable physical deterioration. These are items which are not feasible or economically justifiable to correct, in terms of market conditions as of the date of the appraisal. An example of incurable physical deterioration would be the disintegration of the building foundation. Given modern technology, there are very few items which are technically incurable. The key consideration is whether the anticipated return to the purchaser in increased amenities, utility, and value would be at least as great as the cost to correct the defect.

☐ *Short-Lived Items*. The remaining economic life of some items is less than that of the structure and they will eventually have to be replaced. However, it is not feasible and economically justifiable to replace them at the present time. In a sense, they will become items of curable physical deterioration at some specific future time.

☐ *Long-Lived Items*. The basis structural components such as foundation and framing are considered long-lived items. Their economic lives are normally as long as or longer than the economic life of the structure.

Functional Obsolescence

Functional obsolescence is the inability of a structure to adequately perform the function for which it is currently employed. It is the adverse effect on value resulting from defects in design that impair the utility of the improvement. It may be curable or incurable.

Sources. Functional utility may be the result of changes over time that have made some aspect(s) of the structure, material, or design obsolete by current standards. It is evidenced by poor layout and design, functional inadequacy or overadequacy due to size, style, or age, mechanical inadequacy or overadequacy, changing tastes, and technological advances.

Curable Functional Obsolescence. Functional obsolescence is curable when the cost of replacing the obsolete or unacceptable component is at least offset by the increase in utility and value resulting from the replacement.

☐ *Inadequacy*. Insufficient closet space and a furnace with inadequate heating capacity are examples of curable functional obsolescence resulting from inadequacies.

☐ *Superadequacies*. Utility is also diminished by components or items which are far more than adequate for their intended uses. The test of curability is whether replacement of the component would result in an increase in utility that would offset the cost to cure.

Incurable Functional Obsolescence. Functional obsolescence is incurable when it results from structural deficiencies or superadequacies that the purchaser would not be justified in replacing, adding, or removing because the cost to cure would be greater than the increase in utility resulting from the correction.

☐ *Deficiency*. Some elements considered standard in the current market may be lacking. If the cost to cure such a deficiency exceeds the anticipated addition to utility, the deficiency is classified as an item of incurable functional obsolescence, for example, the lack of a second bath in a three-bedroom residence.

□ *Superadequacy*. Superadequate items add unnecessarily to reproduction cost new and may add to maintenance costs (e.g., two foot thick foundations and twelve foot high ceilings in a residence).

Locational Obsolescence This is also called economic obsolescence or social obsolescence. Locational obsolescence is the adverse effect on value resulting from influences external to the property itself. Because real estate is fixed in location, this type of obsolescence is considered incurable.

Sources. Locational obsolescence may result from changes in land use, the encroachment of inharmonious land uses and nuisances, inadequate public services, and zoning changes.

Special Considerations. When considering locational obsolescence, the appraiser should take into account the following:

□ An adverse influence must be strong enough to be reflected in the market to constitute locational obsolescence. While the odor from a nearby chemical plant may be objectionable, it does not constitute locational obsolescence unless there is market evidence that the prudent purchaser will pay more for a similar residence not in proximity to the plant.

□ Locational obsolescence is usually specific to the subject property and perhaps a few other properties in the immediate neighborhood. A negative influence on an entire neighborhood is not treated as locational obsolescence, but is considered in conjunction with the standards of comparability and competitiveness for the subject property.

□ Locational obsolescence is reflected as part of diminished utility for the improvements only. Any loss in property value attributable to adverse external influences that is experienced by the site is reflected in the market value estimate for the site. Avoid double counting.

MEASURING ACCRUED DEPRECIATION

Remaining Utility Total utility less diminished utility equals remaining utility. Alternatively, the present worth of the improvements is equal to the reproduction cost new less any accrued depreciation.

Economic Life The economic life of the improvements is the standard for measuring accrued depreciation. Economic life is defined as the period of time over which an improvement to real estate contributes to the value of the property of which it is a part. It is the period over which total utility is measured.

Physical Life. This is the period of time over which the structure may be expected to remain in existence as a functioning entity. Generally, physical life has little bearing on the behavior of the prudent buyer.

Useful Life. The useful life of an improvement is the period of time over which it may reasonably be expected to perform the function for which it was intended. At the end of its useful life, a structure becomes valueless. The market behavior of prudent purchasers is rarely influenced by useful life.

Remaining Life. The number of years in the economic life of the structure or the structural component, as of the date of appraisal. This is the period of time that most concerns the purchaser, and therefore the period that the appraiser must ascertain in making the appraisal. The remaining economic life is the basis for estimating remaining utility.

Chronological or Actual Age. The actual age of a structure is the number of years that have elapsed since it was built.

Effective Age. The effective age of a structure is the age of a similar structure of equivalent usefulness, condition, and remaining life expectancy. It is also the difference between the total economic life and the remaining economic life of a structure. Effective age is the basis for estimating diminished utility. The effective age of a structure may be more or less than its actual age, depending on the quality and consistency of maintenance, condition, and acceptability in the market.

Example

A 30 year old residence may have an effective age of 20 due to superior maintenance and some modernization. Conversely, a 10 year old structure may have an effective age of 20 years due to its poor condition.

Property Inspection

The appraiser's inspection of the property and observations as to its condition form the basis for all charges for accrued depreciation due to physical deterioration and functional obsolescence.

Documentation. To substantiate charges for accrued depreciation, the field inspection notes must cover all the conditions for which deductions are to be made from reproduction cost new. Specifically, the description of the improvements and observation of conditions should identify the physical condition of the improvements, their functional adequacy, elements of rehabilitation (restoration to original condition or utility), and whether the improvements are appropriate for the site.

Consistency. The elements for which charges are made must match with the salient characteristics of the improvements used in the adjustment processes of the direct sales comparison approach and the gross rent multiplier analysis. Charges for accrued depreciation cannot be made in the cost approach unless considered in the other two approaches and vice versa.

Market Behavior Accrued depreciation must be estimated on the basis of market evidence. The viewpoint of the typical informed purchaser in the market, as of the date of the appraisal, is the basis for estimating charges for accrued depreciation.

Area and Neighborhood Analysis. Charges for locational obsolescence are identified in the area and neighborhood analysis.

Relationship to Direct Sales Comparison and Gross Rent Multiplier Analysis. The direct estimation of accrued depreciation closely parallels the adjustment processes in the direct sale comparison approach and the gross rent multiplier analysis. The effect of a given condition on sales prices is best indicated by market transaction data. Curability is largely determined on the basis of evidence from the direct sales comparison approach. estimates of rent losses due to specific conditions are justified by data from the gross rent multiplier analysis.

Reliability. The reliability of the estimated present worth of the improvements decreases as the charges for accrued depreciation increase. Consequently, the older and less well maintained a residence is, the less defensible the estimate of value by the cost approach generally is.

Methods There are several methods for the direct measurement of accrued depreciation. Whatever method is selected, it must reflect the way in which an informed, prudent purchaser would react to the conditions encountered in the structure.

Simple Age-Life Method. The three steps involved are:

☐ Estimate the effective age of the improvements by subtracting the remaining economic life from the total economic life. The actual age of the improvements may be used if they have had average maintenance.

☐ Express the effective age as a percentage of the total economic life.

☐ Apply this percentage to the reproduction cost new of the improvements if they have had average maintenance.

☐ *Application.* Depending on the facts and conditions of the situation, use of the simple age-life method is appropriate when an estimate of reproduction cost new has been made on a comparable unit basis. Simplicity is the major advantage of this method.

☐ *Limitations.* The simple age-life method does not recognize curable elements independently nor does it recognize that short-lived items may have remaining economic lives shorter than that of the total structure. Furthermore, this method does not deal directly with either functional or locational obsolescence. This results in a serious understatement of accrued depreciation when significant obsolescence exists.

> ### Example of Simple Age-Life Method
>
> Based primarily on observation. The assumption is that the ratio of effective age to economic life is the same as the ratio of accrued depreciation to reproduction cost new.
>
> $$\frac{\text{Effective Age}}{\text{Economic Life}} = \frac{\text{Accrued Depreciation}}{\text{Reproduction Cost New}}$$
>
> $$\frac{10 \text{ years}}{50 \text{ years}} = \frac{20\%}{100\%}$$
>
> This procedure establishes a percentage to estimate accrued depreciation.
>
> ### Illustration
>
> Assume that the total economic life of the improvement is 60 years and the remaining economic life is 50 years. The reproduction cost new of the structure has been estimated at $50,000. The effective age is thus 10 years (60 − 50 = 10). The estimate of total accrued depreciation is $8,333, calculated by 10/60 x $50,000.
>
> 60 (Total Economic Life)
>
> −50 (Remaining Economic Life
>
> 10 (Effective Age)
>
> $$\frac{10 \text{ (Effective Age)}}{60 \text{ (Economic Life)}} = \frac{8,333 \text{ (Accrued Depreciation)}}{50,000 \text{ (Reproduction Cost New)}}$$

Modified Age-Life Method. The two steps involved are:

- [ ] Estimate the cost to cure all curable items of physical deterioration and functional obsolescence and deduct the total from the estimated reproduction cost new.

- [ ] Next, a percentage lump-sum deduction covering all incurable elements is derived by applying to the remaining reproduction cost new of the improvement the percentage derived from dividing total economic life into effective age.

- [ ] *Applications*. This method is useful in situations where the reproduction cost new is estimated by a comparative unit method. It may be acceptable when there is little or no locational obsolescence or incurable functional obsolescence. Because of its deceptive simplicity, the modified age-life method must be used with particular care.

- [ ] *Limitations*. This approach presumes that utility is reduced on a straight-line basis, which is rarely the case. It tends to understate total accrued depreciation where there is locational or incurable functional obsolescence. The method does not consider the variety of remaining economic lives among components of the structure.

Example of Modified Age-Life Method

Assume that the charge for curable items is $1,000 and that the estimated total reproduction cost new is $50,000. The total economic life of the property is 60 years and the effective age is 10 years. The calculation of present worth of the improvement is:

$50,000	–	$1,000	=	$49,000
10/60	x	$49,000	=	$8,167
$49,000	–	$8,167	=	$40,833

Rounded, the present worth of the improvements via the modified age-life method is $40,800.

Engineering Breakdown Method. A different straight-line percentage is applied to each major structural component. However, all types of depreciation are lumped together for each component.

☐ *Applications.* The engineering breakdown method is actually a detailed form of the straight age-life method, but one which treats the major components individually.

☐ *Limitations.* This method has little applicability to real estate appraisal because it is based on engineering concepts rather than market concepts.

Observed Condition Method. Each of the several variations of this basic method involves separate consideration and measurement of each of the elements of accrued depreciation. The steps below are shown in the usual order of presentation in an appraisal report. However, the appraiser normally considers all curable elements before analyzing the incurable elements of depreciation.

☐ *Physical Deterioration.* The actual weasuring out of a structure through age and use.

Curable. Apply the test for curability and make deductions for any curable items. The cost to cure a component may be greater than its reproduction cost new.

Incurable Short-Lived. Estimate the effective age of each separate component as a percentage of its economic life, on a straight-line basis. For example, if a $4,000 roof would have an expected life of 20 years, the annual straight-line depreciation would be: $4,000 ÷ 20 = $200 or 5% per year. Apply this percentage to the reproduction cost new of that component to estimate the amount of diminished utility.

It may be appropriate to include only a part of a component if a portion of it has already been cured. If the living room carpeting is worn and considered a curable item, then the reproduction cost new of the carpeting is deducted from the reproduction cost new of the total floor covering for the house before the effective age percentage is applied.

Incurable. For the individual basic structural components whose remaining economic life is as great as that of the entire structure, the ratio of effective age to remaining economic life is then applied as a percentage to the reproduction cost new of each component to obtain an estimate of the diminished utility for each component.

- □ The base figure to which this percentage is applied is the reproduction cost new of the specific component less any curable physical deterioration charged against that component.

- □ Overhead, profit and any other indirect costs which were not specifically included in the reproduction cost new of the structural components must also be charged for incurable physical deterioration because they are part of the total reproduction cost new that is used up over the economic life of the structure.

- □ The effective age used in estimating incurable physical deterioration is the effective age after the curable items are cured because the cure extends the remaining economic life of the structure.

□ ***Functional Obsolescence.*** The inability of a structure to perform effeciently the function for which it is currently employed.

Curable. Apply the test for curability and make deductions for any curable items. The cost to cure a component may be greater than its reproduction cost new.

- □ ***Deficiency.*** The measure of a curable functional deficiency is the excess of cost to cure over the reproduction cost new of a standard item installed when the structure is built because the reproduction cost new of the standard item is not included in the reproduction cost new of the entire structure. The cost to cure where the functional deficiency involves replacement is the cost of installing the replacement component less the depreciated value of the existing component.

- □ ***Superadequacy.*** Curable functional superadequacy is measured by the reproduction cost new of the item, less any physical deterioration already charged, plus the cost to install a standard item.

□ ***Incurable.*** Can result from structured deficiencies or superadequacies.

- □ ***Deficiency.*** An incurable functional deficiency is measured by the rent loss attributable to the deficiency, as compared to the "standard" residence, multiplied by the gross rent multiplier. The GRM and the rent loss are derived from the gross rent multiplier analysis. If sufficient data are available, the incurable functional obsolescence may be measured by direct sales comparisons. A comparison of sales prices for otherwise similar properties with and without the specific deficiency should enable the appraiser to determine the deduction in sales price made by the prudent purchaser.

□ *Superadequacy.* These items may be measured by the capitalized value of the rent loss or excess cost of ownership due to the condition. The gross rent multiplier is used to capitalize the monthly rent loss or increased cost for residential properties. In this case, rent loss is based upon the added expense attributable to the superadequacy, plus the excess reproduction cost new of the item over and above the cost that may be supported by an increase in market rental as a result of the existence of the item.

Functional Obsolescence Examples
Using Matched Pairs

These properties are comparable in every way except:

House A:	2 Full Baths	Sales Price:	$ 149,000
House B:	1½ Baths	Sales Price:	$ 147,200
Indicated Value Difference			$ 1,800

Superadequacy Examples

Central air, vinyl kitchen floor.

If these cost	$ 5,000
If they add in value only	–$ 4,000
Functional obsolescence	$ 1,000
Pool cost	$ 10,000
Add to value	–$ 6,000
Functional Obsolescence	$ 4,000

Estimated Incurable Functional
Obsolescence by Rent Loss

1. Consider a house with 1 bath in a market in which 2 baths are standard. Comparable rentals indicate rents of $50 more per month for the 2-bath houses. The GMRM is 135 for this neighborhood. What is the loss in value suffered by the 1-bath house?

    Answer: $50 month x 135 GMRM = $6,750

2.

Monthly Rent House A	3 Bedroom	$750 mo.
Monthly Rent House B	2 Bedroom	$650 mo.
Difference		$100 mo.

GMRM for Neighborhood: 130

Difference ($100 mo. x 130 GMRM)	$13,000

□ **Locational Obsolescence**. The allocation of locational obsolescence charges is normally made on the basis of ratio of site value to building value. There are two methods of measuring locational obsolescence. In both cases, the appraiser must allocate the total locational obsolescence between the site and the improvements because the obsolescence attributable to the site is already included in its estimated market value.

□ **Comparison of Sales Prices**. If sufficient market data are available, a comparison of the sales prices of properties which are subject to the adverse influence with the prices of properties not subject to that influence should indicate the necessary deduction.

□ **Capitalizing Rent**. Usually, locational obsolescence is measured by capitalizing the rent loss attributable to the adverse environmental influence. The amount of the rent loss and the gross rent multiplier used to estimate total locational obsolescence are derived from the gross rent multiplier analysis.

Special Considerations. Use of the observed condition method requires a detailed estimate of reproduction cost new. The necessary detail is found in the segregated cost, unit-in-place, and quantity survey methods of cost estimation.

DERIVATION OF VALUE ESTIMATE BY THE COST APPROACH

The objective of estimating and measuring reproduction cost new, accrued depreciation, and site value is to estimate the value of the subject property by the cost approach. The following examples illustrate the process. The basic formula is as follows:

> **Reproduction cost new of the improvements**
>
> *Less* **all accrued depreciation**
>
> *Equals* **the present worth of the improvements**
>
> *Plus* **the depreciated cost new of the site improvements**
>
> *Equals* **the present worth of all improvements**
>
> *Plus* **the site value**
>
> *Equals* **the estimated value of the subject property**

Depreciation Problem

You are appraising a single-family residence, which has an actual age of 15 years and an effective age of 10 years. An investigation of typical residences in this area supports your conclusion that the subject has a total economic life of 50 years. You estimate that the improvements could be replaced at $46 per square foot. The subject building contains 1200 square feet, and the land is valued at $20,000.

Question: Using the simple age-life method, what is the amount of accrued depreciation in the subject?

Calculation: $\dfrac{\text{Effective age}}{\text{Economic Life}}$ $\dfrac{10}{50}$ = 20%

Estimated cost of improvement new	$46/sq. ft. x 1200	=	$55,200
Amount of accrued depreciation	$55,200 x 20%	=	−$11,040
Answer:			$44,160

Question: What is total indicated value of the property?

Answer: Adding Land Value

	$20,000
TOTAL	$64,160
Say...	$64,200

Depreciation Analysis Illustration

Assume that the subject property is a 1,400 square foot single family residence which is 11 years old. It is typical of the houses in the neighborhood. The improvements have had average maintenance and their effective age is estimated to be 10 years.

The subject is a one-story ranch style house of frame construction on a concrete slab. The exterior walls are stucco and the roof is wood shake. A 2-car garage is attached. There are 3 bedrooms and 2-1/2 baths. The house is heated by an electric forced air unit and there is a fireplace in the living room. All rooms are carpeted except the kitchen and baths. The kitchen is equipped with a built-in gas range and oven.

The property inspection has revealed the need for interior painting and some repairs to the bathroom tile. Overall, the improvements are of average quality and are in average condition. The house suffers some functional obsolescence due to deficiencies in the basic floor plan. Because the property is located on a main street, it is subject to a charge for economic obsolescence due to the noise of rush hour traffic.

(continued, next page)

(Depreciation Analysis Illustration, continued)

Estimate of Physical Depreciation

Curable Physical Deterioration

Item	Cost to Cure
Painting	$ 800
Bath Tile Repair	$ 250
Total Deferred Curable	$1,050

Incurable Physical Deterioration - Short-Lived

Component	Reproduction Cost New	% Depreciation	$ Depreciation
Flooring	$1,750	67	$1,173
Roof	4,620	42	1,940
Heating	1,610	59	950
Plumbing	4,400	33	1,452
Electrical	1,540	33	508
Appliances	575	71	408
			$6,431

Incurable Physical Deterioration - Long Lived

Reproduction Cost New		$45,236
Less: Curable Physical	$1,050	
Incurable	6,431	
Total short Lived		−7,481
		$37,755

Effective Age: 10 years; Economic Life: 50 years

Effective Age/Economic Life	x .20
Total Incurable Physical Long Lived	$7,551

Total Estimate of Accrued Depreciation

Physical Deterioration	
Curable	$ 1,050
Incurable - Short Lived	6,431
Incurable - Long Lived	7,551
Functional Obsolescence Incurable	1,500
Economic Obsolescence	2,000
Total Accrued Depreciation	$18,532
Rounded	$18,500

Summary and Value Estimation by Cost Approach

Estimated Reproduction Cost New	$45,236
Estimated Accrued Depreciation	−18,500
Estimated Value Land and Landscaping	+59,900
Estimated Value by the Cost Approach	$86,636
Rounded	$86,600

Accrued Depreciation

Step 1	Select a house that has sold (sales price)	$129,000
Step 2	Estimate the value of the site (less site improvements)	$25,000
Step 3	Depreciated value of improvements	$104,000
Step 4	Reproduction cost of comparable as of date of sale	$130,000
Step 5	Less depreciated value of improvements	$104,000
	Total amount of depreciation as indicated by the market	$26,000
Step 6	Estimated *effective age*	13 years

Step 7 $\dfrac{\text{Depreciation} \quad [\text{Step 5}]}{\text{Effective Age} \quad [\text{Step 6}]} = \dfrac{26{,}000}{13} = \$2{,}000$ average annual amount

Step 8 $\dfrac{\text{Annual Depreciation (Step 7)}}{\text{Reproduction Cost}} = \dfrac{2000}{130{,}000} = .015$

Step 9 Convert to a percentage .015 = 1.5% average annual % of depreciation

THE URAR COST APPROACH ANALYSIS SECTION

The cost approach to value assumes that a potential purchase will consider building a substitute residence that has the same use as the property that is being appraised. This approach, then, measures value as a cost of production. The reliability of the cost approach depends on valid reproduction cost estimates, proper depreciation estimates, and accurate site values.

Valuation Section   **UNIFORM RESIDENTIAL APPRAISAL REPORT**   **File No.**

Purpose of Appraisal is to estimate Market Value as defined in the Certification & Statement of Limiting Conditions.

BUILDING SKETCH (SHOW GROSS LIVING AREA ABOVE GRADE)
If for Freddie Mac or Fannie Mae, show only square foot calculations and cost approach comments in this space.

COST APPROACH

ESTIMATED REPRODUCTION COST-NEW-OF IMPROVEMENTS:

Dwelling _____	Sq. Ft. @ $ _____	= $ _____	
	Sq. Ft. @ $ _____	= _____	
Extras _____		= _____	
		= _____	
Special Energy Efficient Items		= _____	
Porches, Patios, etc.		= _____	
Garage/Carport _____	Sq. Ft. @ $ _____	= _____	
Total Estimated Cost New		= $ _____	

	Physical	Functional	External
Less			
Depreciation			= $ _____
Depreciated Value of Improvements			= $ _____
Site Imp. "as is" (driveway, landscaping, etc.)			= $ _____
ESTIMATED SITE VALUE			= $ _____
(If leasehold, show only leasehold value.)			
INDICATED VALUE BY COST APPROACH			= $ _____

(Not Required by Freddie Mac and Fannie Mae)
Does property conform to applicable HUD/VA property standards? ☐ Yes ☐ No
If No, explain:

Construction Warranty ☐ Yes ☐ No
Name of Warranty Program _____
Warranty Coverage Expires _____

Building Sketch (Show Gross Living Area Above Grade) Here it is essential that the appraiser understand the client's specific reporting requirements since different agencies have different requirements. In this space, for example, Freddie Mac and Fannie Mae require that the appraiser show only square foot calculations and cost approach comments but require a detailed Sketch Addendum. On the other hand, HUD and the USDVA require the appraiser to provide the following information in this space: a perimeter sketch of the subject property including the exterior dimensions, measurements of all other site improvements reported in the analysis sections of the URAR, and comments on the cost approach.

Estimated Reproduction Cost New of Improvements Prior to completing this section, the appraiser must have inspected the subject property and gathered all relevant data on the neighborhood, the site, and the improvements. The URAR outlines the steps in the cost approach: estimating the reproduction cost of new improvements, subtracting the amount of depreciation from all causes, and adding an estimate of the value for the site as if vacant and available to be developed to its highest and best use. The reproduction cost estimate should reflect the cost of construction based on the current prices of producing a replica of the property being appraised—including all of its positive and negative characteristics. Although construction materials used for the estimate should be as similar as possible to those used for the subject property, they do not have to be exactly the same.

Dwelling Area Calculations This item is the calculated total gross living area and is based on exterior measurements consistent with the specifications presented in the building sketch.

Square-Foot Cost The appraiser compares the subject property in terms of dollars per square foot of gross building area to similar structures recently completed or under construction on which cost information is available. The appraiser may use the actual construction costs of buildings located in the neighborhood, cost manuals, or cost reporting services.

Extras This item should include the square foot areas and related costs for finished basement, finished attic, baths, energy-efficient features, porches, garages. After this has been estimated, all the itemized cost components are summed to arrive at the Total Estimated Cost New.

Depreciation There are three principal types of depreciation—physical, functional, and external, that the appraiser must consider. Physical depreciation—traditionally referred to as physical deterioration—is a loss in value that is caused by deterioration in the physical condition of the improvements. Functional depreciation—traditionally referred to as functional obsolescence—is a loss in value that is caused by defects in the design of the structure. External depreciation—traditionally referred to as economic obsolescence—is a loss in value that is caused by negative influences that are outside of the site. The appraiser's entry here must reflect and be supported by the calculations and comments indicated in previous sections of this form report and be allocated according to physical, functional, and external depreciation.

Depreciated Value of Improvements Accrued depreciation is the difference between an improvement's reproduction or replacement cost new and its market value as of the date of the appraisal. The total estimated cost new, minus depreciation from any and all causes, indicates the depreciated value of improvements and the appraiser should enter this calculated amount in this space.

Site Improvements This category—"Site Improvements 'as is' (driveway, landscaping, etc.)"—requires the appraiser to indicate an estimate of present site improvement value of these features including driveways, patios, fencing, landscaping, etc.

Estimated Site Value On this line the appraiser indicates his or her estimate of the value of the site, usually estimated by comparing sales of similar land parcels transferred within a period reasonably close to the effective date of the appraisal. The method used to estimate site value is similar to the market data approach used for estimating value for improved property.

Indicated Value by Cost Approach On this line the appraiser totals and enters the dollar amount of the depreciated value of the structure, the "as is" value of the site improvements, and the estimated value of the site.

Does Property Conform to Applicable HUD/VA Property Standards? Completion of this section is not required by Freddie Mac and Fannie Mae. However, HUD and the USDVA require a "yes" or "no" answer and an explanation if answered "no." The property standards in question refer to the minimum standards required by local zoning and building codes. If the appraiser is not familiar with these standards, he or she should seek the opinions of qualified professionals to determine compliance or non-compliance.

Construction Warranty A construction warranty guarantees the construction work in a new home or improvement. Some builders and contractors offer construction warranties for a limited time period. The appraiser checks whether or not there is such a warranty on the subject property. If "yes" is checked, the appraiser should enter the name and expiration date of the warranty coverage.

Chapter 9 Quiz

1. Economic obsolescence is:

   (A) Curable
   √(B) Incurable
   (C) Either curable or incurable
   (D) Inherent in the property

2. Which of the following is not a method of estimating accrued depreciation?

   (A) Observed condition
   √(B) Assemblage
   (C) Age-life
   (D) Engineering breakdown

3. A curable item of depreciation would most likely be:

   (A) A change from wood siding to stucco
   (B) An outdated fixture
   (C) A poor floor plan
   (D) A crumbling foundation

4. Accrued depreciation is usually measured as a charge against:

   (A) Replacement cost new as of the date of the acquisition
   (B) Replacement cost new as of the date of the appraisal
   (C) Reproduction cost new as of the date of the acquisition
   √(D) Reproduction cost new as of the date of the appraisal

5. A house with exterior measurements of 50' x 30' would cost $50.00 per square foot to reproduce new today. The 20' x 20' garage would cost $20.00 per sq. ft. to reproduce new today. Assuming that the structure is 10 years old, a 2% annual depreciation rate is appropriate, and the lot value is currently $40,000, what would be the current depreciated value of the improved property?

   (A) $104,600
   (B) $105,500
   (C) $106,400
   (D) $107,600

6. An item of accrued depreciation is curable if the cost to cure is not greater than the:

   (A) Replacement cost
   (B) Reproduction cost new
   √(C) Expected increase in value
   (D) Installation cost

7. Insufficient closet space in a residence is usually an example of:

   (A) Curable economic obsolescence
   (B) Incurable economic obsolescence
   (C) Curable functional obsolescence
   (D) Incurable functional obsolescence

8. Effective age is:

   √(A) Total economic life minus remaining economic life
   (B) Total economic life minus actual age
   (C) Actual age adjusted for obsolescence
   (D) Total utility minus diminished utility

9. One limitation of the age-life method is that it:

   (A) Is based on replacement cost rather than reproduction cost
   (B) Tends to ignore physical deterioration
   (C) Tends to ignore obsolescence
   (D) Cannot be used with detailed estimates of cost new

10. Accrued depreciation is:

    (A) A future loss in value
    (B) A reduction in the original cost
    √(C) A loss in utility
    (D) Proportional with the passage of time

NATURE OF THE SALES COMPARISON APPROACH

This approach to value is based primarily on the economic principle of substitution and the subsidiary principles of anticipation, contribution, and increasing and decreasing returns. The sales comparison approval is also referred to as the market comparison approach. However, since all approaches to value estimation involve market comparisons and use market data, the term sales comparison most accurately describes this approach.

Applicable Principles of Value

Substitution. The sales comparison approach is based on the fundamental principle that an informed buyer would not pay more for a property than it would cost to acquire a satisfactory substitute property with equal utility.

Anticipation. The actions of buyers and sellers in the market reflect their expectations of the future benefits to be derived from the ownership of competitive properties.

Contribution. The value of a component depends upon how much its presence adds to, or its absence detracts from, the value of the whole. The sales adjustment process used in the sales comparison approach is based on the identification and measurement of the effect that the presence, absence, or quantity of a particular characteristic has on the sales price of competitive properties, and therefore on the value of the subject property.

Increasing and Decreasing Returns. The sales adjustment process also shows the effect of larger amounts of variable characteristics in competitive sales properties on their sales prices. This concept is used to determine which comparable sales properties are actually competitive with the subject property.

Use of Market Standards

The standards for comparing sales of competing properties with the subject property are those of the market as indicated by the behavior of purchasers.

Typically Informed Purchaser. All market data are analyzed and evaluated as if through the eyes of typically informed buyers, acting judiciously in their own self-interest based on the information available to them.

Local Market. The standards used in this approach are those of the local market in which the subject property is located, as identified in the area and neighborhood analysis.

Current Market. Because market value is estimated as of the date of the appraisal, the comparable sales data should be as current as possible to be truly comparable. The value of the subject property is directly influenced by the market conditions prevailing on that date.

Highest and Best Use. According to the definition of market value, the purchaser acts rationally on the basis of an awareness of the uses to which the property can be put. Since prudent behavior requires that the purchaser plan to utilize the property at its highest and best use, the value of improved property is always estimated in terms of that highest and best use. This may or may not be the same as the highest and best use of the site as if vacant and available to be developed, depending on whether the improvements are appropriate for the site.

Steps in the Sales Comparison Approach

Gather Data. Research the market to identify similar properties for which pertinent sales, rental, listing, or offering data are available.

Evaluate Data. Qualify the prices as to bona fide nature, motivating forces, and terms and conditions.

Compare. Compare each important characteristic of the comparable properties to the corresponding attribute of the subject under the general categories of time, location, physical characteristics, and conditions of sale.

Conclude. Consider all dissimilarities and their probable effect on the price of each comparable sale property to derive individual market value indications for the subject property.

DATA PROGRAM

A systematic research program is necessary to obtain the appropriate detailed information for each of the comparable sales properties. The pertinent (relevant) and salient (noticeable) characteristics of the subject property must be specifically identified. Those same characteristics should then be analyzed for each comparable sales property. This is the only manner in which meaningful comparisons and adjustments can be made.

Definition of Comparable. The key consideration in selecting a "comparable" sales property is whether it is effectively competitive with the subject property in the mind of a typically informed purchaser.

Conditions of Sale. Market conditions and terms of sale must also be investigated for each comparable sales property.

Basic Data Requirements Certain basic data must be gathered for each sales comparable to establish the characteristics of the property and the transaction.

Property Data. The following information pertaining to the property must be gathered by the appraiser.

☐ Location—market and neighborhood influences

☐ Site—size, shape, topography, etc.

☐ Type of improvements, architectural style

☐ Size—area, room count

☐ Age and condition

☐ Rooms—types, layout

☐ Number of bedrooms and baths

☐ Special features—pool, fireplaces, etc.

☐ Accessory buildings—types, size, age, condition

☐ Listing—price, length of time on market

☐ Zoning and deed restrictions

☐ Tax assessments

☐ Unusual elements of functional or economic obsolescence

☐ Legal description of property.

Transaction Data. The following information must be gathered by the appraiser.

☐ Date of sale

☐ Sales price, as verified by principal or agent

☐ Record volume, page, and document number of deed

☐ Type of deed

☐ Names of grantor (seller) and grantee (buyer)

☐ Amount of consideration, if indicated

☐ Documentary stamps—a useful guide to the amount of consideration, but not to be relied upon without verification

☐ Terms of financing—important because higher prices are sometimes paid when favorable financing is available

☐ Conditions of sale—must be a bona fide, arm's length transaction

☐ Items of personal property included—these must be deducted from the sales price before the transaction can be used as a comparable sale.

Verification All transaction data should be verified with the buyer, the seller, or an authorized agent of either. Unverified data may be subject to misrepresentations or distortions, especially if the motivating forces underlying the transaction have resulted in other than a true arm's length transaction in which neither party has or can gain an advantage at the expense of the other party. Reasons for this may include:

☐ Transactions between related or affiliated parties under nonmarket conditions

☐ Liquidation for inheritance taxes or pressing personal reasons

☐ Better bargaining power on the part of one party to the transaction

☐ Purchase for immediate possession

☐ Special tax considerations in the sale.

Quantity of Data There is no set number of comparable sales which must be analyzed by the appraiser. However, it is generally agreed that the more data there are, the better. This reduces the risk that an atypical sale will distort the value estimate.

Wide Preliminary Survey. While only three or four comparable sales may be presented in the report, the preliminary analysis usually includes consideration of many more comparable properties.

Level of Verification. In the preliminary analysis, it is possible and appropriate to use data gathered and verified by others if they can be considered reliable sources. However, all data included in the appraisal report must be personally verified by the appraiser.

Quality of Data All transaction data must be as accurate and comprehensive as possible. The terms of financing and conditions of sales merit particular attention. The minimum quality requirements for acceptable comparable sales include:

☐ Current market transactions

□ Local market transactions

□ Bona fide sales that are arm's length transactions

□ Truly comparable properties that are competitive with the subject property in the minds of typical purchasers

Sources of Data Two general categories of sources are available to assist the appraiser in gathering data: recorded and nonrecorded sources.

Recorded Sources. These public records are typically found in the offices of the county clerk or some other public office and include:

□ *Recorded Deeds*. Basic transaction data may be obtained from the deed records found in the office of the recorder of deeds, the county clerk, the town clerk, or other appropriate local agency.

□ *Recorded Mortgages and Trust Deeds*. These provide information on the terms of financing.

□ *Transfer Tax Records*. In areas where transfer taxes are levied on real estate, these records will provide data on the transactions.

□ *Assessment Records*. The county or local assessor's office is a source of information on transfers of properties near the subject. Detailed information about taxes and assessments and the physical characteristics of the properties is available.

□ *Zoning Records and Maps*. The local zoning or planning authority provides data on the applicable zoning regulations.

Nonrecord Sources. Additional non-public records usually available to the appraiser include:

□ *Data Banks*. Various services, ranging from the MLS of a local board to private companies, offer access to computerized data on property transactions. The subscriber to such services can obtain rapid information on comparables "on-line" (by phone line), using a terminal or microcomputer.

□ *Appraiser's Files or Data Bank*. The appraiser's own files can be an important source of data if they are accurate and current. Information can be gathered both during appraisal assignments and during slack periods in order to maintain adequate coverage of the local market.

□ *Multiple Listing Services*. Both listing and sales data are reported in detail. In some areas, this information is available to local appraisers.

□ *Subscription Services*. These services operate in some areas, providing information on deed recordings and other transactions which the appraiser can investigate and verify.

□ *USDVA and FHA*. Data on actual transactions are provided by these offices in many areas.

□ *Builders*. Data on new construction is usually available

□ *Real Estate Brokers*

□ *Local Boards of Realtors®*

□ *Other Appraisers*

□ *Local Professional Appraisal Organizations*

□ *Title Companies and Abstract Companies*

□ *Newspaper Stories and Advertisements*

□ *Personal Tours*. Often a tour of the neighborhood reveals "sold" or "for sale" signs on potentially comparable properties. These leads may be investigated with the broker or one of the principals involved.

□ *Principals and Participants*. Buyers, sellers, brokers, attorneys, and lenders are important sources of basic information as well as providing verification of data otherwise obtained.

Sales Data, Listings and Offers to Purchase
Sales data for actual current transactions are the most desirable. Listings and offers to purchase may be utilized on occasion, but this requires a great deal of care and discretion. Listings provide an indication of the upper portion of the price or value range, while offers to purchase tend to represent the lower end of the range. Careful study of listings, offers, and actual sales may indicate an appropriate adjustment which may be applied to listing and offering prices.

Narrative Description
Presentation of the comparable sales data in the comparative analysis in a narrative report should allow the reader to visualize the elements of similarity and dissimilarity between the comparable sales and the subject property. All of the pertinent and salient elements of comparability and dissimilarity should be presented, but only the pertinent and salient features should be listed.

ELEMENTS OF COMPARISON

While it may be possible to find data on sales of properties so current and so comparable that direct comparison can be made without adjustments, it is usually necessary to make a point-by-point comparison of the comparable properties with the subject property.

The pertinent and salient features of each of the comparable sales properties must be identified, just as for the subject property. Identification of these features is followed by a specific comparison process and appropriate adjustments for dissimilarities.

In the comparison process, the subject property is always the standard in terms of which all comparisons are made. The differences in significant property characteristics are measured from the comparable sales property to the subject property. The major elements of comparison are:

Time The date of sale identifies the market conditions existing at the time of the transaction. The appraiser must identify what the comparable sales property would have sold for if it were offered for sale under the market conditions existing as of the valuation date of the appraisal. Any difference between market conditions on the sale date and on the valuation date necessitates an adjustment to the sales price of the comparable property.

Location The true comparability of properties is influenced by the neighborhood environment and any zoning or deed restrictions. Thus, the appraiser must analyze the neighborhood environment for each comparable sales property. Any differences between the locational influences affecting the subject and the comparable sales property require an adjustment to the sales price of the comparable property.

Conditions of Sale Comparisons must be made between the comparable sales properties and the subject property on the basis of:

☐ Bona fide, arm's length transactions

☐ Motivations of the buyers and sellers

☐ Knowledge of market conditions by buyers and sellers

☐ Length of time on the market before sale occurred.

Comparable Sales. Transactions should normally be eliminated from the analysis if there is any evidence that the sale was not an arm's length transaction. However, if very little data is available, an adjustment may be made to the sales price of the comparable sale property to reflect what the property would have sold for if it had been a bona fide transaction.

Terms of Financing Residential sales prices can be influenced by the availability of favorable financing. The terms of financing include:

☐ Downpayment requirements

☐ Interest rate

☐ Loan maturities

☐ Amortization requirements

☐ Seller financing

☐ Buy-downs

☐ Discount points

☐ Assumable loans.

Physical Property Characteristics The salient physical characteristics of the subject property are compared with those of the comparable properties. Each pertinent feature must be analyzed in the comparison process, but only the pertinent features need to be analyzed.

- □ Size—area, volume, or both
- □ Rooms—number and type, especially bedrooms, baths, and separate dining rooms, if any
- □ Architectural style and room layout
- □ Actual age of the improvements
- □ Condition—general maintenance level, deferred maintenance
- □ Structural type and quality
- □ Functional adequacy
- □ Accessory buildings—type, size, function, condition, age
- □ Site and site improvements—size, topography, drainage, curbs and gutters, etc.
- □ Special features—pool, jacuzzi, central air conditioning, fireplaces, etc.

UNITS OF COMPARISON

It is often desirable to reduce properties to some common denominator for analytical purposes and to express the value estimate on a per-unit basis. The appraiser must select a unit of comparison which reflects the thoughts and behavior of the typical purchaser in the market.

Selection of Suitable Units The unit of comparison selected by the appraiser must reflect the types of comparisons made by buyers in the market. What is appropriate for one type of property may not be appropriate for another.

Common Factor. Any common factor which identifies, clarifies and represents typical market behavior may be used.

Direct Comparison. The direct comparison of properties is more appropriate and defensible if the appraiser has correctly chosen units of comparison which represent the salient features of the properties. Relatively small differences in size may be adjusted for by the use of units of comparison. However, significant site differences indicate that the properties are actually in a different market and that the use of units of comparison would be inappropriate.

Types of Units of Comparison **Typical Property.** Direct comparison is sometimes used when comparable sales are considered to be highly competitive with the subject and each other.

Rent Multipliers. The gross rent multiplier is used to compare properties using a ratio of the sales price or value to gross rent unfurnished. Monthly multipliers are often used in the appraisal of residential properties.

Physical Units of Comparison. Units of comparison based on size are widely used in residential valuation. They include:

- Sales price per square foot of living area
- Sales price per cubic foot (in areas where volume is the measurement standard)
- Sales price per room
- Sales price per square foot of foundation area.

THE ADJUSTMENT PROCESS

The objective of the adjustment process is to determine what each of the comparable properties would have sold for if it possessed the salient characteristics of the subject property. It is critical that the salient features of the subject and the comparable properties be properly identified and described in sufficient detail to ensure that the appraiser and the reader of the appraisal report adequately understand the similarities and dissimilarities of the properties. Thus, each category of elements of comparison must be considered in the analysis, whether or not they are included in the adjustment process.

The Standard Adjustments to the sales prices of the comparable properties are always made from the comparable to the subject. The sales prices of comparable properties are used as guides in arriving at the estimated value of the subject property. Adjustments are made to these prices to account for differences between each of the comparables and the subject. The appraiser must work from the known sales prices to an estimate of what each of the comparable properties would have sold for if it possessed the major characteristics of the subject property.

Amount of Adjustment The only valid measure for determining how much of an adjustment should be made to reflect the presence or absence of a particular feature is evidence of the market reactions of buyers to such features.

Paired Sales. Where available, paired sales are especially helpful in determining the proper adjustment. If two properties are identical except for one characteristic, the difference between their sales prices is usually a good indication of what the market estimates that feature to be worth.

Cost. Cost is not an appropriate measure of the adjustment to be made.

Amount of Data. There must be sufficient market data to support the amount and direction of each adjustment made. The question is whether buyers in the market attach any significance to a particular point of superiority or deficiency, regardless of whether the appraiser personally believes this point should be reflected in a sales price differential.

Techniques There are many techniques for comparing or adjusting market data. The appraiser must select the one technique which is most applicable to the appraisal problem at hand and apply it consistently throughout the adjustment process.

Whole Property Comparison. This method involves a single lump-sum adjustment, with no allocation in terms of the specific effect of particular factors contributing to the total.

Plus and Minus Dollar Adjustments. Where there is sufficient market evidence to substantiate dollar differentials, plus and minus dollar adjustments may be applied.

☐ If the comparable property has a deficiency when compared to the subject, the appropriate dollar amount is added to the sales price of the comparable property.

☐ If the comparable property is superior to the subject in some respect, the appropriate dollar amount is subtracted from the sales price of the comparable property.

☐ The sequence of adjustments is generally of little importance because each factor is presumed to have an independent and separate effect on the sales price.

Plus and Minus Percentage Adjustments. A lack of market evidence for specific dollar adjustments often necessitates the use of percentage adjustments. An adjustment for time, if necessary, is generally made first. All other adjustments are then made in terms of the current market. This technique presumes that the adjustment factors are essentially separate and independent of each other.

Mixed Dollar and Percentage Adjustments. In some cases, it may be necessary to mix dollar and percentage adjustments. With this technique, the percentages of the sales prices of the comparables must first be adjusted for time and then converted to dollar amounts to arrive at a value estimate.

Types of Adjustments

Several types of adjustments must be made depending on the elements of comparison including time, location and condition of sale, physical characteristics of the property and the terms of financing.

Time Adjustments. Sales and resales of the same property provide the best method for deriving an appropriate time adjustment. General price level trends may be used, but are less reliable. In any case, the adjustment must be supported by market data.

Example

Assume that a property sold for $50,000 eighteen months ago and has just been resold for $57,500. The time adjustment factor is +15%. (The property value increased by 15% during the 18 month period. Therefore, 15%/18 = .833% per month. .833% per month x 12 months = 10% per year.)

Location and Conditions of Sale. It is often very difficult to find market evidence to substantiate adjustments for location and conditions of sale. To do so requires sales of almost identical properties under the same market conditions. Because it may be impossible to find such sales, comparisons requiring adjustment for the conditions of sale are avoided whenever possible.

Physical Characteristics. Size adjustments are made using the appropriate units of comparison. Adjustments for other physical characteristics are made on the basis of market evidence as to what the presence of a feature adds to, or its absence detracts from, the value of the whole.

Terms of Financing. It is possible to adjust for differences in the terms of financing using the income capitalization techniques presented in Chapter 11. Basically, the cash equivalent price is found by determining the present worth of the monthly payments made under the particular financing terms and then adding the downpayment amount to the present worth. This results in a cash equivalent sales price which is used as the sales price to be adjusted.

Net Adjustment The net adjustment figure derived from the adjustment process is added to, or subtracted from, the sales price of the comparable sale property to arrive at an adjusted sales price. The adjusted sales price represents the appraiser's best estimate of what the comparable property would have sold for if it had the salient characteristics of the subject property.

Amount. As a rule, net adjustments should not exceed 15% to 20% of the sales price. Larger net adjustments suggest that the comparable is not actually competitive with the subject property.

Description of the Adjustment Process To enable the reader to understand the adjustment process, the appraisal report should include a comprehensive and detailed narrative describing each property and the market support for each of the adjustments. In addition, the adjustment process is usually summarized in grid form.

DERIVATION OF THE VALUE ESTIMATE

A value estimate for the subject property is derived from the assembled and adjusted data, using the following principles.

Reconciliation The adjusted sales prices should cluster around a central point of tendency, which is selected as the best indication of market value.

An arithmetic average should not be used to derive the final value estimate unless there are several adjusted sales prices and the appraiser is justified in assuming that each comparable is equally significant.

Those comparables which have required the least adjustment are generally those which are the most reliable.

If a per-unit sales price is derived, it is necessary to multiply the per-unit figure by the number of units to arrive at the final value estimate.

Rounding The estimate of value should be rounded to an appropriate level. Unrounded numbers imply a greater degree of accuracy than is possible in formulating an estimate.

USES AND LIMITATIONS OF THE APPROACH

Reliability Because the sales comparison approach discovers and simulates the behavior of the typical purchaser, great reliance is usually placed upon this approach in arriving at a final estimate of value. This is especially true for residential properties.

Ease and Simplicity Where sufficient quantities of adequate, verified data are available, this approach is the most appropriate and direct of the three standard approaches to value. The sales comparison approach is relatively simple and easy to understand.

Predictability The approach is based on the assumption that past market behavior and forces will continue to occur in the future.

Active vs. Inactive Market A low level of market activity for a specific type of property may make it impossible to apply this approach.

MATCHED PAIRS CALCULATIONS

The following calculations illustrate the sales comparison approach, applied to a group of similar properties examined in terms of a limited number of variables which have been determined to be pertinent to the appraisal of the subject property.

Matched Pairs Illustration

Sale 1	**Sale 2**
3 bedrooms	3 bedrooms
1½ baths	2 baths
good condition	good condition
$138,000	$140,000

Sale 3	**Sale 4**
3 bedrooms	4 bedrooms
1½ baths	2 baths
fair condition	fair condition
$135,000	$145,000

Pair 1 and 2. The only significant difference between Sale 1 and Sale 2 is the half bath. The market can be said to recognize a $2,000 adjustment for this difference.

Pair 1 and 3. Sale 3 can be directly compared with Sale 1. The $3,000 difference in sales price can be attributed to the condition of the properties. Comparing Sales 1 and 2 yields a $2,000 difference for the second full bath.

Pair 2 and 3. There is a $5,000 difference between Sale 2 and Sale 3; $2,000 for the half bath and $3,000 adjustment for the condition, confirming the previous comparisons. (In practice the results would almost always be a range of values.).

Unpaired Sale. Comparable Sale 4 cannot be directly compared with any other sale because there is more than one difference. First the other differences must be adjusted for and the balance will be the net value of a fourth bedroom.

Derived Adjustments. Comparing Sale 4 with the other three sales adjusted to 2 baths and fair condition yields $8,000 as the value of the 4th bedroom. A value can now be estimated for a subject with, e.g., 4 bedrooms, $1\frac{1}{2}$ baths, and in good condition.

THE URAR SALES COMPARISON ANALYSIS SECTION

The valuation section of the URAR enables the appraiser to develop and report in concise format an adequately supported estimate of market value—based on the cost, sales comparison, and income approaches to value. If the appraiser believes that additional information needs to be provided because of the uniqueness of the property or some other condition, he or she should provide the additional supporting data in an addendum to the appraisal report form.

The undersigned has recited three recent sales of properties most similar and proximate to subject and has considered these in the market analysis. The description includes a dollar adjustment, reflecting market reaction to those items of significant variation between the subject and comparable properties. If a significant item in the comparable property is superior to, or more favorable than, the subject property, a minus (–) adjustment is made, thus reducing the indicated value of subject; if a significant item in the comparable is inferior to, or less favorable than, the subject property, a plus (+) adjustment is made, thus increasing the indicated value of the subject.

ITEM	SUBJECT	COMPARABLE NO. 1		COMPARABLE NO. 2		COMPARABLE NO. 3	
Address							
Proximity to Subject							
Sales Price	$		$		$		$
Price/Gross Liv. Area	$	$		$		$	
Data Source							
VALUE ADJUSTMENTS	DESCRIPTION	DESCRIPTION	+ (–) $ Adjustment	DESCRIPTION	+ (–) $ Adjustment	DESCRIPTION	+ (–) $ Adjustment
Sales or Financing Concessions							
Date of Sale/Time							
Location							
Site/View							
Design and Appeal							
Quality of Construction							
Age							
Condition							
Above Grade Room Count	Total / Bdrms / Baths	Total / Bdrms / Baths		Total / Bdrms / Baths		Total / Bdrms / Baths	
Gross Living Area	Sq. Ft.	Sq. Ft.		Sq. Ft.		Sq. Ft.	
Basement & Finished Rooms Below Grade							
Functional Utility							
Heating/Cooling							
Garage/Carport							
Porches, Patio, Pools, etc.							
Special Energy Efficient Items							
Fireplace(s)							
Other (e.g. kitchen equip., remodeling)							
Net Adj. (total)		+ / – $		+ / – $		+ / – $	
Indicated Value of Subject			$		$		$
Comments on Sales Comparison:							

SALES COMPARISON ANALYSIS

INDICATED VALUE BY SALES COMPARISON APPROACH .... $

The sales comparison approach to value—is an analysis of comparable sales, contract offerings, and current listings of properties that are the most comparable to the subject property. However, in this section, the appraiser can report only the comparable sales. The comparable sales must be verified, analyzed, and adjusted for differences between the comparable properties and the subject property. Because the appraiser's estimate of market value is no better than the reliability of the comparable data that is used, the appraiser must exercise due diligence to ensure the reliability of the comparable sales data that he or she uses. The appraiser must report a minimum of three comparable sales as part of the sales comparison approach. Generally, the appraiser should use comparable sales that have been settled or closed within the last 12 months; however, older comparables may be used as additional supporting data if he or she believes that it is appropriate. The appraiser must comment on the reasons for using any comparable sales that are more than six months old.

Address — The address of the subject property and of each comparable should include the city or town. It is recommended that the appraiser include a map referencing each property.

Proximity to Subject — Distance should be indicated in terms of blocks, fractions of a mile, miles, etc. Although there is no standard rule of acceptable distance of the comparable property from the subject property, the appraiser should comment on any comparable property located a substantial distance from the subject property.

Sales Price — On this line the appraiser enters the total purchase price for each property.

Price/Gross Living Area — On this line the appraiser enters the price per square foot of gross living area which is calculated by dividing the sale price of each comparable by the indicated square footage.

Data Source — On this line the appraiser enters the source of his or her data as "personal investigation," "property inspection" or the name of a sale verification source.

Sales or Financing Concessions — On this line the appraiser should include the specific sales or financing concession information for each comparable sale, including the mortgage amount, interest rate, loan type, and any loan fees or concessions paid by the seller. The + (-) dollar adjustment is then entered. The line for the subject property is shaded in this section because the appraiser should state this information in the Subject section or in the Comments section on the first page of the URAR.

Date of Sale/Time — On this line the appraiser should indicate the month and year of the sales contract and the closing date and the appropriate dollar adjustments. As indicated previously, the appraiser must comment on the reasons for using any comparable sales that are more than six months old.

Location   The most reliable and useful comparable sales are those located in the subject property's neighborhood near the subject property. The location adjustment represents any differences in perceived value arising from a comparable located in a different but competing market area. On this line the appraiser should enter in the Description column the ratings "good," "average," or "fair," based on comparison to the subject property; and next to the dotted line, the + (-) dollar adjustment.

Site/View   Here the appraiser gives a general rating of "good," "average," "fair," or "poor" for the subject property and each comparable; and next to the dotted line, the + (-) dollar adjustment.

Design and Appeal   This item includes adjustments for such aspects as appeal of exterior and interior design, special features, and other features which contribute to the subject property's charm or lack of charm. On this line the appraiser rates the subject property and comparables according to the general rating scale and enters the appropriate dollar adjustment.

Quality of Construction   This item considers all aspects of the quality of construction (type of materials and craftsmanship, etc.) for the entire building. The appraiser rates the subject property and comparables according to the general rating scale and enters the appropriate dollar adjustment.

Age   On this line the appraiser reports the actual age of the subject property and each comparable property and then enters the dollar adjustment. If any of the properties have been significantly modernized, their effective age may be reported in parentheses.

Condition   On this line the appraiser rates the subject property according to the general rating scale. Comparable properties are rated against the subject property as "superior," "equal," or "inferior" and appropriate dollar adjustments are then entered.

Above-Grade Room Count— Gross Living Area   On this line the appraiser enters the total number of finished, above-grade rooms, the number of bedrooms and baths, and the total, above-grade, square-foot living area for the subject property and the comparables; then enters the appropriate dollar adjustment for each.

Basement and Finished Rooms Below Grade   On this line the appraiser reports basement improvements (such as finished rooms) found in the subject property and in the comparables; then enters the appropriate dollar adjustments.

Functional Utility This item considers the efficiency of the subject property's use and includes such factors as size, layout, and usability. On this line the appraiser rates the subject property according to the general rating scale. Comparable properties are rated against the subject property as "superior," "equal," or "inferior" and appropriate dollar adjustments are then entered.

Heating/Cooling While the heating system in most homes is adequate-quality forced-air or gravity-air, the presence or absence of air conditioning is a greater variable. On this line the appraiser should indicate the degree of adequacy of these systems and make adjustments on the basis of market value and market expectations.

Garage/Carport On this line the appraiser records the presence or absence of a garage/carport and its total capacity and enters the dollar adjustments. The appraiser should give special attention to added-on garages or to garages converted to living rooms and determine whether these improvements have been completed in accordance with local building requirements.

Porches, Patio, Pools, Etc. On this line the appraiser records and makes adjustments for these building or site improvements. Although cost data may serve as a guide for the adjustment, the adjustments are usually made on the basis of market value and market expectations.

Special Energy Efficient Items An energy-efficient property is one that uses cost-effective design, materials, equipment, and site orientation to conserve nonrenewable fuels. Fannie Mae underwriting guidelines recommend that special energy saving items be recognized in the appraisal process and that borrowers purchasing such properties be given special consideration. On this line the appraiser should list any special energy efficient items for the subject property and the comparable properties and make price adjustments based on the specific contribution of each item to the overall value of the property.

Fireplaces In this section the appraiser records the number and type of fireplaces for the subject and comparable properties and enters an adjustment for the comparable sales.

Other (e.g., Kitchen Equipment, Remodeling) On this line the appraiser should record all interior finish items for the subject property and each of the comparable properties, whether or not an adjustment is necessary. This item provides a basis for comparing interior equipment and should reflect any remodeling or renovation that may have altered the effective age of the properties.

Net Adjustments (Total)   On this line the appraiser reports the net total positive or negative adjustments for all items. Recent Fannie Mae guidelines state that the dollar amount of the net adjustment for each comparison property, in general, should not exceed 15% of the purchase price. Should the adjustments exceed this amount, the appraiser must explain the use of the comparable in the Comments section. Likewise, the dollar amount of gross adjustment for each sale should not exceed 25% of the comparable property's sale price.

Indicated Value of Subject   On this line the appraiser enters the total adjusted sale prices for each of the three comparable properties. The appraiser adds or subtracts the net total adjustment from the sale price of each comparable sale to arrive at a value indication for the subject property. The result of this calculation is an estimated range based on direct market comparison.

Comments on Sales Comparison   The appraiser's comments should reflect his or her reconciliation of the adjusted (or indicated) values for the comparable sales and identify the comparable(s) that were given the most weight in arriving at the indicated value for the subject property.

Indicated Value by Sales Comparison Approach   On this line the appraiser enters the dollar amount of the value estimate.

1. The sales comparison method is based primarily on the principle of:

   (A) Contribution
   (B) Conformity
   (C) Supply and demand
   (D) Substitution

2. Which of the following would require special explanation when used in the direct sales comparison analysis of a residential appraisal?

   (A) Similar homes sold more than six months ago
   (B) A similar residence sold other than "at arm's length"
   (C) Homes of comparable size in a different neighborhood
   (D) All of the above

3. The value estimate is best derived by:

   (A) Averaging the adjusted sales prices of all the comparables
   (B) Selecting the three best comparable sales and averaging their adjusted sales prices
   (C) Using the adjusted sales price of the single least adjusted comparable sale
   (D) Choosing the figure around which the adjusted sales prices tend to cluster

4. Data should be verified:

   (A) If it is obtained from someone who is not an appraiser
   (B) By the appropriate government agency or department
   (C) By at least one of the principals to the transaction
   (D) Just before the report is written to ensure the information is current

5. In the direct sales comparison approach, adjustments are made:

   (A) From the comparable to the norm
   (B) From the subject to the norm
   (C) From the subject to the comparable
   (D) From the comparable to the subject

6. The sales comparison approach serves as strong evidence of value in the appraisal of single family dwellings because of its:

   (A) Simplicity
   (B) Reliability
   (C) Predictability
   (D) All of the above

7. The appropriate adjustment for time is determined to be +9% per year. The time adjustment for a comparable sales property that sold 18 months ago for $50,000 is:

   (A) -$9,000
   (B) -$6,750
   (C) +$6,750
   (D) +$9,000

8. In the sequence of adjustments for plus and minus percentage adjustments, the item adjusted for first should usually be:

   (A) Time
   (B) Location
   (C) Conditions of sale
   (D) None; there is no preferred sequence

9. Which of the following items could be subject to adjustment in the sales comparison approach?

   (A) Ethnic background of the buyer and seller
   (B) Motives of the appraiser
   (C) Location and date of sale
   (D) None of the above

10. Physical units of comparison are a method of adjusting for:

   (A) Time
   (B) Location
   (C) Size
   (D) Age

PREVIEW

Nature of the Income Approach

Gross Rent Multiplier Analysis

Income Capitalization

Steps in the Income Capitalization Process

The URAR Indicated Value by Income Approach Section

NATURE OF THE INCOME APPROACH

The income approach to value deals with the property as an income-producing investment. The purchaser is typically a non-occupant investor seeking investment income rather than the amenities of owner-occupancy.

Definitions   **Income.** Money or other benefits assumed to be received periodically.

Value. A measure of the worth or desirability of a thing, usually expressed in monetary terms. One concept of value states that it is the present worth of anticipated future benefits. These benefits may be in the form of amenities or money income.

Income and Value. When these benefits are in the form of monetary income, the relationship between that income and the market prices of competitive property investments can be measured and expressed as a rate or ratio. Where it is reasonable to assume that this relationship is constant for similar type properties under similar market conditions, the market rate or ratio can be applied to the forecast future income by the capitalization process to derive an estimate of the present value of the subject property.

Multiplier. The relationship between the gross income and the sales price is referred to as a multiplier. It is the ratio of sales price to periodic gross income.

Capitalization Rate. The relationship between the net income and the sales price is referred to as a capitalization rate or factor.

Income Capitalization. In real estate appraisal, income capitalization is the process of applying the appropriate annual rate of capitalization to the annual forecast net income for the subject property to derive an estimate of present worth or value.

Uses The income approach is applicable to any property which is rentable, but as a practical matter, it can be used only when the future income stream for the property can be forecast. Because single-family residential properties are more often purchased for owner occupancy than for rental income, the income approach is rarely used in single-family residential appraisal.

Methods **Gross Rent Multiplier.** Gross rent multiplier analysis has often been called the income approach for residential properties. In reality, it is neither part of the income approach nor income capitalization since they deal only with net income.

☐ A gross income multiplier or gross rent multiplier is one means of comparison in the direct sales comparison process. It compares properties on the basis of their capacity to generate income and the relationship of that income to sales price.

☐ A gross *income* multiplier is used for income-producing real properties because their income may be derived from sources other than rentals. Gross *rent* multipliers are used for residential properties since the only type of income they produce is rental income.

☐ The gross income generating capacity is presumed to be attributable to the real estate itself. The net income is a function of the management by or for the owner-investor.

Income Capitalization. Income capitalization is the process of converting a series of anticipated future periodic installments of net income to their present worth or value. It is always based on net property income, which is usually measured in terms of net operating income.

GROSS RENT MULTIPLIER ANALYSIS

Gross rent multiplier analysis is the appraisal approach which is based on the premise that an informed purchaser would not pay more for a property than the cost of obtaining a return of the same amount with the same level of risk involved in the subject property. It is actually part of sales comparison analysis; it is neither part of the income approach nor is it income capitalization.

Gross Rent The gross rent multiplier is the ratio between sales price and the monthly
Multiplier (GRM) unfurnished rental. For residential properties, monthly gross rent multipliers are calculated using monthly rental income.

Applicable Principles of Value	**Substitution.** An informed purchaser will not pay more for a property than the cost of acquiring a rental income stream of the same size and risk level as that of the subject property.

Anticipation. The value of the subject property is the present worth of the expected rental income stream.

Contribution. The rental income that a residential property is capable of producing, discounted at an appropriate rate, is one measure of the value of the property. The discounting process for residential property valuation consists of multiplying the monthly market rental of the subject property by the gross rent multiplier. |
| **Procedure** | The first step is to estimate the current monthly unfurnished market rental for the subject property.

Deriving GRM. The appropriate gross rent multiplier is calculated from the sales of comparable properties which were rented at the time of sale: GRM = price divided by rent.

Applying to Subject. Multiplying the market unfurnished rental for the subject property by the gross rent multiplier gives an estimate of the market value of the subject property. |
| **Assumptions** | Proper application of gross rent multiplier analysis assumes that the following conditions are met:

□ Sales and rental data are available in the local market for properties which are actually comparable and competitive with the subject.

□ The same market influences and trends operate on the sales price and gross monthly unfurnished rental of residential properties. They will both move in the same direction and in similar proportion in response to changes in these market influences.

□ The operating expenses and costs of ownership of comparable or competitive properties are very similar to one another.

□ Gross monthly unfurnished rental is a good guide to market value in the current local market.

□ The estimated market rental for the subject property will remain essentially unchanged (or predictable) for the foreseeable future. |
| **Ownership Amenities** | The appraiser must make sure that gross rent multiplier actually reflects the amenities of owner occupancy in relating market rental to market value or sales price. The monthly rental does not reflect ownership amenities. They must be reflected in the multiplier to justify the conclusion that the subject property would sell at the same price whether it were offered for rent or for owner occupancy. |

Data Requirements   Since gross multiplier analysis is actually a part of sales comparison analysis, the data requirements are essentially the same as those discussed in Chapter 10. All data must be both reliable and verifiable.

Sales of Comparable Rental Properties.

☐ Market and neighborhood forces affecting the comparable properties must be as similar as possible to those affecting the subject.

☐ The comparable sales properties must be truly comparable to the subject property.

☐ The comparable sales properties should have been rented at the time they were sold.

☐ Sales of comparable properties must be bona fide, arm's length transactions.

☐ The sales price and terms and conditions of sale must be verified by one of the principals to the transaction.

☐ At least eight to ten reliable comparable sales of rented properties should be considered; twelve to fifteen sales would be preferable.

Comparable Unfurnished Rentals.

☐ Gross monthly unfurnished rentals must be obtained. Furnished rentals must either be adjusted or eliminated from the analysis.

☐ The rental properties must be truly comparable to the subject property.

☐ Rental data may be sought for both comparable properties which were rented at the time of a recent sale and for comparable properties which are currently rented.

☐ Rentals must be verified by one of the principals.

☐ At least eight to ten rentals are necessary; more would be preferable.

Data Sources   The data sources are the same as those for direct sales comparison analysis, listed below:

Public Records. Professionals typically make use of these public records when conducting appraisals:

☐ Recorded deeds

☐ Recorded leases

☐ Assessor's records

☐ VA and FHA records.

Private Sources. Additional private sources are also frequently used in the appraisal process:

- ☐ Appraiser's own data bank, appraisal organizations, other appraisers
- ☐ Real estate brokers
- ☐ Multiple Listing Service records
- ☐ Private sales and rental data services
- ☐ Lending institutions
- ☐ Title companies
- ☐ Newspaper advertisements and stories.

Estimation of Market Rent

Using current rental data for comparable properties, the appraiser seeks to estimate the gross monthly unfurnished rent for the subject property.

Nature of Market Rent. Market rent is the most probable rental income that a property would command on the open market as indicated by current rent for comparable space, as of the date of the appraisal.

- ☐ Market rent is not the same as economic rent. Economic rent is a term in economic analysis which means the surplus payment in excess of that necessary to bring the property on the market.

- ☐ Monthly rental data for unfurnished properties must be obtained, because of the wide variation in furnished rentals. Rental data for furnished properties must be adjusted or eliminated from the analysis.

- ☐ In residential property appraisal, rental data is expressed in terms of monthly rates.

- ☐ The rent is gross or contract rent, not net rent. Contract rent is the amount specified by a written or oral lease agreement.

- ☐ Market rent may or may not be the same as contract rent. If the actual current rent is a close approximation of the estimated market rent, then the actual rent may be used to estimate the value of the subject property by gross rent multiplier analysis. In all other cases, market rent must be used.

Example

A lease written two years ago may require monthly rental payments of $600, while an analysis of current comparable rentals indicates that the market rent for the property is now $750.

Use of Comparable Rentals. The rental properties used in the estimation of market rent must be in the same market as the subject property and highly comparable to it.

☐ Rental data must be current, accurate and verified. Rents may not be estimated or imputed.

☐ Sufficient data must be gathered for each rental property to enable the appraiser to justify rent differences based on variations of comparable properties from the subject property.

Adjustments. Generally, adjustments in comparable rents for differences between comparable properties and the subject property should not have to be made and should not be made. If there are sufficient numbers of good comparables, it is preferable to omit a comparable instead of attempting to adjust it.

If it is necessary to adjust the comparable rents, adjustments are made in the same manner as the adjustments are made to comparable sale properties in the direct sales comparison analysis.

☐ Adjustments must be based on market evidence.

☐ Adjustments are made from the comparable rental properties to the subject property.

Indicated Market Rent for the Subject Property. The adjusted monthly rent for the comparable rental properties should lie within a relatively narrow range. The appraiser selects the most probable rent for the subject from this range on the basis of the market data and adjustments.

☐ It is often helpful to reduce the comparable rents to a per-unit basis in the reconciliation process to account for differences in size.

☐ The estimated market rent is generally rounded to a level which reflects market behavior.

Estimation of the Gross Rent Multiplier   The gross rent multiplier is a number which expresses the ratio between the sales price of a residential property and the gross rental income produced by that property at the time it is sold. The estimation process is as follows:

Selection of Comparable Sales Properties. Comparable sales properties for gross rent multiplier analysis are chosen in the same manner as sales comparables used in direct sales comparison analysis.

☐ The salient features of the subject property which are accounted for in the direct sales comparison approach and the cost approach must be considered in the GRM analysis.

☐ At least 8 to 10 comparable sales properties should be included in the analysis; 12 to 15 would be preferable.

☐ The comparable sales must be bona fide, arm's length transactions. All sales data must be reliable and verified by one of the principals to the transactions.

☐ Adjustments should not be necessary if the comparable sales properties are really comparable to the subject. If adjustments are necessary, they should be made in the same proportion for both sales prices and rents on comparable properties. The appraiser must take care not to adjust the sales price for time without making any corresponding change in the rent.

☐ There is no standard gross rent multiplier. The GRM varies according to the property type, market conditions, and time. The appropriate gross rent multiplier is determined by current conditions in the local market.

Formula. The gross rent multiplier is derived by dividing the sales price of a residential property by its gross monthly unfurnished rent as in the following formula:

$$GRM = SP \div GR$$

Example

If the sales price is $100,000 and the monthly rent is $780, the gross rent multiplier is 128.2. ($100,000 ÷ .780 = 128.2)

Rounding. The GRM for a specific property is usually not rounded, except perhaps to the nearest whole number. Rounding is more likely and properly applied to the multiplier selected during the reconciliation.

Reconciliation. If the properties are truly comparable to the subject and to one another, the gross rent multipliers calculated for these properties should fall within a fairly narrow range. The appraiser then selects the appropriate gross rent multiplier indicated by the pattern of GRMs calculated for the comparable properties. This is the GRM that will be applied to the estimated market rent of the subject property to derive an estimate of value.

Estimation of Value The estimate of value is calculated by multiplying the market rent by the gross rent multiplier as in the following formula:

$$V = MR \times GRM$$

Gross rent multipliers are not adjusted.

		Illustration of Gross Monthly Rent Multiplier Analysis		
Sale	**Sales Price**	**Monthly Rent**	**GRM**	
1.	$87,500	$700	125.0	
2.	$89,500	$725	123.4	
3.	$91,650	$750	122.2	
4.	$91,300	$725	125.9	
5.	$92,200	$725	127.2	
6.	$90,200	$700	128.8	
7.	$89,700	$695	129.1	
8.	$89,600	$715	125.3	
9.	$92,500	$730	126.7	
10.	$90,850	$720	126.2	

The selection of an appropriate GRM for the subject property is based largely on the appraiser's judgment of the degree of similarity between each comparable property and the subject. If sales 4, 9, and 10 were found to be the most comparable properties, the indicated GRM for the subject property would be 126. Assuming that the market rent has been estimated as $720 per month, the indicated value of the subject property via gross rent multiplier analysis is $90,720.

$$MR \times GRM = V$$

$$\$720 \times 126 = \$90,720$$

Rounding. The indicated market value is usually rounded to an appropriate level to produce the estimated market value by gross rent multiplier analysis. In the preceding example, the market value would probably be rounded to $91,000.

Advantages **Simplicity**. GRM analysis is relatively simple to use and easy to understand. It is widely accepted.

No Adjustment Necessary. With appropriate data, the use of gross rent multiplier analysis eliminates the need for direct adjustment for individual property differences.

Active Rental Market. Gross rent multiplier analysis reflects market behavior where there is an active rental market for residential properties.

Limitations **Insufficient Reliable Data**. Gross rent multiplier analysis may not be properly applied if there is insufficient reliable data available. A lack of rental market activity may make it impossible to apply GRM analysis.

Distortion. Unusual market forces may distort the relationship between rents and sales prices. Rentals tend to be more sensitive to changes in the environment than owner-occupied properties; while a renter may leave on short notice, an owner cannot usually do so without financial loss.

Sales Prices. Sales prices are more sensitive to changes in zoning regulations, tax burden, and physical deterioration than rents are.

Rent Controls. Rent controls tend to distort the relationship between rents and sales prices.

INCOME CAPITALIZATION

Income capitalization is the process of converting a series of anticipated future periodic installments of net income to their present worth or value. The use of income capitalization in real estate valuation is based on the premise that value is the present worth of anticipated or forecast future benefits in the form of money income.

Definitions **Income**. Income capitalization is always based on net property income which is usually measured in terms of net operating income. NOI, or net operating income, is the before-tax annual net income generated by the property.

Capitalization Rate. The capitalization rate or rates are weighted averages or composites of the rates of return required by equity investors and mortgage lenders to induce them to invest funds in the property.

Value. The estimate of value, as defined for the subject property, is derived by dividing the annual net income by an annual rate of capitalization or by multiplying the annual net income by an annual capitalization multiplier (factor).

Fundamentals **Investment Real Estate**. Income capitalization is the third approach to value. While the direct sales comparison and cost approaches are applicable to all types of properties, income capitalization is applicable only to investment real estate which is capable of producing money income and where the motivation of the buyers is a return on investment including income tax considerations.

Net Income. Income capitalization differs from gross rent multiplier analysis in that net income, rather than gross income, is processed to a value estimate.

Characteristics of Income-Producing Properties. Valuation is undertaken from the viewpoint of the typical informed investor and is based on the money income produced by the property. The market is stratified in terms of comparable, competitive investments.

Formula. The indicated value can be estimated by dividing the income by the capitalization rate, as in the following formula:

$$V = I/R$$

where: V = **Value Indicated**
        I = **Income Produced**
        R = **Capitalization Rate**

Example

If the net operating income (I) is $50,000 and the capitalization rate (R) is 10%, then the indicated value (V) is calculated:

V = I/R = $50,000 ÷ .10 = $500,000

Investment Principles Investment analysis is essentially a matter of determining who gets what, and when. It points out the amount and timing of anticipated income receipts and expenses.

Amount. More is preferable to less for income. The reverse is true for expenses and capital outlays. The investor would prefer to receive $5,000 rather than $500 on an investment, and would prefer to spend $500 rather than $5,000.

Timing. Sooner is preferable to later for income. The reverse is true for expenses and capital outlays. Because a dollar received today is worth more than a dollar received a year from now, the investor would prefer to receive any income from the investment as soon as possible.

Return of Investment. The investor's primary concern is to maintain capital intact. This is return of investment and means that the entire amount of the original investment is returned to the investor.

Return on Investment. The investor typically seeks a profit or gain on the investment, in addition to the return of capital. This gain is referred to as the return on investment.

Cap Rate. The capitalization rate is a composite of the rate of return on an investment and the rate of return of an investment.

STEPS IN THE INCOME CAPITALIZATION PROCESS

While there are several methods of capitalization, only direct capitalization will be discussed in this chapter. The study of alternate capitalization techniques is reserved for advanced appraisal courses.

Estimate Future Gross Annual Income
The income estimation process seeks to determine the quantity, quality, and duration of the forecast income.

Quantity. The amount of income that is likely to be received.

Quality. The likelihood that the forecast income will actually be received.

Duration. The period of time over which the income is forecast to be received.

Determine the Potential Gross Income (PGI)
Potential gross income this is the total amount of rental income, assuming 100% occupancy. It is always expressed on an annual basis.

Example

If each apartment in a ten unit building rents for $500 per month, the Potential Gross Income for that property is $500 x 10 x 12, or $60,000.

Estimate the Effective Gross Income (EGI)
This is derived by subtracting an allowance for vacancy and income loss and adding any other income to potential gross income.

Example

If there is a 5% vacancy rate and $50 per month of other income from laundry and vending machines, then the annual Effective Gross Income is $57,600.

$60,000 x .05	=	$ 3,000
$60,000 − $3,000 + $600	=	$57,600

Compute the Net Operating Income (NOI)
Effective gross income less the annualized operating expenses results in the net operating income. Operating expenses are the expenditures that the owner-investor must make by law, custom, or contract to protect the generation of gross income by the property. The four categories of operating expenses are:

Fixed Expenses. Expenses which tend not to vary with occupancy, e.g., insurance and property taxes.

Variable Expenses. Expenses which usually vary with occupancy, such as utilities and management fees.

Reserves for Replacements. Reserves for personal property such as furniture, carpeting, etc., which must be replaced periodically.

Repairs and Maintenance. Expenses incurred in keeping a property in condition to perform its function efficiently.

Example

Effective Gross Income	$57,600
Less Operating Expenses of 40%	− $23,560
Net Operating Income	$34,560

Derive the Capitalization Rate The two most frequently used methods of deriving a capitalization rate are the comparative sales method and the band of investment method.

Comparative Sales Method. This method is based upon an analysis of recent sales of comparable properties. The indicated capitalization rate is derived by dividing the net incomes from the properties by their sales prices.

Example

An apartment building with an annual net income of $30,000 recently sold for $300,000. Therefore the indicated capitalization rate is 10%.

$$\$30,000 \div \$300,000 = .10 \text{ or } \underline{10\%}$$

☐ The sales must be reasonably recent transactions to accurately reflect current market conditions.

☐ Properties must be comparable to the subject, particularly in respect to location, investment quality, and other salient characteristics.

☐ Net income for the comparable properties must be derived in the same manner as for the subject in order to be meaningful.

☐ Use of this method is often limited by a lack of necessary income data for the comparable properties.

Band of Investment Method. This method derives a capitalization rate which is a composite of the rates of return required by the lender and by the owner of the equity interest. Theoretically, the rate of return required by the lender reflects the relative attractiveness of the loan compared with alternate permitted investments for the lender's funds. Similarly, the equity component reflects the competitive alternate returns to equity, both on a before and after tax basis.

☐ *Mortgage Interest Technique*. The capitalization rate is computed as a weighted average of the most probable mortgage terms and the return required by the equity investor.

Example

Assume that a long-term loan of 75% of the property value is available at 9.5% interest and investors require 12% interest on their equity.

Interest	Portion		Rate		Product
First Mortgage	.75	x	.095	=	.071
Equity	.25	x	.12	=	<u>.030</u>
Capitalization Rate				=	.101
					or <u>10.1%</u>

This form of Band of Investment method is seldom used by investors or appraisers because it makes no allowance for either amortization of the loan principal or for recapture of the investment in the wasting asset. Compare the rate for the same transaction using the Mortgage Constant Technique, in the next example.

□ *Mortgage Constant Technique*. The mortgage constant is the total annual payment of principal and interest on a mortgage with level payment amortization, expressed as a percentage of the initial principal amount of the loan. Constants are readily available in published financial tables or can be determined with a financial calculator. This technique uses a weighted average of the mortgage constant and the return on equity required by investors.

Example

Assume a 75% loan for 25 years at 9.5% interest represents the prevailing financing terms. The mortgage constant is found to be .104844. If investors require 12% return on equity, the capitalization rate is calculated by:

	Portion		Rate		Product
First					
Mortgage	.75	x	.104844	=	.0786
Equity	.25	x	.12	=	<u>.0300</u>
Overall Capitalization Rate				=	.1086 or
					<u>10.86%</u>

Use of the mortgage constant technique provides for recapture (return of the investment) in addition to the return on the investment. This technique is the preferred method for arriving at an overall capitalization rate and is the one most used by both appraisers and investors. However, it should be noted that it assumes that the amortization of loan principal satisfies all of the capital recapture requirements.

Apply the Direct Capitalization Formula To determine the present value of the property by the income approach, the net operating income is divided by the capitalization rate, according to the formula:

$$V = \frac{I}{R}$$

Example

Assume the net operating income for the property is $34,560 and the overall capitalization rate is 10%.

$$\text{Value} = \frac{\text{Income}}{\text{Rate}} = \frac{\$34,560}{.10} = \$345,600$$

Illustration of Property Valuation With Income Capitalization

Assume the subject property is a new 20-unit apartment building with a potential gross income of $100,000. The vacancy and income loss allowance is estimated to be 5% of the scheduled gross income. Operating expenses are estimated at $45,000. The expected life of the building is 50 years.

The prevailing financing terms for this type of property are a 75% loan-to-value ratio at 9.5% interest for 25 years. Investors typically require a 12% return on comparable properties.

Computation of the Indicated Value of the Property

Potential Gross Income	$100,000
Less: Allowance for Vacancy and Income Loss (5%)	5,000
Effective Gross Income	$ 95,000
Less: Operating Expenses	45,000
Net Operating Income	$ 50,000

Comparative Sales Method

Assume the analysis of comparable sales indicates that 10% is the appropriate capitalization rate.

$$\text{Value} = \frac{I}{R} = \frac{\$50,000}{.10} = \$500,000$$

Band of Investment Method

First Mortgage	.75 x .1048	=	.0786
Equity	.25 x .12	=	.03
Capitalization Rate		=	.1086

where .104844 is the mortgage constant for the given loan terms.

$$\text{Value} = \frac{I}{R} = \frac{\$50,000}{.1086} = \$460,405, \text{ rounded to } \$460,500$$

THE URAR INDICATED VALUE BY INCOME APPROACH SECTION

The income approach to value is based on the assumption that market value is related to the market rent or income that a property can be expected to earn. Its use generally is appropriate in neighborhoods of single-family properties when there is a substantial rental market, and it is an important approach in the valuation of a two- to four-family property. However, it generally is not appropriate in areas that consist mostly of owner-occupied properties since adequate rental data generally does not exist for those areas. To arrive at the indicated value by the income approach, the appraiser multiplies the estimated monthly market rent for the subject property by a gross rent multiplier.

■ **INDICATED VALUE BY INCOME APPROACH** (If Applicable) Estimated Market Rent $ _____ /Mo. x Gross Rent Multiplier _____ = $ _____ |

Estimated Market Rent   The estimated market rent is based on an analysis of comparable rentals in the neighborhood. After appropriate adjustments are made to the comparables, their adjusted (or indicated) values are reconciled to develop an estimated monthly market rent for the subject property.

Gross Rent Multiplier   The gross rent multiplier is determined by dividing the sales prices of comparable properties that were rented at the time of sale by their monthly market rent, which is then reconciled to create a single gross rent multiplier (or a range of multipliers) for the subject property.

Indicated Value   The estimated market rent is multiplied by the gross rent multiplier to arrive at an indicated value by the income approach. Results of this calculation are reported in this section.

1. The use of the gross income multiplier in real estate appraisal is based upon:

    (A) Scheduled gross income and expected net income

    (B) Gross income in relation to capitalized value

    (C) Gross income and anticipated gross income

    √(D) Relationship between rent and sales price of property

2. A gross rent multiplier is:

    √(A) Based on gross income, not net income

    (B) Used to estimate the overall capitalization rate if the properties are truly comparable

    (C) Rarely applicable or acceptable

    (D) None of the above

Questions 3-5:

A property containing 25 apartments has 15 two-bedroom units renting for $400 per month and 10 one-bedroom units renting for $300 per month. There are 14 two-bedroom units occupied and 8 one-bedroom units occupied.

3. The potential gross income is:

    (A) $ 8,500

    (B) $ 9,000

    (C) $102,000

    √(D) $108,000

4. The allowance for vacancy and income loss is:

    (A) $ 1,000

    (B) $ 1,100

    (C) $10,400

    √(D) $12,000

5. The effective gross income is:

    (A) $ 7,500

    (B) $ 7,900

    (C) $91,600

    √(D) $96,000

6. A single-family rental unit which rents for $700 per month recently sold for $105,000. What gross rent multiplier is indicated by this sale?

    (A) 13

    (B) 150

    (C) 700

    (D) 8400

Questions 7-10:

A property has a potential gross income of $50,000. Vacancy and income loss is estimated at 5%. Management fees are 2% of rent collections. Insurance is $1,000, property taxes are $500, and other operating expenses are $18,700.

7. The effective gross income is:

    (A) $43,750

    (B) $45,000

    (C) $47,500

    (D) $49,600

8. Total operating expenses are:

    (A) $19,250

    (B) $20,200

    (C) $21,150

    (D) $29,700

9. Net operating income is:

    (A) $19,900

    (B) $24,500

    (C) $24,800

    (D) $26,350

10. Assuming that the appropriate capitalization rate is 10.5%, what is the indicated market value of the above property?

    (A) $190,000

    (B) $251,000

    (C) $236,000

    (D) $233,000

PREVIEW

Valuation

Evaluation

Measures of Investment Performance

VALUATION

Valuation is a systematic process of estimating value. The purpose of valuation in appraisal is to estimate a defined value of a property or an interest in property. There are many different types of value which might be appraised.

Types of Value **Market Value.** The most probable selling price for the property, given a willing and able buyer and a willing seller.

Insurable Value. The value of portions of a property which are destructible. This often determines the amount of insurance that should be carried to protect the owner in the event of loss.

Assessed Value. The value established for property tax purposes; often different from market value.

Liquidation Value. The value which an owner must accept when the property must be sold without reasonable market exposure.

Value in Use. The current monetary worth of the property.

Value After Taking. The market value of the remaining parcel in a partial taking in condemnation.

Value Before Taking. The market value of the entire property affected by the taking in a condemnation.

Investment Value. The value of an investment to a particular investor, as distinguished from market value.

Exchange Value. The monetary value of real estate in a typical market.

Functions The function or use of an appraisal is the manner in which the client employs the information from the appraisal report. Uses might include any of the following, as examples:

☐ To assist a prospective buyer in determining an offering price.

☐ To assist an owner in establishing a listing price.

☐ To establish a basis for exchanges.

☐ To evaluate the adequacy of property as security for a mortgage.

☐ To establish a "just compensation" in condemnation proceedings.

☐ To set up income tax depreciation schedules.

☐ To determine gift, inheritance, or property taxes.

☐ To assist company purchase of a transferred employee's home.

☐ To estimate liquidation value in bankruptcy proceedings.

Methods To review, the three appraisal approaches that are traditionally used are summarized as follows:

The Cost Approach. The approach based on the principle that a prudent purchaser would not pay more for a property than the cost to reproduce it, provided that it could be reproduced without costly delay. (Chapter 8)

The Sales Comparison Approach. The approach based on the premise that an informed buyer would not pay more for a property than it would cost to acquire an existing property with the same utility. (Chapter 10)

The Income Approach. The procedure which converts anticipated benefits to be derived from the ownership of property into a value estimate (Chapter 11). Use of the income approach often goes beyond *valuation* to *evaluation*.

EVALUATION

Appraisers often perform services for clients that go quite beyond the derivation of an estimate of market value of a property, but which assist clients in making transaction and investment decisions.

Definitions **Evaluation.** The American Institute of Real Estate Appraisers defined evaluation as "A study of the nature, quality, or utility of a parcel of real estate or interests in, or aspects of, real property, in which a value estimate is not necessarily required."

Market Value. Market value is the price in cash for which a willing seller would sell, and which a willing buyer would pay, in a competitive market, with both acting prudently and neither being under undue pressure to act. Market value is based on the assumption that market behavior does not depend on any one participant's personal characteristics or objectives. However, buyers and sellers may agree on a price even though each has an entirely different idea about the value of the property.

Investment Value. Investment value is related to the specific requirements and characteristics of an individual investor or group of investors. Investment value may be equal to market value in many circumstances; however, investment value to the client may reflect many other considerations in the evaluation of the investment.

MEASURES OF INVESTMENT PERFORMANCE

There are several commonly used calculations which an investor may use to evaluate a property.

Direct Capitalization As a measure of economic productivity, direct capitalization is expressed in the formula:

$$R = \frac{I}{V}$$

where:

R	=	Overall Rate of Return
I	=	Projected Annual Net Operating Income
V	=	Value

Example

A property purchased for $300,000 (V) which produces an annual net operating income of $36,000 (I) may be said to produce an overall rate of return of 12% (R).

$$\frac{\$36,000}{\$300,000} = .12, \text{ or } \underline{12\%}$$

This overall rate is a device used in valuation of a property in the income approach, assuming that normal financing is available, and such rates are established in the market through the interaction of buyers and sellers. This rate would tend to evaluate the investment only with 100% equity investment, a rare occurrence, and reversion (future sale) is not considered.

Cash-on-Cash Return The same technique that is used in direct capitalization can be applied to the evaluation of equity investments by using cash-on-cash returns. The cash on cash return method gives a prospective investor a much better evaluation of the investment than an estimate of value based on direct capitalization alone.

$$R = \frac{I}{V}$$

where:
   I = Cash flow after debt service
   V = Equity Investment
   R = Rate of Return on Cash Invested

Example

A property purchased for $300,000 with $75,000 cash downpayment, and producing a net annual operating income of $36,000, would require a debt service of $23,700 on a $225,000 mortgage at 10%, leaving a cash flow of $12,300.

$12,300/$75,000 = .164 or <u>16.4%</u>

While this technique presents a better analysis of the investment, it still fails to take into consideration the fact that debt service includes some equity build-up through amortization, and that there is a possibility of reversion in the property. The reversion will come from the sale of the property at some predicted time in the future.

Band of Investment Analysis
If the purchase of the property is financed, each component of financing represents a "band of investment." By analyzing the proportion of an overall capitalization rate which is allocated to each band of investment, an equity yield rate can be established.

Example

Assume that an investment property can be purchased at an overall capitalization rate of 12%. If a first trust deed loan of 80% of the purchase price can be obtained for 30 years at an annual interest rate of 10%, this represents the first "band of investment." The equity band is the remaining 20% of the purchase price.

Assume the first TD loan has a mortgage constant of .105309 (the annual debt service divided by the original principal amount of the loan).

By multiplying the percentage of the total purchase price which this band of investment represents (80%) by the mortgage constant for this available financing (.105309), a capitalization rate is derived for this band of investment. This capitalization rate is then subtracted from the overall capitalization rate to determine what portion of the overall rate is available to apply to the next band of investment, the equity band.

80% x .105309 = .0842 or 8.42% of the capitalization rate to apply to the first band of investment.

   12.00%   overall capitalization rate
  <u>−8.42%</u>   applied to the first band
    3.58%   to apply to the equity band
  .0358/.20 = .179 or <u>17.9% equity yield</u>

This greatly increased equity yield, significantly higher than the overall capitalization rate, reflects the advantage of leverage, and shows clearly that a capitalization rate alone does not analyze a leveraged investment. It also becomes clear that an overall capitalization rate alone is not an adequate tool for a direct comparison between a real estate investment and other types of investments which will compete for the investor's funds.

Pay-Back Period   The pay-back period is the length of time required for the stream of cash flows produced by the investment to equal the original cash outlay. By measuring this period, the investor determines how long the investment funds are at risk. The cash outlay is divided by the annual cash flow.

> ### Example
> $75,000/$12,300 = 6.10 years

Pay-back periods are used to compare investment opportunities. A different investment might have higher returns in early years and nothing thereafter. In general, the shorter the pay-back period the more attractive the investment. However, the total return may be more significant to some investors.

Proceeds Per Dollar Invested   An investment may be evaluated according to the total anticipated proceeds from income and reversion upon sale of the property. The problem with this technique is that each dollar received is treated the same, regardless of when received, even though it is generally recognized that a dollar to be received one year from now is worth less than a dollar received today. Next year's dollar, if discounted to present value at the rate of 10% per year, would be worth only $.91 today; one dollar to be received two years from now would be worth only $.83 today. (These figures are derived from compound interest tables or a financial calculator.)

Discounted Cash Flows   Based on the theory that a dollar to be received in the future is worth less than a dollar in hand today (compound interest theory), a discounted cash flow analysis can be used to evaluate a series of negative and positive cash flows over the anticipated ownership of a property. The cash flows used can be either before-tax or after-tax calculations, but the more complete investment analysis for the client would require the use of after-tax cash flows. The mathematics of this procedure is relatively simple but lengthy, and is accomplished by the following formula:

$$PV = \frac{CF_1}{(1+i)} + \frac{CF_2}{(1+i)^2} + \cdots + \frac{CF_n}{(1+i)^n}$$

Where: PV = Present Value of the Discounted Cash Flows

CF = Cash Flow

i = Discount Rate used to reflect the time value of money

This laborious arithmetic is accomplished quickly and easily with a financial calculator or a computer.

Net Present Value (NPV) An evaluation of the investment is frequently accomplished by determining the net present value (NPV) of a series of negative and positive discounted cash flows, where the first cash flow is the initial cash outlay, subsequent cash flows are the after-tax cash flows projected for the property, and the final cash flow is the anticipated value of the reversion from the sale of the property in 5, 10, or 15 years.

Interpretation. A positive NPV indicates that the financial value of the investor's assets would be increased by this investment. A NPV of exactly zero means that the future cash flows have been discounted exactly to present value. NPV for one investment can be compared with NPV for another investment, and these comparisons can provide useful data in investment decision-making. The greater the NPV, the greater would be the increase in the value of the investor's assets.

Internal Rate of Return (IRR) The American Institute of Real Estate Appraisers defines the internal rate of return (IRR) as "The annualized rate of return on capital that is generated or capable of being generated within an investment or portfolio over the period of ownership; similar to the equity yield rate; often used to measure profitability after income taxes, i.e., the after-tax equity yield rate; the rate of discount that makes the net present value of an investment equal to zero; discounts all returns from an investment, including returns from its termination, to equal the original investment."

Calculation. A series of discount rates is applied to a projected series of negative and positive cash flows to determine the net present value (NPV) of the cash flows at each discount rate. First a high discount rate is used, then a low discount rate. Next a slightly less high rate is used, then a slightly less low rate, etc. These calculations continue in a reiterative process until a certain discount rate produces a NPV of approximately zero. This discount rate is the internal rate of return (IRR).

☐ The calculation of IRR, being a reiterative process, is accomplished quickly and easily with a financial calculator, but the application of this arithmetic is beyond the scope of this course.

Application. The procedure enables the prospective investor in real estate to make direct comparisons of the real estate investment with other investments such as bonds, notes, and other securities.

Quiz Chapter 12

1. Market value and investment value:

   (A) Are never the same
   (B) Are always the same
   (C) Will be the same for any one investor
   (D) May be the same but may be different

2. Buyers and sellers can agree on a price for a property:

   (A) Only when they agree on the value of the property
   (B) Even though each has an entirely different idea about the value of the property
   (C) Only when there is a formal written appraisal of the property
   (D) Easily when the market establishes the value

3. An overall capitalization rate will accurately evaluate an investment:

   (A) If the capitalization rate is accurate
   (B) If the property is properly appraised
   (C) Only with 100% equity investment
   (D) Always

4. A cash-on-cash return is based on:

   (A) Gross income
   (B) Effective gross income
   (C) Net operating income
   (D) Cash flow

5. A $62,000 cash down payment toward a $300,000 purchase price and a $10,300 annual cash flow would produce a cash-on-cash return of approximately:

   (A) 4%
   (B) 6%
   (C) 16%
   (D) 24%

6. An anticipated reversion from an investment:

   (A) Would come from tax savings
   (B) Would come from the sale of the property at some future time
   (C) Would exist only if the property was leased
   (D) Would be the lessee's interest in the property

7. A band-of-investment analysis will establish:

   (A) An equity yield rate
   (B) An annual interest rate on a mortgage
   (C) Both A and B
   (D) None of the above

8. An equity yield rate is normally expected to be:

   (A) The same as an overall capitalization rate
   (B) Less than an overall capitalization rate
   (C) Greater than an overall capitalization rate
   (D) Any of the above

9. A net present value (NPV) is:

   (A) The sum of a series of cash flows
   (B) The initial investment minus a series of cash flows
   (C) The initial investment plus a series of cash flows
   (D) The present value of a series of negative and positive discounted cash flows

10. Internal rate of return (IRR) is:

    (A) The same as cash flow
    (B) The easiest way of estimating the yield of an investment
    (C) Useful to the investor in comparing competing investment opportunities
    (D) All of the above

Chapter 13
Reconciliation and
the Final Value Estimate

PREVIEW

Nature of the Reconciliation Process

Review of the Valuation Process

Reconciliation

The Final Value Estimate

The URAR Reconciliation Section

NATURE OF THE RECONCILIATION PROCESS

The reconciliation of value estimates is the final step in the valuation process. The appraiser typically utilizes several approaches—the cost approach, the income approach, and the sales comparison approach—to obtain value estimates, and each approach may yield different indications of value. Reconciliation is the process by which the appraiser evaluates these preliminary indications of value and from them selects a range of final values or a single final estimate of value. The final reconciliation of value is not an average of the different value estimates or based on some appraisal formula. It is a value based on the appraiser's judgment and experience and the application of appropriate appraisal techniques.

Purpose The purpose of the reconciliation process is to reconcile the range of value estimates resulting from the various approaches to value into a single estimate of value as of the valuation date.

Steps **Review.** The appraiser reviews all the previous work and analysis. checking and verifying the data, logic, techniques, and conclusions.

Reconciliation. The final estimate of value or range of values is reached by applying logic and judgment through the reconciliation process. Confidence in this estimate is directly related to the quality and quantity of the data used as well as the appropriateness of the valuation approaches utilized for the particular property being appraised.

As mentioned, the application of two or more of the different approaches to value will usually result in somewhat different indications of value. This occurs because all required data are not always available, real estate markets are not perfect, and judgments are not always perfect. The appraiser should review the work to understand any variations in the value estimates. If there is a wide discrepancy among the value indications, the appraiser must carefully review all the work to determine whether revisions are necessary. Data cannot be revised because they are the facts of the market. However, the application of logic and the various valuation techniques are subject to change if the review indicates that they are improper or inadequate.

General Points **Applicability**. Are the approaches and procedures used appropriate to the appraisal problem? The purpose of most residential appraisals is to estimate market value for lending or employee relocation purposes. Does the appraisal answer the client's specific question?

Data Reliability. The data collected must be accurate and adequate. Has the information been documented and verified? Was it obtained first hand from reliable sources? Are the data representative of the market?

Mechanics. Simple arithmetic errors can lead to incorrect value estimates. Are the calculations, adjustments, and techniques correct? Have they been double checked, preferably by another person?

Logic and Analysis. What are the assumptions underlying the judgments made in the analysis? Are they appropriate and logical?

Consistency. The items and findings of the analysis must be consistent if the value indications are to be compatible with each other. The following checklist may be used to review the analysis for consistency:

☐ Are the same size, areas, and dimensions used in the direct sales comparison and cost approaches?

☐ Are the salient property features, as identified in the property inspection and described in the property description, used in the adjustment process of the direct sales comparison approach?

☐ Are the charges for locational obsolescence consistent with the environmental influences identified in the property description and the neighborhood analysis?

☐ Is the highest and best use of the improved property compatible with the existing improvements?

☐ Do the patterns of sales prices and unit prices from the direct sales comparison analysis and the gross rent multiplier analysis support each other?

☐ Is the time adjustment (if any) used in the direct sales comparison analysis in line with the sales price trends identified in the area and neighborhood analysis?

□ Is the highest and best use assigned to the site legally and physically feasible, based on the findings of the site analysis? Is there evidence of market acceptability for this use in the area and neighborhood analysis?

□ Are the elements for which adjustments are made in the direct sales comparison approach the same as those for which charges for accrued depreciation are made in the cost approach?

□ Is each item of condition and functional or locational obsolescence that is identified in the property description or neighborhood analysis included as a sales adjustment factor in the direct sales comparison approach and as an element of accrued depreciation in the cost approach?

□ Is the method of rounding the value estimate consistent among the valuation approaches used?

□ Are the items or conditions for which charges for accrued depreciation are made described fully and adequately in the property description? Is the basis for all accrued depreciation charges fully supported and justified in the description of the improvements?

□ Are the adjustments in comparable rentals compatible with the adjustments made in the direct sales comparison approach and with accrued depreciation charges made in the cost approach?

Approaches to Value   **Sales Comparison Approach.** This appraisal approach is based on the premise that an informed buyer would not pay more for a property than it would cost to acquire an existing property with the same utility. The appraiser should review the following:

□ Adequacy and reliability of the market data. All data must be verified. Are there enough data to justify the analysis?

□ Adequacy of comparable sales properties' descriptions, particularly as a basis for adjustments on the salient features of the subject property.

□ Comparability of the comparable sales properties to the subject property.

□ Market evidence which supports the adjustments between the comparable sales and subject property.

□ Applicability of units of comparison. Are they used consistently? Check for mathematical errors.

□ Accuracy of measurements and area and unit computations.

□ Directions of adjustments, the arithmetic in the adjustments, and the consistency of size of the adjustments among the comparable sales properties.

- [ ] Terms of sale and conditions of sale for the comparable sales properties.

- [ ] Reconciliation of the adjusted sales prices for the comparable sales properties to an indication of value. Is it logical and defensible?

Cost Approach. This approach in appraisal analysis is based on the principle that a prudent purchaser would not pay more for a property than the cost to reproduce it, provided that it could be reproduced without costly delay. The appraiser should review the following:

- [ ] Comparability of the comparable sales sites to the subject site.

- [ ] Reliability and adequacy of the market data used in making adjustments from the comparable sales sites to estimate site value.

- [ ] Selection and use of units of comparison in estimating site value. Check for mathematical errors.

- [ ] Appropriateness of the reconciliation and the selection of the estimated site value.

- [ ] Field observations and the property description, for indications of the components, condition, and quality of the subject property. Are the measurements and size and area calculations correct?

- [ ] Selection of appropriate unit cost type.

- [ ] Completeness of coverage of the cost of new elements.

- [ ] Appropriateness of the method of estimating reproduction cost new. Check for arithmetic errors.

- [ ] Market evidence for accrued depreciation charges.

- [ ] Description and observational basis of the types and amount of accrued depreciation charged.

- [ ] Relationship and consistency of depreciation charges to measures used in the direct sales comparison approach and in the gross rent multiplier analysis.

- [ ] Accrued depreciation charges, for omissions and double counting. Have the depreciation charges been properly deducted from the reproduction cost new estimate?

- [ ] Market data basis for assigning present worth to the site improvements.

- [ ] Summation of the site value estimate and the present worth of the improvements for mathematical errors.

Income Approach. This approach in appraisal analysis is based on the premise that an informed purchaser would not pay more for a property than the cost of obtaining a return of the same amount with the same level of risk involved in the subject property. The appraiser should review the following:

☐ Adequacy and reliability of the comparable rental and comparable sales data. All data must be verified. Is there enough information to justify the analysis?

☐ Comparability of comparable rentals and comparable sales to the subject property.

☐ Adequacy of descriptions of comparable rental and sales properties as a basis for adjustments on the salient features of the subject property.

☐ Market evidence on which adjustments are based.

☐ Appropriateness of the market rental selected from indications provided by comparable rental properties.

☐ Appropriateness of the gross rent multiplier selected.

☐ Arithmetic for errors.

RECONCILIATION

Reconciliation is the process by which the appraiser evaluates the preliminary indications of value and from them selects a range of final values or a single final estimate of value. Reconciliation occurs, consciously or unconsciously, every time the appraiser makes a selection from among several alternatives anywhere in the appraisal analysis. Reconciliation does not include corrections of technique and logic—this is part of the review phase which precedes reconciliation. It is not the application of a mathematical formula. It requires the application of careful judgment and analysis. In particular, arithmetic averaging by itself is not reconciliation. Reconciliation does not narrow the range of possible values. Although the steps in the review phase may provide a basis for narrowing the range, a review of the data and analyses may also support widening of the range. In any event, the final estimate of value is most likely to be within the indicated range of values.

Limitations The appraiser's selection of a final value estimate is constrained by the availability and reliability of verified market data and the appropriateness of the particular approach to the current appraisal problem.

Choice of Approach The appraiser must review the data, analyses, and logic to determine the best approximation to the type of value being sought, based on the applicability of the underlying theory to the appraisal problem and the reliability and availability of required data.

Adequacy of Data. There may not be enough reliable, verified data available to support a particular approach, even if it is the most appropriate approach theoretically. This should be explained in the report.

Appropriateness. The indication of value derived from one or more of the approaches may be ignored if it proves to be improper or inappropriate in the final analysis. This should also be explained in the report.

Best Indication. The greatest reliance must be placed on that indication of value which represents the best combination of applicability to the appraisal problem, with support from adequate, verified data.

Assumptions   **Market Behavior**. The reconciliation process, as all other steps in the appraisal process, is approached from the viewpoint of the typically informed, rational purchaser in the pertinent market. The final analysis should reflect the attitudes, responses, and behavior of such a purchaser.

Other Assumptions. Indicate the impact of the limiting conditions and assumptions identified during the definition of the appraisal problem.

Consistency   The final value estimate must be consistent with:

- ☐ The behavior and reactions of the typically informed, rational purchaser operating in the open market in competition with other informed, rational buyers.

- ☐ The property rights to be appraised, as identified in the definition of the appraisal problem.

- ☐ The market conditions existing on the date of the appraisal.

THE FINAL VALUE ESTIMATE

After thoroughly reviewing the valuation process, the final step is to reconcile the various value estimates. Practical experience indicates that clients frequently expect the appraiser to provide *the* worth of the particular property. In reality, though, the final value estimate may be expressed as a single value or a range of values.

Single Value vs. Range of Values   **Single Value**. The single value is the traditional manner of expressing the final value estimate—e.g., $300,000. Single value estimates are usually required by lenders and insurance companies, for tax purposes, condemnation proceedings, and for employee relocation.

Range of Values. Now and then an appraiser will choose to express the final value estimate by reporting a range of value indicating that the actual value of the property is probably no lower than the low end of the range and no higher than the high end of the range.

Rounding It is conventional for the final value estimate to be rounded—usually to two or three digits. This custom reflects the imprecision associated with the conclusions of the valuation process.

Characteristics In conclusion, the final value estimate:

☐ Is based on the definition of value sought.

☐ Is the appraiser's opinion of the most logical and defensible conclusion of value, based on knowledge, analysis, professional judgment, and experience.

☐ May be the same as the value indicated by one of the approaches or may be another, different figure.

☐ Is valid only as of the date of the appraisal and only under certain stipulated conditions.

☐ Will generally be expressed as a single point estimate. However, it is sometimes more useful and appropriate to identify a range of indicated values.

☐ Must always be rounded to avoid any implication of excessive accuracy or precision. The final value estimate is just that—an estimate.

THE URAR RECONCILIATION SECTION

The reconciliation process that leads to the estimate of market value is an ongoing process throughout the appraiser's analysis. In the final reconciliation, the appraiser must reconcile the reasonableness and reliability of each approach to value and the reasonableness and validity of the indicated values and the available data, and then must select and report the approach or approaches that were given the most weight. The final reconciliation must never be an averaging technique. If the appraiser has provided a comprehensive and logical analysis of the neighborhood and the property, the lender's underwriter should be able to reach a sound conclusion on the adequacy of the property as security for the mortgage.

RECONCILIATION

This appraisal is made ☐ "as is" ☐ subject to the repairs, alterations, inspections or conditions listed below ☐ completion per plans and specifications.
Comments and Conditions of Appraisal: _____

Final Reconciliation: _____

This appraisal is based upon the above requirements, the certification, contingent and limiting conditions, and Market Value definition that are stated in
☐ FmHA, HUD &/or VA instructions.
☐ Freddie Mac Form 439 (Rev. 7/86)/Fannie Mae Form 1004B (Rev. 7/86) filed with client _____ 19 ____ ☐ attached.
I (WE) ESTIMATE THE MARKET VALUE, AS DEFINED, OF THE SUBJECT PROPERTY AS OF _____ 19 ____ to be $ _____
I (WE) certify: that to the best of my (our) knowledge and belief the facts and data used herein are true and correct; that I (we) personally inspected the subject property, both inside and out, and have made an exterior inspection of all comparable sales cited in this report; and that I (we) have no undisclosed interest, present or prospective therein.
Appraiser(s) SIGNATURE _____ Review Appraiser SIGNATURE _____ ☐ Did ☐ Did Not
NAME _____ (if applicable) NAME _____ Inspect Property

Conditions of Valuation The appraiser must check the appropriate box indicating whether the subject property was appraised "as is", "subject to the repairs, alterations, inspections or conditions listed below", or "completion per plans and specifications."

Comments and Conditions of Appraisal On this line the appraiser itemizes the cost of necessary repairs, and comments on details concerning other conditions of valuation or any previous section of the report form.

Final Reconciliation The final reconciliation is the last step in the appraisal process. Space is provided here for the appraiser to explain the relevance and validity of each of the three approaches to value and to justify his or her final value estimate.

Basis The appraiser must check the appropriate box, regardless of whether the actual form is attached or is on file with the lender, indicating whether the appraisal is based on the requirements, the certification, contingent and limiting conditions, and market value definition that are stated in FMHA, HUD and/or VA Instructions, or Freddie Mac Form 439/Fannie Mae Form 1004B.

Date and Market Value On this line the appraiser indicates the effective date of the appraisal—usually the date of principal inspection. The dollar amount is the same as the final value estimate listed above in the Final Reconciliation.

Certification and Signature By signing this section, the appraiser certifies that he or she has personally inspected the exterior and interior of the subject property, and the exteriors of all comparable sale properties, and has no undisclosed interest, present or prospective, in the subject property. If there has been a review appraisal, the reviewer signs and checks the appropriate box indicating whether he or she has or has not inspected the property.

1. The process of checking the data, analysis, and preliminary conclusions is known as:

    (A) Review
    (B) Reconciliation
    (C) Correlation
    (D) Mediation

2. The following value indications were produced in a single-family residential appraisal: direct sales comparison approach, $87,900; cost approach, $89,200; and gross rent multiplier analysis, $86,000. Barring any special circumstances, the indicated final value estimate for the property is most likely:

    (A) $90,000
    (B) $87,900
    (C) $88,500
    (D) $89,200

3. Which of the following is not an essential element of every appraisal report prepared by a professional appraiser?

    (A) Identification of the property
    (B) Statement of the objectives of the appraisal
    (C) Statement of the cost of the appraisal
    (D) Statement of limiting conditions and assumptions

4. Reconciliation requires a review of the:

    (A) Relevance of each approach
    (B) Relevance of each approach based on the value definition
    (C) Reliability of data
    (D) All of the above

5. If any of the three approaches to value is omitted:

    (A) The omission should be explained and supported in the report
    (B) It is understood that only applicable approaches are used
    (C) It must be agreed between the appraiser and the client
    (D) None of the above is true because the three must always be used.

6. The process of evaluating the preliminary indications of value and selecting a single final estimate of value is:

    (A) Averaging
    (B) Review
    (C) Reconciliation
    (D) Summarization

7. The reconciliation process is used:

    (A) Only to estimate the final value
    (B) Throughout the appraisal
    (C) Whenever the indications of value deviate from one another by more than 10%
    (D) Whenever the indications of value deviate from one another by more than 25%

8. For a final value estimate, most lenders prefer a range of values rather than a single figure.

    (A) True
    (B) False

9. The last step in establishing the final estimate of value is to reconcile the indications of value obtained through the three approaches. The final estimate of value is obtained by:

    (A) Averaging the three indications of value
    (B) Assigning weights to the individual indications of value and computing a weighted average of the three
    (C) Either of the above, at the appraiser's discretion
    (D) None of the above

10. The URAR appraisal report reconciliation section requires a review appraiser's signature on all appraisals.

    (A) True
    (B) False

Chapter 14
The Appraisal Report and Review

PREVIEW

The Appraisal Report

Types of Written Appraisal Reports

The Review Appraisal

THE APPRAISAL REPORT

The appraisal report communicates the appraiser's opinion of value to the client. It should begin with the definition of the problem, include relevant descriptive data and analyses, and conclude with a final value estimate. The final report may take a variety of shapes (e.g., oral, letter, narrative, form) and should include the essential elements listed below.

Objectives The objective of every appraisal report is to communicate to the client what the appraiser did, how and why it was done, and what the conclusions are. Whatever form the appraisal report takes, there must be a complete analysis of the market data and property characteristics underlying the report. The field notes and working papers should be retained in the appraiser's files for future reference. The entire appraisal framework should be applied in every appraisal assignment, regardless of the form and manner of reporting the findings and conclusions.

Essential Elements As a minimum, every report prepared by a professional appraiser should include the following nine items:

Identification of the Client. The report should include the name of the party for whom the appraisal is made.

Identification of the Property. The legal description, physical description, and identification of the property rights being appraised.

Purpose. A statement of the objectives of the appraisal, including a definition of the type of value sought.

Date. The appraisal report should indicate the valuation date.

Data and Analysis. The appraiser should state the underlying logic which supports the conclusion of value. The omission of any of the three approaches to value should be explained and supported.

Final Value Estimate. The report should include the final estimate of value for the subject property.

Assumptions and Limitations. The report should include a statement of limiting conditions and assumptions.

Certification by the appraiser.

Signature of the appraiser.

Professional Standards To ensure the quality of appraisal report, professional appraisal organizations have set minimum standards for the factual content, descriptive material, and statements of work and purpose included in all types of appraisal reports. As an example, to comply with the requirements set by the American Institute of Real Estate Appraisers (now, the Appraisal Institute), an appraiser should:

☐ Identify and describe the real estate being appraised.

☐ Specify the real property interest(s) being appraised by analyzing the ownership, financial, and legal interests in the property.

☐ Define the opinion that is the purpose of the appraisal and describe the use of the appraisal.

☐ Specify the date of valuation and the date when the report was completed.

☐ Determine the highest and best use of the real estate being appraised, when this is necessary and appropriate.

☐ Describe the appraisal procedures used.

☐ Provide supporting data and the reasoning behind the analyses, opinions, and conclusions in the report.

☐ Explain all assumptions and limiting conditions that affect the analyses, opinions, and conclusions set forth in the report and disclose any extraordinary assumptions and limiting conditions in the relevant sections of the report.

☐ Identify related personal property that is included in the appraisal opinion.

☐ Discuss the history of the property, including recent sales transactions and current listings, offers, leases, and contracts.

Certification. Written appraisal reports prepared by members or candidates of the Appraisal Institute must contain a certification that includes the following items:

□ A statement that, to the best of the appraiser's knowledge and belief, the facts in the report are true and correct and all assumptions and limiting conditions that affect the appraiser's analyses, opinions, and conclusions are set forth in the report.

□ A statement disclaiming or acknowledging any personal interest in the subject property.

□ A statement disavowing or disclosing any personal bias on the part of the appraiser with respect to the parties involved.

□ A statement that the appraiser's compensation is or is not contingent on any action or event resulting from the analyses, opinions, or conclusions in, or the use of, the report.

□ A statement that the analyses, opinions, and conclusions in the report have been developed in conformity with the requirements of the Code of Professional Ethics and the Standards of Professional Practice.

□ A statement that the use of the report is subject to the requirements of the Appraisal Institute regarding review by its duly authorized representatives.

□ A statement that the appraiser is or is not currently certified under the Appraisal Institute's voluntary continuing education program (not required for candidates).

□ A statement confirming that a personal inspection of the subject property was or was not made, and identifying the individual(s) who carried out the inspection.

□ An acknowledgment of any significant professional assistance that the appraiser received in conducting the appraisal.

TYPES OF WRITTEN APPRAISAL REPORTS

As mentioned previously, the appraisal report may be oral or written. The three basic types of written reports are letter reports, form reports, and narrative reports.

Letter Report   Occasionally an appraiser will communicate his or her results to the client in the form of a letter report. Although the letter report is typically brief, it should include at least the following:

□ Identification of the client for whom the appraisal is made.

□ Identification of the property.

□ Statement of the purpose of the appraisal.

□ Date of valuation, date of the report, and all limiting conditions.

□ Certification by the appraiser.

□ Signature of the appraiser.

Narrative Report The narrative appraisal report presents the appraiser with an opportunity to support his or her opinions and conclusions and persuade the client of the soundness and completeness of the entire valuation process, including the final estimate of value. The narrative report should be formatted to maximize communication with the reader. Although the organization of the report may vary, AIREA (now the Appraisal Institute) suggests the following example of an outline that can be used as a general rule:

Part I. Introduction

- Title page
- Letter of transmittal
- Table of contents
- Photograph (optional)
- Summary of important facts and conclusions
- Purpose and use of the appraisal
- Date of value estimate
- Property rights appraised
- Definition of value and property rights

Part II. Factual Description

- Identification of the property
- History, including sales history
- Regional and city data
- Neighborhood data
- Zoning
- Tax and assessment data
- Site description
- Improvement description

Part III. Analysis of Data and Opinions of the Appraiser

- Highest and best use analysis
- Site value estimate
- The cost approach

  Estimate of current reproduction or replacement cost

  Estimate of accrued depreciation

  Summary of conclusions

□ The sales comparison approach

General content and depth of the market research

Choice of the most indicative comparable sales

Description of each selected comparable sale

Analysis of major value-influencing characteristics of the comparables and the subject

Market-oriented adjustments for differences between the comparables and the subject

□ The income capitalization approach

Estimate of market rent for subject

Estimate of GRM for subject

□ Reconciliation and final value estimate

□ Certification of value

□ Assumptions and limiting conditions

□ Qualifications of the appraiser

Addenda

□ Additional photographs of the subject property

□ Photographs of street views in the immediate area

□ Maps of secondary importance

□ City and regional statistical data

□ Supplemental material that may help the reader visualize the property or understand the appraisal.

Form Reports In most appraisals, form reports meet the needs of the client, whether lenders, insurance companies, governmental agencies, or corporations. Use of a standardized form makes for more efficient review and greater convenience. The three most common single-family form reports are described below.

Uniform Residential Appraisal Report (URAR). In 1986 representatives of FHA, USDVA, FNMA and other actors in the primary and secondary mortgage markets agreed to adopt this standardized residential appraisal form. The URAR, identified as Freddie Mac Form 70 10/86 and Fannie Mae Form 1004 10/86, is shown in Appendix B and consists of two parts: a property description and analysis section and a valuation section. The appraiser completes the following descriptive information:

□ *Subject*. Property address, legal description, owner/occupant, sale price and date, seller-paid loan charges or concessions, real estate taxes, and property rights appraised.

□ *Neighborhood*. Location—urban/suburban/rural, degree of development, growth rate, trend in property values, demand and supply balance, marketing time, neighborhood analysis, present land use, likelihood of change in use, predominant type of occupant, and price and age range of single-family housing.

□ *Site*. Dimensions, area, zoning classification, zoning compliance, highest and best use, utilities, site improvements, and physical characteristics.

□ *Improvements*. General description, exterior description, foundation, basement, and insulation.

□ *Room List*

□ *Interior*. Surfaces, heating, kitchen equipment, attic, and improvement analysis.

□ *Car Storage Facility*.

□ *Comments*. Any remarks by the appraiser relative to additional features of the subject property, the market, etc.

The appraiser completes the following entries for the valuation section:

□ *Cost Approach*. Building sketch, estimates of the reproduction cost of the main improvement and accessory buildings, accrued depreciation, and site value, and construction warranty.

□ *Sales Comparison Approach*. Market data grid for transaction, locational, physical, and other adjustments.

□ *Income Approach*. Value indication from the income approach.

□ *Conditions*. Of the valuation (as is, or subject to repairs or completion according to plans.

□ *Conditions*. Of the appraisal (itemized cost of necessary repairs).

□ *Final Reconciliation*.

□ *Certification Signature*.

A certification and statement of limiting conditions (FHLMC Form 439/FNMA Form 1004B) must be attached to all URAR form reports unless the appraiser has placed the attachment on file with the client.

Individual Condominium or PUD Unit Appraisal Report.
Known as FHLMC Form 465/FNMA Form 1073, this form, shown in
Appendix B, is a two page form. The appraiser completes information for
the following entries:

☐ Names of the mortgagor, lender, and occupant; legal description of the
unit, property rights appraised, and transaction and tax data

☐ Neighborhood land use, occupancy, and rating

☐ Site dimensions, zoning, utilities, and offsite improvements

☐ Project improvements, type, and rating

☐ Description and rating of the condo or PUD unit

☐ Budget analysis for the unit

☐ Cost approach value indication

☐ Market data analysis

☐ Market data and income approach value indications

☐ Final reconciliation

☐ Certification signature.

☐ *Addendum A*. Freddie Mac requires completion of this addendum
for project analysis. If fewer than 70% of the individual units have
been sold, Part I must be completed. If the project is in the process of
conversion or has been converted within the past two years, Part II
must be completed.

☐ *Addendum B*. Freddie Mac requires completion of this form—the
operating budget—by the seller or servicer or an agent for the owners'
association or property management.

Employee Relocation Council Residential Appraisal Report.
This four page form, shown in Appendix B, is used by ERC members
including corporations, relocation service companies, brokers, etc.,
concerned with the transfer of business employees. The first two pages of
the form provide information relative to relocation appraisals and a grid
for a building sketch. On the third page, the appraiser completes the
following information:

☐ Address and legal description of the subject property and the property
rights appraised

☐ Neighborhood land use and occupancy

☐ Site dimensions, zoning, and utilities

☐ Description of the improvements and basement

☐ Room list

☐ Description of the interior finish and equipment

☐ Property rating.

The fourth page consists of the valuation section which contains a market data grid, a supplementary section for reconciling differences between the subject property and individual comparables, and a line for recording the indicated value of the subject by the market data approach. The fifth and sixth pages consist of information on competing listings and value-related differences between these properties and the subject. The appraiser completes sections on:

- □ Special features
- □ Condition
- □ Acreage, taxes, and fees
- □ Personal property included
- □ Special financing
- □ Information on the current list price and length of market exposure

The final section of the form addresses current market conditions, including the availability of financing, the present supply and demand situation, and future economic trends, and additional comments as the appraiser may wish to include.

Small Residential Income Property Appraisal Report. The Small Residential Income Property Appraisal Report (FHLMC Form 72/FNMA Form 1025), shown in Appendix B, is a two-page form containing the following entries:

- □ Names of the mortgagor, lender, and occupant, legal description of the property, property rights appraised, and transaction and tax data.
- □ Neighborhood land use, occupancy, and rating
- □ Site dimensions, zoning, utilities, and offsite improvements
- □ Description and analysis of the improvements
- □ Cost approach value indication
- □ Rental data on comparable properties
- □ Schedule of actual and forecast rents for subject property
- □ Analysis of market data for deriving gross rent multipliers and reconciliation of GRMs
- □ Market data approach value indication
- □ Analysis of actual and forecast expenses
- □ Certification signature.

APPRAISAL REVIEWS

Where there is a formal independent appraisal review section within an organization, it is usually the reviewer's responsibility to interpret the appraisal report for management. The reviewer must assure that an appraisal is well substantiated and contains a reasonableness in the appraisal logic. The reviewer should see that the appraisal is in compliance with the assignment and is in conformity with generally accepted appraisal practices. These field reviews may be done by the primary lender, the investor, Fannie Mae or Freddie Mac if the loan is sold to one of them, or by the mortgage insurance company if insurance is required. For these reasons, professional appraisers do not need to be reminded of the value of carrying errors and omissions insurance to protect themselves against honest errors and omissions.

Most Common Errors A private survey of over 300 reviewers was conducted by the National Association of Review Appraisers and Mortgage Underwriters and the following were found to be the most common problem areas (not necessarily in order of frequency). The following can serve as a check list when the appraiser is reviewing his or her own work.

☐ Contract specifications not followed.

☐ Typing, grammar, and punctuation errors.

☐ Mathematical errors

☐ Poorly reproduced copies of supporting data and reports.

☐ Poor exhibits—quality and relevance.

☐ Poor overall format.

☐ Failure to understand the client's requirements or procedures.

☐ Loading the appraisal with "Chamber of Commerce" type data without relating factual data to subject.

☐ Inadequate history of property.

☐ Errors in land area or building size.

☐ Failure to consider zoning or potential zoning.

☐ Failure to consider easements on property.

☐ Inadequate discussion of "highest and best use."

☐ Not adequately searching market for sales and leases.

☐ Using comparables too far afield in size and use.

☐ Failure to fully analyze and adjust all comparable data.

- [ ] Abundant sales or rental data with little or no discussion relating it to the subject.

- [ ] Not using the same methods of measurement between comparables and subject.

- [ ] Inconsistent adjustment patterns.

- [ ] Relying on mathematical exercise, formulas, curves, etc., without relating them to the subject.

- [ ] Failure to follow through in the analysis of data in the factual presentation.

- [ ] Values derived on assumptions not consistent with the "highest and best use" statement.

- [ ] Inconsistencies between cost, market, and income approaches.

- [ ] Inadequate treatment of remaining economic life, depreciation, net return.

- [ ] Unsupported adjustments for time.

- [ ] Use of techniques and procedures not appropriate to the problem.

- [ ] Capitalization rates not current or adequately supported from the market.

- [ ] Lack of clarity or explanation of the appraiser's reasoning or procedures.

- [ ] Photographs of the subject do not adequately show the property.

- [ ] Report missing neighborhood data trends of the subject area.

- [ ] Appraiser employing inexperienced personnel without adequate supervision.

- [ ] Failure to state why an approach to value has not been used.

- [ ] Overall report too short to adequately cover the property.

- [ ] Positive or negative features of property not mentioned.

- [ ] Failure to deliver report in a reasonable time or meet deadlines.

Quiz Chapter 14

1. The basic components of an appraisal report include:

   (A) Definition of the problem
   (B) Data and analysis
   (C) Final value estimate
   (D) All of the above

2. An appraisal report may be oral as well as written.

   (A) True
   (B) False

3. The steps the appraiser took in reaching the final estimate:

   (A) Are irrelevant as long as the value estimate is correct
   (B) Should be supported by working papers and notes retained in the appraiser's files
   (C) Should be clearly communicated to the client in the appraisal report
   (D) Both B and C

4. Every report prepared by a professional appraiser should include:

   (A) Identification of client and property
   (B) Explanation if any of the three approaches to value was not used
   (C) Signature of the appraiser
   (D) All of the above

5. The certification required by the Appraisal Institute includes statements disclosing the appraiser's:

   (A) Personal bias or personal interest in the property
   (B) Basis of compensation
   (C) Reliance on professional assistance
   (D) All of the above

6. The three basic types of written appraisal report include all *except*:

   (A) Competitive market analysis
   (B) Narrative report
   (C) Letter
   (D) Form report

7. The type of appraisal report which maximizes communication with the client is the:

   (A) Letter report
   (B) Oral report
   (C) Narrative report
   (D) Uniform residential appraisal report

8. The recommended sections in a narrative report are:

   (A) Introduction, factual description, analysis and opinions, addenda
   (B) Cost approach, sales comparison approach, reconciliation
   (C) FHLMC Form 465 and FNMA Form 1073
   (D) Brief identification of client and property, statement of purpose, date and signatures

9. In most appraisals, form reports are acceptable to:

   (A) Individual single-family buyers only
   (B) Lenders and insurance companies
   (C) Governmental agencies
   (D) All of the above

10. An appraisal review would commonly look for inadequacies in:

    (A) Searching the market for comparable sales and leases
    (B) Handling the concept of "highest and best use"
    (C) Fully analyzing and adjusting data
    (D) All of the above

Chapter 15
Special Types and Special Purpose Residence Appraisals

PREVIEW

Condominiums

PUDs

Cooperatives

Mobilehomes

Modular and Prefabricated Houses

Timeshares

Residences on Leased Land

Mansions

Historic Houses

Solar and Underground Houses

Experimental Houses

Resort Homes

Farm and Ranch Houses

Housing for the Elderly

SPECIAL TYPES AND SPECIAL PURPOSE RESIDENCE APPRAISALS

Thus far this text has dealt primarily with the conventional single-family detached home. Newer forms of single-family residential ownership and special-purpose residences present a new category of single-family residential appraisal problems. For example, an owner of a condominium owns interest in both privately held and commonly held areas. An owner in a planned unit development (PUD) owns interest in a single-family residence but has access to commonly held areas and facilities. These and other special types of residences (e.g., residences on leased lands, mobilehomes, modular and prefabricated houses) and special-purpose residences (e.g., vacation and resort homes, farm and ranch houses) are discussed briefly in this chapter.

Condominiums **Definition.** A condominium consists of two elements: (1) a separate interest in spaced called a unity, and (2) an undivided interest in common in a portion of real property. Both elements must be present to constitute a condominium. In a typical condominium project, the condominium owner receives a separate interest in a three-dimensional block of airspace within a building and an undivided interest in common with the other owners in the building (other than the units), the land underlying the building, and the airspace surrounding the building.

Appraisal Considerations. The appraisal technique typically used for condominiums is the market approach. The best comparables are resales of similar units in the same building or a similar building. Comparable properties must be carefully analyzed for differences in common area, recreational facilities, design and size, and common assessments. Consideration should be given to both the sales price of similar new units and resale prices of units in the same or similar building—which are frequently lower than the sales price of comparable new units. Since numerous condo associations have been found to have inadequate reserves, some lenders require an examination of the entire project when estimating value of a single unit. The appraiser should consider the present common assessments as well as their projected increases.

PUDs **Definition.** A planned development is the catch-all category of common interest developments. It is a common interest development, other than a community apartment project, condominium project, or stock cooperative, having either or both of the following elements:

☐ Lots, parcels, or areas in which owners of separately-owned lots are owners in common with rights to use and enjoy the commonly-owned property.

☐ An association with the power to enforce the owners' obligations by means of an assessment which can become a lien on the separately-owned lot, parcel, or area.

Appraisal Considerations. The considerations and problems associated with appraising PUDs are similar to those associated with condominiums and fee simple properties.

Cooperatives **Definition.** A stock cooperative is a development in which a corporation holds title to the property and the shareholders of the corporation receive a right of exclusive occupancy in a portion of the real property. The price per unit determines the number of shares that a tenant must purchase to acquire a proprietary lease. In establishing a stock cooperative, a builder typically will transfer title to the property to the corporation at the outset and agree to build the improvements on the property in exchange for a master proprietary lease of all the units in the building. Typically, the lease will run for 99 years. This form of common interest development is rather rare in California although it is common on the East Coast.

Appraisal Considerations. As with condominiums, the appraisal technique typically used for stock cooperatives is the market approach by analyzing of the sale of ownership shares for comparables in the same or similar building. The appraiser should take into account not only the sales price, which is usually low and misleading, but also the shareholder's portion of the mortgage on the entire building. For example, a unit may be offered for $50,000. However, the shareholder's portion of the entire building's mortgage of $1,000,000 might be $100,000; thus the shareholder's total mortgage debt will be $150,000. When comparables are from other buildings, the appraiser must take into account the corporations' mortgage obligations which might be quite dissimilar. If the corporation permits rentals, the income approach can be used to establish the relationship between rent and value.

Mobilehomes **Definition**. A mobilehome is a complete inhabitable dwelling unit that is equipped with wheels so it can be towed from one place to another. In terms of cost per square foot, mobilehomes are attractive and can provide considerable savings. Sizes range from 12 feet wide by 60 feet long to double units 28 feet wide by 60 feet long. Mobilehomes can be found on leased or owned lots, but they are frequently placed on foundations in mobilehome parks and sometimes become real property. Mobilehome parks can offer a wide range of amenities.

Appraisal Considerations. The two approaches to value commonly used with mobilehomes are the market approach and the income approach. Valuation books for mobilehomes (similar to the books used for used cars and trucks) are available which report national or regional average sales. These books should be used with discretion by the appraiser since quality of construction varies considerably among different models and manufacturers and since they do not take into account the value of the location of the subject property. Many mobilehomes are sold in place, and their value estimate will be affected by their environment or the mobilehome park's amenities.

Modular and Prefabricated Houses **Definition**. Modular and prefabricated homes are partially factory-built in three dimensions. Entire rooms are transported to a site for installation, with little labor required for assembly. When assembly is complete (frequently only several days) some of these homes resemble mobilehomes and others look like conventionally constructed homes. Modular homes range from small (12 feet by 60 feet) to large (several segments similar to double mobilehomes). Although still a small portion of the housing market, because of the efficiency resulting from mass production, these homes offer affordable housing. Another advantage for buyers is that they can see complete model houses and not have to base their decisions on architectural plans which they may or may not understand.

Appraisal Considerations. The appraisal of modular and prefabricated houses is similar to conventionally constructed houses of similar quality, design, and size. Traditional appraisal techniques and procedures are typically utilized.

Timeshares **Definition.** According to California law, (a) a *time-share project* is one in which a purchaser receives the right in perpetuity, for life, or for a term of years, to the recurrent exclusive use or occupancy of a lot, parcel, unit, or segment of real property, annually or on some other periodic basis, for a period of time that has been allotted from the use or occupancy periods into which the project has been divided; (b) a *time-share estate* is a right of occupancy in a time-share project which is coupled with an estate in the real property; (c) a *time-share use* is a license or contractual or membership right of occupancy in a time-share project which is not coupled with an estate in the real property. Generally timeshares apply to vacation and resort properties.

Appraisal Considerations. The first step in the appraisal of a timeshare is to establish the rights of ownership and use. Ownership rights may take the form of fee simple, joint tenancy, tenancy in common, condominium, stock cooperative, limited partnership, or a real estate investment trust (REIT). In addition, the portion of the property to be assigned to the shareholder must also be identified. Many timeshares are sold fully furnished and the appraiser must consider this personal property. If new timeshares are being constructed in the area, the cost approach may be used to estimate value. New sales of similar property may be used as comparables but resales in the timeshare property being appraised or similar properties typically provide a more reliable estimate of value, since new sales may be the result of the developer's intensive advertising efforts. The market approach can also help determine the relationship between the rent a timeshare unit can charge and its resale value.

Residences on Leased Land **Definition.** Some of California's favorite neighbors (Hawaii and Mexico) have homes built on land that is leased for as long as 30 to 99 years. When the lease or trust expires, the improvements on the property revert back to the landowner, which may be an individual or the country.

Appraisal Considerations. When appraising a residence on leased land the appraiser typically uses the same valuation techniques applicable to residences in other forms of ownership. To estimate the leasehold interest, the appraiser may capitalize the ground rent and adjust to reflect differences between the ground rents and the lease terms of the subject property.

Mansions **Definition.** Mansions are a special type of house, large and opulent, with extra rooms for guests and staff, recreation and entertainment rooms, and often extensive landscaping and a pool. Many have custom features created for the owner's individual tastes and requirements. Mansions are associated with wealthy owners who can afford the high maintenance costs associated with this special type of house. Some have significant historical value due to their uniqueness or previous owners.

Appraisal Considerations. Due to their limited numbers and the fact that they are not frequently sold, mansions can present peculiar valuation difficulties. If the highest and best use is to remain a single-family residence, the market data approach will usually produce the most reliable estimate of value. Finding comparable property sales may be difficult and may mean the appraiser will have to look outside the subject property's community. This necessitates an adjustment for location which is extremely important but extremely difficult. If the highest and best use is other than a single-family residence (such as a multifamily residence, bed and breakfast facility, etc.) the appraiser will most likely need to conduct additional investigations and analyses considering such factors as excess land. In these instances the income approach and cost approach will be appropriate.

Historic Houses

Definition. Prior to the 1960s, most historic houses were identified with notable individuals or significant historical events. However, since then there has been an increasing trend to include both architecturally significant buildings and entire neighborhoods. The preservation of designated historic sites and districts can be regulated by municipal zoning, state and/or federal legislation. In recent years, federal tax incentives have been provided for rehabilitation of some of these sites and districts. Houses are usually designated as historic landmarks as a result of their facade's contribution to the street or district, although infrequently a *room* inside a building may be designated. While a historic designation may increase value and provide special tax benefits, it may also restrict the owner's rights.

Appraisal Considerations. Appraising historic properties is complex and the appraiser should consult current literature published by the National Trust for Historic Preservation. Use of the market data approach can be difficult since comparable data are frequently limited and the appraiser will usually have to look outside the neighborhood and include a wider area. Use of the cost approach is limited since it is difficult to estimate the value of a property's historical significance or to replicate the conditions of construction. The market data approach is probably the most reliable but the appraiser should consider the historic importance of each comparable property. Location of the subject property and the comparables is especially important. The appraiser should also consider applicable regulations and tax incentives, if any.

Solar and Underground Houses

Definition. Solar houses are designed to utilize energy from the sun, typically by use of solar collectors situated on the building's exterior to absorb energy for space or water heating. Some solar houses are designed to allow the sun to provide interior heating directly. Underground houses are so constructed for their architectural uniqueness or, more practically, to benefit from the moderate year round temperatures.

Appraisal Considerations. Use of the market data approach with solar houses is difficult due to the scarcity of comparable properties. The value of solar homes is also difficult to estimate since some buyers will pay a premium due to the solar home's uniqueness and status while other buyers value them lower due to their nonconforming nature. The appraiser must take great care in determining whether the estimate of value is the actual market value or the value for a particular owner. Most underground houses are found in the central and southwest United States where reduced energy costs and storm protection are important concerns. The market data is regarded as the most reliable approach with this type of property.

Experimental Houses

Definition. Experimental houses are those which are constructed of unconventional materials such as fiberglass, plastics, ceramics, foams, etc. These houses are usually unique, and frequently incorporate unusual architectural designs and features.

Appraisal Considerations. Use of the market data approach is considered the best for appraising experimental houses. As with solar and underground houses, the value of experimental homes is difficult to estimate since their nonconformity may subtract value or their status may increase value. Again, the appraiser should clarify if the value estimate is for use by a specific owner or the actual market value.

Resort Homes

Definition. Of the several million resort homes in this country, most are occupied by their owners as second homes on a seasonal or periodic basis. Many are in or near recreational areas and can range from the modest to the magnificent. Current federal tax laws continue to permit second home mortgage interest deductions.

Appraisal Considerations. The resort home market tends to be quite changeable. Initial sales can be somewhat unreliable since they may be the result of the developer's advertising and promotion campaigns. Resales tend to provide a more reliable and more accurate indication of value. If the resort home is used as a rental unit, which is typical in seasonal homes, the income capitalization approach is applicable. If land is available for development and new resort homes are still being built, the cost approach may also be applicable.

Farm and Ranch Houses

Definition. The appraisal of rural properties demands special skills and experience. Rural land may have value as a working farm, as an ordinary residence, or for its development potential. The appraiser must be able to distinguish and analyze all these scenarios.

Appraisal Considerations. Briefly, the two usual approaches to estimating value of farm and ranch houses are the market approach, when most of the subject property's value is in the improvement, and the cost approach, when most of the subject property's value is in the land.

Housing for the Elderly

Definition. A variety of special housing accommodations are available for the elderly including single-family residences, seniors' apartments, adult congregate living facilities (ACLF), continuing-care retirement centers (CCRC), and others. The elderly market is often viewed as consisting of two age groups: 50 to 65 (preretirement) and over 65 (retirement). Depending on age and health, the latter group varies considerably in terms of their needs for independence, privacy, leisure, and health care. Housing for the elderly should take into account these needs.

Appraisal Considerations. More and more properties and even entire communities are restricted to the elderly—usually 50 or 55 years of age or over. The courts have ruled that age restrictions for seniors are legal. Since these restrictions affect the value of the properties, the appraiser should take care to find comparable sales located in the same or a similar community. Some facilities for the elderly are recipients of government subsidies, either directly or indirectly through rent subsidies paid to the residents. Use of the market data approach is the first choice but can be problematic due to the need to use a wide geographic area for comparables.

1. Single-family residences present special appraisal problems if they are:

    (A) Condominiums
    (B) Planned unit developments
    (C) Mobilehomes
    (D) Any of the above

2. Condominiums are usually appraised using the _____ approach:

    (A) Market
    (B) Cost
    (C) Income
    (D) None of the above

3. Special considerations in appraising a condominium unit include:

    (A) Interest in common areas
    (B) Difference in prices of new and resale units
    (C) Association reserves
    (D) All of the above

4. The catch-all category of common interest development is:

    (A) Condominiums
    (B) Stock cooperatives
    (C) Planned developments
    (D) Community apartment projects

5. The property owner normally owns the land underlying the building in a:

    (A) Condominium
    (B) Stock cooperative
    (C) Planned development
    (D) Mobilehome park

6. The appraisal of modular and prefabricated houses is similar to appraisal of:

    (A) Mobilehomes
    (B) Conventional single family dwellings
    (C) Condominium units
    (D) Commercial buildings

7. The first step in appraising a timeshare is to establish:

    (A) The purpose for which the unit is occupied
    (B) The nature of ownership rights involved
    (C) Sales prices of comparable new units
    (D) Value trends

8. Appraisal of homes built on leased land:

    (A) Is impossible because there is no ownership interest
    (B) Is the same as appraisal of time-share
    (C) May involve capitalization of ground rent
    (D) None of the above

9. Mansions present special appraisal issues because:

    (A) There are few comparable sales
    (B) The highest and best use may be other than a single-family residence
    (C) They may have historical significance
    (D) All of the above

10. Resale prices may be a better value indicator than new sales prices for:

    (A) Condominiums
    (B) Timeshares
    (C) Resort properties
    (D) All of the above

Appraisal Report
Of A
Single Family Residence
Located At
4377 San Juan Avenue
Fremont, California 94536

Prepared For
Anthony Bank
15942 Foothill Blvd.
San Leandro, CA 94578

By
Paul M. Kullman
446 Skyline Drive
Oakland, California 94651

As Of
December 29, 1985

i

Paul M. Kullman
446 Skyline Drive
Oakland, California 94651

November 21, 1985

Anthony Bank
15942 Foothill Blvd.
San Leandro, CA 94578

At the bank's request I have prepared the attached narrative
appraisal of a single family residence located at 4377 San Juan
Avenue, Fremont, California, more specifically described in the
accompanying report.

The purpose of the appraisal is to estimate the market value of
the property in fee simple.

I personally inspected the property on September 7, 1985, and
have gathered all the data I considered necessary to arrive at
the value conclusion.

As a result of my investigation and my analysis of the
information gathered, I estimate the market value of the property
as of December 29, 1985, to be:

ONE HUNDRED THIRTY THOUSAND DOLLARS

($130,000)

Respectfully submitted,

Paul M. Kullman

ii

TABLE OF CONTENTS

SUMMARY OF SALIENT FACTS AND CONCLUSIONS

Type of Property: Single Family Residence

Location: 4377 San Juan Avenue
                                     Fremont, California 94536

Zoning: Single Family Residential R1-6

Objective of the Appraisal: To estimate the market value of
                                     fee simple ownership as of
                                     December 29, 1985

Neighborhood Highlights: Most of the homes in the area
                                     are part of the 500 dwelling
                                     "Fair Oaks Development" of
                                     average quality, tract-type
                                     houses. They range in price from
                                     $110,000 to $145,000 and from 15
                                     to 30 years in age.

Site: A level lot with 61 foot
                                     frontage on San Juan Avenue and
                                     a depth of 100 feet with a total
                                     area of 6,1000 square feet.

Improvements: A 24 year old one story wood
                                     framed stucco exterior ranch
                                     style dwelling containing 1,617
                                     square feet of living area and
                                     an attached 2 car garage. It has
                                     3 bedrooms, 2 baths, kitchen
                                     with dining area, living room
                                     and family room.

Site Valuation:

Market Value Indicated by
   the Cost Approach: Site: $49,000
                                     Improvements: $78,500
                                     Total: $127,500

Market Value Indicated by
   the Market Data Approach $130,000

Final Estimate of Market
   Value: $130,000

Date of Appraisal: December 29, 1985

iv

ASSUMPTIONS AND LIMITING CONDITIONS

I assume no responsibility for legal matters, nor do I render an opinion as to the title to subject property, but I assume said title to be in fee simple.

The property is being appraised as though free of encumbrances. The legal description given in this report was furnished, and is assumed to be correct.

The plot plan of the property was drawn to approximate scale, but no survey was made of the property.

The information, estimates and opinions furnished to me and contained in this report were obtained from sources considered reliable and believed to be true and accurate. However, no responsibility for accuracy can be assumed by me. I reserve the right to change or alter this appraisal report after submission if new facts are received that, in the opinion of this appraiser, warrant a change in this report. The report shall be used for its intended purpose only, and by the parties to whom it is addressed. Possession of this report does not include the right of publication.

If attendance in court for testimony is required as a result of this report, arrangements and fees shall be agreed on prior to appearance for testimony.

The statements of value and all conclusions shall apply as of the date shown in the letter of transmittal.

v

<u>QUALIFICATIONS OF PAUL M. KULIMAN</u>

EDUCATION

Attended University of Southern California.

    Real estate related courses successfully completed.
    (1) College level:
        Real Estate Practice
        Real Estate Law
        Real Estate Financing
        Residential Real Estate Appraising

    (2) American Institute of Real Estate Appraisers courses
        successfully completed:
        Real Estate Appraisal Principles
        Residential Valuation
        Standards of Professional Practice

PROFESSIONAL ACTIVITIES

Although not a member of the American Institute of Real Estate
Appraisers, I am a candidate for the RM Designation, and attend
AIREA chapter meetings and workshops.

TEN YEARS WORK EXPERIENCE

7-76 to 9-80   California Federal Savings and Loan Association.
                Northern California Insurance Vice President.

9-80 to 2-83   Golden State Realty. Real estate sales and fee
                appraiser.

2-83 to 1-85   Mills and Associates Appraisal Service. Fee
                appraiser.

2-85 to -   Independent residential fee appraiser.

DATA SOURCES

I am a Real Estate Broker and MLS member of the Southern Alameda
County Board of Realtors. I have a computer terminal in my office
for MLS access. I am a subscriber to California Market Data
Service and the Marshall and Swift Handbook.

TYPES OF ASSIGNMENTS

My appraisal practice includes the following types of property:

Single Family Residential
Condominiums, Townhouses and Planned Unit Developments
Small Income Properties - Two to Eight Residential Units

vi

PHOTOGRAPH OF 4377 SAN JUAN AVENUE

ADDITIONAL PHOTOGRAPHS OF THE SUBJECT WILL BE FOUND
IN THE ADDENDA

THE REPORT:

DESCRIPTION, ANALYSIS AND CONCLUSIONS

IDENTIFICATION OF THE PROPERTY

The subject property is a 24 year old one story ranch style
single family residence. It is legally described as: Lot 37,
block 1, "Tract 2253," filed April 11, 1962, Map Book 45, Pages
23 and 24, Alameda County Records. Its commonly known address is:
4377 San Juan Avenue, Fremont, California 94536.

OBJECTIVE OF THE APPRAISAL AND DEFINITION OF MARKET VALUE

The objective of this appraisal is to estimate market value as of
December 29, 1985.

Market value, as defined by the Dictionary of Real Estate
Appraisal (American Institute of Real Estate Appraisers of the
National Association of Realtors®) is:
> The most probable price in cash, terms equivalent to cash, or
> in other precisely revealed terms, for which the appraised
> property will sell in a competitive market under all
> conditions requisite for fair sale, with the buyer and seller
> each acting prudently, knowledgeably, and for self-interest,
> and assuming that neither is under undue duress.

Fundamental assumptions and conditions presumed in this
definition are:
1. Buyer and seller are motivated by self-interest.
2. Buyer and seller are well informed and are acting
   prudently.
3. The property is exposed for a reasonable time on the open
   market.
4. Payment is made in cash, its equivalent, or in specified
   financing terms.
5. Specified financing, if any, may be the financing
   actually in place, or on terms generally available for
   the property type in its locale on the effective
   appraisal date.
6. The effect, if any, on the amount of market value of
   atypical financing, service, or fees shall be clearly and
   precisely revealed in the appraisal report.

PROPERTY RIGHTS APPRAISED

The property rights being appraised are fee simple. Fee simple,
as defined (source previously referenced), is:

Absolute ownership unencumbered by any other interest or estate;
subject only to the limitations of eminent domain, escheat,
police power, and taxation.

1

<u>AREA - CITY DATA</u>

Fremont is located approximately 40 miles southeast of San Francisco and five miles north of San Jose. It is a rapidly growing suburban city with almost all development occurring after 1960. Land use has changed in the Fremont area from primarily agricultural to modern suburban development during recent decades. Fremont is the second largest city in the Bay Area with a land area or 96 square miles. The city was incorporated in 1956 when five towns - Niles, Mission San Jose, Irvington, Warm Springs, and Centerville - merged.

The population of Fremont has increased over threefold since 1960. The population reached 131,945 in 1980, a gain of 31,136 or 30.9 percent since 1970. The population is estimated to have grown by nearly 15,000 persons since 1980, or 11 percent. The estimated current population of Fremont is 153,900. It ranks as the fourth most populous city in the Bay Area.

Fremont is well served by transportation facilities. Two major freeways on the east side of San Francisco Bay, Interstate 880 and Interstate 680, run through Fremont. Travel to the the west side of the bay has been facilitated with the recent opening of the new Dumbarton Bridge and a freeway connecting the bridge to Interstate 880. The freeway and the new bridge provide good access to Silicon Valley. Fremont is also served by Bay Area Rapid Transit (BART) as well as two major railroads, Santa Fe-Southern Pacific and Western Pacific.

The local economic base in Fremont has been expanding in recent years. The largest manufacturing employers are the New United Motors Manufacturing, Inc. with 2,200 employees, and the Diablo Systems Division of Xerox with 1,400 employees. Other major employers include Tri Valley Growers, Gemini Company, and Nicolet Industries. The largest nonmanufacturing employers include the Fremont School District, Washington Hospital, Safeway Stores, and First Interstate Bank. The latter has a major credit card processing center in Fremont as does J.C. Penney Company.

Educational, religious, cultural, and recreational facilities are excellent throughout the county. All utilities are available throughout the metropolitan area, and excellent medical, police, fire, and community services exist.

The Central School District administers all schools in the city of Fremont including a high school, three junior high schools, and five elementary schools. There are also adequate preschool facilities, a special education district, and a community college in the county. It appears that the city of Fremont will continue to attract solid middle class residents for the foreseeable future.

2

The subject property is located approximately in the middle of northwestern Fremont. This area is predominantly. It encompasses roughly four square miles, and is considered a desirable living area – comparable to the Mission District in southeastern Fremont, and Glenmoor in central Fremont. The subject is situated in the approximate center of the neighborhood generally considered to be bounded on the northwest by Decoto city limits, on the southeast by Thornton Avenue, on the southwest by the Nimitz Freeway, and on the northeast by Paseo Padre Boulevard. These are all well known streets in the area and comprise a total of about two square miles. The neighborhood is approximately 90 percent developed. Most of this development has taken place during the past 30 years. Developed land use is roughly 70 percent single family residential, ten percent apartments, ten percent commercial, five percent churches and five percent schools.

Commercial use consists of one story strip development, mostly of concrete tilt-up construction, along the major streets of Fremont Boulevard and Thornton Avenue. There is a shopping center on Fremont Boulevard of approximately five acres with a supermarket, chain drug store, and small shops such as dry cleaners, photo developers, and shoe stores. Thornton Avenue has primarily "in and out" fast food restaurants and a 24 hour convenience market. Street parking is permitted on the residential streets. This parking is usually utilized as additional parking space for the residents of that street. The business district offers adequate off-street parking for its tenants and customers, and the only apparent competition of parking is in the immediate area of the local apartment houses. There are two apartment complexes of around 200 units each on Fremont Boulevard at the intersection of Nicolet Street. They are well maintained, and appear to have adequate management. However, there is assigned off-street parking for only one car per unit. Parking space on the street is therefore competitive. The subject is far enough removed as to be unaffected. Most of the commercial buildings are somewhat newer than the residential buildings and, therefore, have a longer physical life expectancy. However, their economic life is dependent upon the economy of the neighborhood.

The Hub shopping mall is within three miles in downtown Fremont. An outdoor mall, it has been losing considerable business to Newpark Mall which is approximately four miles away, just across the Nimitz Freeway in nearby Newark.

The neighborhood is within the Fremont Unified School District. Oliveira grade school is located three blocks away on Alder Avenue, serving grades Kindergarten through eighth grade. Due to its proximity, no school bus transportation is necessary.

3

American High School serves grades nine through twelve. It is approximately five blocks away and does not provide bus service to local residents for the same reason. Ohlone College (grades 13-14) is approximately five miles to the southeast. It is an accredited community college and tuition is free to Fremont residents. Hayward State University is approximately eight miles northeast. It is a fully accredited four year institution, with typical State of California tuition fees.

Public transportation is provided by the Alameda County Transit Authority and by the Bay Area Rapid Transit System (BART). There is a bus stop at the corner of San Juan and Coronado street, one block away. BART serves most of the Bay Area. There is a BART station in downtown Fremont, about 3 miles away.

Churches of most denominations are readily available. Recreational facilities, such as fishing, camping, golf, hiking and swimming are within a short drive.

Employment centers are generally within a 20 minute commute. Fremont, and its neighbor Newark, has recently attracted several "hi-tech" industries, opening new employment. The former General Motors plant has reopened as New United Motor, producing the Nova automobile and employing about 3,000. Other heavy industry jobs are located in Hayward and Oakland, to the north.

Houses in the neighborhood of the subject range in price from approximately $110,000 to $140,000 and in age from 15 to 30 years. Homes are usually upgraded and generally well maintained. Most of the homes in the area are part of the "Fairoaks Development" of average quality, tract-type dwellings by Kay builders. They built approximately five hundred homes in the area, over a period of about five years, beginning 25 years ago. Although there is a good mix of exterior elevations, the interiors have a similar 6 room configuration: kitchen with dining area, living room, family room, three bedrooms, and two baths. There are very few rentals in the area. Residents, as a group, tend to be older, have higher incomes, and fewer children living at home than the general Fremont population. This contributes to a large number of two income families with total family incomes ranging between $25,000 and $50,000 per year.

The nearest new residential development is approximately 4 miles to the north. It is farther away from the desirable shopping and business facilities of central Fremont, and competes with a similar development located across the border in Union City. The local neighborhood, on the other hand, is essentially built out.

There is not enough buildable land to support a new development of any consequence, and there is therefore little likelihood of excess of new housing starts developing. Primarily, housing

4

competition comes from the two established communities previously mentioned, and they also share the lack of available new building sites. The neighborhood appears to be in a long term "stable cycle" stage with residents spending their higher incomes on maintenance and investments as opposed to selling and moving to newer developments. The majority of the residents have lived here several years creating a fairly well balanced environment.

There are no obvious indications of transition in the neighborhood. Due to its stable condition, the lack of major adverse influences, the general high level of upkeep, owner occupancy, and diversity of employment opportunities, no downturn trends in the area are evident. Subject to the general condition of the region's and the country's economic health no local adverse economic influences are discernible in the immediate or foreseeable future of subject's remaining economic life.

ZONING

The subject property is located in the city limits of Fremont and is zoned R1-6 by that city. The principal permitted uses are:

    (a) Single-family detached dwellings
    (b) Agricultural - except retail sales on the premises
    (c) Special residential care facilities

The following are conditional uses in an R1-6 district:

    (a) Public and quasi-public buildings and uses; cultural, recreational, educational, religious, or public service
    (b) Children's nursery schools
    (c) Community clubs and other noncommercial recreation, such as country clubs, golf courses, and swimming pools

The following requirements apply to R1-6:

    30 feet maximum building height. 6,000 square feet minimum lot size. 55 feet minimum lot width. 20 feet minimum front yard set back. 5 feet minimum side yard set back, 12 feet minimum both sides. 20 feet minimum rear yard set back.

Off-street parking requirements are determined according to the use of the property. Typical parking requirements are:

One family dwellings	two spaces
Churches	one space per four seats
Rest homes	one space per bed
Private clubs	one space per 200 square feet of building area

The property conforms to all the R1-6 zoning requirements.

5

<u>ASSESSMENT AND TAX DATA</u>

In June, 1978 the voters of the State of California passed the Jarvis-Gann initiative, commonly known as "Prop 13." It amended the State Constitution to establish a maximum <u>ad valorem</u> tax on property of one percent of "full cash value." Assessed values were rolled back to the 1975-1976 tax year level. A two percent yearly increase was then permitted. Property is assessed at its current market value only when there is a change in ownership. In addition, new construction improvements to the property are added to the existing tax base. The State also provides a $7,000 Homeowners Exemption for owner-occupied dwellings.

This describes the "full cash value" base to which the one percent maximum rate would be applied.

The tax rate limitation does not apply to taxes required to pay off bonded indebtedness authorized by voters before the measure took effect.

In 1978 the assessed value of the subject property was set at $35,831. There have been no new construction improvements in the interim. Since 1978, the assessed value of the subject has been increasing at the approved rate of 2%. Against this base, a 1.1903% yearly tax has been levied. This tax consists of the approved state 1% tax plus pre-existing bonded indebtedness of .1903%.

VOTER APPROVED DEBT SERVICE (IN PERCENT)

City of Fremont	.0095
School - Fremont Unified	.0889
School - Community College	.0122
Washington Hospital	.0090
Bay Area Rapid Transit	.0508
Alameda County Water District	.0199
TOTAL	.1903

1985-1986 ASSESSMENT
Assessment number 501-109-107

Land	$10,711
Improvements	31,271
TOTAL	$41,982

TAX COMPUTATION

Gross Assessment and Tax	$41,982	x .01 =	$419.82
Less Homeowners Exemption	−7,000	x .01 =	−70.00
Bonded Indebtedness	34,982	x .001903 =	66.57
TOTAL TAX	34,982	x 011903 =	$416.39

Since the present owners do not intend any new improvements or to sell the property, there should be no change in the subject's tax pattern in the immediate future.

6

SITE DATA AND DESCRIPTION

There is a "Declaration of Restriction" recorded April 16, 1962 which permits the site to be used only for the purpose of single family occupancy and states no income producing activity, such as, but not limited to trade, commercial, professional, or manufacturing enterprises be conducted.

Site Description, Size and Easements

The subject has an interior site. It is rectangular in shape, having 61 feet of frontage on the northwestern side of San Juan Avenue. It has a depth of 100 feet, totaling 6,1000 square feet. The nearest intersection is Alicante Drive, approximately 55 feet to the southeast. Alicante Drive terminates at San Juan Avenue. See Assessor's Map in the Addenda for visual illustration. There is an easement affecting the northeasterly ten feet and northwesterly two feet for the purpose of servicing public utilities. This is usual and customary in this area of above ground electrical and telephone utilities, and has little effect on the utility of the site. The site is large enough to meet zoning requirements and is adequate for residential needs. It is typical for the neighborhood, with no evident adverse influences.

DESCRIPTION OF IMPROVEMENTS

The subject property is improved with a twenty four year old one story wood framed, stucco exterior dwelling containing 1,617 square feet of living area, and an attached garage containing 360 square feet. The residence is divided into 6 rooms; three bedrooms, two baths, kitchen with dining area, living room, and family room. Laundry facilities are located in the garage. The interior has sheetrock walls, acoustical ceilings, wood floors with wall to wall carpeting. The kitchen, dining area, and baths have sheet vinyl floors. The exterior is freshly painted stucco with wood trim and wood siding in the front. The roof is wood shingle with galvanized iron gutters and downspouts. Windows are aluminum sash with screens. It has a raised floor crawl space under the house, on a concrete perimeter foundation, with concrete support piers.

All the interior walls are recently painted, except for the family room and kitchen, which are papered. Baths have ceramic tile wainscot over the tub and in the shower. The front door is solid wood. All interior doors are hollow core. Both the family room and the living room have sliding glass doors leading to the back yard patio area. Molding and trim are of average quality. There is 100 amp electric service from the overhead wires at the rear property line. The circuit breaker box has nine circuits, two of which are 220 volts for the washer and dryer. There are additional spots available for circuit expansion, if needed. All waterlines, both from the street, and within the structure are

7

galvanized iron. The sewer lines are cast iron. Room sizes and layout are functional. There is a foyer, with Italian flagstone tile floor and guest closet, leading to the guest and dining areas. Sleeping rooms are conveniently located off an opposite hall. The laundry facilities are in the garage, which is typical for most homes in the area. The garage interior has been fully finished in sheetrock and painted. There are several shelves and a work bench. The driveway is paved with concrete. Landscaping is average. The rear yard is minimum maintenance. Approximately two thirds of the back yard is in concrete. There is a ten by twenty foot aluminum awning extending from the rear of the house. The rear and side yards are fully fenced in wood.

OVERALL CONDITION AND EFFECTIVE AGE

The overall quality of the house is average. It has been generally maintained, and is in average condition for dwellings in this neighborhood.
The wood shingle roof is original and appears to have a short remaining life.
The forced air heating unit is also original and will probably need at least a new motor soon.
The 60 gallon hot water heater is three years old.
The original wood kitchen cabinets were refinished five years ago and are in good condition.
The electric stove and oven are thirteen years old but show little wear.
Sheet vinyl in kitchen is one year old.
All carpeting is new.
Both baths were refurbished, including new fixtures, cabinets, and sheet vinyl, about two years ago.
The dishwasher is five years old.
The dwelling's interior and exterior have been freshly painted. Functional utility is average. Laundry facilities in the house rather than in the attached garage would be desirable, however none of the Fairoaks homes have this amenity.

The principal deferred maintenance consists of the original roof and forced air furnace. A few new roofs are appearing in the neighborhood, however, most are still originals. This 24 year old house appears very similar to the 20 year old houses in the area, and is therefore estimated to have an effective age of 20 years.

HISTORY OF THE PROPERTY

As are most of the homes in the area, subject is part of the "Fairoaks Development" of average quality, ranch-type homes built by Kay Builders, AKA Fairoaks Development Company, Limited. They built approximately 500 homes over a period of five years, beginning twenty five years ago. The Horrills are the original owners, paying $18,950.00 in 1961. They presently owe $8,427.22, at an interest rate of six percent. The existing layout has been satisfactory for their needs, there have consequently been no major additions or alterations over the years.

8

HIGHEST AND BEST USE ANALYSIS

Highest and best use is defined as:

1. The reasonable and probable use that supports the highest
    present value of vacant land or improved property, as defined,
    as of the date of the appraisal.
2. The reasonably probable and legal use of land or sites as
    though vacant, found to be physically possible, appropriately
    supported, financially feasible, and that results in the
    highest present land value.
3. The most profitable use.

Implied in these definitions is that the determination of highest
and best use takes into account the contribution of a specific
use to the community development goals as well as the benefits of
that use to individual property owners. Hence, in certain
situations the highest and best use of land may be for parks,
greenbelts, preservation, conservation, wildlife habitats, and
the like.
(The Dictionary of Real Estate Appraisal, previously cited).

The analysis is divided into two parts:

(1) The first assumes the site is vacant and ready to be
improved. The site is presently zoned R1-6. This zoning, as
described in a previous heading, allows farming, churches, clubs,
etc. The size of the site makes it impractical for agricultural
use. Due to the size of the site and the city's off-street
parking requirements, alternate legal uses of the property, as
presently zoned, are not feasible.

Zanny Staff, a Fremont city planner, states that the city master
plan calls for low density single family dwellings in this area.
According to Staff, it is very improbable that the city would
approve a zoning change, a variance, or a conditional use permit
for any other purpose. Finally, a recorded "Declaration of
Restriction" specifically restricts the use of the site to single
family occupancy. The immediate area is developed with primarily
one story single family dwellings in the range of $110,000 to
$140,000 and between 15 to 30 years in age. Demand is good and
marketing time is usually less than ninety days. It is reasonable
to presume that a new single family dwelling could be profitably
built on that site. There is a wide variety of styles, materials,
quality, etc., that a builder may select to best utilize the site
and maximize profit. The predominant house in this neighborhood,
and which most readily sells, is a one story with 3 bedrooms, 2
baths, of average quality, and approximately 1,600 square feet of
living area. A small additional area should be added to
accommodate an inside laundry area - an amenity much in demand

9

today and missing in virtually all homes in this community. This feature would add considerable sales appeal to the property, and should more than offset its cost. In order for a new home, with today's building prices, to compete with the older homes in the neighborhood, all other improvements should be no better than the city code and competitive neighborhood quality demands. The design, size, quality, and layout of the homes in the area are so uniform that any additional building features would be superadequate.

A one story, 3 bedroom, 2 bath, wood frame residence with approximately 1,650 to 1,675 square feet similar to the existing homes in the neighborhood is estimated to be the highest and best use of the site, if vacant.

(2) In the second part of the analysis, we must consider what changes, if any should be made to the improvements that presently occupy the site. These changes should be made only if they can be shown to add value in excess of cost. The roof and the forced air furnace are both original. The roof would be very expensive to replace. Few of the neighborhood homes have replaced theirs as yet. The subject's roof appears to be in the same condition as most of the neighborhood. It seems to be sound and does not leak. It should be repaired as, and if, needed but not replaced. The only powered moving part of the forced air furnace is the motor. Although in comparison to a new roof, the relative cost of replacing the motor is minor, it is a sealed, maintenance free unit and there is no particular reason to replace it at this time.

The present improvements, with roof repairs as needed, is estimated to be the highest and best use of the site as improved.

10

<u>THE COST APPROACH</u>

The cost approach is a set of procedures in which a value indication is derived by estimating the value of the land as if vacant, adding the current cost to reproduce or replace the existing improvements, and finally deducting for all accrued depreciation in the improvements.

The procedure is best explained by quoting the American Institute of Real Estate Appraisers' book <u>Appraising The Single Family Residence</u> (4th Edition ©1984, Page 212):

> "There are five basic steps to the cost approach. Essentially they provide for an estimate of the site (land) value, to which is added the depreciated reproduction cost (new) of the improvements as of the date of the appraisal.
> The appraiser:
> 1. Estimates the value of the site (land) in its highest and best use as if vacant.
> 2. Estimates the reproduction cost or replacement cost new of all the improvements (excluding any that were included as part of the site value).
> 3. Estimates accrued depreciation from all causes.
> 4. Deducts the total of all accrued depreciation (step 3) from the cost new of the improvements (step 2) to arrive at a depreciated value of the improvements recognized as the market value.
> Steps 2, 3, and 4 are the process of converting cost to value.
> 5. Adds the site (land) value (step 1) to the depreciated valued of the improvements (step 4) to arrive at a market value of the property indicated by the cost approach."

LAND VALUATION

To estimate the value of the site, four comparable site sales were found in the subject's market area. Residential land in this area is typically bought and sold based on total square footage. Therefore, sales price per square foot is the most convenient method of comparing the comparables to the subject. The differences between the comparables and the subject are then adjusted by the use of paired data analysis. Paired data analysis is a procedure in which sales are compared in pairs to identify the effect of specific differences on sale price. (<u>The Dictionary of Real Estate Appraisal</u>, previously cited). The adjustments are discussed following the description of the comparables, followed by an adjustment grid. The final decision of market value of the land is then explained.

11

Address: 4335 Blueridge St. Fremont

Location: 3 Blocks southwest
Grantor: Jack N. Mills
Grantee: Kevin P. Hart
Date of Sale: 5/15/85
Sale Price: $43,000
Terms of Sale: Cash
Data Source: County Recorder
Confirmed By: Jack N. Mills
Assessment: Full Sales Price (State Law)
Topography: Level and Cleared
Special Conditions: City Square Footage Variance
Frontage: 55 Feet
Average Depth: 100 Feet
Square Feet: 5,500
Available Utilities: Gas, water, electricity,
                                   sewers, telephone
Easements or Restrictions: Utility Service Easement
                                   Northeasterly Ten Feet
Additional Information: On quiet, residential street
Sales Price Per Square Foot: $7.82

12

Address:	34072 Fremont Bl. Fremont
Location:	1.6 Miles Northwest
Grantor:	Rose Soares
Grantee:	Michael Johnson
Date of Sale:	8/30/85
Sale Price:	$85,000
Terms of Sale:	Cash
Data Source:	County Recorder
Confirmed By:	Rose Soares
Assessment:	Full Sales Price (State Law)
Topography:	Level and Cleared
Special Conditions:	None Reported
Frontage:	75 Feet
Average Depth:	148 Feet
Square Feet:	11,100
Available Utilities:	Gas, water, electricity, sewers, telephone
Easements or Restrictions:	None
Additional Information:	Fremont Bl. is an arterial, with the resultant moderate to heavy traffic noise
Sales Price Per Square Foot:	$7.66

13

COMPARABLE SITE SALE NUMBER THREE

Address:	33911 Milton St. Fremont
Location:	1.5 Miles Northwest
Grantor:	Saia Gabriel
Grantee:	Amar Nader
Date of Sale:	9/30/85
Sale Price:	$68,000
Terms of Sale:	Cash
Data Source:	County Recorder
Confirmed By:	Amar Nader
Assessment:	Full Sales Price (State Law)
Topography:	Level and Cleared
Special Conditions:	None Reported
Frontage:	90 Feet
Average Depth:	94 Feet
Square Feet:	8,460
Available Utilities:	Gas, water, electricity sewers, telephone
Easements or Restrictions:	Utility Easement-Easterly 4 Feet
Additional Information:	On a quiet, residential street
Sales Price Per Square Foot:	$8.04

14

<u>COMPARABLE SITE SALE NUMBER FOUR</u>

Address:	36656 Fremont Bl. Fremont
Location:	4 Blocks Southeast
Grantor:	Amos Picker
Grantee:	Ahmad Siddiq
Date of Sale:	11/20/85
Sale Price:	$50.180
Terms of Sale:	Cash
Data Source:	County Recorder
Confirmed By:	Ahmad Siddiq
Assessment:	Full Sales Price (State Law)
Topography:	Level and Cleared
Special Conditions:	None Reported
Frontage:	60 Feet
Average Depth:	109 Feet
Square Feet:	6,540
Available Utilities:	Gas, water, electricity, sewers, telephone
Easements or Restrictions:	None
Additional Information:	Fremont Bl. is an arterial, with the resultant moderate to heavy traffic noise
Sales Price Per Square Foot:	$7.65

15

	APPRAISED PROPERTY	SITE SALE NO. 1	SITE SALE NO. 2	SITE SALE NO.3	SITE SALE NO.4
ADDRESS	4379 San Juan Ave.	4323 Blueridge	34072 Fremont Bl.	33919 Milton	36656 Fremont Bl.
SALE PRICE		$43,000	$85,000	$68,000	$50,000
SIZE	6,100 Sq. Ft.	5,500 Sq. Ft.	11,000 Sq. Ft.	8,460 Sq. Ft.	6,540 Sq. Ft.
SALE PRICE PER SQUARE FOOT		$7.82	$7.66	$8.04	$7.65
DATE OF SALE		5-15-85 +$.22	8-85	9-30-85	11-20-85
LOCATION	Quiet Street	Quiet Street -0-	Traffic Noise +$.39	Quiet Street -0-	Traffic Noise +$.39
PHYSICAL CHARACTERISTICS	Level and Cleared	Similar	Similar	Similar	Similar
SPECIAL CONDITIONS	None Reported	City Variance -0-	Similar -0-	Similar -0-	Similar -0-
TOTAL ADJUSTMENTS		+$.22	+$.38	-0-	+$.45
ADJUSTED SALE PRICE PER SQUARE FOOT		$8.04	$8.05	$8.04	$8.04

ADJUSTMENT COMMENTS

The four vacant site sales were in the Subject's market area.
They appear to be similar except for size, location, and date of
sale. Site sale no. 1 is 500 square feet under the required 6,000
square feet minimum site size. A city variance was applied for
and granted. As with the other site sales, the size difference
was satisfied by using the unit price per square foot approach.
The grid then called for adjustments in two specific areas of
comparison — time and location.

Location Adjustment

Sale no. 2 and sale no. 4 are adversely affected by the traffic
noise on Fremont Blvd. Sale no. 3 is located on a quiet street
but is otherwise similar to sale no. 4. Sale no. 3 sold for $8.04
per sq. ft. and sale no. 4 sold for $7.65 per sq. ft. There then
appears to be an adjustment required of $.39 per sq. ft. for
traffic noise.

Sale no. 3 (no traffic noise)	$8.04 per sq. ft.
Sale no. 4 (traffic noise)	−7.65 per sq. ft.
Location adjustment	$ .39 per sq. ft.

The location adjustment can also be estimated by comparing sale
no. 2 with sale no. 3.

Sale no. 3 (no traffic noise)	$8.04 per sq. ft.
Sale no. 2 (traffic noise)	−7.66 per sq. ft.
Location adjustment	$ .38 per sq. ft.

The two adjustments are within one cent of each other. Therefore,
the use of the $.39 per sq. ft. figure appears reasonable.

Time Adjustment

Sale no. 1 is approximately eight months old. The other 3 sales
are relatively recent. Sale no. 4 is the most recent sale and is
similar to the subject except for location. The adverse location
of sale no. 4 can be adjusted for by the use of the $.39 traffic
noise adjustment.

Sale no 4 (11/20/85)	$7.65 per sq. ft.
(Traffic noise adjustment)	+.39 per sq. ft.
Sale no 4 (as adjusted)	$8.04 per sq. ft.
Sale no. 1 (5/15/85)	−7.82 per sq. ft.
Difference attributed to time	$.22 per sq. ft.

It appears that a six month time differential calls for an
adjustment of $.22 per sq. ft.

16

SUMMARY:

The preceding grid demonstrates how the adjustments were applied to each sale and how the adjusted sale prices and final indication of market value of the site was reached.

Sale no. 1 has the weakness of having a special condition. In most cases, this would cause the sale to be suspect and disregarded for consideration as a reliable comparable. However, an examination of the condition on its own merits first, is permissible. Jack Mills, the buyer, is a local builder. After obtaining a zoning variance due to the lot being 500 square feet less than required, he constructed a 3 bedroom 2 bath single family residence with a living room and family room. Total living area = 1,404 square feet, and an attached garage of 370 square feet. Total gross building area = 1,774. He used average quality materials and built a structure essentially similar to those recommended in this report in the "Highest And Best Use Of The Land As If Vacant" section.

The total square footage of building area is proportional to those on 6,000 square feet of land and was sold for $139,500. After deducting for the cost of the land ($43,000), the improvement sold for $54.40 per square foot of gross building area. In the following pages it will be shown that this amount is very close to the estimated new building costs as derived from a cost estimate publication, and the market. For the preceding reasons, sale no. 1 is considered to be appropriate. Because of similarities to the subject and its location in the same development, it is considered to be the strongest sale. Sales 2, 3, and 4 have sufficient similarities in elements of comparison, or property characteristics, to also establish reliability, hence their strong support of sale no. 1. Therefore, $8.04 per sq. ft. is selected as the vacant land value.

Subject's Total Vacant Site Value:

$8.04 x 6,100 = $49,000 (rounded)

17

ESTIMATE OF COST NEW

The next step in the cost approach is to estimate the cost to build the improvements new on the date of the appraisal. One estimate was made by using the Marshall-Swift Residential Handbook square foot costs, as adjusted for the local market. The total building cost by the Marshall-Swift approach is $107,312 or $54.28 per square foot of gross building area, including yard improvements and landscaping. A unit breakdown of costs will be found in the addenda.

As a check, a newly constructed dwelling in the area was located and building costs analyzed. Igor Satan of Diablo Properties, Inc. was interviewed concerning the recently constructed property located at 37861 Tacchella Street, Fremont. It is a three bedroom two bath home with a two car garage. It is located approximately one and one half miles southwest of the subject. Total direct and indirect building costs, including a living area of 1447 square feet, garage area of 400 square feet, yard improvements, and landscaping, was $100,980 or $54.67 per square foot. This is very consistent with the handbook approach, above.

COST NEW CONCLUSION

Based on the cost of subject's improvements at $54.28 x gross building area of 1977 square feet, the estimated reproduction cost of the subject is $107,312.

18

DEPRECIATION ANALYSIS

The next step in the cost approach is to determine the amount of depreciation to subtract from the cost new of the improvements.

"Depreciation is a loss in value from any cause. Deterioration, or physical depreciation, is evidenced by wear and tear, dry rot, cracks, encrustations, or structural defects. Other types of depreciation are caused by obsolescence, either functional or external. Functional obsolescence may be caused by such items as inadequacy or superadequacy in size, style, or mechanical equipment. Physical deterioration and functional obsolescence are evident in the improvement. External obsolescence is caused by changes external to a subject property, such as changes in demand, changes in general property uses in the subject property's area, and changes in zoning, financing, and national regulations" (The Appraisal of Real Estate, previously cited).

There are a variety of approaches available to an appraiser in estimating accrued depreciation – such as the breakdown method, the sales comparison method, and the economic age-life method.

BREAKDOWN METHOD

The breakdown method is done by estimating total loss in value due to accrued depreciation by analyzing each cause of depreciation separately and measuring the amount of each. The estimates are then totaled to derive a lump-sum deduction from the estimated replacement cost.

The five basic elements of accrued depreciation in structures are:

1. Curable physical deterioration
2. Incurable physical deterioration
3. Curable functional obsolescence
4. Incurable functional obsolescence
5. External obsolesence

Due to the extensive detail involved, the full breakdown method is rarely practical in appraising single family dwellings. However, the fundamentals of arriving at cost of improvements new using the square footage approach (see previous "Estimate of Cost New"), and the age-life method of depreciation (explanation to follow) are directly derived from the breakdown method.

19

SALES COMPARISON METHOD

Sales comparison to determine accrued depreciation is done by subtracting the market-derived contribution of the improvements to current market value from the reproduction or replacement cost on the date of the appraisal. This approach is extremely sensitive to the availability of comparable sales, both of improved and vacant sites. The sale must be open-market, the site value market-supported, and the estimate of replacement or reproduction cost accurate.

ECONOMIC AGE-LIFE METHOD

In the economic age-life method, the ratio of effective age to total economic life is applied to the current cost of the improvements to obtain a lump sum deduction for accrued depreciation.

$$\frac{\text{Effective age x current cost of improvements}}{\text{Total economic life}} = \text{accrued depreciation}$$

The economic age-life method is the approach used in this report. It was selected because of its simplicity and directness. It is also easily understood by the reader.

Homes in this neighborhood range in age from 15 to 30 years. In appearance, the subject is similar to most of the 20 year old homes. Therefore, the effective age of the subject was estimated to be 20 years. Two long time local building contractors, John Alan of Alan and Rogers Builders and J. E. Bachmann of Bachmann Construction Co, Inc. state that, considering the typical quality of building materials used in local construction, the level of skilled labor available over the last several years, and Fremont's code requirements, dwellings built in the subject's neighborhood within the past 15 to 30 years should reasonably expect a total physical life in excess of 75 years. The city of Fremont has several small communities that have been recognized as distinct localities for nearly 75 years (the Niles District in northeastern Fremont, the Irvington District in central Fremont, and the Warm Springs District in southern Fremont are examples). There is today little apparent diminution in their existence as viable, economically functioning communities. The subject's community is at least economically equal to these districts in the city and should reasonably expect at least a similar economic longevity. Therefore, the economic life of the subject is estimated to be 75 years.

Subject's estimated Accrued Depreciation by Economic Age-Life:

$$\frac{20 \text{ years}}{75 \text{ years}} = 26.7 \text{ total depreciation}$$

SUMMARY

The depreciation estimated by the age-life method is:

Reproduction cost	$107,312
Total % of depreciation	x .267
Total depreciation	$28,652

SUMMARY OF THE COST APPROACH

The age-life method of depreciation was selected. The functional utility and physical layout of the dwelling is adequate and very similar to the other homes in the area. Therefore, no functional obsolescence was assigned. The subject is located on a quiet street. There are no factories, railroad tracks, freeways, or other adverse influences in the immediate area, nor is there evidence of any change in property use, zoning, etc., impacting upon the neighborhood. Therefore, no external obsolescence was assigned.

INDICATION OF VALUE

The total age-life depreciation was estimated to be $28,652.

Estimated market value of the site		$49,000
Estimated replacement cost of the improvements	$107,312	
Estimated depreciation (.267 x $107,312)	-28,652	
Depreciated value of the improvements (rounded)		+ 78,500
		$127,500

Total indicated market value via the cost approach:

$127,500

21

THE DIRECT SALE OR MARKET DATA APPROACH

THE MARKET COMPARABLES

The market data approach is a set of procedures in which the appraiser derives a value indication by comparing the property being appraised to similar properties that have been sold recently, applying appropriate units of comparison - such as time of sale, location, financing, and physical characteristics. Adjustments are then made to the sales, based upon these comparisons. Finally, adjusted sale prices are reconciled into an indication of value for the market data approach.

Address: 4371 San Juan Ave.
No. of Families: one. Type: one story. Style: ranch.
Date of Sale: 12/27/85   Grantor: James O'Sullivan.
Sale Price: $133,000   Grantee: Wilfredo Zambrano
Financing: new VA mortgage.
Data Source: MLS. Verification: W. Zambrano.
Lot Dimensions: 61' x 100'.   Lot Size: 6,100 sq. ft.
Site Improvements /Landscaping/Topography: avg/avg/level.
Zoning: residential. Conforming: yes. View: average.
Neighborhood Life Cycle: stable.
Improvement Conformity: conforms.
No. of Rooms: 6. No. of baths: 2. No. of bedrooms: 3.
Other Rooms: living room, family room.
Car Storage: 2 car garage. Functional Utility: average.

SERVICES AND MECHANICAL EQUIPMENT
Water: County. Type of Heat: forced air. Sewage: City.
Fuel: Gas. Electricity: public. Hot Water: gas 60 gals.
Gas: public. Plumbing: galvanized iron/cast iron waste.
ASSESSMENT: full sales price (State tax code).

CONSTRUCTION
Type:frame. Quality: average. Condition: average.
Appeal: average. Date Inspected: 12/30/85
Effective Age: 20 years
Foundation: concrete perimeter with crawl space.
Special Considerations: no special conditions
Sq. Ft. of GLA: 1,617 Sales Price/Sq. Ft. of GLA: $82.25.

23

Address: 3617 Oak Street.
No. of Families: one. Type: one story. Style: ranch
Date of Sale: 11/21/85   Grantor: Hsiang Maa.
Sale Price: $130,000   Grantee: Miguel Egea.
Financing: new conventional mortgage.
Data Source: MLS. Verification: M. Egea.
Lot Dimensions: 60 x 105 (avg. depth) Lot Size: 6,000
Site Improvements /Landscaping/Topography: avg/avg/level.
Zoning: residential. Conforming: yes. View: average.
Neighborhood Life Cycle: stable.
Improvement Conformity: conforms.
No. of Rooms: 6. No. of baths: 2. No. of bedrooms: 3.
Other Rooms: living room, family room.
Car Storage: 2 car garage. Functional Utility: average

SERVICES AND MECHANICAL EQUIPMENT
Water: County. Type of Heat: forced air. Sewage: City.
Fuel: Gas. Electricity: public. Hot Water: gas 50 gals.
Gas: public. Plumbing: galvanized iron/cast iron waste.
ASSESSMENT: full sales price (State tax code).

CONSTRUCTION
Type: frame. Quality: average. Condition: average.
Appeal: average. Date Inspected: 12/27/85.
Effective Age: 20 years.
Foundation: concrete perimeter with crawl space.
Special Considerations: no special conditions.
Sq. Ft. of GLA: 1,617 Sales Price/Sq. Ft. of GLA: $80.40.

24

COMPARABLE SALE NO. 3

Address: 3147 Isherwood Way
No. of Families: one. Type: one story. Style: ranch.
Date of Sale: 11/11/85   Grantor: Jaime A. Lee
Sale Price: $137,000   Grantee: Baxter Ross
Financing: new conventional mortgage.
Data Source: MLS. Verification: B. Ross
Lot Dimensions: 63' x 100'.   Lot Size: 6,300 sq. ft.
Site Improvements /Landscaping/Topography: avg/avg/level.
Zoning: residential. Conforming: yes. View: average.
Neighborhood Life Cycle: Stable.
Improvement Conformity: conforms
No. of Rooms: 6. No. of baths: 2. No. of bedrooms: 3.
Other Rooms: living room, family room.
Car Storage: 2 car garage. Functional Utility: average

SERVICES AND MECHANICAL EQUIPMENT
Water: County. Type of Heat: forced air. Sewage: City.
Fuel: Gas. Electricity: public. Hot Water: gas 50 gals.
Gas: public. Plumbing: galvanized iron/cast iron waste.
ASSESSMENT: full sales price (State tax code).

CONSTRUCTION
Type: frame. Quality: average. Condition: average.
Appeal: average. Date Inspected: 12/27/85.
Effective Age: 15 years.
Foundation: concrete perimeter with crawl space.
Special Considerations: no special conditions.
Sq. Ft. of GLA: 1,615 Sales Price/Sq. Ft. of GLA: $84.83.

25

COMPARABLE SALE NO. 4

Address: 3510 Dumbar Court
No. of Families: one. Type: one story. Style: ranch.
Date of Sale: 10/18/85.   Grantor: Theodore Danniels
Sale Price: $129,000   Grantee: Jerry Pederson
Financing: new conventional mortgage.
Data Source: MLS. Verification: J. Pederson
Lot Dimensions: 60' x 101'.   Lot Size: 6,100 sq. ft.
Site Improvements /Landscaping/Topography: avg/avg/level.
Zoning: residential. Conforming: yes. View: average.
Neighborhood Life Cycle: Stable.
Improvement Conformity: conforms.
No. of Rooms: 6. No. of baths: 2. No. bedrooms: 3.
Other Rooms: living room, family room.
Car Storage: 2 car garage. Functional Utility: average

SERVICES AND MECHANICAL EQUIPMENT
Water: County. Type of Heat: forced air. Sewage: City.
Fuel: Gas. Electricity: public. Hot Water: gas 45 gals.
Gas: public. Plumbing: galvanized iron/cast iron waste.
ASSESSMENT: full sales price (State tax code).

CONSTRUCTION
Type: frame Quality: average. Condition: average.
Appeal: average. Date Inspected: 12/27/85.
Effective Age: 20 years.
Foundation: concrete perimeter with crawl space.
Special Considerations: no special conditions.
Sq. Ft. of GLA: 1,607 Sales Price/Sq. Ft. of GLA: $80.27.

26

DESCRIPTIONS, ANALYSES, AND ADJUSTMENTS

The preceding four sales are all in the Fairoaks Development.
They are three bedroom, two bath ranch style single family
resales of similar quality, utility, design, and appeal on quiet
streets. They are all recent sales, therefore no time adjustments
were assigned.

They were inspected and found to materially differ only in terms
of sale, and effective age. Any additional minor differences did
not appear to affect the sales price.

The sales will now be compared to each other to obtain
adjustments for their differences. Paired data analysis was used
in both adjustment procedures. Unit of comparison used was price
per square foot of living area, for the reasons explained in the
cost approach. The information is summarized and displayed on a
comparable sale adjustment grid. Finally, all the data is
reconciled to give an indicated market value.

Finance Adjustment

Comparable Sale No. 1 and Comparable Sale No. 4 appear to be
similar except for their terms of sale. The seller of Sale No. 1
paid $3,000 in financing "points" for the VA loan obtained by the
buyer. It sold for $82.25 per sq. ft. of GLA. Sale No. 4 sold for
$80.27 per sq. ft. of GLA.

    Comparable Sale No. 1 (base sale)
      Paid financing charge $82.25 per sq. ft. of GLA

    Comparable Sale No. 2
      No financing charge to seller   <u>-80.27</u> per sq. ft. of GLA

    Difference in sales price
    attributable to financing $1.98

Effective Age Adjustment

Comparable Sale No. 2 and Comparable Sale No. 3 appear to be
similar except for effective age. Sale No. 2 has an effective age
of 20 years and Sale No. 3 has an effective age of 15 years. Sale
No. 3 sold for $8483 per sq. ft. of GLA. Sale No. 2 sold for
$80.40 per sq. ft. of GLA.

    Comparable Sale No. 3 (base sale)
      15 year effective age   84.83 per sq. ft. of GLA

    Comparable Sale No. 2
      20 year effective age   <u>-80.40</u> per sq. ft. of GLA

    Difference in sale price per $4.43
    sq. ft. of GLA attributable
    to difference in effective age

27

	Appraised Property	Site Sale No. 1	Site Sale No. 2	Site Sale No. 3	Site Sale No. 4
Address	4379 San Juan Ave.	4371 San Juan Ave.	36717 Oak St.	3147 Isherwood Pl.	3510 Dunbar Ct.
Sales Price	—	$133,000	$130,00	$137,00	$129,000
GLA	1,617 Sq. Ft.	1617 Sq. Ft.	1617 Sq. Ft.	1615 Sq. Ft.	1607 Sq. Ft.
Sales Price GLA	—	$82.25	$80.40	$84.83	$80.27
Date of Sale	—	12-27-85	11-8-85	11-11-85	10-18-85
Location	Quiet Street	Quiet Street	Quiet Street	Quiet Street	Quiet Street
Lot Size	61' x 100' 6,100 Sq. Ft.	61' x 100' 6,100 Sq. Ft.	60' x 105' 6,300 Sq. Ft.	63' x 100' 6,300 Sq. Ft.	61' x 101' 6,100 Sq. Ft.
Car Storage	2 Car Garage	2 Car Garage	2 Car Garage	2 Car Garage	2 Car Garage
Effective Age	20 Years	20 Years	20 Years	15 Years -$4.43	20 Years
Terms of Sale	—	VA Mortgage -$1.98	New Conventional Mortage	New Conventional Mortage	New Conventional Mortage
Total Adjustments	—	-$1.98	0	-$4.43	0
Adjusted Sales Price Sq. Ft. GLA	—	$80.27	$80.40	$80.40	$80.27
Adjusted Sale Price	—	$130,000 (Rounded)	$130,000 (Rounded)	$130,000 (Rounded)	$130,000 (Rounded)

Comparable Sale No. 1
4371 San Juan Avenue, Fremont, CA

	Adjustments (per sq. ft. GLA)	Explanation
Sale Price	$133,000	
Gross Living Area	1,617 sq. ft.	
Sale price per sq. ft. of gross living area	$82.25	
Date of Sale	0	12/27/85
Location	0	Quiet street
Lot Size	0	Typical
Car Storage	0	2 car garage
Effective Age	0	20 year. Same as subject
Special Conditions	-$1.98	VA loan charge
Total Adjustments	-$1.98	
Adjusted sale price per sq. ft. of gross living area	$80.27	
Adjusted Sale Price	$130,000	Sale price per sq. ft. of GLA x GLA of house being appraised ($80.40 x 1,617)

28

Comparable Sale No. 2
36717 Oak Street, Fremont, CA

	Adjustments (per sq. ft. GLA)	Explanation
Sale Price	$133,000	
Gross Living Area	1,617 sq. ft.	
Sale price per sq. ft. of gross living area	$80.40	
Date of Sale	0	11/21/85
Location	0	Quiet street
Lot Size	0	Typical
Car Storage	0	2 car garage
Effective Age	0	20 year. Same as subject
Special Conditions	0	None
Total Adjustments	0	
Adjusted sale price per sq. ft. of gross living area	$80.40	
Adjusted Sale Price	$130,000	Sale price per sq. ft. of GLA x GLA of house being appraised ($80.40 x 1,617)

29

Comparable Sale No. 3
3147 Isherwood Place, Fremont, CA

	Adjustments (per sq. ft. GLA)	Explanation
Sale Price	$137,000	
Gross Living Area	1,615 sq. ft.	
Sale price per sq. ft. of gross living area	$84.83	
Date of Sale	0	11/11/85
Location	0	Quiet street
Lot Size	0	Typical
Car Storage	0	2 car garage
Effective Age	$4.43	15 years
Special Conditions	0	None
Total Adjustments	$4.43	
Adjusted sale price per sq. ft. of gross living area	$80.40	
Adjusted Sale Price	$130,000	Sale price per sq. ft. of GLA x GLA of house being appraised ($80.40 x 1,617)

30

Comparable Sale No. 4
36717 Oak Street, Fremont, CA

	Adjustments (per sq. ft. GLA)	Explanation
Sale Price	$129,000	
Gross Living Area	1,607 sq. ft.	
Sale price per sq. ft. of gross living area	$80.27	
Date of Sale	0	10/18/85
Location	0	Quiet street
Lot Size	0	Typical
Car Storage	0	2 car garage
Effective Age	0	20 year. Same as subject
Special Conditions	0	None
Total Adjustments	0	
Adjusted sale price per sq. ft. of gross living area	$80.27	
Adjusted Sale Price	$130,000	Sale price per sq. ft. of GLA x GLA of house being appraised ($80.03 x 1,619)

31

<u>INDICATION OF VALUE</u>

Seven sales from the subject's development were initially considered. Of these, four were selected as being the most comparable to the subject, and are as substitutionally equal as possible.

Sale no. 1 is the same model as subject and is located next door. The only significant difference in elements of comparison for consideration is in the VA financing. An adjustment for this factor was taken from the market. Sale no. 2 is also the same model as the subject, and required no adjustments. Although within the same development, sales 3 and 4 are somewhat farther away from the subject. Sale no. 3 is a very similar model. It has an apparent economic age five years less than the other sales and the subject. This factor too was adjusted for from the market. Sale no. 4 is a similar model in all important respects. It required no adjustments.

Based on sales 1 and 2 being the same models, and the close support of sales 3, 4, and other similar sales in this market, the indicated market value of 4377 San Juan Avenue is:

$130,000

32

RECONCILIATION

4377 San Juan Avenue, Fremont, CA is a single family, one story, ranch-style, six-room house with a two car garage. It is located in a stable neighborhood of homes of similar age, quality, condition, design and appeal. The nearest new home development is on the northern outskirts of the city. They are higher priced and further removed from the shopping and public facilities amenities that the subject's neighborhood enjoys. There are no apparent adverse influence exposures. Homes in the area are generally well maintained. For these reasons, the economic outlook for the foreseeable future should remain stable.

The subject has a typical interior site for the neighborhood. The street is fully improved and all public utilities are available. Supply and demand are relatively in balance, with marketing time usually less than 90 days.

Subject's room size and layout is typical for the neighborhood and no functional utility problems were noted. The subject lacks an inside laundry area, but laundry facilities in the garage are standard for the neighborhood. The market does not seem to recognize this as a defect.

Tax increases are limited by state law, applying to all neighborhoods equally. Therefore there should be no unforeseen tax burden levied against this community.

With minor repairs, the present improvements represent the highest and best use of the property.

Two approaches to value have been utilized in this appraisal. The final values indicated for each are:

           Cost approach $127,500
           Market approach $130,000

Very few of the homes in this area are rentals, therefore the income approach to value was not used.

The two values are within a narrow range. However, a definite final value must now be determined - a choice must be made between the two approaches. Greatest weight will be given that method which is most reliable in both quantity and quality of data, and is most appropriate to this appraisal assignment.

The market is a strong and usually reliable source of data because it is directly observable in a "real life" environment. When sufficient and creditable information is available, it is the preferred data source. For example, market data was used as the basis for confirmation and corroboration in both value approaches used in this report.

33

The cost approach value was reached in three steps: derive land value, determine reproduction cost of the improvements, and estimate depreciation of improvements (land does not wear out and therefore is not depreciated). Four site sales from the subject's area were used to obtain site value. There were sufficient similarities to the subject to establish reliability. Cost of improvements was determined by referring to a valuation service publication, and verifying results with a local builder on an actual property. Accurately estimating depreciation is the most difficult aspect of the cost approach, particularly in older homes. The age-life approach is a simple and direct method of measuring accrued depreciation, and was the approach utilized in this report.

There were ample data to draw upon in the market approach. There have been sufficient sales in the area to allow the selection of sales that were very similar to the subject. Two comparables that were used in the sales comparison section were the same model as the subject, and the two additional sales used varied only slightly from the subject.

CONCLUSION

Because of the creditable amount of data provided, the market approach value was selected as the final market value. As previously discussed, the cost approach has the inherent difficulty of accurately establishing accrued depreciation when appraising older properties. However, in this case the market approach determined by paired data analysis that comparable dwellings in this area apparently depreciated $7,000 over a period of five years, or $1,400 per year. The cost approach, using the age-life method, indicated the subject depreciated $1,433 per year ($28,652 divided by 20 years). This is a very strong correlation. The cost approach value then, of $127,500, reinforces the market approach value of $130,000; differing by somewhat less than 2%.

The indicated market value of 4377 San Juan Avenue as of December 29, 1985 is:

One Hundred Thirty Thousand Dollars ($130,000)

34

CERTIFICATE OF VALUE

I certify that to the best of my knowledge and belief:

The statements of fact contained in this report are true and correct.

The reported analyses, opinions, and conclusions are limited only by the reported assumptions and limiting conditions, and are my personal, unbiased professional analyses, opinions, and conclusions.

I have no present or prospective interest in the property that is the subject of this report, and I have no personal interest or bias with respect to the parties involved.

My compensation is not contingent on any action or event resulting from the analyses, opinions, or conclusions in, or the use of, this report.

Although not a member of the Institute, my analyses, opinions, and conclusions were developed, and this report has been prepared, in comformity with the requirements of the Code of Professional Ethics and the Standards of Professional Practice of the American Institute of Real Estate Appraisers.

The use of this report is subject to the requirements of the American Institute of Real Estate Appraisers relating to review by its duly authorized representatives.

I have made a personal inspection of the property that is the subject of this report.

No one provided significant professional assistance to the person signing this report.

SUBJECT FRONT - NORTHEASTERLY VIEW

SUBJECT FRONT - SOUTHWESTERLY VIEW

SUBJECT REAR - NORTHEASTERLY VIEW

SUBJECT REAR - SOUTHWESTERLY VIEW

SAN JUAN AVENUE - NORTHEASTERLY VIEW

SAN JUAN AVENUE - SOUTHWESTERLY VIEW

Appendix B—Standard Appraisal Report Forms

1. Uniform Residential Appraisal Report
   FHLMC 70/FNMA 1004 (10/86)

2. Definition of Market Value/Statement of Limiting Conditions/Certification
   FHLMC 439/FNMA 1004B (7/86)

3. Sketch Addendum

4. Location Map & Sketch Addendum

5. Photograph Addendum: Subject Property

6. Photograph Addendum: Comparable Sales

7. Single Family Comparable Rent Schedule
   FHLMC 1000/FNMA 1007 (8/88)

8. Appraisal Report—Individual Condominium or PUD Unit
   FHLMC 465/FNMA 1073 (9/80)

9. Project Analysis—Individual Condominium or PUD Unit
   FHLMC 465, Addendum A (9/80)

10. Analysis of Annual Income and Expenses—Operating Budget
    FHLMC 465, Addendum B/FNMA 1073, Addendum B (9/80)

11. Employee Relocation Council Residential Appraisal Report
    ERC (4/86)

12. Small Residential Income Property Appraisal Report
    FHLMC 72, 2-4 units/FNMA 1025, 2-4 units (10/89)

13. Operating Income Statement
    FHLMC 998/FNMA 216 (8/88)

14. Appraisal Report—Residential Income Property
    FHLMC 71B (8/77)

15. Mobile Home Appraisal Report

16. Land Appraisal Report

17. Satisfactory Completion Certificate
    FHLMC 442 (6/78)

18. Residential Appraisal Field Review Report
    FHLMC 1032, 1-4 Family/FNMA 2000, 1-4 Family (1/90)

19. Loan Valuation for Second Mortgage
    FNMA 219 (10/85)

☒

Property Description & Analysis   **UNIFORM RESIDENTIAL APPRAISAL REPORT**   File No. ___

SUBJECT

Property Address		Census Tract	**LENDER DISCRETIONARY USE**
City ___ County ___ State ___ Zip Code ___			Sale Price $ ___
Legal Description			Date ___
Owner/Occupant		Map Reference	Mortgage Amount $ ___
Sale Price $ ___ Date of Sale ___		PROPERTY RIGHTS APPRAISED	Mortgage Type ___
Loan charges/concessions to be paid by seller $ ___		☐ Fee Simple	Discount Points and Other Concessions
R.E. Taxes $ ___ Tax Year ___ HOA $/Mo. ___		☐ Leasehold	Paid by Seller $ ___
Lender/Client		☐ Condominium (HUD/VA)	
		☐ De Minimis PUD	Source ___

NEIGHBORHOOD

LOCATION	☐ Urban	☐ Suburban	☐ Rural	NEIGHBORHOOD ANALYSIS	Good	Avg.	Fair	Poor
BUILT UP	☐ Over 75%	☐ 25-75%	☐ Under 25%	Employment Stability	☐	☐	☐	☐
GROWTH RATE	☐ Rapid	☐ Stable	☐ Slow	Convenience to Employment	☐	☐	☐	☐
PROPERTY VALUES	☐ Increasing	☐ Stable	☐ Declining	Convenience to Shopping	☐	☐	☐	☐
DEMAND/SUPPLY	☐ Shortage	☐ In Balance	☐ Over Supply	Convenience to Schools	☐	☐	☐	☐
MARKETING TIME	☐ Under 3 Mos.	☐ 3-6 Mos.	☐ Over 6 Mos.	Adequacy of Public Transportation	☐	☐	☐	☐

PRESENT LAND USE %	LAND USE CHANGE	PREDOMINANT	SINGLE FAMILY HOUSING		Recreation Facilities	☐	☐	☐	☐
Single Family ___	Not Likely ☐	OCCUPANCY	PRICE $(000)	AGE (yrs)	Adequacy of Utilities	☐	☐	☐	☐
2-4 Family ___	Likely ☐	Owner ☐			Property Compatibility	☐	☐	☐	☐
Multi-family ___	In process ☐	Tenant ☐	Low		Protection from Detrimental Cond.	☐	☐	☐	☐
Commercial ___	To: ___	Vacant (0-5%) ☐	High		Police & Fire Protection	☐	☐	☐	☐
Industrial ___		Vacant (over 5%) ☐	Predominant		General Appearance of Properties	☐	☐	☐	☐
Vacant ___			—		Appeal to Market	☐	☐	☐	☐

Note: Race or the racial composition of the neighborhood are not considered reliable appraisal factors.

COMMENTS: ___

SITE

Dimensions ___			Topography ___
Site Area ___		Corner Lot ___	Size ___
Zoning Classification ___		Zoning Compliance ___	Shape ___
HIGHEST & BEST USE: Present Use ___		Other Use ___	Drainage ___

UTILITIES	Public	Other	SITE IMPROVEMENTS	Type	Public	Private		
Electricity	☐		Street		☐	☐	View	___
Gas	☐		Curb/Gutter		☐	☐	Landscaping	___
Water	☐		Sidewalk		☐	☐	Driveway	___
Sanitary Sewer	☐		Street Lights		☐	☐	Apparent Easements	___
Storm Sewer	☐		Alley		☐	☐	FEMA Flood Hazard Yes* ___ No ___	
							FEMA* Map/Zone	___

COMMENTS (Apparent adverse easements, encroachments, special assessments, slide areas, etc.): ___

IMPROVEMENTS

GENERAL DESCRIPTION	EXTERIOR DESCRIPTION	FOUNDATION	BASEMENT	INSULATION
Units ___	Foundation ___	Slab ___	Area Sq. Ft. ___	Roof ☐
Stories ___	Exterior Walls ___	Crawl Space ___	% Finished ___	Ceiling ☐
Type (Det./Att.) ___	Roof Surface ___	Basement ___	Ceiling ___	Walls ☐
Design (Style) ___	Gutters & Dwnspts. ___	Sump Pump ___	Walls ___	Floor ☐
Existing ___	Window Type ___	Dampness ___	Floor ___	None ☐
Proposed ___	Storm Sash ___	Settlement ___	Outside Entry ___	Adequacy ☐
Under Construction ___	Screens ___	Infestation ___		Energy Efficient Items:
Age (Yrs.) ___	Manufactured House ___			
Effective Age (Yrs.) ___				

ROOM LIST

ROOMS	Foyer	Living	Dining	Kitchen	Den	Family Rm.	Rec. Rm.	Bedrooms	# Baths	Laundry	Other	Area Sq. Ft.
Basement												
Level 1												
Level 2												

Finished area **above** grade contains: ___ Rooms; ___ Bedroom(s); ___ Bath(s); ___ Square Feet of Gross Living Area

INTERIOR

SURFACES	Materials/Condition	HEATING		KITCHEN EQUIP.		ATTIC		IMPROVEMENT ANALYSIS	Good	Avg.	Fair	Poor
Floors	___	Type	___	Refrigerator	☐	None	☐	Quality of Construction	☐	☐	☐	☐
Walls	___	Fuel	___	Range/Oven	☐	Stairs	☐	Condition of Improvements	☐	☐	☐	☐
Trim/Finish	___	Condition	___	Disposal	☐	Drop Stair	☐	Room Sizes/Layout	☐	☐	☐	☐
Bath Floor	___	Adequacy	___	Dishwasher	☐	Scuttle	☐	Closets and Storage	☐	☐	☐	☐
Bath Wainscot	___	COOLING		Fan/Hood	☐	Floor	☐	Energy Efficiency	☐	☐	☐	☐
Doors	___	Central	☐	Compactor	☐	Heated	☐	Plumbing-Adequacy & Condition	☐	☐	☐	☐
		Other	___	Washer/Dryer	☐	Finished	☐	Electrical-Adequacy & Condition	☐	☐	☐	☐
		Condition	___	Microwave	☐			Kitchen Cabinets-Adequacy & Cond.	☐	☐	☐	☐
Fireplace(s)	# ___	Adequacy	___	Intercom	☐			Compatibility to Neighborhood	☐	☐	☐	☐

AUTOS

CAR STORAGE:		Attached ☐	Adequate ☐	House Entry ☐	Appeal & Marketability	☐	☐	☐	☐
No. Cars	Garage ___ Carport ___	Detached ☐	Inadequate ☐	Outside Entry ☐	Estimated Remaining Economic Life ___ Yrs.				
Condition	None ___	Built-In ☐	Electric Door ☐	Basement Entry ☐	Estimated Remaining Physical Life ___ Yrs.				

Additional features: ___

COMMENTS

Depreciation (Physical, functional and external inadequacies, repairs needed, modernization, etc.): ___

General market conditions and prevalence and impact in subject/market area regarding loan discounts, interest buydowns and concessions: ___

Freddie Mac Form 70 10/86 10CH.   AMERICAN REALTY FORMS, INC. • ALEXANDRIA, VIRGINIA • 1 (800) 642-9494 • 703-684-3500   Fannie Mae Form 1004 10/86

Exhibit 1.1

UNIFORM RESIDENTIAL APPRAISAL REPORT   File No.

COST APPROACH

Purpose of Appraisal is to estimate Market Value as defined in the Certification & Statement of Limiting Conditions.

BUILDING SKETCH (SHOW GROSS LIVING AREA ABOVE GRADE)
If for Freddie Mac or Fannie Mae, show only square foot calculations and cost approach comments in this space.

ESTIMATED REPRODUCTION COST – NEW – OF IMPROVEMENTS:

Dwelling _____ Sq. Ft. @ $ _____	= $ _____	
_____ Sq. Ft. @ $ _____	= _____	
Extras _____	= _____	
	= _____	
Special Energy Efficient Items _____	= _____	
Porches, Patios, etc. _____	= _____	
Garage/Carport _____ Sq. Ft. @ $ _____	= _____	
Total Estimated Cost New	= $ _____	

	Physical	Functional	External
Less			
Depreciation			= $ _____
Depreciated Value of Improvements			= $ _____
Site Imp. "as is" (driveway, landscaping, etc.)			= $ _____
ESTIMATED SITE VALUE			= $ _____
(If leasehold, show only leasehold value.)			
INDICATED VALUE BY COST APPROACH			= $ _____

(Not Required by Freddie Mac and Fannie Mae)
Does property conform to applicable HUD/VA property standards? ☐ Yes ☐ No
If No, explain: _____

Construction Warranty ☐ Yes ☐ No
Name of Warranty Program _____
Warranty Coverage Expires _____

The undersigned has recited three recent sales of properties most similar and proximate to subject and has considered these in the market analysis. The description includes a dollar adjustment, reflecting market reaction to those items of significant variation between the subject and comparable properties. If a significant item in the comparable property is superior to, or more favorable than, the subject property, a minus (–) adjustment is made, thus reducing the indicated value of subject; if a significant item in the comparable is inferior to, or less favorable than, the subject property, a plus (+) adjustment is made, thus increasing the indicated value of the subject.

SALES COMPARISON ANALYSIS

ITEM	SUBJECT	COMPARABLE NO. 1		COMPARABLE NO. 2		COMPARABLE NO. 3	
Address							
Proximity to Subject							
Sales Price	$	$		$		$	
Price/Gross Liv. Area	$ ⊠	$ ⊠		$ ⊠		$ ⊠	
Data Source							
VALUE ADJUSTMENTS	DESCRIPTION	DESCRIPTION	+ (–) $ Adjustment	DESCRIPTION	+ (–) $ Adjustment	DESCRIPTION	+ (–) $ Adjustment
Sales or Financing Concessions							
Date of Sale/Time							
Location							
Site/View							
Design and Appeal							
Quality of Construction							
Age							
Condition							
Above Grade Room Count	Total ¦ Bdrms ¦ Baths	Total ¦ Bdrms ¦ Baths		Total ¦ Bdrms ¦ Baths		Total ¦ Bdrms ¦ Baths	
Gross Living Area	Sq. Ft.	Sq. Ft.		Sq. Ft.		Sq. Ft.	
Basement & Finished Rooms Below Grade							
Functional Utility							
Heating/Cooling							
Garage/Carport							
Porches, Patio, Pools, etc.							
Special Energy Efficient Items							
Fireplace(s)							
Other (e.g. kitchen equip., remodeling)							
Net Adj. (total)		☐+ ☐– $		☐+ ☐– $		☐+ ☐– $	
Indicated Value of Subject		$		$		$	

Comments on Sales Comparison: _____

INDICATED VALUE BY SALES COMPARISON APPROACH .... $ _____

INDICATED VALUE BY INCOME APPROACH (If Applicable) Estimated Market Rent $ _____ /Mo. x Gross Rent Multiplier _____ = $ _____

This appraisal is made ☐ "as is" ☐ subject to the repairs, alterations, inspections or conditions listed below ☐ completion per plans and specifications.

Comments and Conditions of Appraisal: _____

Final Reconciliation: _____

RECONCILIATION

This appraisal is based upon the above requirements, the certification, contingent and limiting conditions, and Market Value definition that are stated in
☐ FmHA, HUD &/or VA instructions.
☐ Freddie Mac Form 439 (Rev. 7/86)/Fannie Mae Form 1004B (Rev. 7/86) filed with client _____ 19 ___ ☐ attached.
I (WE) ESTIMATE THE MARKET VALUE, AS DEFINED, OF THE SUBJECT PROPERTY AS OF _____ 19 ___ to be $ _____

I (We) certify: that to the best of my (our) knowledge and belief the facts and data used herein are true and correct; that I (we) personally inspected the subject property, both inside and out, and have made an exterior inspection of all comparable sales cited in this report; and that I (we) have no undisclosed interest, present or prospective therein.

APPRAISER(S)	REVIEW APPRAISER (if applicable)	
Signature _____	Signature _____	☐ Did ☐ Did Not
Name _____	Name _____	Inspect Property

Freddie Mac Form 70   10/86   10CH.   AMERICAN REALTY FORMS, INC. • ALEXANDRIA, VIRGINIA • 1 (800) 642-9494 • 703-684-3500   Fannie Mae Form 1004   10/86

Exhibit 1.2

DEFINITION OF MARKET VALUE: The most probable price which a property should bring in a competitive and open market under all conditions requisite to a fair sale, the buyer and seller, each acting prudently, knowledgeably and assuming the price is not affected by undue stimulus. Implicit in this definition is the consummation of a sale as of a specified date and the passing of title from seller to buyer under conditions whereby: (1) buyer and seller are typically motivated; (2) both parties are well informed or well advised, and each acting in what he considers his own best interest; (3) a reasonable time is allowed for exposure in the open market; (4) payment is made in terms of cash in U.S. dollars or in terms of financial arrangements comparable thereto; and (5) the price represents the normal consideration for the property sold unaffected by special or creative financing or sales concessions* granted by anyone associated with the sale.

*Adjustments to the comparables must be made for special or creative financing or sales concessions. No adjustments are necessary for those costs which are normally paid by sellers as a result of tradition or law in a market area; these costs are readily identifiable since the seller pays these costs in virtually all sales transactions. Special or creative financing adjustments can be made to the comparable property by comparisons to financing terms offered by a third party institutional lender that is not already involved in the property or transaction. Any adjustment should not be calculated on a mechanical dollar for dollar cost of the financing or concession but the dollar amount of any adjustment should approximate the market's reaction to the financing or concessions based on the appraiser's judgment.

CERTIFICATION AND STATEMENT OF LIMITING CONDITIONS

CERTIFICATION: The Appraiser certifies and agrees that:

1. The Appraiser has no present or contemplated future interest in the property appraised; and neither the employment to make the appraisal, nor the compensation for it, is contingent upon the appraised value of the property.

2. The Appraiser has no personal interest in or bias with respect to the subject matter of the appraisal report or the participants to the sale. The "Estimate of Market Value" in the appraisal report is not based in whole or in part upon the race, color, or national origin of the prospective owners or occupants of the property appraised, or upon the race, color or national origin of the present owners or occupants of the properties in the vicinity of the property appraised.

3. The Appraiser has personally inspected the property, both inside and out, and has made an exterior inspection of all comparable sales listed in the report. To the best of the Appraiser's knowledge and belief, all statements and information in this report are true and correct, and the Appraiser has not knowingly withheld any significant information.

4. All contingent and limiting conditions are contained herein (imposed by the terms of the assignment or by the undersigned affecting the analyses, opinions, and conclusions contained in the report).

5. This appraisal report has been made in conformity with and is subject to the requirements of the Code of Professional Ethics and Standards of Professional Conduct of the appraisal organizations with which the Appraiser is affiliated.

6. All conclusions and opinions concerning the real estate that are set forth in the appraisal report were prepared by the Appraiser whose signature appears on the appraisal report, unless indicated as "Review Appraiser." No change of any item in the appraisal report shall be made by anyone other than the Appraiser, and the Appraiser shall have no responsibility for any such unauthorized change.

CONTINGENT AND LIMITING CONDITIONS: The certification of the Appraiser appearing in the appraisal report is subject to the following conditions and to such other specific and limiting conditions as are set forth by the Appraiser in the report.

1. The Appraiser assumes no responsibility for matters of a legal nature affecting the property appraised or the title thereto, nor does the Appraiser render any opinion as to the title, which is assumed to be good and marketable. The property is appraised as though under responsible ownership.

2. Any sketch in the report may show approximate dimensions and is included to assist the reader in visualizing the property. The Appraiser has made no survey of the property.

3. The Appraiser is not required to give testimony or appear in court because of having made the appraisal with reference to the property in question, unless arrangements have been previously made therefor.

4. Any distribution of the valuation in the report between land and improvements applies only under the existing program of utilization. The separate valuations for land and building must not be used in conjunction with any other appraisal and are invalid if so used.

5. The Appraiser assumes that there are no hidden or unapparent conditions of the property, subsoil, or structures, which would render it more or less valuable. The Appraiser assumes no responsibility for such conditions, or for engineering which might be required to discover such factors.

6. Information, estimates, and opinions furnished to the Appraiser, and contained in the report, were obtained from sources considered reliable and believed to be true and correct. However, no responsibility for accuracy of such items furnished the Appraiser can be assumed by the Appraiser.

7. Disclosure of the contents of the appraisal report is governed by the Bylaws and Regulations of the professional appraisal organizations with which the Appraiser is affiliated.

8. Neither all, nor any part of the content of the report, or copy thereof (including conclusions as to the property value, the identity of the Appraiser, professional designations, reference to any professional appraisal organizations, or the firm with which the Appraiser is connected), shall be used for any purposes by anyone but the client specified in the report, the borrower if appraisal fee paid by same, the mortgagee or its successors and assigns, mortgage insurers, consultants, professional appraisal organizations, any state or federally approved financial institution, any department, agency, or instrumentality of the United States or any state or the District of Columbia, without the previous written consent of the Appraiser; nor shall it be conveyed by anyone to the public through advertising, public relations, news, sales, or other media, without the written consent and approval of the Appraiser.

9. On all appraisals, subject to satisfactory completion, repairs, or alterations, the appraisal report and value conclusion are contingent upon completion of the improvements in a workmanlike manner.

Date:. . . . .　Appraiser(s) . . . .

Exhibit 2

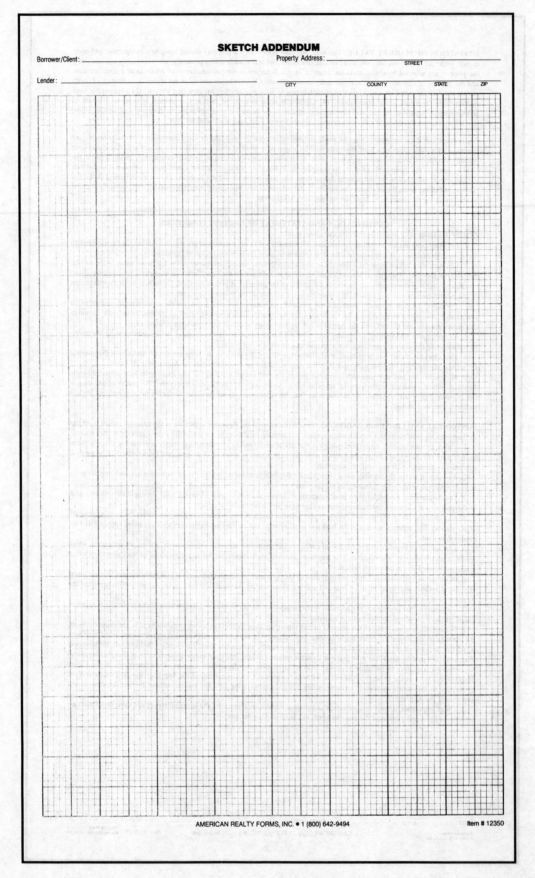

SKETCH ADDENDUM

Borrower/Client: _____

Property Address: _____
STREET

Lender: _____

CITY   COUNTY   STATE   ZIP

AMERICAN REALTY FORMS, INC. ● 1 (800) 642-9494   Item # 12350

Exhibit 3

LOCATION MAP & SKETCH ADDENDUM

Borrower/Client: _____

Lender: _____

Property Address: _____
STREET

CITY   COUNTY   STATE   ZIP

BUILDING SKETCH

LOCATION MAP

N

Exhibit 4

PHOTOGRAPH ADDENDUM: SUBJECT PROPERTY

Borrower/Client: _____

Lender: _____

Property Address: _____
STREET

CITY   COUNTY   STATE   ZIP

FRONT VIEW OF SUBJECT PROPERTY

REAR VIEW OF SUBJECT PROPERTY

STREET SCENE

☐ ADDITIONAL PHOTOGRAPHS ON REVERSE SIDE

AMERICAN REALTY FORMS, INC • ALEXANDRIA, VIRGINIA • 1 (800) 642-9494 • 703-684-3500

Exhibit 5

PHOTOGRAPH ADDENDUM: COMPARABLE SALES

Borrower/Client: _____   Property Address: _____

Lender: _____

CITY	COUNTY	STATE ZIP

COMPARABLE SALE #1

COMPARABLE SALE #2

COMPARABLE SALE #3

☐ ADDITIONAL PHOTOGRAPHS ON REVERSE SIDE

AMERICAN REALTY FORMS, INC. ● ALEXANDRIA, VIRGINIA ● 1 (800) 642-9494 ● 703-684-3500

Exhibit 6

SINGLE FAMILY COMPARABLE RENT SCHEDULE

This form is intended to provide the appraiser with a familiar format to estimate the market rent of the subject property. Adjustments should be made only for items of significant difference between the comparables and the subject property.

ITEM	SUBJECT	COMPARABLE NO. 1		COMPARABLE NO. 2		COMPARABLE NO. 3	
Address							
Proximity to Subject							
Date Lease Begins Date Lease Expires							
Monthly Rental	If Currently Rented: $	$		$		$	
Less: Utilities Furniture	$	$		$		$	
Adjusted Monthly Rent	$	$		$		$	
Data Source							
RENT ADJUSTMENTS	DESCRIPTION	DESCRIPTION	+(−) $ Adjustment	DESCRIPTION	+(−) $ Adjustment	DESCRIPTION	+(−) $ Adjustment
Rent Concessions							
Location/View							
Design and Appeal							
Age/Condition							
Above Grade Room Count	Total Bdrms Baths	Total Bdrms Baths		Total Bdrms Baths		Total Bdrms Baths	
Gross Living Area	Sq. Ft.	Sq. Ft.		Sq. Ft.		Sq. Ft.	
Other (e.g., basement, etc.)							
Other:							
Net Adj. (total)		+ − $		+ − $		+ − $	
Indicated Monthly Market Rent		$		$		$	

Comments on market data, including the range of rents for single family properties, an estimate of vacancy for single family rental properties, the general trend of rents and vacancy, and support for the above adjustments. (Rent concessions should be adjusted to the market, not to the subject property.)

Final Reconciliation of Market Rent:

I (WE) ESTIMATE THE MONTHLY MARKET RENT OF THE SUBJECT AS OF _____ 19____ TO BE $_____

Appraiser(s) SIGNATURE _____   Review Appraiser SIGNATURE _____
(If applicable)

NAME _____   NAME _____

Freddie Mac Form 1000 (8/88)   AMERICAN REALTY FORMS, INC. • ALEXANDRIA, VIRGINIA • 1 (800) 642-9494 • 703-684-3500   Fannie Mae Form 1007 (8/88)

Exhibit 7

APPRAISAL REPORT – INDIVIDUAL ☐ CONDOMINIUM OR ☐ PUD UNIT   File No. _____

To be completed by Lender

Borrower _____ Census Tract _____ Map Reference _____
Unit No. _____ Address _____ Project Name/Phase No. _____
City _____ County _____ State _____ Zip Code _____
Actual Real Estate Taxes $ _____ (yr.) Sales Price $ _____ Property Rights Appraised ☐ Fee ☐ Leasehold
Loan Charges to be Paid by Seller $ _____ Other Sales Concessions _____
Lender/Client _____
Occupant _____ Appraiser _____ Instructions to Appraiser _____
☐ FNMA 1073A required   ☐ FHLMC 465 Addendum A required   ☐ FHLMC 465 Addendum B required

NEIGHBORHOOD

	Urban	Suburban	Rural
Location	☐	☐	☐
Built Up	☐ Over 75%	☐ 25% to 75%	☐ Under 25%
Growth Rate ☐ Fully Developed	☐ Rapid	☐ Steady	☐ Slow
Property Values	☐ Increasing	☐ Stable	☐ Declining
Demand/Supply	☐ Shortage	☐ In Balance	☐ Oversupply
Marketing Time	☐ Under 3 Mos.	☐ 4-6 Mos.	☐ Over 6 Mos.

Present Land Use ____ % 1 Family ____ % 2-4 Family ____ % Apts. ____ % Condo
____ % Commercial ____ % Industrial ____ % Vacant
Change in Present Land Use ☐ Not Likely ☐ Likely* ☐ Taking Place*
*From _____ To _____

Predominant Occupancy ☐ Owner ☐ Tenant ____ % Vacant
Condominium   Price Range $ ____ to $ ____ Predominant $ ____
Age ____ yrs. to ____ yrs. Predominant ____ yrs.
Single Family: Price Range $ ____ to $ ____ Predominant $ ____
Age ____ yrs. to ____ yrs. Predominant ____ yrs.
Describe potential for additional Condo/PUD units in nearby area _____

NEIGHBORHOOD RATING	Good	Avg.	Fair	Poor
Adequacy of Shopping	☐	☐	☐	☐
Employment Opportunities	☐	☐	☐	☐
Recreational Facilities	☐	☐	☐	☐
Adequacy of Utilities	☐	☐	☐	☐
Property Compatibility	☐	☐	☐	☐
Protection from Detrimental Conditions	☐	☐	☐	☐
Police and Fire Protection	☐	☐	☐	☐
General Appearance of Properties	☐	☐	☐	☐
Appeal to Market	☐	☐	☐	☐

	Distance	Access or Convenience
Public Transportation	☐	☐
Employment Centers	☐	☐
Neighborhood Shopping	☐	☐
Grammar Schools	☐	☐
Freeway Access	☐	☐

NOTE: FHLMC/FNMA do not consider race or the racial composition of the neighborhood to be reliable appraisal factors.
Describe those factors, favorable or unfavorable, affecting marketability (e.g. public parks, schools, noise, view, mkt. area, population size and financial ability)

SITE

Lot Dimensions (if PUD) _____ = _____ Sq. Ft. ☐ Corner Lot   Project Density When Completed as Planned ____ Units/Acre
Zoning Classification _____ Present improvements ☐ do ☐ do not conform to zoning regulations
Highest and best use: ☐ Present use ☐ Other (specify) _____

	Public	Other (Describe)
Elec.	☐	_____
Gas	☐	_____
Water	☐	_____
San. Sewer	☐	_____
Underground Elec. & Tel.	☐	

OFF-SITE IMPROVEMENTS
Street Access: ☐ Public ☐ Private
Surface _____
Maintenance: ☐ Public ☐ Private
☐ Storm Sewer ☐ Curb/Gutter
☐ Sidewalk ☐ Street Lights

Project Ingress/Egress (adequacy) _____
Topo _____
Size/Shape _____
View Amenity _____
Drainage/Flood Conditions _____
Is the property located in a HUD identified Special Flood Hazard Area? ☐ No ☐ Yes

Comments (including any easements, encroachments or other adverse conditions) _____

PROJECT IMPROVEMENTS

☐ Existing   Approx. Year Built 19____   Original Use _____
☐ Condo ☐ PUD   ☐ Converted (19____)
TYPE ☐ Proposed   ☐ Under Construction
PROJECT ☐ Elevator   ☐ Walk-up No. of Stories ____
☐ Row or Town House   ☐ Other (specify) ____
☐ Primary Residence   ☐ Second Home or Recreational

If Completed: No. Phases ____ No. Units ____ No. Sold ____
If Incomplete: Planned No. Phases ____ No. Units ____ No. Sold ____
Units in Subject Phase: Total ____ Completed ____ Sold ____ Rented ____
Approx. No. Units for Sale: Subject Project ____ Subject Phase ____

Exterior Wall _____ Roof Covering _____ Security Features _____
Elevator: No. ____ Adequacy & Condition _____ Soundproofing: Vertical _____ Horizontal _____
Parking: Total No. Spaces ____ Ratio ____ Spaces/Unit ____ Type _____ No. Spaces for Guest Parking ____
Describe common elements or recreational facilities _____
Are any common elements, rec. facilities or parking leased to Owners Assoc.? _____ If yes, attach addendum describing rental, terms and options.

PROJECT RATING	Good	Avg.	Fair	Poor
Location	☐	☐	☐	☐
General Appearance	☐	☐	☐	☐
Amenities and Recreational Facilities	☐	☐	☐	☐
Density (units per acre)	☐	☐	☐	☐
Unit Mix	☐	☐	☐	☐
Quality of Constr. (mat'l & finish)	☐	☐	☐	☐
Condition of Exterior	☐	☐	☐	☐
Condition of Interior	☐	☐	☐	☐
Appeal to Market	☐	☐	☐	☐

SUBJECT UNIT

☐ Existing ☐ Proposed ☐ Under Constr.   Floor No. ____ Unit Livable Area ____ ☐ Basement ____ % Finished
Parking for Unit: No. ____ Type ____ ☐ Assigned ☐ Owned   Convenience to Unit _____

Room List	Foyer	Liv	Din	Kit	Bdrm	Bath	Fam	Rec	Lndry	Other
Basement										
1st Level										
2nd Level										

Floors: ☐ Hardwood ☐ Carpet over _____
Int. Walls: ☐ Drywall ☐ Plaster
Trim/Finish: ☐ Good ☐ Average ☐ Fair ☐ Poor
Bath Floor: ☐ Ceramic   ☐ Wainscot ☐ Ceramic
Windows (type): _____ ☐ Storm Sash ☐ Screens ☐ Combo
Kitchen Equipment: ☐ Refrigerator ☐ Range/Oven ☐ Fan/Hood ☐ Washer ☐ Dryer
☐ Intercom ☐ Disposal ☐ Dishwasher ☐ Microwave ☐ Compacter
HEAT: Type ____ Fuel ____ Cond. ____
AIR COND: ☐ Central ☐ Other   ☐ Adequate ☐ Inadequate
☐ Earth Sheltered Housing Design ☐ Solar Design/Landscape ☐ Solar Space Heat/Air Cond. ☐ Solar Hot Water
☐ Flue Damper ☐ Elec./Mech. Gas Furn. Ignition ☐ Auto Setback Thermostat ☐ Dble./Triple Glazed Windows ☐ Caulk/Weatherstrip
INSULATION (state R-Factor if known) ____ ☐ Walls ☐ Ceiling ☐ Floor ☐ Roof/Attic ☐ Water Heater
If rehab proposed, do plans and specs provide for adequate energy conservation? _____ If no, attach description of modification needed.
ENERGY EFFICIENCY APPEARS: ☐ High ☐ Adequate ☐ Low   Energy Audit: ☐ Yes (attach, if available) ☐ No
COMMENTS (special features, functional or physical inadequacies, modernization or repairs needed etc.) _____

UNIT RATING	Good	Avg.	Fair	Poor
Condition of Improvement	☐	☐	☐	☐
Room Sizes and Layout	☐	☐	☐	☐
Adequacy of Closets and Storage	☐	☐	☐	☐
Kit. Equip, Cabinets & Workspace	☐	☐	☐	☐
Plumbing = Adequacy and Condition	☐	☐	☐	☐
Electrical = Adequacy and Condition	☐	☐	☐	☐
Adequacy of Soundproofing	☐	☐	☐	☐
Adequacy of Insulation	☐	☐	☐	☐
Location within Project or View	☐	☐	☐	☐
Overall Livability	☐	☐	☐	☐
Appeal and Marketability	☐	☐	☐	☐
Est. Effective Age		____ to ____ yrs.		
Est. Remaining Economic Life		____ to ____ yrs.		

FHLMC Form 465 9/80   10 CH   AMERICAN REALTY FORMS, INC. • ALEXANDRIA, VIRGINIA • 1-800-642-9494 • 703-684-3500   FNMA Form 1073 9/80

Exhibit 8.1

Unit Charge $ _____ / Mo. x 12 = $ _____ /Yr. ($ _____ /Sq. Ft./year of livable area) Ground Rent (if any) $ _____ /yr.

Utilities included in unit charge: ☐ None ☐ Heat ☐ Air Cond. ☐ Electricity ☐ Gas ☐ Water ☐ Sewer

Note any fees, other than regular Condo/PUD charges, for use of facilities _____

To properly maintain the project and provide the services anticipated, the budget appears: ☐ High ☐ Adequate ☐ Inadequate

Compared to other competitive projects of similar quality and design subject unit charge appears: ☐ High ☐ Reasonable ☐ Low

Management Group: ☐ Owners Association ☐ Developer ☐ Management Agent (identify)

Quality of Management and its enforcement of Rules and Regulations appears: ☐ Superior ☐ Good ☐ Adequate ☐ Inadequate

Special or unusual characteristics in the Condo/PUD Documents or otherwise known to the appraiser that would affect marketability (if none, so state) _____

Comments _____

NOTE: FHLMC does not require the cost approach in the appraisal of condominium or PUD units.

Cost Approach (to be used only for detached, semi-detached, and town house units)

Reproduction Cost New _____ Sq. Ft. @ $ _____ per Sq. Ft. = ... $ _____

Less Depreciation: Physical $ _____ Functional $ _____ Economic $ _____ .... (_____)

Depreciated Value of Improvements: .... _____

Add Land Value (if leasehold, show only leasehold value-attach calculations) .... _____

Pro-rata Share of Value of Amenities .... $ _____

Total Indicated Value: ☐ FEE SIMPLE ☐ LEASEHOLD .... $ _____

Comments regarding estimate of depreciation and value of land and amenity package _____

The appraiser, whenever possible, should analyze two comparable sales from within the subject project. However, when appraising a unit in a new or newly converted project, at least two comparables should be selected from outside the subject project. In the following analysis, the comparable should always be adjusted to the subject unit and not vice versa. If a significant feature of the comparable is superior to the subject unit, a minus (-) adjustment should be made to the comparable; if such a feature of the comparable is inferior to the subject, a plus (+) adjustment should be made to the comparable.

LIST ONLY THOSE ITEMS THAT REQUIRE ADJUSTMENT

ITEM	Subject Property	COMPARABLE NO. 1		COMPARABLE NO. 2		COMPARABLE NO. 3	
Address-Unit No:							
Project Name							
Proximity to Subject							
Sales Price	$	$		$		$	
Price/Living Area	$	$		$		$	
Data Source							
Date of Sale and	DESCRIPTION	DESCRIPTION	+ (-) $ Adjustment	DESCRIPTION	+ (-) $ Adjustment	DESCRIPTION	+ (-) $ Adjustment
Time Adjustment							
Location							
Site/View							
Design and Appeal							
Quality of Constr.							
Age							
Condition							
Living Area, Room Count & Total	Total / B-rms / Baths	Total / B-rms / Baths		Total / B-rms / Baths		Total / B-rms / Baths	
Gross Living Area	Sq. Ft.	Sq. Ft.		Sq. Ft.		Sq. Ft.	
Basement & Bsmt.							
Finished Rooms							
Functional Utility							
Air Conditioning							
Storage							
Parking Facilities							
Common Elements and Recreation Facilities							
Mo. Assessment							
Leasehold/Fee							
Special Energy Efficient Items							
Other (eg. fire-places, kitchen equip. remodeling)							
Sales or Financing Concessions							
Net Adj. (total)		☐ + ☐ — $		☐ + ☐ — $		☐ + ☐ — $	
Indicated Value of Subject		$		$		$	

Comments on Market Data Analysis _____

INDICATED VALUE BY MARKET DATA APPROACH .... $ _____

INDICATED VALUE BY INCOME APPROACH (If applicable) Economic Market Rent $ _____ /Mo. x Gross Rent Multiplier _____ = $ _____

This appraisal is made ☐ "as is" ☐ subject to repairs, alterations, or conditions listed below ☐ subject to completion per plans and specifications

Comments and Conditions of Appraisal: _____

Final Reconciliation: _____

Construction Warranty ☐ Yes ☐ No Name of Warranty Program _____ Warranty Coverage Expires _____

This appraisal is based upon the above requirements, the certification, contingent and limiting conditions and Market Value definition that are stated in

☐ FHLMC Form 439 (Rev. 7/86) / FNMA Form 1004B (Rev. 7/86) filed with client _____ , 19 ____ ☐ attached

I ESTIMATE THE MARKET VALUE, AS DEFINED, OF SUBJECT PROPERTY AS OF _____ , 19 ____ to be $ _____

Appraiser(s) _____ Review Appraiser (if applicable) _____

Date Report Signed _____ , 19 ____ ☐ Did ☐ Did Not Physically Inspect Property

FHLMC Form 465 9/80 10 CH   REVERSE   AMERICAN REALTY FORMS, INC. • ALEXANDRIA, VIRGINIA • 1-800-642-9494 • 703-684-3500   FNMA Form 1073 9/80

Exhibit 8.2

PROJECT ANALYSIS ☐ CONDOMINIUM OR ☐ PUD – ADDENDUM A TO FHLMC FORM 465 9/80

INSTRUCTIONS

The following outlines the appraisal documentation required on each Condominium or PUD Unit loan submitted to FHLMC. The Individual Unit Appraisal Report and Project Analysis must be signed by an appraiser approved by the Seller/Servicer submitting the loan to FHLMC. It is preferred, but not required, that each of these forms be signed by the same appraiser. FHLMC does not require the cost approach in the appraisal of an individual condominium or PUD unit; however, if the lender or appraiser desires, the Cost Approach Section may be completed.

APPRAISAL REPORT INDIVIDUAL CONDOMINIUM OR PUD UNIT (FHLMC Form 465/FNMA Form 1073)

This must be submitted with each individual loan and the date of the estimate of Market Value must be within ninety (90) days of the date of closing of the mortgage.

PROJECT ANALYSIS (FHLMC Form 465 ADDENDUM A)

PART I: This must be submitted if less than 70% of the individual units in the project or section/phase have been sold. To establish this 70% requirement, a sale under an option to purchase contract cannot be counted, and multiple sales to one owner must be counted as one sale. A section/phase is one established by the Condo/PUD documents and is of sufficient size to contain an adequate number of units to support any common elements or recreational facilities, which are included in the sale price or appraised value of an individual unit. Subject section/phase may be combined with other completed, sold and occupied section(s)/phase(s) to meet this requirement, provided all are under a common Owners Association.

PART II: This must be submitted if the project is in the process of conversion or the conversion process has been completed less than two years.

ANALYSIS OF ANNUAL INCOME & EXPENSES—OPERATING BUDGET (FHLMC Form 465 ADDENDUM B/FNMA Form 1073A, Page 1)

This must be submitted ONLY if the project or section/phase has not been operated and managed by the Owners Association for at least two years. The upper portion is to be completed in detail by the Developer, Owners Association or Management Agent. The completion of the lower portion is the responsibility of the Seller/Servicer. It can be prepared by a staff member of the Seller/Servicer, a property manager or an approved appraiser, provided the person who signs is qualified, in the opinion of the Seller/Servicer, to make the required analysis.

To facilitate the submission, the Seller/Servicer may submit a clearly reproduced signed copy of Addendum A and/or Addendum B, if required, provided each is dated within 12 months of the date of the estimate of Market Value of the Individual Unit. If reproduced copies of the Addendum A and/or Addendum B are furnished the Appraiser, and submitted to FHLMC, the Appraiser who signs the Individual Condominium or PUD Unit Appraisal Report should note in the following Comments Section any significant changes or variances which are observed when making the inspection.

COMMENTS SECTION

Date _____ 19 _____ Signature(s) _____

PROJECT ANALYSIS

Part I must be completed if less than 70% of the individual units in the project or section/phase have been sold. To establish this 70% requirement, a sale under an option to purchase contract cannot be counted, and multiple sales to one owner must be counted as one sale. Part II must be completed if the project is in the process of conversion or the conversion process has been completed less than two years.

Project Name _____ Phase No._____

Address or Location _____ City _____ State _____ Zip _____

If the project is not completed, discuss the proposed overall development or conversion plan and stage of completion including the number of sections, units and recreational facilities per section and the estimated completion date of each section

Describe the common elements and recreational facilities, and comment on their adequacy, quality and condition _____

Are the recreational facilities available for use by individuals other than unit owners and guests? If yes, comment as to effect on marketability _____

Describe and comment on the adequacy of the following:

Storage space _____

Laundry facilities _____

Trash removal _____

Parking facilities _____

Soundproofing material _____

PART I

FHLMC Form 465 ADDENDUM A 9/80   AMERICAN REALTY FORMS, INC. ● ALEXANDRIA, VIRGINIA ● 1 (800) 642-9494 ● 703-684-3500

Exhibit 9.1

PROJECT ANALYSIS

Individual Unit Room Count			Livable Area Sq. Ft.	Price Range		Price Per Sq. Ft.		Monthly Assoc. Dues	Number of Units		
Total	Bedrooms	Baths							Planned	Sold	Completed
				$	to $	$	to $				
						TOTAL					

Discuss sales performance to date (per phase/section, if applicable) _____

Estimated absorption time, after completion, for _____ unsold units, at existing prices, in subject project/phase is _____ months.

Comment on any unit type(s) on which sales appear to be slow _____

Discuss project density as it compares to others in the area from a standpoint of marketability _____

State the approximate number of units currently for sale by developer in prior phases. If more than one prior phase, list for each phase _____

Discuss any rental or sales concessions being offered (if none known, so state) _____

If the developer(s) plans to retain any unsold units for rental, discuss number, voting rights and comparability of unit charges _____

Describe nearby competition including sale prices, rate of sales, sellout time, etc. _____

Describe potential for additional Condo/PUD units in nearby area, considering land availability, zoning, utilities, apartments subject to conversions, etc. _____

General comments including any probable changes in the economic base or neighborhood which would either favorably or unfavorably affect Condo/PUD sales

Date _____ 19 _____ Appraiser(s) Signature: _____

THIS SECTION MUST BE COMPLETED IF THE PROPERTY IS IN THE PROCESS OF CONVERSION OR RECENTLY CONVERTED

Itemize major alterations, modernization and repairs _____

Describe any incomplete items including estimated completion date _____

Has the Appraiser reviewed engineering reports on the structural integrity of the buildings and the condition of the major physical components and systems of the project? _____ If yes, describe any unfavorable conditions indicated _____

How many of the units were sold to tenants? _____ Percentage of sales price discount to tenants: _____ %.

Describe other sales concessions to tenants _____

Estimated absorption time for _____ unsold units is _____ months. How many of the unsold units are rented? _____

General Comments _____

Date _____ 19 _____ Appraiser(s) Signature: _____

FHLMC Form 465, ADDENDUM A 9/80   (REVERSE)

Exhibit 9.2

ANALYSIS OF ANNUAL INCOME AND EXPENSES — OPERATING BUDGET

For FNMA submissions complete both pages of this form. For FHLMC submissions complete this side only. Note: If developer control has terminated and the Home Owners Association has been controlled by Unit Owners for two or more years, FHLMC does not require this form.

Project Name _____

Address or Location _____ City _____ State _____ Zip _____

STATEMENT OF ANNUAL PROJECT OPERATING BUDGET AND RESERVES FOR THE YEAR 19_____

COMPLETE ONLY THOSE ITEMS WHICH ARE PAID BY OWNERS ASSOCIATION WHICH INCLUDES SUBJECT UNIT.

Budget below is for ☐ Entire project ☐ Phase No. _____

ADMINISTRATIVE EXPENSES

Office expenses, supplies, equipment rental, etc. . . . . $ _____

Telephone . . . . _____

Office salaries (itemize) _____ _____

Management fee (name of management firm) _____ _____

Legal and audit . . . . _____

_____ _____

OPERATING EXPENSES

Fuel . . . . _____

Utilities (Gas $ _____ Electricity $ _____ Water & Sewer $ _____) _____

Trash & Garbage Removal . . . . _____

Exterminating . . . . _____

Supplies . . . . _____

REPAIRS AND MAINTENANCE

Decorating (exterior and interior) . . . . _____

Cleaning expenses and supplies . . . . _____

Snow removal . . . . _____

Building maintenance and repairs . . . . _____

Elevator maintenance and repairs . . . . _____

Heating and air conditioning maintenance and repairs . . . _____

Pool maintenance and repairs . . . . _____

Parking area maintenance and repairs . . . . _____

Private street maintenance and repairs . . . . _____

Gardening and yard maintenance and repairs including shrub replacement . . . _____

Other (specify) _____ _____

Salaries (itemize including employee benefits and payroll taxes) _____

_____ _____

_____ _____

_____ _____

FIXED EXPENSES

Real estate taxes (if PUD) . . . . _____

Other (Taxes $ _____ Assessments $ _____ Regime Fees $ _____) . . . _____

Licenses . . . . _____

Insurance premiums . . . . _____

Ground rent . . . . _____

Recreational or other facilities rental . . . . _____

_____

TOTAL EXPENSES . . . . _____

REPLACEMENT RESERVES List Each Item	Yrs. of Estimated Remaining Life	Expected Replacement Cost	Average Yearly Cost
		$ _____	$ _____

TOTAL REPLACEMENT RESERVES . . . . $ _____

TOTAL ANNUAL EXPENSES AND REPLACEMENT RESERVES . . . . $ _____

Project Annual Income from: Condo/PUD charges $ _____ Other $ _____ Total $ _____

Itemize other income _____

If the income is less than the budget, discuss deficit _____

Actual funds now held: for payment of operating expenses $ _____ in Replacement Reserve fund $ _____

No. of Unit Owners over 30 days delinquent in Association charges _____ in Special Assessment charges _____

Explain any indebtedness or leases on the common area or parking, utilities or other facilities (if none, so state) _____

Certified Correct: Organization _____

Date _____ By _____ Title _____

I certify that I have analyzed the above Statement of Operating Budget and Reserves. In my opinion, except as stated below, the items as set forth in this Budget appear sufficient to maintain the project, including replacement of major items, in a manner adequate to protect its marketability.

Comments on Budget and Reserves _____

_____

_____

_____

Date _____ 19____ Organization _____

By _____ Title _____

TO BE COMPLETED BY SELLER/SERVICER, OWNERS ASSOCIATION OR MANAGEMENT AGENT

Seller/Servicer's Use Only

FHLMC Form 465 ADDENDUM B 9/80

FNMA Form 1073A 9/80
1 of 2

AMERICAN REALTY FORMS, INC. ● ALEXANDRIA, VIRGINIA ● 1 (800) 642-9494 ● 703-684-3500

Exhibit 10.1

Required for FNMA · FHLMC does not require this page.

STATEMENT OF ANNUAL PROJECT INCOME AND EXPENSES FOR THE YEAR 19____
COMPLETE ONLY THOSE ITEMS WHICH WERE RECEIVED OR PAID BY THE OWNERS ASSOCIATION WHICH INCLUDES SUBJECT UNIT.

GROSS ANNUAL INCOME:
Condo/PUD charges $ _____ per mo. X _____ units X 12 = ... $ _____
Other Income (itemized) : _____
TOTAL INCOME FROM ALL SOURCES $ _____

ADMINISTRATIVE EXPENSES
Office expenses, supplies, equipment rental, etc. . . . . $ _____
Telephone . . . .
Office salaries (itemized) _____
Management fee (name of management firm) _____
Legal and audit . . . .
_____

OPERATING EXPENSES
Fuel . . . .
Utilities (Gas $ _____ Electricity $ _____ Water & Sewer $ _____) . . . .
Trash and Garbage Removal . . . .
Exterminating . . . .
Supplies . . . .
_____

REPAIRS AND MAINTENANCE
Decorating (exterior and interior) . . . .
Cleaning expenses and supplies . . . .
Snow removal . . . .
Building maintenance and repairs . . . .
Elevator maintenance and repairs . . . .
Heating and air conditioning maintenance and repairs . . . .
Pool maintenance and repairs . . . .
Parking area maintenance and repairs . . . .
Private street maintenance and repairs . . . .
Gardening and yard maintenance and repairs including shrub replacement . . . . .
Replacement expenses (itemize) _____
_____
_____

Other (specify) _____
_____
_____

Salaries (itemize including employee benefits and payroll taxes) _____
_____
_____

FIXED EXPENSES
Real estate taxes (if PUD) . . . .
Other taxes or assessments . . . .
Licenses . . . .
Insurance premiums . . . .
Ground rent . . . .
Recreational or other facilities rental . . . .

TOTAL EXPENSES . . . . $ _____

TOTAL ANNUAL NET SURPLUS (deficit) . . . . $ _____

Discuss disposition of surplus or, if (deficit), method of funding: _____
_____
_____

Does inspection of project indicate that funds spent during preceding year for maintenance and repairs were sufficient to maintain project in a manner likely to be acceptable to the market? If answer is no, explain _____
_____
_____
_____
_____

Above statement of income and expenses is certified to be correct.
Organization _____

By _____   Title _____   Date _____

AMERICAN REALTY FORMS, INC. ● ALEXANDRIA, VIRGINIA ● 1 (800) 642-9494 ● 703-684-3500   884   FNMA Form 1073A 9/80
2 of 2

Exhibit 10.2

E-R-C
is a non-profit membership
organization concerned with the
transfer of corporate employees.

EMPLOYEE RELOCATION COUNCIL
RESIDENTIAL APPRAISAL REPORT

Client File No.: _____

Homeowner: _____

Address: _____

_____

Date: _____

Appraiser File No.: _____

Appraiser: _____

DEFINITIONS RELATING TO THE RELOCATION APPRAISAL

Purpose of the Relocation Appraisal:

To establish the most probable sales price for a relocated employee's primary residence, assuming an arm's length transaction.

Definition of the Relocation Appraisal:

The most probable sales price of a residential housing unit, using the market approach to value.

Definition of Market Data Approach to Value:

The price at which a property would most probably sell, if exposed to the market for a reasonable period of time in an "as is" condition, where payment is made in cash or its equivalent.

Implicit in this definition is the consummation of the sale with passing of title from seller to buyer under conditions whereby:

1. Both parties are well informed and acting in what they consider their best interests.

2. A reasonable amount of time is allowed for exposure in the local market. (A reasonable period is typically up to 120 days unless market conditions indicate otherwise.)

3. Financing, if any, is on terms generally available in the community and typical for the property type in its locale. (If an assumption or special financing is available, justify its specific effect on the appraised value on page four in the "Sales or Financing Concessions" grid section, and discuss the impact if any, on page six in the "Special Financing" section.)

4. Forecasting is applied in making an estimate of a future happening or condition, based on an analysis of trends in the recent past, tempered with analytical judgment concerning the probable extent to which these trends will continue into the future and reflecting an estimated impact, if any, upon value.

INSTRUCTIONS TO APPRAISERS

General Guidelines

The appraiser must observe the following general guidelines in determining the appraised value opinion. The appraiser is to:

1) Estimate the appraised value considering the property in an "as is" condition as of the date of inspection. "As is" condition should reflect the cost of those items (e.g., repairs, decorations, etc.) required to make the subject comparable with similar properties in that market area from a buyer's point of view. If there is a circumstance where the appraiser is unable to determine the "as is" condition (e.g., in-process construction or improvements, suspected structural problems, water related problems, roof, etc.) notify the client immediately.

2) Stress what the property should sell for in the current marketplace. In this regard, give particular attention to the analysis of comparable sales (or homes under contract), competitive listings, supply and demand, and overall market conditions. The appraiser should also consider other factors and make necessary adjustments such as the residence's exposure to the market, availability and terms of financing, over-improvements and location.

3) Reflect in your appraised value opinion as of the date of the appraisal:

   a) An adjustment for any value that may have been created by comparable sale prices (or homes under contract) that were influenced by discount points paid by the seller of FHA, VA, or conventional mortgages; or those comparables which were sold by loan assumption, installment contract, seller carry back, or any form of preferential financing. This also applies to situations where the seller pays certain buyer costs such as buy downs, fees, or credits. In these situations, adjustments should be noted and described for the specific comparable sale.

   b) The difference in discount points between those charged on the comparable sales (or homes under contract) and those charged currently if it is the custom of lenders to charge discount points to sellers on conventional mortgages.

4) Develop the appraised value opinion, assuming the property is free and clear of all non-mortgage encumbrances with the owner responsible for discharging all liens and unpaid installments of special assessments for improvements completed. If the special assessments are still pending and the improvements are not yet completed, the appraiser should include any additional value which may attribute to the pending improvements. If paying off an assessment provides the subject property with an advantage over the comparable sales and competitive listings, this should be reflected in the appraised value.

Page 1 of 6

© Copyright 1986, Employee Relocation Council

Exhibit 11.1

Appendix B—Appraisal Report Forms **257**

Procedural Guidelines

In addition to the aforementioned general guidelines, the appraiser must be aware of and follow these specific guidelines:

1. Appraisers are frequently the sole visible representative of the client to the relocated homeowner. Therefore, a professional and courteous manner should be presented.

2. When an appraiser assignment is directed to a specific individual, that appraiser must personally inspect the property and complete the assignment unless approval for a substitution is obtained from the client.

3. On the day the appraiser is contacted with the appraisal request, contact should be made with the employee (or spouse) for an appointment. If the employee (or spouse) cannot be reached on the same day, let the client know so they can assist in locating the homeowner.

4. Inspect the property within two working days and contact the client with the verbal figure within four working days of the original request (unless the transferring employee delays the process). If the appraisal cannot be completed in the required time frame, or if the appraiser will be unavailable to discuss the assignment after completion, the assignment should not be accepted.

5. If access to the property cannot be gained, if valuation problems arise, or if an inspection is required for clarification (such as a structural engineer's report, etc.), the client should be called immediately.

6. Completed copies of the typewritten appraisal report should be mailed within seven working days of the original request (providing there are not delays created by the homeowner).

7. Sufficient time should be taken when inspecting the subject property to impart confidence to the homeowner even if the appraiser is familiar with the property.

8. Consider any information that the homeowner feels is important to the value of his/her home.

9. The appraiser should not discuss his/her appraisal opinions or reveal sensitive information to anyone other than the client. If the homeowner (or spouse) asks general questions as it relates to the appraisal process, feel free to discuss generalities.

10. The appraiser who arrives at the homeowner's property while another appraiser or broker is present, should leave the property immediately and reschedule the appointment.

11. An appraiser will not accept an appraisal assignment if there is a conflict of interest such as: recently appraising the house for another party, an association with the listing agent/company, etc.

12. Appraisers will not solicit a listing or generate a referral as a result of an appraisal assignment.

13. Call the client to clarify the instructions if they are not completely understood.

14. Include the following exhibits:

    a. Photos of the front and rear view of the residence, street scene of the property, factors in near-by vicintiy which affect subject property, either favorably or adversely.
    b. Photos of all comparables. (Please attach all photos separately.)
    c. Sketch of the floor plan of subject property (not necessarily to scale).
    d. Sketch of plot plan showing all improvements (not necessarily to scale).
    e. Map of the subdivision or area depicting locations of the subject, comparable sold properties and competitive listings.

BUILDING SKETCH (if grid is inadequate, please attach separate grid)

ERC-2 Rev. 4/86

Exhibit 11.2

EMPLOYEE RELOCATION COUNCIL
RESIDENTIAL APPRAISAL REPORT

SUBJECT INFORMATION

Homeowner

Property Address

City   County   State   Zip Code

Legal Description

Property Rights Appraised ☐ Fee ☐ Leasehold ☐ DeMinimis PUD

Client   Address

Occupant   Appraiser

NEIGHBORHOOD

				Good	Avg.	Fair	Poor
Location	☐ Urban	☐ Suburban	☐ Rural				

Built Up ☐ Over 75% ☐ 25% to 75% ☐ Under 25% Employment Stability

Growth Rate ☐ Fully Dev. ☐ Rapid ☐ Steady ☐ Slow Convenience to Employment

Property Values ☐ Increasing ☐ Stable ☐ Declining Convenience to Shopping

Demand/Supply ☐ Shortage ☐ In Balance ☐ Over Supply Convenience to Schools

Marketing Time ☐ Under 4 Mos. ☐ 4-6 Mos. ☐ Over 6 Mos. Adequacy of Public Transportation

Present Land Use ____ % 1 Family ____ % 2-4 Family ____ % Apts. ____ % Condo ____ % Commercial Recreational Facilities

____ % Industrial ____ % Vacant ____ %   Adequacy of Utilities

Change in Present Land Use ☐ Not Likely ☐ Likely (*) ☐ Taking Place (*) Property Compatibility

(*) From _____ To _____ Protection from Detrimental Conditions

Predominant Occupancy ☐ Owner ☐ Tenant ____ % Vacant Police and Fire Protection

Single Family Price Range $ _____ to $ _____ Predominant Value $ _____ General Appearance of Properties

Single Family Age _____ Yrs. to _____ Yrs. Predominant Age _____ Yrs. Appeal to Market

Comments including those factors, favorable or unfavorable, affecting marketability (e.g. public parks, schools, view, noise) _____

SITE

Dimensions _____ = _____ Sq. Ft. or Acres ☐ Corner Lot

Zoning Classification _____ Present Improvements ☐ do ☐ do not conform to zoning regulations

Highest and Best Use ☐ Present Use ☐ Other (specify) _____

	Public	Other (Describe)	OFF SITE IMPROVEMENTS	Topo _____
Elec.			Street Access: ☐ Public ☐ Private	Size _____
Gas			Surface _____	Shape _____
Water			Maintenance: ☐ Public ☐ Private	View _____
San. Sewer			☐ Storm Sewer ☐ Curb/Gutter	Drainage _____
	☐ Undergrnd. Elect. & Tel.		☐ Sidewalk ☐ Street Lights	Is the property located in a HUD Identified Special Flood Hazard Area? ☐ No ☐ Yes

Comments (favorable or unfavorable including any apparent adverse easements, encroachments or other adverse conditions) _____

IMPROVEMENTS

☐ Existing ☐ Under Constr. VALID PERMIT? ☐ No. Units ____ Type (det., duplex, semi-det., etc.) Design (rambler, split level, etc.) Exterior Walls

Yrs. Actual ____ Effective ____ to ____ No. Stories

Roof Material Gutters and Downspouts ☐ NONE Window (Type): Insulation ☐ None ☐ Floor

☐ Storm Sash ☐ Screens ☐ Combination ☐ Ceiling ☐ Roof ☐ Wall

☐ Manufactured Housing BSMT. ____ % Basement ☐ Floor Drain Finished Ceiling _____

Foundation Walls ☐ Outside Entrance ☐ Sump Pump Finished Walls _____

☐ Concrete Floor ____ % Finished Finished Floor _____

☐ Slab on Grade ☐ Crawl Space Evidence of: ☐ Dampness ☐ Termites ☐ Settlement

Refer comments on improvements and property condition to page 5 in the Supplement under "PROPERTY CONDITION."

ROOM LIST

Room List	Foyer	Living	Dining	Kitchen	Den	Family Rm.	Rec. Room	Bedrooms	No. Baths	Laundry	Other
Basement											
1st Level											
2nd Level											

Finished area above grade contains a total of ____ rooms ____ bedrooms ____ baths. *Gross Living Area ____ Sq. Ft. Bsmt. Area ____ Sq. Ft.

INTERIOR FINISH AND EQUIPMENT

Kitchen Equip.: ☐ Refrigerator ☐ Range/Oven ☐ Disposal ☐ Dishwasher ☐ Fan/Hood ☐ Compact. ☐ Washer ☐ Dryer

HEAT: Type ____ Fuel ____ Cond. ____ AIR COND.: ☐ Central ☐ Other ____ ☐ Adequate ☐ Inadequate

						PROPERTY RATING	Good	Avg.	Fair	Poor
Floors	☐ Hardwood	☐ Carpet Over ____				Quality of Construction (Materials and Finish)				
Walls	☐ Drywall	☐ Plaster				Condition of Improvements				
Trim/Finish	☐ Good	☐ Average ☐ Fair	☐ Poor			Room sizes and layout				
Bath Floor	☐ Ceramic					Closets and Storage				
Bath Wainscot	☐ Ceramic					Insulation - adequacy				

Energy related (including energy efficient items) _____

Plumbing - adequacy and condition

Electrical - adequacy and condition

ATTIC: ☐ Yes ☐ No ☐ Stairway ☐ Drop-Stair ☐ Scuttle ☐ Floord. Compatibility to Neighborhood

Finished (Describe) _____ ☐ Heated Overall Livability

CAR STORAGE ☐ Garage ☐ Blt. In ☐ Attached ☐ Detach ☐ Car Port Appeal and Marketability

No. Cars ____ ☐ Adequate ☐ Inadequate Condition

Describe specialty items (e.g. FIREPLACES, PATIOS, POOL, FENCES, etc.) and detail your comments of functional or physical inadequacies, repairs needed, modernization, etc. on page 5 of the Supplement under "SPECIAL FEATURES" and/or "PROPERTY CONDITION."

*See definition on page 4 and reflect same in the "Gross Living Area" section of the "MARKET DATA ANALYSIS."

Exhibit 11.3

ERC ⌂
VALUATION SECTION

IMPORTANT

*GROSS LIVING AREA (square footage) is defined as the calculation of the total living area, which is a measurement taken around the outside of the house and includes finished and habitable above-grade living area only. Finished (and unfinished) basement areas are calculated and shown separately (in both the Room List and Market Data Analysis sections of the appraisal report) but are not included in the total gross living area.

The appraiser has recited three recent sales of properties most similar and proximate to subject and has considered these in the market analysis. The description includes a dollar adjustment, reflecting market reaction to those items of significant variation between the subject and comparable properties. If a significant item in the comparable property is superior to, or more favorable than, the subject property, a minus (-) adjustment is made, thus reducing the indicated value of subject; if a significant item in the comparable is inferior to, or less favorable than, the subject property, a plus (+) adjustment is made, thus increasing the indicated value of the subject.

MARKET DATA ANALYSIS

ITEM	Subject Property	COMPARABLE NO. 1		COMPARABLE NO. 2		COMPARABLE NO. 3	
Address							
Proximity to Subj							
Sales Price		$		$		$	
Closing Date							
Data Source							
Market / Time Adjustments	DESCRIPTION	DESCRIPTION	+ (-) $ Adjustment	DESCRIPTION	+ (-) $ Adjustment	DESCRIPTION	+ (-) $ Adjustment
Location							
Site/View							
Design and Appeal							
Quality of Const.							
Age							
Condition							
Living Area Room Count and Total	Total / B-rms. / Baths	Total / B-rms. / Baths		Total / B-rms. / Baths		Total / B-rms. / Baths	
*Gross Living Area	Sq. Ft.	Sq. Ft.		Sq. Ft.		Sq. Ft.	
Basement & Bsmt. Finished Rooms							
Functional Utility							
Air Conditioning							
Garage/Car Port							
Porches, Patio, Pools, etc.							
Energy Related Items (e.g. solar, heat pumps, etc.)							
Special Features (e.g. fireplaces, kit. equipment, remodeling, etc.)							
Other							
Sales or Financing Concessions							
Net Adj. (Total)		Plus / Minus	$	Plus / Minus	$	Plus / Minus	$
Indicated Value of Subject			$		$		$

Describe "other" for Subject: _____

SUPPLEMENT TO MARKET DATA ANALYSIS

The Market Data Analysis for each comparable sale should include adjustments as appropriate for market condition and **days-on-market** under the heading "Market/Time Adjustment." "Sales or Financing Concessions" should include adjustments for terms of sale.
Reconcile each of the value-related differences between the subject property and the individual comparables, including but not limited to *financing, terms, condition, location, appeal, deferred maintenance, utility, style, view, days-on-market, and other amenities.*

Comparable Sale #1 _____

Comparable Sale #2 _____

Comparable Sale #3 _____

Comments on Market Data and Final Reconciliation: _____

INDICATED VALUE BY MARKET DATA APPROACH .... $ _____

The above indicated value by the market data approach is also to appear on page 6.

Construction Warranty ☐ Yes ☐ No   Name of Warranty Program _____   Warranty Coverage Expires _____

If yes, is it transferable? ☐ Yes ☐ No

TO ORDER: BLAKEWOOD BUSINESS FORMS 1 (800) 443-1004
© Copyright 1986, Employee Relocation Council

ERC-2 Rev. 4-86

Exhibit 11.4

**EMPLOYEE RELOCATION COUNCIL SUPPLEMENT TO THE
RESIDENTIAL APPRAISAL REPORT**

Describe the value related differences between the subject property and the competing listings (including *financing, terms, condition, location, appeal, deferred maintenance, utility, style, view, days-on-market, and other amenities*). Are seller financing, discount points and/or other seller concessions being offered? *If yes, explain below.*

COMPETING LISTINGS

Listing #1 Address: _____
Original List Price $ _____ Current List Price $ _____ Date of Most Recent Price Revision _____

Proximity to Subject	Style	Approx. Gross Living Area	Total Rms.	Bed-Rms.	Baths	Garage and Type	Lot Size	Approx. Yr. Blt.	Days-On-Market

Comments: _____

Listing #2 Address: _____
Original List Price $ _____ Current List Price $ _____ Date of Most Recent Price Revision _____

Proximity to Subject	Style	Approx. Gross Living Area	Total Rms.	Bed-Rms.	Baths	Garage and Type	Lot Size	Approx. Yr. Blt.	Days-On-Market

Comments: _____

Listing #3 Address: _____
Original List Price $ _____ Current List Price $ _____ Date of Most Recent Price Revision _____

Proximity to Subject	Style	Approx. Gross Living Area	Total Rms.	Bed-Rms.	Baths	Garage and Type	Lot Size	Approx. Yr. Blt.	Days-On-Market

Comments: _____

SPECIAL FEATURES

Specifically describe any special features which affect the appraised value of the subject property such as upgrades, additions, improvements, etc.

PROPERTY CONDITION

Is Urea-Formaldehyde Foam Insulation (UFFI) present or suspected? ☐ Yes ☐ No
Explain _____
Has the owner secured the necessary permits for all additions and improvements? ☐ Yes ☐ No
How was this verified? _____
List any required inspections (e.g., municipal, state, certificate of occupancy, federal, etc.).

List any recommended inspections and why (e.g., structural, mechanical, roof, etc.).

As required in paragraph 1 of the General Guidelines relative to "as is" condition, list in descending order of importance any repairs and improvements you recommend to put the home in marketable condition. Estimate the cost of each recommended repair/improvement. Furnish photographs if warranted.

PROPERTY ACREAGE, TAXES & FEES

Is the property size excessive for the area? ☐ Yes ☐ No   Is the subject comprised of more than one parcel? ☐ Yes ☐ No
Explain: _____
What are the actual real estate taxes? _____
Period covered from _____ to _____
Are taxes typical for the area and price range? ☐ Yes ☐ No
If no, explain: _____

List any special assessments (including municipal, Homeowner Association dues, etc.) or additional encumbrances/liens (existing or pending).

TO ORDER: BLAKEWOOD BUSINESS FORMS, PHONE 1-800-443-1004   ERC-2 Rev. 4/86

Exhibit 11.5

PERSONAL PROPERTY

Note all personal property in your estimated appraised value.

_____
_____
_____
_____

SPECIAL FINANCING

Does the subject property have an assumable loan? ☐ Yes ☐ No

If yes, how was this verified? _____

Is any value for it included in the final appraised value estimate on pages 4 and 6? ☐ Yes ☐ No

If yes, describe the terms of the assumption and discuss its impact on potential purchasers. _____
_____
_____

How does this "Special Financing," if any, compare with the noted COMPETING LISTINGS? (Indicate by listing order)
_____
_____
_____
_____
_____

LISTING INFORMATION

Is the subject property currently listed? ☐ Yes ☐ No

List price(s): Original $ _____ Current $ _____

Listing company/address _____

Listing agent _____ Phone (_____) _____

How long has property been exposed to market? _____

MARKET CONDITIONS

Describe current local financing availability, interest rates, and terms. _____
_____
_____

Describe current local supply/demand and other pertinent economic issues. _____
_____
_____

Describe future economic trends in these and other pertinent factors and how they may impact on the subject property.
_____
_____
_____
_____
_____
_____

ADDITIONAL COMMENTS

_____
_____
_____
_____
_____
_____
_____
_____
_____
_____
_____
_____
_____
_____

I certify that I have personally inspected both the exterior and interior of the foregoing described property, and I have no interest in such, either present or contemplated. I further certify that I have adhered to the terms of the assignment set forth in the definitions and appraiser instructions. (If more than one appraiser is involved in this assignment, including inspection and review, two signatures are required.) My appraised value estimate (as shown on page 4) for the subject property based on the aforementioned statement is $ _____ .

Appraiser(s) Signature _____

Appraiser(s) (please type) _____ Date _____

Review Appraiser(s) Signature (if applicable) _____

Review Appraiser(s) (if applicable please type) _____ Date _____

Tax I.D. Number: _____

ERC-2 Rev.4/86

Exhibit 11.6

SMALL RESIDENTIAL INCOME PROPERTY APPRAISAL REPORT

File No. _____

Subject

Property address			
City	County	State	Zip code
Legal description			
Owner/occupant	Tax year	R.E. taxes $	
Sale price $	Date of sale	Census tract	Map reference

Property rights appraised ☐ Fee simple ☐ Leasehold ☐ Condominium or ☐ PUD HOA$ _____ /Mo.

Borrower _____ Project Name _____

Loan charges/concessions to be paid by seller $ _____

Lender/client _____

Appraiser _____

Lender discretionary use

Sale price $ _____
Gross monthly rent $ _____
Closing date _____
Mortgage amount $ _____
Mortgage type _____
Discount points and other concessions
Paid by seller $ _____
Source _____

Neighborhood

Location	☐ Urban	☐ Suburban	☐ Rural
Built up	☐ Over 75%	☐ 25-75%	☐ Under 25%
Growth rate	☐ Rapid	☐ Stable	☐ Slow
Property values	☐ Increasing	☐ Stable	☐ Declining
Demand/supply	☐ Shortage	☐ In balance	☐ Over supply
Marketing time	☐ Under 3 mos.	☐ 3-6 mos.	☐ Over 6 mos.

Predominant occupancy
☐ Owner
☐ Tenant
☐ Vacant (0-5%)
☐ Vacant (over 5%)

Single family housing
PRICE $ (000) / AGE (yrs)
Low
High
Predominant

Typical 2-4 family bldg. Type _____
No. stories _____ No. units _____
Age _____ yrs. Condition _____
Typical rents $ _____ to $ _____
☐ Increasing ☐ Stable ☐ Declining
Est. neighborhood apt. vacancy _____ %
☐ Increasing ☐ Stable ☐ Declining

Present land use %
One family _____
2-4 family _____
Multifamily _____
Commercial _____
Industrial _____
Vacant _____

Land use change
☐ Not likely
☐ Likely
☐ In process
To: _____

2-4 family housing
PRICE $ (000) / AGE (yrs)
Low
High
Predominant

Rent controls ☐ Yes* ☐ No ☐ Likely*

Neighborhood analysis	Good	Avg.	Fair	Poor
Employment stability	☐	☐	☐	☐
Convenience to employment	☐	☐	☐	☐
Convenience to shopping	☐	☐	☐	☐
Convenience to schools	☐	☐	☐	☐
Adequacy of public transportation	☐	☐	☐	☐
Recreation facilities	☐	☐	☐	☐
Adequacy of utilities	☐	☐	☐	☐
Property compatibility	☐	☐	☐	☐
Protection from detrimental cond.	☐	☐	☐	☐
Police & fire protection	☐	☐	☐	☐
General appearance of properties	☐	☐	☐	☐
Appeal to market	☐	☐	☐	☐

Note: Race and the racial composition of the neighborhood are not considered reliable appraisal factors.

Description of neighborhood boundaries: _____

Description of those factors, favorable or unfavorable, that affect marketability (including neighborhood stability, appeal, property conditions, vacancies, *rent control, etc.). _____

The following available listings represent the most current, similar, and proximate competitive properties to the subject property in the subject neighborhood. This analysis is intended to evaluate the inventory currently on the market competing with the subject property in the subject neighborhood and recent price and marketing time trends affecting the subject property. (Listings outside the subject neighborhood are not considered applicable). The listing comparables can be the rental or sale comparables if they are currently for sale.

ITEM	SUBJECT	COMPARABLE LISTING NO. 1	COMPARABLE LISTING NO. 2	COMPARABLE LISTING NO. 3
Address				
Proximity to subject				
Listing price	$	☐ Unf. ☐ Furn. $	☐ Unf. ☐ Furn. $	☐ Unf. ☐ Furn. $
Approximate GBA				
Data source				
# Units/Tot. rms./BR/BA				
Approximate year built				
Approx. days on market				

Comparison of listings to subject property: _____

Reconciliation: Description and analysis of the general market conditions that affect 2-4 family properties in the subject neighborhood (including the above neighborhood indicators of growth rate, property values, demand/supply, and marketing time) and the prevalence and impact in the subject market area regarding loan discounts, interest buydowns, and concessions; and identification of trends in listing prices, average days on market and any change over past year, etc.: _____

Site

Dimensions _____
Site area _____ Corner lot ☐ No ☐ Yes
Specific zoning classification and description _____
Zoning compliance ☐ Legal ☐ Legal nonconforming (Grandfathered use) ☐ Illegal ☐ No zoning
Highest & best use as improved: ☐ Present use ☐ Other use (explain) _____

Topography _____
Size _____
Shape _____
Drainage _____
View _____
Landscaping _____
Driveway _____
Apparent easements _____

Utilities	Public	Other	Off-site Improvements	Type	Public	Private
Electricity			Street			
Gas			Curb/gutter			
Water			Sidewalk			
Sanitary sewer			Street lights			
Storm sewer			Alley			

FEMA Special flood hazard area ☐ Yes* ☐ No
*FEMA Zone/Map Date _____
*FEMA Map No. _____

Comments (apparent adverse easements, encroachments, special assessments, slide areas, illegal or legal nonconforming zoning, use, etc.): _____

Freddie Mac Form 72 10/89 2-4 units   PAGE 1 OF 4   Fannie Mae Form 1025 2-4 units 10/89

AMERICAN REALTY FORMS, INC. • (800) 642-9494

Exhibit 12.1

PROPERTY DESCRIPTION
& ANALYSIS, continued

SMALL RESIDENTIAL INCOME PROPERTY APPRAISAL REPORT

Description of improvements

General description	Exterior description (Materials/condition)	Foundation	Insulation (R-value if known)
Units/bldgs. _____ /	Foundation _____	Slab _____	☐ Roof
Stories _____	Exterior walls _____	Crawl space _____	☐ Ceiling
Type (det./att.) _____	Roof surface _____	Sump Pump _____	☐ Walls
Design (style) _____	Gutters & dwnspts. _____	Dampness _____	☐ Floor
Existing/proposed _____	Window type _____	Settlement _____	☐ None
Under construction _____	Storm sash/Screens _____	Infestation _____	Adequacy _____
Year Built _____	Manufactured housing* ☐ Yes ☐ No	Basement _____ % of 1st floor area	Energy efficient items: _____
Effective age(yrs.) _____	*(Complies with the HUD Manufactured Housing Construction and Safety Standards.)	Basement finish _____	

Units	Level(s)	Foyer	Living	Dining	Kitchen	Den	Family rm.	# Bedrooms	# Baths	Laundry	Other	Sq. ft./unit	Total ☑

Improvements contain: _____ Rooms; _____ Bedroom(s); _____ Bath(s); _____ Square feet of GROSS BUILDING AREA

GROSS BUILDING AREA (GBA) IS DEFINED AS THE TOTAL FINISHED AREA (INCLUDING COMMON AREAS) OF THE IMPROVEMENTS BASED UPON EXTERIOR MEASUREMENTS.

Surfaces	(Materials/condition)	Heating		Kitchen equip. (# / unit- cond.)		Attic		Improvement analysis	Good	Avg.	Fair	Poor
Floors	_____	Type	_____	Refrigerator	_____	☐ None		Quality of construction	☐	☐	☐	☐
Walls	_____	Fuel	_____	Range/oven	_____	☐ Stairs		Condition of improvements	☐	☐	☐	☐
Trim/finish	_____	Condition	_____	Disposal	_____	☐ Drop stair		Room sizes/layout	☐	☐	☐	☐
Bath floor	_____	Adequacy	_____	Dishwasher	_____	☐ Scuttle		Closets and storage	☐	☐	☐	☐
Bath wainscot	_____	Cooling		Fan/hood	_____	☐ Floor		Energy efficiency	☐	☐	☐	☐
Doors	_____	Central	_____	Compactor	_____	☐ Heated		Plumbing—adequacy & condition	☐	☐	☐	☐
		Other	_____	Washer/dryer	_____	☐ Finished		Electrical—adequacy & condition	☐	☐	☐	☐
		Condition	_____	Microwave	_____	☐ Unfinished		Kitchen cabinets—adequacy & cond.	☐	☐	☐	☐
Fireplace(s)	# _____	Adequacy	_____	Intercom	_____			Compatibility to neighborhood	☐	☐	☐	☐
Car storage:		☐ Garage		☐ Attached		☐ Adequate		☐ None	Appeal & marketability	☐	☐	☐	☐
No. cars:		☐ Carport		☐ Detached		☐ Inadequate		☐ Offstreet	Estimated remaining economic life			_____ years	

Comments on repairs needed, additional features, modernization, etc.: _____

_____

_____

_____

_____

Additional comments on neighborhood, site and description of improvements

Depreciation (physical, functional, and external inadequacies, etc.): _____

_____

_____

_____

Environmental conditions observed by or known to the appraiser: _____

_____

_____

VALUATION ANALYSIS

Purpose of Appraisal is to estimate Market Value as defined in the Certification & Statement of Limiting Conditions.

Cost approach

Comments on cost approach, accrued depreciation, and estimated site value:

ESTIMATED REPRODUCTION COST—NEW—OF IMPROVEMENTS:

_____ Sq. Ft. @ $ _____	= $ _____	
_____ Sq. Ft. @ $ _____	= _____	
_____ Sq. Ft. @ $ _____	= _____	
_____ Sq. Ft. @ $ _____	= _____	
Extras _____	= _____	
	= _____	
Special Energy Efficient Items _____	= _____	
Porches, Patios, etc. _____	= _____	
Total Estimated Cost New	= $ _____	

	Physical	Functional	External
Less			
Depreciation			= $ _____

Depreciated Value of Improvements .... = $ _____

Site Imp. "as is" (driveway, landscaping, etc.) ..... = $ _____

ESTIMATED SITE VALUE .... = $ _____
(If leasehold, show only leasehold value.)

INDICATED VALUE BY COST APPROACH .... = $ _____

Exhibit 12.2

VALUATION ANALYSIS, continued   **SMALL RESIDENTIAL INCOME PROPERTY APPRAISAL REPORT**

Comparable rental data

At least three rental comparables should be reported and analyzed in this section. The rental comparables should represent the most current rental information on properties as similar and proximate to the subject property as possible. (This comparison is based on current rental data, therefore, the rental comparables typically are not the same comparables used in the sales comparison analysis.) The appraisal report should assure the reader that the units and properties selected as comparables are comparable to the subject property (both the units and the overall property) and accurately represent the rental market for the subject property (unless otherwise stated within the report).

ITEM	SUBJECT	COMPARABLE RENTAL NO. 1	COMPARABLE RENTAL NO. 2	COMPARABLE RENTAL NO. 3
Address				
Proximity to subject				
Lease dates (if available)				
Rent survey date				
Data source				
Rent concessions				
Description of property—units, design, appeal, age, vacancies, and conditions	No. Units No. Vac. Yr. Blt.:	No. Units No. Vac. Yr. Blt.:	No. Units No. Vac. Yr. Blt.:	No. Units No. Vac. Yr. Blt.:

	Rm. Count	Size		Rm. Count	Size	Total	Rm. Count	Size	Total	Rm. Count	Size	Total
	Tot Br Ba	Sq. Ft.		Tot Br Ba	Sq. Ft.	Monthly Rent	Tot Br Ba	Sq. Ft.	Monthly Rent	Tot Br Ba	Sq. Ft.	Monthly Rent
Individual unit breakdown						$			$			$

Utilities, furniture, and amenities included in rent				

Functional utility, basement, heating/cooling, project amenities, etc.				

Reconciliation of rental data and support for estimated market rents for the individual subject units (including the adjustments used, the adequacy of comparables, rental concessions, etc.) _____

Subject's rent schedule   The rent schedule reconciles the applicable indicated monthly market rents to the appropriate subject unit, and provides the estimated rents for the subject property. The appraiser must review the rent characteristics of the comparable sales to determine whether estimated rents should reflect actual or market rents. For example, if actual rents were available on the sales comparables and used to derive the gross rent multiplier (GRM), actual rents for the subject should be used. If market rents were used to construct the comparables' rents and derive the GRM, market rents should be used. The total gross estimated rent must represent rent characteristics consistent with the sales comparable data used to derive the GRM. The total gross estimated rent is not adjusted for vacancy.

				ACTUAL RENTS			ESTIMATED RENTS		
Unit	Lease Date		No. Units Vacant	Per Unit		Total Rents	Per Unit		Total Rents
	Begin	End		Unfurnished	Furnished		Unfurnished	Furnished	
				$	$	$	$	$	$
						$			$

Other monthly income (itemize) _____ $ _____

Vacancy: Actual last year ____ % Previous year ____ % Estimated: ____ % $ ____ Annually   **Total gross estimated rent** $ _____

Utilities included in estimated rents: ☐ Electric ☐ Water ☐ Sewer ☐ Gas ☐ Oil ☐ Trash collection ☐ _____

Comments on the rent schedule, actual rents, estimated rents (especially regarding differences between actual and estimated rents), utilities, etc.: _____

Exhibit 12.3

SMALL RESIDENTIAL INCOME PROPERTY APPRAISAL REPORT

Sales comparison analysis

The undersigned has recited three recent sales of properties most similar and proximate to the subject property and has described and analyzed these in this analysis. If there is a significant variation between the subject and comparable properties, the analysis includes a dollar adjustment reflecting the market reaction to those items or an explanation supported by the market data. If a significant item in the comparable property is superior to, or more favorable than, the subject property, a minus (–) adjustment is made, thus reducing the indicated value of subject; if a significant item in the comparable is inferior to, or less favorable than, the subject property, a plus (+) adjustment is made, thus increasing the indicated value of the subject. **[(1) Sales Price ÷ Gross Monthly Rent)]**

ITEM	SUBJECT	COMPARABLE SALE NO. 1	COMPARABLE SALE NO. 2	COMPARABLE SALE NO. 3
Address				
Proximity to subject				
Sales price	$	Unf. Furn. $	Unf. Furn. $	Unf. Furn. $
Sales price per GBA	$	$	$	$
Gross monthly rent	$	$	$	$
Gross mo. rent mult. (1)				
Sales price per unit	$	$	$	$
Sales price per room	$	$	$	$
Data source				

ADJUSTMENTS	DESCRIPTION	DESCRIPTION	+(–) $ Adjustment	DESCRIPTION	+(–) $ Adjustment	DESCRIPTION	+(–) $ Adjustment
Sales or financing concessions							
Date of sale/time							
Location							
Site/view							
Design and appeal							
Quality of construction							
Year built							
Condition							
Gross Building Area	Sq. ft.	Sq. ft.		Sq. ft.		Sq. ft.	
Unit breakdown	No. of units / Rm. count (Tot Br Ba) / No. Vac.	No. of units / Rm. count (Tot Br Ba) / No. Vac.		No. of units / Rm. count (Tot Br Ba) / No. Vac.		No. of units / Rm. count (Tot Br Ba) / No. Vac.	
Basement description							
Functional utility							
Heating/cooling							
Parking on/off site							
Project amenities and fee (If applicable)							
Other							
Net Adj. (total)		+ – $		+ – $		+ – $	
Adj. sales price of comparables		$		$		$	

Comments on sales comparison (including reconciliation of all indicators of value as to consistency and relative strength and evaluation of the typical investors'/purchasers' motivation in that market): _____

INDICATED VALUE BY SALES COMPARISON APPROACH $ _____

Analysis of any current agreement of sale, option, or listing of the subject property and analysis of any prior sales of subject and comparables within one year of the date of appraisal: _____

Income Approach

Total gross monthly estimated rent $ _____ x gross rent multiplier (GRM) _____ = $ _____ INDICATED VALUE BY INCOME APPROACH

Comments on income approach (including expense ratios, if available, and reconciliation of the GRM) _____

Reconciliation

INDICATED VALUE BY SALES COMPARISON APPROACH .... $ _____
INDICATED VALUE BY INCOME APPROACH .... $ _____
INDICATED VALUE BY COST APPROACH .... $ _____

This appraisal is made [ ] "as is" [ ] subject to the repairs, alterations, inspections or conditions listed below [ ] subject to completion per plans and specifications.

Comments and conditions of appraisal: _____

Final reconciliation: _____

This appraisal is based upon the above conditions and the certification, contingent and limiting conditions, and Market Value definition that are stated in Freddie Mac Form 439/Fannie Mae Form 1004B (Rev. _____) [ ] attached or [ ] filed with client on _____ or [ ] other attached.

I (WE) ESTIMATE THE MARKET VALUE, AS DEFINED, OF THE SUBJECT PROPERTY AS OF _____ to be $ _____

I (We) certify that to the best of my (our) knowledge and belief the facts and data used herein are true and correct; that I (we) personally inspected the subject property, both inside and out, and have personally made an exterior inspection of all comparables cited in this report; and that I (we) have no undisclosed interest, present or prospective therein.

APPRAISER(S) SIGNATURE _____
NAME _____

REVIEW APPRAISER (if applicable) SIGNATURE _____
NAME _____
[ ] Did [ ] Did not inspect property

Freddie Mac Form 72 10/89 2-4 units   PAGE 4 OF 4   Fannie Mae Form 1025 2-4 units 10/89

Exhibit 12.4

Operating Income Statement
One- to Four-Family Investment Property and Two- to Four-Family Owner-Occupied Property

Property Address

Street	City	State	Zip Code

General Instructions: This form is to be prepared jointly by the loan applicant, the appraiser, and the lender's underwriter. The applicant must complete the following schedule indicating each unit's rental status, lease expiration date, current rent, market rent, and the responsibility for utility expenses. Rental figures must be based on the rent for an "unfurnished" unit.

	Currently Rented	Expiration Date	Current Rent Per Month	Market Rent Per Month	Utility Expense	Paid By Owner	Paid By Tenant
Unit No. 1	Yes ___ No ___	_____	$_____	$_____	Electricity.............	☐	☐
Unit No. 2	Yes ___ No ___	_____	$_____	$_____	Gas...................	☐	☐
Unit No. 3	Yes ___ No ___	_____	$_____	$_____	Fuel Oil	☐	☐
Unit No. 4	Yes ___ No ___	_____	$_____	$_____	Fuel (Other)	☐	☐
Total			$_____	$_____	Water/Sewer	☐	☐
					Trash Removal	☐	☐

The applicant should complete all of the income and expense projections and for existing properties provide actual year-end operating statements for the past two years *(for new properties the applicant's projected income and expenses must be provided)*. This Operating Income Statement and any previous operating statements the applicant provides must then be sent to the appraiser for review, comment, and/or adjustments next to the applicant's figures *(e.g., Applicant/Appraiser 288/300)*. If the appraiser is retained to complete the form instead of the applicant, the lender must provide to the appraiser the aforementioned operating statements, mortgage insurance premium, HOA dues, leasehold payments, subordinate financing, and/or any other relevant information as to the income and expenses of the subject property received from the applicant to substantiate the projections. The underwriter should carefully review the applicant's/appraiser's projections and the appraiser's comments concerning those projections. The underwriter should make any final adjustments that are necessary to more accurately reflect any income or expense items that appear unreasonable for the market. *(Real estate taxes and insurance on these types of properties are included in PITI and not calculated as an annual expense item.)* Income should be based on current rents, but should not exceed market rents. When there are no current rents because the property is proposed, new, or currently vacant, market rents should be used.

Annual Income and Expense Projection for Next 12 months

Income *(Do not include income for owner-occupied units)*	By Applicant/Appraiser	Adjustments by Lender's Underwriter
Gross Annual Rental *(from unit(s) to be rented)*	$_____	$_____
Other Income *(include sources)*	+_____	+_____
Total	$_____	$_____
Less Vacancy/Rent Loss	−_____ (%)	−_____ (%)
Effective Gross Income	$_____	$_____

Expenses *(Do not include expenses for owner-occupied units)*

Electricity	_____	_____
Gas	_____	_____
Fuel Oil	_____	_____
Fuel ....(Type - _____)	_____	_____
Water/Sewer	_____	_____
Trash Removal	_____	_____
Pest Control	_____	_____
Other Taxes or Licenses	_____	_____
Casual Labor	_____	_____
This includes the costs for public area cleaning, snow removal, etc., even though the applicant may not elect to contract for such services.		
Interior Paint/Decorating	_____	_____
This includes the costs of contract labor and materials that are required to maintain the interiors of the living units.		
General Repairs/Maintenance	_____	_____
This includes the costs of contract labor and materials that are required to maintain the public corridors, stairways, roofs, mechanical systems, grounds, etc.		
Management Expenses	_____	_____
These are the customary expenses that a professional management company would charge to manage the property.		
Supplies	_____	_____
This includes the costs of items like light bulbs, janitorial supplies, etc.		
Total Replacement Reserves - See Schedule on Pg. 2..................	_____	_____
Miscellaneous	_____	_____
....	_____	_____
....	_____	_____
....	_____	_____
....	_____	_____
....	_____	_____
....	_____	_____
....	_____	_____
Total Operating Expenses	$_____	$_____

Freddie Mac
Form 998 Aug 88

Page 1 of 2

Fannie Mae
Form 216 Aug 88

AMERICAN REALTY FORMS, INC. • ALEXANDRIA, VIRGINIA • 1 (800) 642-9494 • 703-684-3500

Exhibit 13.1

Replacement Reserve Schedule

Adequate replacement reserves must be calculated regardless of whether actual reserves are provided for on the owner's operating statements or are customary in the local market. This represents the total average yearly reserves. Generally, all equipment and components that have a remaining life of more than one year—such as refrigerators, stoves, clothes washers/dryers, trash compactors, furnaces, roofs, and carpeting, etc.—should be expensed on a replacement cost basis.

Equipment	Replacement Cost	Remaining Life		By Applicant/ Appraiser	Lender Adjustments
Stoves/Ranges	@ $ _____	ea. ÷ ____ Yrs. x	_____ Units = $ _____		$ _____
Refrigerators	@ $ _____	ea. ÷ ____ Yrs. x	_____ Units = $ _____		$ _____
Dishwashers	@ $ _____	ea. ÷ ____ Yrs. x	_____ Units = $ _____		$ _____
A/C Units	@ $ _____	ea. ÷ ____ Yrs. x	_____ Units = $ _____		$ _____
C. Washer/Dryers	@ $ _____	ea. ÷ ____ Yrs. x	_____ Units = $ _____		$ _____
HW Heaters	@ $ _____	ea. ÷ ____ Yrs. x	_____ Units = $ _____		$ _____
Furnace(s)	@ $ _____	ea. ÷ ____ Yrs. x	_____ Units = $ _____		$ _____
(Other)	@ $ _____	ea. ÷ ____ Yrs. x	_____ Units = $ _____		$ _____
Roof	@ $ _____	÷ ____ Yrs. x One Bldg. =	$ _____		$ _____

Carpeting (Wall to Wall)

Remaining Life

(Units) _____ Total Sq. Yds. @ $____ Per Sq. Yd. ÷ ____ Yrs. = $ _____ $ _____

(Public Areas) _____ Total Sq. Yds. @ $____ Per Sq. Yd. ÷ ____ Yrs. = $ _____ $ _____

Total Replacement Reserves. (Enter on Pg. 1) $ _____ $ _____

Operating Income Reconciliation

$ _____ − $ _____ = $ _____ ÷ 12 = $ _____
Effective Gross Income Total Operating Expenses Operating Income Monthly Operating Income

$ _____ − $ _____ = $ _____
Monthly Operating Income Monthly Housing Expense Net Cash Flow

(Note: Monthly Housing Expense includes principal and interest on the mortgage, hazard insurance premiums, real estate taxes, mortgage insurance premiums, HOA dues, leasehold payments, and subordinate financing payments.)

Underwriter's instructions for 2-4 Family Owner-Occupied Properties

- If Monthly Operating Income is a positive number, enter as "Net Rental Income" in the "Gross Monthly Income" section of Freddie Mac Form 65/Fannie Mae Form 1003. If Monthly Operating Income is a negative number, it must be included as a liability for qualification purposes.

- The borrower's monthly housing expense-to-income ratio must be calculated by comparing the total Monthly Housing Expense for the **subject** property to the borrower's stable monthly income.

Underwriter's instructions for 1-4 Family Investment Properties

- If Net Cash Flow is a positive number, enter as "Net Rental Income" in the "Gross Monthly Income" section of Freddie Mac Form 65/Fannie Mae Form 1003. If Net Cash Flow is a negative number, it must be included as a liability for qualification purposes.

- The borrower's monthly housing expense-to-income ratio must be calculated by comparing the total monthly housing expense for the borrower's **primary residence** to the borrower's stable monthly income.

Appraiser's Comments (Including sources for data and rationale for the projections)

_____   _____   _____
Appraiser Name   Appraiser Signature   Date

Underwriter's Comments and Rationale for Adjustments

_____   _____   _____
Underwriter Name   Underwriter Signature   Date

Freddie Mac
Form 998 Aug 88

Page 2 of 2

Fannie Mae
Form 216 Aug 88

AMERICAN REALTY FORMS, INC. • ALEXANDRIA, VIRGINIA • 1 (800) 642-9494 • 703-684-3500

Exhibit 13.2

APPRAISAL REPORT—RESIDENTIAL INCOME PROPERTY
This Form may be used for appraisal of income producing properties provided the loan requested does not exceed $750,000.

TO BE COMPLETED BY LENDER

Borrower/Client _____   File No. _____
Property Address _____   Map Reference _____
City _____ County _____ State _____ Zip Code _____   Census Tract
Legal Description _____

Current Sale Price (if applicable) $_____ Date of Sale _____ Loan Requested $ _____
Terms of Sale _____
Property Rights Appraised ☐ Fee   ☐ Leasehold (attach completed Lease Analysis FHLMC Form 461)
Lender _____ Lender's Address _____

Instructions to Appraiser: The purpose of this Appraisal is to estimate the current Market Value of the Subject Property. The Definition of Market Value is as set forth in Certification And Statement Of Limiting Conditions (FHLMC 439).

Note: FHLMC/FNMA do not consider the racial composition of the neighborhood to be a relevant factor and it must not be considered in the appraisal.

Other Information _____
Appraisal requested from _____ Date _____ 19 ___ By _____

Items 1, 2, 4, 5 & 6 are required. Attach additional items and check box if items are considered appropriate for this appraisal or are requested by Lender.
1. ☐ Descriptive photographs of subject property
2. ☐ Descriptive photographs of street scene
3. ☐ Photographs of _____
4. ☐ Sketch or floor plan of typical units
5. ☐ Owner's current certified rent roll if existing, or pro forma if proposed or incomplete
6. ☐ Owner's income and expense statement 19 ___, or pro forma income and expense statement
7. ☐ Map(s)
8. ☐ Plot plan or survey
9. ☐ Qualifications of Appraiser
10. ☐ Lease Analysis FHLMC Form 461 (required if leasehold interest appraised)
11. ☐ Summary of reciprocal agreements with other owners for use of parking, driveways, recreational facilities, private streets, (required if applicable)
12. ☐
13. ☐

NEIGHBORHOOD

Location ☐ Urban ☐ Suburban ☐ Rural
Built-up ☐ Over 75% ☐ 25% to 75% ☐ Under 25%
Present land use ___ % Condominiums ___ % 1-Family ___ % Apartments
___ % Commercial ___ %
Change in present land use ☐ Not Likely ☐ Likely (*) ☐ Taking Place (*)
(*) From _____ To _____
Property values ☐ Increasing ☐ Stable ☐ Declining
Housing demand/supply ☐ In Balance ☐ Shortage ☐ Oversupply
Predominant occupancy ☐ Owner ☐ Tenant ___ % Vacant
Condominium: Price range $_____ to $_____ Predominant $_____
Age _____ yrs. to _____ yrs. Predominant _____ yrs.
Single Family: Price range $_____ to $_____ Predominant $_____
Age _____ yrs. to _____ yrs. Predominant _____ yrs.
Typical apartment: Type _____ No. Stories _____
No. Units _____ Age _____ yrs. Condition _____
Rent Levels: ☐ Increasing ☐ Stable ☐ Declining
Estimated neighborhood apartment vacancy rate _____ % ☐ Decreasing ☐ Stable ☐ Increasing   Rent Controls ☐ No ☐ Yes (comments on page 4 if Yes)

OVERALL RATING	Good	Avg.	Fair	Poor
Employment Stability				
Adequacy of Utilities				
Convenience of Schools				
Police and Fire Protection				
Recreational Facilities				
Property Compatibility				
Protection from Detrimental Conditions				
General Appearance of Properties				
Appeal to Market				

	Distance	Access or Convenience
Public Transportation		
Employment Centers		
Shopping Facilities		
Grammar Schools		
Freeway Access		

Describe any incompatible land uses and overall property appeal and maintenance level _____

Describe any oversupply of units in area by type and rental _____

Describe any shortage of units in area by type and rental _____

Describe potential for additional units in area considering land availability, zoning, utilities, etc. _____

Is population of relevant market area of insufficient size, diversity and financial ability to support subject property and its amenities? _____ If yes, specify.

Describe any probable changes in the economic base of neighborhood which would favorably or adversely affect apartment rentals (e.g. employment centers, zoning)

General comments including either favorable or unfavorable elements not mentioned (e.g. public parks, view, noise, parking congestion) _____

SITE

Dimensions _____ Area _____ Sq. ft. or Acres
Zoning (classification, uses and densities permitted) _____
Present improvements ☐ do ☐ do not conform to zoning regulations
Highest and best use ☐ Present use ☐ Other (specify) _____

	Public	Comm.	Individual
Electricity	☐	☐	☐
Gas	☐	☐	☐
Water	☐	☐	☐
Sanitary Sewer	☐	☐ Sep. Tnk.	☐

☐ Underground Electricity & Telephone

Street Surface ☐ Public ☐ Private
☐ Storm Sewer
☐ Curb & Gutter
☐ Sidewalk ☐ Alley
☐ Street Lights

Ingress and Egress (Adequacy) _____
Topography _____
View Amenity _____
Drainage and Flood Conditions _____

Is the property located in a HUD Identified Special Flood Hazard Area?

COMMENTS (including any easements or encroachments or any nonconforming use(s) of present improvements) _____

FHLMC Form 71B-Rev. 8/77   AMERICAN REALTY FORMS, INC. • ALEXANDRIA, VIRGINIA • 1 (800) 642-9494 • 703-684-3500   Page 1

Exhibit 14.1

DESCRIPTION OF IMPROVEMENTS

☐ Existing Approx. Year Built 19___ ☐ Proposed ☐ Under Construction ☐ Elevator ☐ Walk-up No. of Stories _____ ☐ Row or Townhouse

No. of Bldgs. _____ No. of Units _____ No. of Rooms _____ No. of Baths _____ Parking Spaces: No. _____ Type _____

Basic Structural System _____ Exterior Walls _____ Roof Covering _____

Interior Walls _____ Floors _____ Bath Floor and Walls _____

Insulation _____ Adequacy _____ Adequacy and Soundproofing _____

Heating: ☐ Central ☐ Individ. Type _____ Fuel _____ Condition _____

Air Conditioning: ☐ Central ☐ Individ. Describe _____ Adequacy and Condition _____

Elevator(s): Number _____ Automatic _____ Adequacy and Condition _____

Security Features _____

Kitchen cabinets, drawers and counter space ☐ Adequate ☐ Inadequate
☐ Range/Oven ☐ Fan/Hood ☐ Dishwasher ☐ Disposal
☐ Refrigerator ☐ Washer ☐ Dryer ☐ _____

Hot Water Heater(s) _____

Plumbing Fixtures _____

Electrical Service _____

Recreational Facilities _____

OVERALL PROPERTY RATING	Good	Avg.	Fair	Poor
General appearance of property				
Quality of construction (materials and finish)				
Condition of improvements				
Rooms size and layout				
Closets and storage				
Plumbing-adequacy and condition				
Electrical-adequacy and condition				
Amenities and parking facilities				
Appeal to Market				

Effective Age _____ Yrs. **Estimated Remaining Economic Life** _____ Yrs.

COMMENTS: (Special features, functional or physical inadequacies, repairs needed, modernization etc.) _____

COST APPROACH

LAND SALES (complete ONLY if appropriate for this appraisal)	Zoning	Area	Sales Price	Date	Price per Sq. Ft. or per Unit	
1.		☑ $			$	Per
2.		☑ $			$	Per
3.		☑ $			$	Per

Comments & Reconciliation

Estimated Land Value $ _____

APARTMENT BUILDING(S)-ESTIMATED REPRODUCTION COST NEW

___ x ___ = ___ Sq. ft. x ___ (Stories) = ___ Sq. ft. x $ ___ $ _____
___ x ___ = ___ Sq. ft. x ___ (Stories) = ___ Sq. ft. x $ ___ $ _____
___ x ___ = ___ Sq. ft. x ___ (Stories) = ___ Sq. ft. x $ ___ $ _____

OTHER IMPROVEMENTS _____ $ _____
$ _____
$ _____

TOTAL ESTIMATED COST NEW OF IMPROVEMENTS $ _____

LESS DEPRECIATION _____

DEPRECIATED VALUE OF IMPROVEMENTS $ _____
ADD-ESTIMATED LAND VALUE $ _____
INDICATED VALUE BY THE COST APPROACH (IN FEE SIMPLE) $ _____
IF LEASEHOLD DEDUCT VALUE OF FEE INTEREST (ATTACH CALCULATIONS) $ _____
INDICATED VALUE BY THE COST APPROACH (LEASEHOLD) $ _____

COMPARABLE RENTAL DATA

ITEM	COMPARABLE NO. 1	COMPARABLE NO. 2	COMPARABLE NO. 3
Address			
Proximity to subj.			
Rental survey date			
Brief description of property improvements	No. Units / No. Vacant / Age / Yrs	No. Units / No. Vacant / Age / Yrs	No. Units / No. Vacant / Age / Yrs
Individual unit breakdown	Rm. Count (Tot BR b) / Size Sq. Ft. / Monthly Rent ($ ☑ Rm)	Rm. Count (Tot BR b) / Size Sq. Ft. / Monthly Rent ($ ☑ Rm)	Rm. Count (Tot BR b) / Size Sq. Ft. / Monthly Rent ($ ☑ Rm)
Utilities, furniture and amenities included in rent			
Comparison to subject including rental concessions, if any			

MONTHLY RENT SCHEDULE SUBJECT

Utilities included in actual rents: ☐ Water ☐ Gas ☐ Heat ☐ Electric ☐ Air Conditioning ☐ _____
Utilities included in forecasted rents: ☐ Water ☐ Gas ☐ Heat ☐ Electric ☐ Air Conditioning ☐ _____

No. of Units	Unit Rm Count (Tot. BR b)	Total Rooms	Sq Ft Area Per Unit	No. Units Vacant	ACTUAL RENTS Per Unit Unfurnished	ACTUAL RENTS Per Unit Furnished	Total Rents	FORECASTED RENTS Per Unit Unfurnished	FORECASTED RENTS Per Unit Furnished	Total Rents	Per Sq. Ft. or Room
					$	$	$	$	$		c $
TOTAL							$			$	

FHLMC FORM 71B - Rev. 8/77

Page 2

Exhibit 14.2

270 *Appendix B—Appraisal Report Forms*

ITEM	SUBJECT	COMPARABLE NO. 1	COMPARABLE NO. 2	COMPARABLE NO. 3
Address				
Proximity to subject				
Map code				
Lot size				
Brief description of building improvements	No. Units: ____ No. Vac ____ Year Built: 19 ____	No. Units: ____ No. Vac ____ Year Built: 19 ____	No. Units: ____ No. Vac ____ Year Built: 19 ____	No. Units: ____ No. Vac ____ Year Built: 19 ____
Quality				
Condition				
Recreational facilities				
Parking				
Tenant appeal				

MARKET APPROACH

	No. of Units	UNIT ROOM COUNT Total	BR	Bath	No. of Units	UNIT ROOM COUNT Total	BR	Bath	No. of Units	UNIT ROOM COUNT Total	BR	Bath	No. of Units	UNIT ROOM COUNT Total	BR	Bath
Unit breakdown																

ITEM	SUBJECT	COMPARABLE NO. 1	COMPARABLE NO. 2	COMPARABLE NO. 3
Util. paid by owner				
Data source				
Price	$ □ Unf. □ F	$ □ Unf. □ F	$ □ Unf. □ F	$ □ Unf. □ F
Sale-Listing-Offer				
Date of sale				
Terms (Including conditions of sale and financing terms)				

Complete as many of the following items as possible using data effective at time of sale

ITEM	SUBJECT	COMPARABLE NO. 1	COMPARABLE NO. 2	COMPARABLE NO. 3
Gross Annual Income	$	$	$	$
Gross Ann. Inc. Mult. (1)				
Net Annual Income	$	$	$	$
Expense Percentage (2)	%	%	%	%
Overall Cap. Rate (3)	%	%	%	%
Price per unit	$	$	$	$
Price per room	$	$	$	$
Price gross bldg. area	$ /sq. ft. bldg. area	$ /sq. ft. bldg. area	$ /sq. ft. bldg. area	$ /sq. ft. bldg. area

(1) Sale Price ÷ Gross Annual Income   (2) Total Annual Expenses ÷ Total Gross Annual Income   (3) Net Annual Income ÷ Price

RECONCILIATION: _____

INDICATED VALUE BY MARKET APPROACH

INCOME APPROACH

INCOME		EXPENSES	ACTUAL	FORECASTED
Total Monthly Apartment Forecasted Rents .... $____		Real Estate Taxes* .... $____		$____
Other Monthly Income (Itemize) ____		Other taxes or licenses		
____ $____		Insurance		
Total Gross Monthly Forecasted Income .... $____		Unsubordinated ground rent		
Total Gross Annual Forecasted Income .... $____		Fuel		
Less Forecasted Vacancy and Collection Loss (___ %) $ (____)		Gas		
Effective Gross Annual Income .... $____		Electricity		
Less Forecasted Expenses & Replacement Reserves ... $ (____)		Water and sewer		
Net Annual Income from Total Property .... $____		Trash removal		
Less Return on and Recapture of Depreciated Value of		Pest control		
Furnishings ($____ " ___ %) .... $ (____)		Maintenance and repairs		
Net Annual Income from Real Property .... $____		Interior and exterior decorating		
Capitalized as follows:		Cleaning expenses and supplies		
		Management (Off-site)		
		Res. Mgr. salary & apartment		
		Janitor(s) salary & apartment		
		Miscellaneous		
*Real Est. Taxes □ Actual □ Est. Tax Rate Per $100 $____				
Total Assessed Value $		REPLACEMENT RESERVES		
Comments: ____		Carpeting and drapes		
		Ranges and refrigerators		
		Dishwashers and disposals		
		Individual heating & AC units		
		TOTAL EXPENSES & REPL. RES. .... $____		$____

INDICATED VALUE BY INCOME APPROACH $

FHLMC Form 71B-Rev. 8/77

Page 3

Exhibit 14.3

GENERAL COMMENTS (Including comments on any items rated poor or fair) _____

_____

_____

_____

_____

_____

_____

CONDITIONS AND REQUIREMENTS OF APPRAISAL (include required repairs, replacements, painting, termite inspections, etc.) _____

_____

_____

_____

RECONCILIATION AND VALUE CONCLUSION

Indicated Value by the Cost Approach .... $ _____

Indicated Value by the Market Approach .... $ _____

Indicated Value by the Income Approach .... $ _____

FINAL RECONCILIATION _____

_____

_____

_____

_____

_____

_____

_____

I certify, that to the best of my knowledge and belief, the statements made in this report are true and I have not knowingly withheld any significant information; that I have personally inspected subject property, both inside and outside, and have made an exterior inspection of all comparable sales listed herein; that I have no interest, present or contemplated, in subject property or the participants in the sale; that neither the employment nor compensation to make said appraisal is contingent upon any value estimate; and, that all contingent and limiting conditions are stated herein. ☐ Certification and Statement of Limiting Conditions. (FHLMC Form 439 Rev. 9/75) applies (☐ on file with Client ☐ Attached).

As a result of my investigation and analysis, my estimate of Market Value of the subject property as of _____ 19 ___ is ....

$ _____

Date _____ Appraiser _____

If applicable, complete the following

Date _____ Appraiser _____

Date _____ ☐ Supervising or ☐ Review Appraiser _____

☐ Did ☐ Did Not Physically Inspect Property

FOR LENDER'S USE ONLY (completion optional)

Loan Recommended $ _____ @ ___ %. Term ___ yrs. Principal & Interest $ _____ /mo. $ _____ /annually

Subject to: _____

Borrower's Cost or Purchase Price $ _____ Appraised Value $ _____ Loan to Appraised Value _____ %

Loan: Per Unit $ _____ Per Room $ _____ Per Sq. Ft. of Building Area $ _____

Gross Annual Forecasted Income $ _____ Gross Annual Income Multiplier _____ Overall Capitalization Rate _____ %

Forecasted Annual Expenses and Replacement Reserves $ _____ (_____ % of Gross Annual Forecasted Income)

Break-even Point (this loan): (Annual Exp. & RR $ _____ + Annual P & I pymts. $ _____) ÷ (Gross Annual Income $ _____) = _____ %

(All financing) : (Annual Exp & RR $ _____ + Annual P & I pymts. for all financing $ _____) ÷ (Gross Annual Inc. $ _____) = _____ %

Borrower's Return on Appraised Equity   (Net Annual Inc. $ _____ (-) Annual P & I pymts $ _____) = $ _____ (1)

(Appraised Value $ _____ (-) Loan Amt. $ _____) = $ _____ (2)

$ _____ (1) ÷ $ _____ (2) = _____ %

Comments or Committee Action _____

_____

FHLMC Form 71B-Rev. 8/77

AMERICAN REALTY FORMS, INC. • ALEXANDRIA, VIRGINIA • 1 (800) 642-9494 • 703-684-3500

Page 4

Exhibit 14.4

MOBILE HOME APPRAISAL REPORT

IDENTIFICATION

Borrower	Census Tract	Map Reference
Unit No.	Address	Project Name/Phase No.
City	County	State	Zip Code
Make	Model	Year	Serial No.	Property Rights Appraised ☐ Fee ☐ Personal
Length	Width	Tip-out	Wanigan	Porches	Decks
Lender/Client		Lender's Address
Occupant	Appraiser	Instructions to Appraiser
Sale Price	Date of Sale	Loan Terms	Actual RE Taxes

NEIGHBORHOOD

Location	☐ Urban	☐ Suburban	☐ Rural
Built Up	☐ Over 75%	☐ 25% to 75%	☐ Under 25%
Growth Rate	☐ Fully Dev ☐ Rapid	☐ Steady	☐ Slow
Property Values	☐ Increasing	☐ Stable	☐ Declining
Demand/Supply	☐ Shortage	☐ In Balance	☐ Oversupply
Marketing Time	☐ Under 3 Mos.	☐ 4-6 Mos.	☐ Over 6 Mos.

Present Land Use _____ % 1 Family _____ % 2-4 Family_____ % Apts. _____ % Condo
_____ % Commercial _____ % Industrial _____ % Vacant_____ % MBHM's
Change in Present Land Use: ☐ Not Likely ☐ Likely (*) ☐ Taking Place (*)
(*) From _____ To_____
Predominant Occupancy: ☐ Owner ☐ Tenant _____ % Vacant
Mobile Homes: Price Range $_____ to $_____ Predominant $_____
Age _____ yrs. to _____ yrs. Predominant _____ yrs.
Single Family: Price Range $_____ to $_____ Predominant $_____
Age _____ yrs. to _____ yrs. Predominant_____ yrs.
Describe potential for additional MBHM Parks units in nearby area _____

NEIGHBORHOOD RATING

	Good	Avg.	Fair	Poor
Adequacy of Shopping	☐	☐	☐	☐
Employment Opportunities	☐	☐	☐	☐
Recreational Facilities	☐	☐	☐	☐
Adequacy of Utilities	☐	☐	☐	☐
Property Compatibility	☐	☐	☐	☐
Protection from Detrimental Conditions	☐	☐	☐	☐
Police and Fire Protection	☐	☐	☐	☐
General Appearance of Properties	☐	☐	☐	☐
Appeal to Market	☐	☐	☐	☐

	Distance	Access or Convenience			
		Good	Avg.	Fair	Poor
Public Transportation		☐	☐	☐	☐
Employment Centers		☐	☐	☐	☐
Neighborhood Shopping		☐	☐	☐	☐
Grammar School		☐	☐	☐	☐
Freeway Access		☐	☐	☐	☐

Describe those factors, favorable or unfavorable, affecting marketability (e.g. public parks, schools, noise, view, mkt. area, population size and financial ability)
_____
_____
_____

SITE

Describe Site ONLY if it is included in the Final Value Estimate.

Dimensions _____ = _____ Sq. Ft. or Acres ☐ Corner Lot
Zoning Classification_____ Present improvements ☐ do ☐ do not conform to zoning regulations
Highest and Best Use ☐ Present Use ☐ Other (specify)_____

	Public	Other (Describe)	OFF SITE IMPROVEMENTS	
Electricity	☐		Street Access ☐ Public ☐ Private	Topo _____
Gas	☐		Surface	Size _____
Water	☐		Maintenance ☐ Public ☐ Private	Shape _____
San.Sewer	☐		☐ Storm Sewer ☐ Curb/Gutter	View _____
	☐ Underground Elect. & Tel.	☐ Sidewalk ☐ Street Lights	Drainage _____

Is the property located in a HUD Identified Special Flood Hazard Area? ☐ No ☐ Yes
Comments (favorable or unfavorable including any apparent adverse easements, encroachments or other adverse conditions) _____

PROJECT RATING

Complete only if subject is located in a Mobile Home Park.
Name _____
No. of Mobile Homes_____ Density per Acre_____
Zoning Classification_____
Approx. No. Units for Sale_____ Approx. No. Units Rented_____
Monthly Space Rent $_____ (includes ☐ water ☐ sewer ☐ garbage)
Access (Ingress/Egress) _____
Drainage/Flood Conditions_____
Describe common elements or recreation facilities _____

PROJECT RATING

	Good	Avg.	Fair	Poor
Location	☐	☐	☐	☐
General Appearance	☐	☐	☐	☐
Amenities and Recreational Facilities	☐	☐	☐	☐
Density (units per acre)	☐	☐	☐	☐
Unit Mix	☐	☐	☐	☐
Quality of Constr. (mat'l & finish)	☐	☐	☐	☐
Condition of Exterior	☐	☐	☐	☐
Condition of Interior	☐	☐	☐	☐
Appeal to Market	☐	☐	☐	☐

SUBJECT UNIT

☐ Existing ☐ Proposed Mobile Home Living Area (including Expandos, Tipouts, etc.)
Built-on Additions (Finished and Unfinished Areas)

Room List	Foyer	Liv	Din	Kit	Bdrm	Bath	Fam	Rec	Lndry	Other
Mobile Home										
Additions										

Floors:	☐ Hardwood ☐ Carpet over _____ ☐ _____
Interior Walls:	☐ Paneling ☐ Presboard
Trim/Finish:	☐ Good ☐ Average ☐ Fair ☐ Poor
Bath Floor:	☐ Vinyl ☐ Wainscot: ☐ Marlite ☐
Windows (type):	☐ Storm Sash ☐ Screens ☐ Combo
Kitchen Equip:	☐ Refrigerator ☐ Range/Oven ☐ Fan/Hood ☐ Washer ☐ Dryer
☐ Intercom	☐ Disposal ☐ Dishwasher ☐ Microwave ☐ Compactor
HEAT:	Type_____ Fuel_____ Cond._____
AIR COND:	☐ Central ☐ Other _____ ☐ Adequate ☐ Inadequate

Comments: _____

RATING	Good	Avg.	Fair	Poor
Condition of Improvements	☐	☐	☐	☐
Room Sizes and Layout	☐	☐	☐	☐
Adequacy of Closets and Storage	☐	☐	☐	☐
Kit. Equip. Cabinets & Workspace	☐	☐	☐	☐
Plumbing – Adequacy and Condition	☐	☐	☐	☐
Electrical – Adequacy and Condition	☐	☐	☐	☐
Skirting – Adequacy and Condition	☐	☐	☐	☐
Adequacy of Insulation	☐	☐	☐	☐
Location within Project or View	☐	☐	☐	☐
Overall Livability	☐	☐	☐	☐
Appeal and Marketability	☐	☐	☐	☐
Est. Effective Age	_____ to _____ Yrs.
Est. Remaining Economic Life	to _____ Yrs.

Mobile Home Appraisal Report

Exhibit 15.1

VALUATION SECTION

The undersigned has recited three recent sales of properties most similar and proximate to subject and has considered these in the market analysis. The description includes a dollar adjustment, reflecting market reaction to those items of significant variation between the subject and comparable properties. If a significant item in the comparable property is superior to, or more favorable than, the subject property, a minus (-) adjustment is made, thus reducing the indicated value of subject; if a significant item in the comparable is inferior to, or less favorable than the subject property, a plus (+) adjustment is made, thus increasing the indicated value of the subject.

ITEM	SUBJECT	COMPARABLE NO. 1		COMPARABLE NO. 2		COMPARABLE NO. 3	
Address or Space Number							
Proximity to Subject							
Sales Price	$	$		$		$	
Price / sf. GLA	$	$		$		$	
Date of Sale	DESCRIPTION	DESCRIPTION	+(-) $ Adjustment	DESCRIPTION	+(-) $ Adjustment	DESCRIPTION	+(-) $ Adjustment
Time Adjustment							
Location							
Make							
Year							
Condition							
Living Area: Room Count & Total	Total · Bdrms · Bath	Total · Bdrms · Bath		Total · Bdrms · Bath		Total · Bdrms · Bath	
Gross Living Area	Sq. Ft.	Sq. Ft.		Sq. Ft.		Sq. Ft.	
Tip-out							
Additions							
Furnishings							
Wood Stove							
Extras							
Site Value							
Financing							
Total Adjustments		☐ Plus ☐ Minus $		☐ Plus ☐ Minus $		☐ Plus ☐ Minus $	
Indicated Value of Subject		$		$		$	

Comments on Market Data: _____

INDICATED VALUE BY MARKET DATA APPROACH .... $ _____

INDICATED VALUE BY INCOME APPROACH (If applicable) Economic Market Rent $ _____ /Mo. x Gross Rent Multiplier _____ = $ _____

This appraisal is made ☐ "as is" ☐ subject to repairs, alterations, or conditions listed below ☐ completion per plans and specifications.

Comments and Conditions of Appraisal: _____

Final Reconciliation: _____

Construction Warranty ☐ Yes ☐ No Name of Warranty Program _____ Warranty Coverage Expires _____

This appraisal is based upon the above requirements, the certification, contingent and limiting conditions, and Market Value definition that are stated in ☐ FHLMC Form 439 (Rev. 7/86)/FNMA Form 1004B (Rev. 7/86) filed with client _____ 19 _____ ☐ attached

I (WE) ESTIMATE THE MARKET VALUE, AS DEFINED, OF SUBJECT PROPERTY AS OF _____ 19 _____ to be $ _____

Appraiser(s) _____ Review Appraiser (If applicable) _____ ☐ Did ☐ Did Not Physically Inspect Property

Mobile Home Appraisal Report   AMERICAN REALTY FORMS, INC. • ALEXANDRIA, VIRGINIA • 1 (800) 642-9494 • 703-684-3500

Exhibit 15.2

LAND APPRAISAL REPORT

Borrower _____ Census Tract _____ Map Reference _____

Property Address _____

City _____ County _____ State _____ Zip Code _____

Legal Description _____

Sale Price $ _____ Date of Sale _____ Loan Term _____ yrs. Property Rights Appraised ☐ Fee ☐ Leasehold ☐ De Minimis PUD

Actual Real Estate Taxes $ _____ (yr) Loan charges to be paid by seller $ _____ Other sales concessions _____

Lender/Client _____ Address _____

Occupant _____ Appraiser _____ Instructions to Appraiser _____

NEIGHBORHOOD

Location	☐ Urban	☐ Suburban	☐ Rural	
Built Up	☐ Over 75%	☐ 25% to 75%	☐ Under 25%	
Growth Rate ☐ Fully Dev.	☐ Rapid	☐ Steady	☐ Slow	
Property Values	☐ Increasing	☐ Stable	☐ Declining	
Demand/Supply	☐ Shortage	☐ In Balance	☐ Oversupply	
Marketing Time	☐ Under 3 Mos.	☐ 4-6 Mos.	☐ Over 6 Mos.	

Present Land Use ____% 1 Family ____% 2-4 Family ____% Apts. ____% Condo ____% Commercial ____% Industrial ____% Vacant ____%

Change in Present Land Use ☐ Not Likely ☐ Likely (*) ☐ Taking Place (*)

(*) From _____ To _____

Predominant Occupancy ☐ Owner ☐ Tenant ____% Vacant

Single Family Price Range $ _____ to $ _____ Predominant Value $ _____

Single Family Age _____ yrs. to _____ yrs. Predominant Age _____ yrs

	Good	Avg.	Fair	Poor
Employment Stability	☐	☐	☐	☐
Convenience to Employment	☐	☐	☐	☐
Convenience to Shopping	☐	☐	☐	☐
Convenience to Schools	☐	☐	☐	☐
Adequacy of Public Transportation	☐	☐	☐	☐
Recreational Facilities	☐	☐	☐	☐
Adequacy of Utilities	☐	☐	☐	☐
Property Compatibility	☐	☐	☐	☐
Protection from Detrimental Conditions	☐	☐	☐	☐
Police and Fire Protection	☐	☐	☐	☐
General Appearance of Properties	☐	☐	☐	☐
Appeal to Market	☐	☐	☐	☐

Comments including those factors, favorable or unfavorable, affecting marketability (e.g. public parks, schools, view, noise): _____

SITE

Dimensions _____ = _____ Sq. Ft. or Acres ☐ Corner Lot

Zoning classification _____ Present improvements ☐ do ☐ do not conform to zoning regulations

Highest and best use ☐ Present use ☐ Other (specify) _____

	Public	Other (Describe)	OFF SITE IMPROVEMENTS			
Elec.	☐		Street Access ☐ Public ☐ Private	Topo		
Gas	☐		Surface _____	Size		
Water	☐		Maintenance ☐ Public ☐ Private	Shape		
San. Sewer	☐		☐ Storm Sewer ☐ Curb/Gutter	View		
	☐ Underground Elect. & Tel.	☐ Sidewalk ☐ Street Lights	Drainage			

Is the property located in a HUD Identified Special Flood Hazard Area? ☐ No ☐ Yes

Comments (favorable or unfavorable including any apparent adverse easements, encroachments or other adverse conditions): _____

MARKET DATA ANALYSIS

The undersigned has recited three recent sales of properties most similar and proximate to subject and has considered these in the market analysis. The description includes a dollar adjustment reflecting market reaction to those items of significant variation between the subject and comparable properties. If a significant item in the comparable property is superior to or more favorable than the subject property, a minus (-) adjustment is made thus reducing the indicated value of subject; if a significant item in the comparable is inferior to or less favorable than the subject property, a plus (+) adjustment is made thus increasing the indicated value of the subject.

ITEM	SUBJECT PROPERTY	COMPARABLE NO. 1		COMPARABLE NO. 2		COMPARABLE NO. 3	
Address							
Proximity to Subject							
Sales Price	$	$		$		$	
Price	$	$		$		$	
Data Source							
	DESCRIPTION	DESCRIPTION	+(-)$ Adjustment	DESCRIPTION	+(-)$ Adjustment	DESCRIPTION	+(-)$ Adjustment
Date of Sale and Time Adjustment							
Location							
Site/View							
Sales or Financing Concessions							
Net Adj. (Total)		☐ Plus ☐ Minus $		☐ Plus ☐ Minus $		☐ Plus ☐ Minus $	
Indicated Value of Subject		$		$		$	

Comments on Market Data: _____

RECONCILIATION

Comments and Conditions of Appraisal: _____

Final Reconciliation: _____

I ESTIMATE THE MARKET VALUE, AS DEFINED, OF SUBJECT PROPERTY AS OF _____ 19____ to be $ _____

Appraiser(s) _____ Review Appraiser (if applicable) _____ ☐ Did ☐ Did Not Physically Inspect Property

AMERICAN REALTY FORMS, INC. • ALEXANDRIA, VIRGINIA • 1 (800) 642-9494 • 703-684-3500

Exhibit 16

SATISFACTORY COMPLETION CERTIFICATE

On _____ 19 _____ the property situated at

_____

_____

_____

was appraised by me or _____

The appraisal report was subject to: _____ satisfactory completion, _____ repairs, or _____

_____

I certify that I have reinspected subject property, the requirements or conditions set forth in the appraisal report have been met, and any required repairs or completion items have been done in a workmanlike manner.

Itemized below are substantial changes from the data in the appraisal report, and these changes do not adversely affect any property ratings or final estimate of value in the report:

Date _____ 19 _____   Inspector _____

FHLMC 442 Rev. 6/78   C   Forms and Worms,® Incorporated, 315 Whitney Avenue, New Haven, CT 06511 583   Item # 116360

Exhibit 17

Residential Appraisal Field Review Report

The purpose of this review is to determine the completeness and accuracy of the data in an appraisal report and to verify the accuracy of the market value estimate as of the effective date of the original appraisal. The appraisal review must address all factual, judgmental, and appraisal technique discrepancies. This field review is a spot-check on the original appraisal report as part of a mortgage quality review. It is not intended to be used as a new appraisal. (Please attach a copy of the original appraisal report to this report.)

Property Address		City	State	Zip Code

Legal Description

Property Rights Appraised	Client Reference Number

Effective Date of Original Appraisal and Field Review

Borrower

Review Appraiser	Company Name

Address

Telephone Number	Soc. Sec. or Tax ID. Number

Instructions: The review appraiser must personally inspect (by, at least, driving by) the exterior of the subject property and the comparables used in the analysis. Photographs are required for: the front of the comparables; the front of the subject; and a street scene of the subject property. Additional photographs are suggested if any adverse conditions that were not noted in the original appraisal report are observed. (NOTE: The review appraiser is not required to inspect the interior of the subject property. The review appraiser should verify the data in the original appraisal report, using the assessment records, the real estate broker, or any other data source that he or she considers to be reliable and reasonably available.) Based on the exterior inspection of the subject and the comparables, a thorough desk review of the appraisal report, and a review of the relevant market data for the subject market area, respond to the following questions, form an opinion about the appropriateness of the appraisal methods and techniques that were used, and indicate any areas of disagreement (giving reasons for the differences). Do not limit your responses to the space provided: attach an addendum, if necessary:

1. Provide a sales and refinance history for the subject property for the last three years (if it is reasonably available for a data source that the review appraiser considers to be reliable).

Conveyance Recordation Date	Sales Price	Asking Price	Mortgage Amount	Grantor/Grantee	Data Source

2. Is the appraiser's overall description of the neighborhood complete and accurate (location, general market conditions [i.e., plant closings, crop failures, etc.], property values, demand/supply, marketing time, general appearance of properties, appeal to market, etc.)? ☐ Yes ☐ No (If no, explain.) _____

3. Is the appraiser's overall description of the site complete and accurate (zoning compliance, apparent adverse conditions, apparent environmental hazards, size, flood hazard, etc.)? ☐ Yes ☐ No (If no, explain.) _____

4. Is the appraiser's overall description of the improvements complete and accurate (property description, depreciation, condition, apparent environmental hazards, etc.)? ☐ Yes ☐ No (If no, explain.) _____

5. Are the design and appeal, quality of construction, and size of the subject similar to others in this area? ☐ Yes ☐ No (If no, how is the subject different?) _____

6. Are the comparables used in the analysis truly comparable to the subject property, representative of the subject market, and were they the best ones available as of the effective date of the appraisal? ☐ Yes ☐ No (If no, explain and provide an adjustment grid with the appropriate comparables and adjustments on an addendum.) _____

7. (a) Can the date of sale (contract date and/or closing/settlement date), sales price, and sales or financing concessions for the comparables be confirmed through the data source that the appraiser indicated? ☐ Yes ☐ No (If no, explain.) _____

(b) Were the comparables actual closed or settled sales as of the effective date of the original appraisal? ☐ Yes ☐ No (If no, explain.)

Freddie Mac Form 1032 1/90
1-4 Family Properties

Page 1 of 2

Forms and Worms Inc.,® 315 Whitney Ave., New Haven, CT 06511 1(800) 243-4545 Item #237360

Fannie Mae Form 2000 1/90
1-4 Family Properties

Exhibit 18.1

Residential Appraisal Field Review Report

8. Is the specific data for the comparables accurate (time, location, design and appeal, quality of construction, age, condition, size, sales or financing concessions, etc.)? ☐ Yes ☐ No   (If no, explain.) _____

_____
_____
_____
_____
_____

9. Are the individual adjustments to the comparables reasonable and supported (time, location, design and appeal, quality of construction, age, condition, size, sales or financing concessions, etc.)? ☐ Yes ☐ No   (If no, explain.) _____

_____
_____
_____
_____
_____

10. If the subject property is a small residential income property (2–4 unit) or a single-family investment property, are the comparable rental and expense data accurate and reasonable? ☐ Yes ☐ No ☐ N/A   (If no, explain.) _____

_____
_____
_____
_____
_____

11. If the subject property is an individual unit in a condominium or PUD project, is the project description complete and accurate? ☐ Yes ☐ No ☐ N/A   (If no, explain.) _____

_____
_____
_____
_____

12. Is the estimate of market value for the subject property reasonable as of the effective date of the appraisal? ☐ Yes ☐ No   (If no, provide an appropriate estimate of market value for the subject property and state the assumptions [exterior inspection only, property description and condition, etc.] that the opinion is subject to.) _____

_____
_____
_____
_____
_____

13. Has there been a substantial change in the base economy in the area since the effective date of the appraisal? ☐ Yes ☐ No   (If yes, please explain.) _____

_____
_____
_____

14. If the subject property is a cooperative unit, the review appraiser must address the completeness and accuracy of the original appraiser's description and analysis of the cooperative project and specifically comment on the accuracy of: (a) the number of shares attributable to the unit; (b) the pro-rata share of the blanket mortgage payments; and (c) the treatment of the monthly assessments of the comparable sales.

_____
_____
_____

I certify that, to the best of my knowledge and belief, the facts and data used herein are true and correct; that I personally inspected the exterior of the subject property and the comparables used in the report; that the reported analyses, opinions, and conclusions are limited only by the reported assumptions and limiting conditions, and are my personal, unbiased professional analyses, opinions, and conclusions; that I have no present or prospective interest in the property that is the subject of this report, and I have no personal interest in or bias with respect to the parties involved; that my compensation is not contingent on any action or event resulting from the analyses, opinions, or conclusions in, or the use of, this report; and that my analyses, opinions, and conclusions were developed, and this report was prepared, in conformity with the Uniform Standards of Professional Appraisal Practice.

Signature of Review Appraiser	Date

Client Use Only

Review Underwriter's Comments _____

_____
_____

Signature of Review Underwriter	Date

Freddie Mac Form 1032 1/90   Page 2 of 2   Fannie Mae Form 2000 1/90
1-4 Family Properties   Forms and Worms.® 315 Whitney Ave., New Haven, CT 06511 1(800) 243-4545 Item #237360   1-4 Family Properties

Exhibit 18.2

FannieMae

Loan Valuation Summary for Second Mortgages

To Be Completed by Lender

Subject Property Address _____ City _____

County _____ Street _____ State _____ Zip _____ Census Tract _____

Legal Description _____ Property rights appraised ☐Fee ☐Leasehold

Lender/Client _____ Address _____

Name of Applicant(s) _____ Telephone No. _____

Appraisal to be made of property in: ☐ "as is" condition; or, ☐ "as completed" (if improvements to be made).

Improvement to be completed _____

To Be Completed by Appraiser

Neighborhood

					Good Avg Fair Poor
Location	☐Urban	☐Suburban	☐Rural	Property Compatibility	☐ ☐ ☐ ☐
Built Up	☐Over 75%	☐25% to 75%	☐Under 25%	Protection from Detrimental Conditions	☐ ☐ ☐ ☐
Growth Rate [ ] Fully Dev.	☐Rapid	☐Steady	☐Slow	General Appearance of Properties	☐ ☐ ☐ ☐
Property Values	☐Increasing	☐Stable	☐Declining	Appeal to Market	☐ ☐ ☐ ☐
Predominant Occupancy	☐Owner	☐Tenant	____ % Vacant		

Single Family Price Range $_____ to $_____ Predominant Value $_____ Age _____ yrs. to _____ yrs.

Note: Fannie Mae does not consider race or the racial composition of the neighborhood to be reliable appraisal factors.

Site

Highest and best use: ☐Present use ☐Other (specify) _____

Improvements upon completion conform to zoning ☐Yes ☐No

Utilities:	Public	Other		Briefly describe and rate:
Electricity	☐	_____	Topo	_____
Gas	☐	_____	Size	_____
Water	☐	_____	Shape	_____
Sanitary Sewer	☐	_____	View	_____
	Underground Elec. & Tel. ☐Yes ☐No		Drainage	_____

Describe visible easements, if any, affecting subject property _____

Is the property located in an HUD-identified Special Flood Hazard Area? ☐No ☐Yes

Improvements

	Good Avg Fair Poor
Design _____	Exterior Condition ☐ ☐ ☐ ☐
Type _____	Interior Condition ☐ ☐ ☐ ☐
Exterior Walls _____ Roof _____	Overall Livability ☐ ☐ ☐ ☐
Approximate Age (Actual) _____ Yrs. (Effective) _____ Yrs.	Compatibility to Neighborhood ☐ ☐ ☐ ☐
Comments:	Appeal and Marketability ☐ ☐ ☐ ☐

Room List

Room List	Foyer	Living	Dining	Kitchen	Den	Family Rm.	Rec. Rm.	Bedrooms	No. Baths	Laundry	Other
Basement											
1st Level											
2nd Level											

Finished area above grade contains a total of ____ rooms ____ bedrooms ____ baths. Gross Living Area _____ sq. ft. Bsmt Area _____ sq. ft.

If cost and income approaches are appropriate, include them in an addendum to this report.

Market Data Analysis

Comparable No. 1:

Address _____ Street _____ City, State _____ Proximity to subject _____

Sale price of comparable $_____ Date of sale _____

Overall comparison to subject property: ☐Equal ☐Inferior Indicated value of subject $_____

Comparable No. 2:

Address _____ Street _____ City, State _____ Proximity to subject _____

Sale price of comparable $_____ Date of sale _____

Overall comparison to subject property: ☐Equal ☐Inferior Indicated value of subject $_____

Comparable No. 3:

Address _____ Street _____ City, State _____ Proximity to subject _____

Sale price of comparable $_____ Date of sale _____

Overall comparison to subject property: ☐Equal ☐Inferior Indicated value of subject $_____

This appraisal is based upon the above requirements, the certification, contingent and limiting conditions, and Market value definition that are stated in

Fannie Mae Form 1004B (Rev. 7/86) filed with client _____ , 19___ ☐attached.

Estimated "as completed" value of subject property as of _____ , 19___ is $_____

_____ _____
Appraiser's Name   Date

Attach descriptive photographs of subject property and street scene.

Forms and Worms, Inc.® 315 Whitney Ave., New Haven, CT 06511 1(800) 243-4545

EQ

Fannie Mae
Form 219 Oct. 85
Item # 233000

Exhibit 19

Appendix C—Measures, Formulas and Conversions

THE ENGLISH SYSTEM

Linear Measure

12	inches	=	1 foot
3	feet	=	1 yard
5.5	yards	=	1 rod
40	rods	=	1 furlong
8	furlongs	=	1 mile

Square Measure

144	square inches	=	1 square foot
9	square feet	=	1 square yard
43,560	square feet	=	1 acre
640	acres	=	1 square mile

Cubic Measure

1,728	cubic inches	=	1 cubic foot
27	cubic feet	=	1 cubic yard
128	cubic feet	=	1 cord
24.75	cubic feet	=	1 perch

Measures of Angles and Acres

60	seconds	=	1 minute
60	minutes	=	1 degree
90	degrees	=	1 quadrant
360	degrees	=	1 full circle

Surveyor's or Land Measure

1 link	=	7.92 inches
1 rod (or pole)	=	25 links = 16-1/2 feet
1 chain	=	100 links = 4 rods = 66 feet
1 furlong	=	40 rods = 10 chains = 1/8 mile
1 mile	=	320 rods = 80 chains = 5,280 feet
1 acre	=	160 square rods = 43,560 square feet
1 square mile	=	640 acres

THE METRIC SYSTEM

Measures of Length

10 millimeters (mm.)	=	1 centimeter
10 centimeters	=	1 decimeter
10 decimeters	=	1 meter
10 meters	=	1 dekameter
10 dekameters	=	1 hectometer
10 hectometers	=	1 kilometer
	=	39.37 inches
1 meter	=	3.28083 feet
	=	1.0936 yards
1 centimeter	=	.3937 inch
	=	.03937 inch, or
1 millimeter	=	approximately 1/25 inch
1 kilometer	=	0.62137 mile
1 foot	=	0.3048 meter
1 inch	=	2.54 centimeters
		25.4 millimeters
1 yard	=	0.9144 meters
1 rod	=	5.029 meters
1 mile	=	1.6093 kilometers

MEASURES OF SURFACE

Myriameter	10,000 meters		6.2137 miles
Kilometer	1,000 meters		0.62137 miles
Hectometer	100 meters		328 feet 1 inch
Dekameter	10 meters		393.7 inches
Meter	1 meter		39.37 inches
Decimeter	0.1 meter		3.937 inches
Centimeter	0.01 meter		0.3937 inches
Millimeter	0.001 meter		0.0394 inches

1 square meter	=	(10.764 sq. ft.
		(1.196 sq. yds.
		(1 dentiare
1 square centimeter	=	.155 square inch
1 square millimeter	=	.00155 square inch
1 square yard	=	.836 square meter
1 square foot	=	.0929 square meter
1 square inch	=	(6.452 square centimeters
		(645.2 square millimeters
1 square rod	=	25.29 square meters
1 acre	=	0.4047 hectares
1 square mile	=	259 hectares

Cuerda	3,930.40 square meters	=	0.97123 acres
Hectare	10,000 square meters	=	2.471 acres
Are	100 square meters	=	119.6 square yards
Centiare	1 square meter	=	1,550 square inches

MATHEMATICAL FORMULAS

Square
A side multiplied by 1.4142 equals diameter of its circumscribing circle.
A side multiplied by 4.443 equals circumference of its circumscribing circle.
A side multiplied by 1.128 equals diameter of an equal circle.
A side multiplied by 3.547 equals circumference of an equal circle.

To Find Side of an Equal Square
Multiply diameter by	0.8862
Or divide diameter by	1.1284
Or multiply circumference by	0.2821
Or divide circumference by	3.545

To Find Side of an Inscribed Square
Multiply diameter by	0.7071
Or multiply circumference by	0.2251
Or divide circumference by	4.4428

To Find Circumference
Multiply diameter by	3.1416
Or divide diameter by	0.3183

To Find Diameter
Multiply circumference by	0.3183
Or divide circumference by	3.1416

To Find Radius
Multiply circumference by	0.15915
Or divide circumference by	6.28318

To Find the Area of a Circle
Multiply circumference by one-quarter of the diameter
Or multiply the square of diameter by	0.7854
Or multiply the square of circumference by	0.07958
Or multiply the square of 1/2 diameter by	3.1416

To Find the Square of a Sphere or Globe
Multiply the diameter by the circumference
Or multiply the square of diameter by	3.1416
Or multiply four times the square of radius by	3.1416

To Find the Cubic Inches (Volume) in a Sphere or Globe
Multiply the cube of the diameter by	0.5236

SELECTED CONVERSION FACTORS

1 kilogram per meter	=	.6720 pounds per foot
1 gram per square millimeter	=	1.422 pounds per square inch
1 kilogram per square meter	=	.2084 pounds per square foot
1 kilogram per cubic meter	=	.0624 pounds per cubic foot
1 degree centigrade	=	1.8 degrees Fahrenheit
1 pound per foot	=	1.488 kilograms per meter
1 pound per square foot	=	4.882 kilograms per square meter
1 pound per cubic foot	=	16.02 kilograms per cubic meter
1 degree Fahrenheit	=	.5556 degrees centigrade
1 calorie (French Thermal Unit)	=	3.968 B.T.U. (British Thermal Unit
1 horsepower	=	(33,000 foot pounds per minute
		(746 watts
1 watt (unit of electrical power)	=	(.00134 horsepower
		(44.22 foot pounds per minute
		(1,000 watts
1 kilowatt	=	(44,220 foot pounds per minute
		(1.34 horsepower

Length Conversion Factors

Symbol	Given	Multiply by	To Find	Symbol
in.	inches	2.54	centimeters	cm
ft.	feet	30.48	centimeters	cm
yd.	yards	0.9144	meters	m
mi.	miles	1.6093	kilometers	km
mm	millimeters	0.0394	inches	in.
cm	centimeters	0.3937	inches	in.
m	meters	3.281	feet	ft.
m	meters	1.0936	yards	yd.
km	kilometers	0.62137	miles	mi.

Area Conversion Factors

Symbol	Given	Multiply by	To Find	Symbol
in.^{2}	sq. inches	6.452	sq. centimeters	cm^2
ft.^{2}	sq. feet	0.0929	sq. meters	m^2
yd.^{2}	sq. yards	0.836	sq. meters	m^2
mi.^{2}	sq. miles	2.590	sq. kilometers	km^2
ac	acres	0.4047	hectares	ha
cm^2	sq. centimeters	0.155	sq. inches	in.^{2}
m^2	sq. meters	1.196	sq. yards	yd.^{2}
km^2	sq. kilometers	0.386	sq. miles	mi.^{2}
ha	hectares (10,000m)	2.471	acres	ac.

Volume Conversion Factors

Symbol	Given	Multiply by	To Find	Symbol
in.^{3}	cubic inches	16.393	cubic centimeters	cm^3
ft.^{3}	cubic feet	0.028	cubic meters	m^3
yd.^{3}	cubic yards	0.765	cubic meters	m^3
cm^3	cubic centimeters	0.061	cubic inches	in^3
m^3	cubic meters	35.7143	cubic feet	ft.^{3}
m^3	cubic meters	1.3072	cubic yards	yd.^{3}

Capacity Conversion Factors

Symbol	Given dry measure	Multiply by	To Find	Symbol
pt.	pints	.5506	liters	l
qt.	quarts	1.1012	liters	l
gal.	gallons	4.545	liters	l
pk.	pecks	0.009	cubic meters	m^3
bu.	bushels	0.036	cubic meters	m^3
l	liters	1.8162	pints	pt.
l	liters	0 .9081	quarts	qt.
l	liters	0.2270	gallons	gal.
m^3	cubic meters	111.1111	pecks	pk.
m^3	cubic meters	27.7778	bushels	bu.

Liquid Measure Conversion Factors

Symbol	Given	Multiply by	To Find	Symbol
fl. oz.	fluid ounces	29.573	milliliters	ml
pt.	pints	0.4732	liters	l
qt.	quarts	0.9463	liters	l
gal.	gallons	3.7853	liters	l
ml	milliliters	0.0338	fluid ounces	fl.oz.
l	liters	2.1134	pints	pt.
l	liters	1.0567	quarts	qt.
l	liters	0.2642	gallons	gal.

Mass Weight Conversion Factors

Symbol	Given	Multiply by	To Find	Symbol
oz.	ounces	28.35	grams	g
lb.	pounds	0.4536	kilograms	kg
	short tons (2000 lbs.)	0.9072	tonnes (1000 kg)	†
g	grams	0.035	ounces	oz.
kg	kilograms	2.2046	pounds	lb.
†	tonnes (1000 kg)	1.1023	short tons (2000 lbs.)	

Temperature Conversion Factors

Symbol	Given	Multiply by	To Find	Symbol
°F	Fahrenheit	5/9 (after subtracting 32)	Celsius	°C
°C	Celsius	9/5 (then add 32)	Fahrenheit	°F

Appendix D - Statistical Concepts

MEASURES OF CENTRAL TENDENCY

In order to make data more manageable and understandable, we frequently calculate certain numbers which describe the entire set of data. A familiar example of this is an average or a measure of central tendency. Whenever the word "average" is used in statistics it refers to the calculation of either the mean, median or mode each of which is designed to yield a different number of the "typical" (i.e., average) value of a set of data.

Mean. The arithmetic mean (represented by the symbol $\overline{X}$) is the type of average or typical score calculated by adding up all the numbers in the set of data and dividing by how many numbers there are in the set (the total number of numbers). Suppose we had the following dollar estimates for a dimmer switch: 5, 6, 6, 6, 7, 7, 8, 8, 8, 8. To calculate the mean, the first step is to add up all the numbers: $5 + 6 + 6 + 6 + 7 + 7 + 8 + 8 + 8 = 69$. The total number of estimates is 10. Therefore, $69 \div 10 = 6.9$. The mean of these estimates is $6.90.

Median. Although the mean is the more common average, the median is more simple to calculate. The median is the type of average or typical score which divides a distribution of numbers in half. It is the mid-point of the whole distribution of numbers. Suppose we had the following dollar estimates for a dimmer switch: 8, 6, 8, 5, 7, 6, 8, 9, 8, 6. To calculate the median, simply line up all the scores from smallest to largest, and find the middle one: 5, 6, 6, 6, 7, 8, 8, 8, 9. The median is 7 since four scores are larger than 7 and for scores are smaller than 7. When there is an odd number of numbers, the median is easily found since there is a natural middle score—a middle score which has the same number of scores above and below it. When there is an even number of numbers, there is no natural middle score, so we calculate the mean of the middle two numbers. Supose we had the following data: 7, 9, 6, 3. The median is the "average" of the two middle scores, 6 and 7. The median is 6.5

Mode. The mode is the easiest type of average to find. It is simply the most frequently occurring number in a set of data. Suppose we had the following data: 2, 2, 3, 4, 4, 5, 5, 5, 6, 6, 7. The mode is 5. There is no formula for finding the mode. It is simply the number which occurs most frequently. Sometimes there are two scores which occur with the highest frequency. In such situations, both scores are considered the modes of the distribution. Distributions with two modes are called *bimodal* distributions. When there are three or more modes in a distribution, they are called *multimodal* distributions. Suppose we had the following data: 3, 4, 5, 5, 5, 6, 6, 6, 7, 7. This is a bimodal distribution with two modes: 5 and 6.

The Appropriate Average. When a distribution of scores is symmetrical (i.e., when the two halves of the graph are identical as in Figure 1) the mean, median and mode will be identical, or very close together. In such cases it makes little difference which "average" is used, but the mean is preferred because it is used in many statistical callculations. When a distribution of scores is skewed (i.e., the highest point is to one side and not in the middle as in Figures 2 and 3) the mean is drawn toward the tail (the low part of the graph) of the distribution. In other words, the mean is unduly influenced by the extremely high or low scores. In such instances the median, or the mode, or possibly both, could be considered the "typical" score rather thsn the mean.

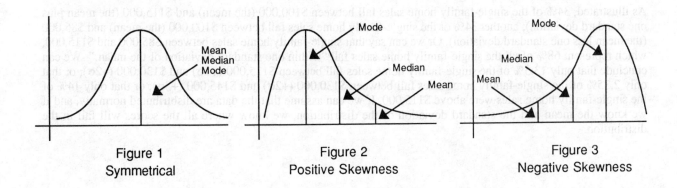

Figure 1	Figure 2	Figure 3
Symmetrical	Positive Skewness	Negative Skewness

MEASURES OF VARIABILITY

A measure of variability is a score which describes a distribution in terms of how spread out or how compact the scores are. The two most common measures of variability are the range, and standard deviation.

Range. The range indicates the distance from the smallest score to the largest score. It is calculated by subtracting the smallest score from the largest score. Suppose we had the following data: 2, 2, 3, 4, 4, 5, 5, 5, 6, 6, 7. The Range is 7 – 2 = 5. Although the range gives only limited information, it does tell us how far the highest score is from the lowest.

Standard Deviation. The standard deviation (represented by the letter σ) indicates how *all* the scores, not just the lowest and highest, are spread out in relation to the mean. The computation of the standard deviation is somewhat tedious and outside the scope of this text, but it can be computed easily with many calculators and computer programs. Of greater significance is the interpretation of the standard deviation when used in conjunction with a normal distribution of scores. By definition, one of the characteristics of the normal distribution is that the curve is spread out in a specific way so that whatever the standard deviation is, 68% of all the scores will fall within ±1 standard deviation of the mean; 95% of the scores will fall within ±2 σ; 99.7% of the scores will fall within ±3 σ. Figure 4 illustrates these characteristics of the normal distribution using single-family home sales data with a mean of $100,000 and a standard deviation of $15,000.

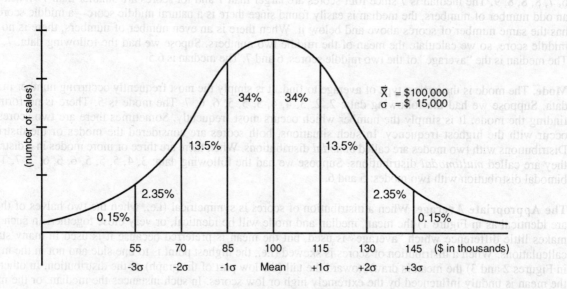

Figure 4
Normal Distribution of Single-family Home Sales

As illustrated, 34% of the single-family home sales fall between $100,000 (the mean) and $115,000 (the mean plus one standard deviation); another 34% of the single-family home sales fall between $100,000 (the mean) and $85,000 (the mean less one standard deviation). Or we can say that single-family home sales between $85,000 and $115,000, which represent 68% of all the single-family home sales fall "within one standard deviation of the mean." We can conclude that only 13.5% of the single-family home sales fall between $115,000 (+1σ) and $130,000 (+2σ); or that only 2.35% of the single-family home sales fall between $130,000 (+2σ) and $145,000 (+3σ); or that only 14% of the single-family home sales were above $115,000. If we can assume that the data are disbtributed normally, and if we know the mean and the standard deviation of the distribution, we know where all the scores will fall in the distribution.

Appraisal Foundation
1029 Vermont Ave., N.W., Suite 900
Washington, D.C. 2005
(202) 347-7722

Bureau of the Census
Data User Services Division
Customer Services (Publications)
Bureau of Census
Washington, D.C. 20233
(301) 763-4100

**California Department of Veterans Affairs
(Cal-Vet)**
Division of Farm and Home Loans
POB 942895
Sacramento, CA 94295-0001
(800) 952-5626

Farmers Home Administration (FmHA)
194 West Main Street, Suite F
Woodland, CA 95695-2915
(916)-551-1708

**Federal Deposit Insurance Corporation
(FDIC)**
Western Regional Office
25 Ecker Street
San Francisco, CA 94105
(415) 546-0160

**Federal Home Loan Mortgage Corp.
Freddie Mac (FHLMC)**
Western Regional Office
15303 Ventura Blvd., Suite 500
Sherman Oaks, CA 91403
(818) 905-0070

Federal Housing Administration (FHA)
San Francisco Regional Office
450 Golden Gate Avenue
San Francisco, CA 94102
(415) 556-4752

Los Angeles Area Office
1615 West Olympic Blvd.
Los Angeles, CA 90015-3801
(213) 251-7122

**Federal National Mortgage Association
Fannie Mae (FNMA)**
Western Regional Office
10920 Wilshire Blvd.
Suite 1800
Los Angeles, CA 90024-6519
(213) 208-6234

Federal Reserve Board of San Francisco
101 Market Street
San Francisco, CA 94105
(415) 974-2000

National Credit Union Administration
2300 Clayton Road
Concord, CA 94520
(415) 825-6125

National Decision Systems
539 Encinitas Boulevard
Encinitas, CA 92034
ATTN: Mapping Department
(619) 942-7000

**Office of The Comptroller of The
Currency**
Western Regional Office
50 Fremont Street
San Francisco, CA 94105
(415) 545-5900

Office of Thrift Supervision
Western Regional Office
P.O. Box 7165
San Francisco, CA 94120
(415) 393-1225

Resolution Trust Corporation
Western Regional Office
1515 Arapahoe St.
Tower 3, Suite 800
Denver, CO 80202
(300) 556-6500

Superintendent of Documents
U.S. Government Printing Office
Washington, D.C. 20402
(202) 783-3238

U.S. Department of Housing and Urban Development (HUD)
Headquarters
451 Seventh Street, S.W.
Washington, D.C. 20410
(202) 655-4000

San Francisco Regional Office
450 Golden Gate Avenue
San Francisco, CA 94102
(415) 556-4752

Fresno Field Office
1315 Van Ness Street, Suite 200
Fresno, CA 93721-1775
(209) 487-5036

Los Angeles Office
2500 Wilshire Boulevard
Los Angeles, CA 90057-4361
(213) 688-5973

Sacramento Office
777 12th Street, Suite 200
POB 1978
Sacramento, CA 95809-1978
(916) 440-3471

San Diego Office
Federal Office Building
880 Front Street
San Diego, CA 92188-0100
(619) 293-5310

Santa Ana Office
34 Civic Center Plaza
POB 12850
Santa Ana, CA 92712-2850
(714) 836-2451

Indian Program Office
Western Regional Office
1 North First Avenue, Suite 400
Phoenix, Arizona 85004-2360
(602) 261-4156

U.S. Department of Veterans Affairs (USDVA)
Western Regional Office
Federal Building
11000 Wilshire Boulevard
Los Angeles, CA 90024
(213) 479-4011

San Francisco Office
211 Main Street
San Francisco, CA 94105

Western Economic Research*
15910 Ventura Boulevard
Encino, CA 91436
(818) 981-9762
*California maps only

Glossary

Abstraction Technique: A site valuation technique; the estimated value of the improvements is subtracted from the sales price of an improved property to obtain an indicated value of the site.

Accrual for Depreciation: A provision in a capitalization rate to provide for a recapture of investment out of income to compensate for future loss of value.

Accrued Depreciation: The difference between the reproduction cost new or the replacement cost new of the improvements and their present worth, as of the date of the appraisal; also referred to as diminished utility.

Acre: An area of earth surface containing 43,560 square feet, measured as if the earth were flat. If in the form of a square, the length on a side is 208.71 feet.

Acreage: Land, measured in acres.

Actual Age: The number of years that have elapsed since a structure was built.

Adjusted Sale Price: A sale price adjusted for elements of comparison.

Ad Valorem: According to value.

Ad Valorem Tax: A tax, such as real property taxes, based on the value of property.

Adverse Possession: The possession of property adverse to the interests of the owner. Title to real property can be acquired by adverse possession if all specific requirements are met.

Affidavit: A written declaration either sworn or affirmed.

Affirmative Easement: A positive right in the land of another, such as a right of way.

After-Tax Cash Flow: Net income remaining after debt service and income tax are deducted. Also called net spendable.

After-Tax Cash Proceeds of Sale: The estimated resale price less all costs of sale, outstanding debt and taxes.

After-Tax Equity Yield Rate: An annualized rate of return on equity based on a series of after-tax cash flows. Also called internal rate of return (IRR).

Age-Life Method: A method of estimating accrued depreciation as a percentage applied to the current reproduction cost new of the improvements.

Age-Life Method, Modified: A method of estimating accrued depreciation which recognizes the possibility of curing certain items of accrued depreciation.

Agency: A fiduciary relationship in which one party (the agent) acts on behalf of another (the principal) in dealing with third persons.

Agent: One who acts in behalf of another, called the principal, in dealing with third persons.

Agents in Production: The four agents of production which create wealth: labor, management, capital, and land.

Agricultural Property: Improved or unimproved land used for or suitable for the production of crops, timber, livestock, etc.

Agricultural Use Value: A value of land based solely on its agricultural use, affecting property taxes on land devoted to agricultural use.

Airport Zoning: A zoning that controls land uses around an airport to eliminate hazards to aircraft, e.g., smoke, electronic interference, tall buildings, etc.

Air Rights: Rights to the use, control, and regulation of air space over a parcel of real estate.

Allocation: An appraisal technique in which the appraiser establishes a typical ratio of site value to total value and applies that ratio to a subject property to estimate land value.

Amenities: The tangible and intangible benefits of property ownership.

Amortization Rate: The rate at which principal on a loan is repaid over the contract term of the loan.

Amortized Loan: A loan requiring periodic payments which include both a partial repayment of the debt and interest on the outstanding balance.

Anchor Tenant: In a shopping center the major tenant, one that attracts patronage for the center. Usually a supermarket in a neighborhood shopping center, and a department store in a regional shopping center.

Annual Percentage Rate: A ratio of total finance charges, not just interest alone, to the amount financed, as defined by the Federal Truth in Lending law.

Annuity: An income in the form of a series of payments receivable at even intervals; a periodic income.

Anticipation, Principle of: The principle that states that value of real property is a function of the expected benefits of ownership.

Apartment: A dwelling unit within a larger building, designed to provide complete living facilities.

Appraisal: A supportable or defensible estimate of value as of a particular point in time.

Appraisal Date: The effective date of the appraisal identifying the market conditions existing when the appraisal was made.

Appraisal Process: A systematic analysis of the factors which influence the value of real property.

Appraisal Report: A report of the results of an appraisal which begins with the definition of an appraisal problem and leads to a specific conclusion using reasoning and relevant descriptive data.

Appraiser: The person who performs an appraisal.

Appreciation: An increase in value.

Approaches to Value: The procedures used by appraisers to derive value indications. The three fundamental approaches are (1) sales comparison approach, (2) cost approach and (3) income approach.

Appurtenances: Rights which run with the land and are thus real property rights, such as easements or mineral rights.

Arm's Length Transaction: A transaction arrived at between parties acting in their own interests in an open market, neither being under undue pressure.

Assemblage: The process of combining two or more parcels into a single unit, usually for the purpose of increasing utility of the larger unit and thus increasing value. *See* Plottage.

Assessed Value: The value established for property tax purposes. Often different from market value.

Asset: Anything of value which is owned, whether encumbered with liens or owned clear.

Assignee: One to whom rights are assigned.

Assignment: The process of conveying rights or interests, such as in a lease or other contract.

Assisted Housing: Housing for which the government provides assistance in occupancy, construction, or financing.

Assumable Mortgage: A debt which is capable of being assumed by a buyer of property. The mortgage instrument has no enforceable due-on-sale clause.

Assumed Mortgage: The purchaser assumes primary liability for payment of an existing mortgage. The seller remains secondarily liable for repayment unless specifically released from the obligation by the lender.

Attachment: Seizure of a property by the court to hold as security for a judgment which may later be obtained. Makes title unmarketable until removed.

Attorney in Fact: A person holding power of attorney to act for another.

Avigation Easement: The right to the use of air space above a property for the flight of aircraft, including the associated noises, etc.

Avulsion: The sudden tearing away of soil from the land of an owner by the action of water. Title to land so removed does not transfer during the year in which the owner has the right to reclaim his land.

Axial Theory: The theory that land uses develop in relation to the transportation axes that radiate from the central business district.

Backfill: The soil used to replace earth in an excavation, usually against foundations, etc.

Balance, Principle of: The principle which states that the point of maximum productivity and maximum value is achieved when all factors of production are in balance with one another.

Balance Sheet: A financial sheet showing assets, liabilities and net worth of an individual or business.

Balloon Payment: The unamortized principal amount of a mortgage which is paid off in a lump sum at the end of the term.

Band of Investment: A technique in which the weighted averages of capitalization rates attributable to the various components of invested capital are combined to derive an overall capitalization rate.

Basic Demand: The desire to buy; a measure of the total need for shelter; a function of population size and characteristics, representing the number of households needing housing.

Basic Industry: An industry which purchases and sells more goods or services than are consumed locally, bringing outside money into the local economy.

Basic Multiplier: The ratio of an area's total economic activity, e.g., total employment, to basic activities, e.g., basic employment.

Basis: In income taxation, the taxpayer's capital investment in the property. Also called cost basis or book value.

Basis Point: One one-hundredth of one percentage point. Written as .0001 decimally.

Bearing Wall: A wall that supports a part of the ceiling, roof, or upper floors.

Before-and-After Rule: Just compensation is measured as the difference between the value of the entire property before the taking and the value of the remainder, in eminent domain situations.

Before-Tax Cash Flow: An investor's cash flow from a property before that investor's tax liabilities are deducted.

Benchmark Property: A property typical for an area or location, the standard against which other properties are judged in determining accrued depreciation.

Beneficiary: The lender on a trust deed.

Blanket Mortgage: A mortgage which encumbers several properties.

Blight: Decay in a community caused by deferred maintenance in many properties or by negative social influences.

Blighted Area: A neighborhood or district suffering loss of property value because of negative and detrimental influences.

Bona Fide Sale: A sale made in good faith. Similar to arm's length transaction.

Book Value: The capital amount at which property is shown in the account books. Cost of acquisition, plus capital improvements, less depreciation allowed or taken.

Breakdown Method: A method of estimating accrued depreciation in which each type of depreciation is measured separately.

Break-Even Point: In real estate analysis, the point at which before-tax cash flow is zero, because effective gross income equals operating expenses and debt service.

B.T.U.: Abbreviation for "British thermal unit," a unit of heat measure. BTUs per hour rate the capacities of furnaces.

Building Code: A local or state regulation that controls the design, construction, materials, use, and occupancy of any building in its jurisdiction; enforced by police power in the interest of public health, safety, and welfare.

Building Line: The closest point to the street upon which a building may be placed, as established by local ordinance.

Building Residual Technique: A capitalization technique for estimating the value of the building alone, separate from the value of the land.

Bundle of Rights Theory: The concept that compares property ownership to a bundle of sticks with each stick representing a distinct and separate right of the property owner, e.g., the right to use real estate, to sell it, to lease it, to give it away, or to choose to exercise all or none of these rights. (AIREA).

Business Valuation: An appraisal of a business, to determine the present and future value of complete or partial ownership of the business.

Buydown: A lump-sum payment to a lender that reduces the interest rate on a loan for a period of time. The lump sum is usually added to the price of the property.

Buyer's Market: Many properties available, few buyers. Prices tend to decline.

Cap: A ceiling or limit on interest rate or payment changes which can be made as in an adjustable rate mortgage.

Capital Gain: Profit made in the sale of a capital asset.

Capital Improvement Plan: A schedule of capital improvement projects that a property owner (public or private) intends to complete over a specified period of time; includes project descriptions, schedule of priorities, cost estimates, and methods of financing.

Capitalization: The conversion of a future stream of income into current value.

Capitalization Rate: The sum of a Capital Recovery Rate and a Discount Rate; it is applied to any income stream with a finite term over which the invested principal is returned to the investor or lender. It is referred to as the "Installment To Amortize One" in compound interest tables.

Capital Loss: A loss suffered in the sale of a capital asset.

Capital Recapture Rate: The annual return of invested capital, expressed as an annual rate; also referred to as the Capital Recovery Rate.

Capital Recovery Period: The period of time during which an investor receives a return of invested capital.

Capital Recovery Rate: The annual return of invested capital, expressed as an annual rate; also referred to as the Capital Recapture Rate or Accrual for Future Depreciation.

Cash Flow: The balance remaining from net operating income of a property after deducting debt service.

Cash Throw-Off to Equity: A measure of before-tax cash flow derived by subtracting annual debt service from net operating income.

Casualty Loss Appraisal: An appraisal to establish loss in value due to fire, storm, etc.

Caveat Emptor: "Let the buyer beware." A doctrine that a buyer purchases at his own risk. Has little application in modern real estate practice.

Census Tracts: Relatively uniform areas of about 4,000 residents into which cities and adjacent areas are divided by the U.S. Census Bureau.

Certificate of Reasonable Value: A document required for a federally insured or guaranteed loan, most commonly a USDVA loan, that states the value on which the loan amount may be granted.

Certificate of Title: A certificate given to a property buyer, stating an opinion that title is good, based on a search of the records of title.

Chain of Title: A history of the title to property.

Change, Principle of: The principle which states that change is a fundamental characteristic of the real estate market, evidenced by continual shifts in supply and demand.

Chattel: Personal property.

Chattel Mortgage: A mortgage against personal property.

Chattels Real: Leasehold estates.

Class of Construction: Buildings are classified according to the fire-resistant qualities of their materials, e.g., structural steel, reinforced concrete, masonry, frame.

Climatic Zone: A section of the country with similar climatic conditions, commonly defined by the number of heating and cooling degree days.

Cloud on Title: Any doubt about the certainty of title which might make the property unmarketable.

Cluster Zoning: Zoning designed to preserve open space by permitting houses to be built in groups or clusters on smaller parcels than would normally be permitted.

Commercial Paper: Promissory notes written by a corporation and sold to other businesses for short-term funds.

Common Area: An area owned in common by the owners of the separate parcels of space in a condominium project.

Common Property: Land that is considered public or group property, in which all members of the group enjoy equal rights.

Community Property: Real or personal property owned by husband and wife together, unless taken in a different tenancy such as joint tenancy.

Comparables: Competitive property sales, rentals, or operating expenses used for comparison in the valuation process. Also called comps.

Comparative Unit Method: A method of estimating construction costs which involves grouping all the components together on a unit basis such as the cost per square foot of building area or the cost per cubic foot of building volume.

Competition, Principle of: The principle which states that moderate profits or benefits attract healthy competition; excess profits or benefits bring damaging competition, eventually reducing profits.

Compound Interest: Interest applied periodically to principal, earning additional interest on the accrued interest.

Condemnation: The legal process by which government exercises the right of eminent domain.

Conditional Sales Contract: A financing device by which a seller extends credit, conveys possession of the property, but retains legal title as security for the credit extended. Commonly called a "land contract."

Condominium: A real property estate consisting of a separate interest in the space within a unit, together with an undivided interest in the common areas.

Condominium Conversion: Conversion of rental properties (residential, commercial, office, or industrial) into condominium ownership.

Conformity, Principle of: The principle which states that a reasonable degree of conformance tends to maximize value; however, monotonous uniformity may result in a reduction in value.

Conservation Easement: An easement held by a nonprofit organization, limiting use of property to preserve natural areas, animal habitats, etc.

Consistent Use: The concept that land cannot be valued on the basis of one use while improvements to the land are valued on the basis of another.

Construction Loan: A short-term loan to finance construction of real estate improvements.

Constructive Notice: Notice to the world, presumed at law, based on the public records or on the rights of persons in possession of real property.

Contract: A binding promise, usually enforceable in court.

Contract Rent: The amount of rent contracted for in a lease. Compare with economic rent.

Contribution, Principle of: The principle that states that the value of a component depends upon how much its presence adds to or its absence detracts from the value of the whole.

Conventional Home: A home constructed on site, as distinct from a "manufactured home" or "mobilehome."

Conventional Loan: A permanent loan which is not made, insured, or guaranteed by an agency of the federal government.

Conveyance: A document which conveys an interest in real property, such as a deed or a lease.

Cooperative Apartment Project: An apartment building in which each owner purchases a share in the ownership of the property, along with a proprietary lease on a specific unit.

Cooperative Ownership: A form of ownership in which each owner of stock in a building or housing corporation pays a share of operating expenses and debt service on the underlying mortgage, which is paid by the corporation. The share is usually based on the proportion of the total stock owned.

Corner Influence: The increase in value that may accrue to a property because of its location at or near an intersection.

Corporation: An organization recognized at law as a separate entity, an artificial but legal person.

Cost Approach: The approach in appraisal analysis which is based on the principle that a prudent purchaser would not pay more for a property than the cost to reproduce it, provided that it could be reproduced without costly delay.

Cost Estimating: In appraisal, the estimation of the reproduction or replacement cost of an improvement. In construction, estimating the cost to build a structure based on the costs of all materials and labor and other essential expenses.

Cost of Development Method: A method of valuing undeveloped acreage. Development costs are deducted from the probable proceeds from the sale of the developed sites to estimate the maximum amount an investor would be warranted in paying for the land.

Cost to Cure: The estimated cost to eliminate accrued depreciation.

Co-Tenancy: A co-ownership of real property, as distinguished from sole ownership or tenancy in severalty.

Covenant: One form of private restriction, limiting the use of real property, usually running with the land, and which may affect its value.

Cul-de-Sac: A short street with one open end and a turn-around at the closed end.

Curable Depreciation: Items of physical deterioration and functional obsolescence that are economically feasible to cure at the time of the appraisal.

Curable Functional Obsolescence: The cost of replacing the obsolete or unacceptable component is at least offset by

the increase in utility and value resulting from the replacement.

Curable Physical Deterioration: Items which the prudent buyer would anticipate correcting upon purchase of the property; the cost to correct the item would not be more than the anticipated addition to utility and value associated with the cure.

Data: Information or facts, usually in numerical form.

Debt Coverage: The ability of a property to meet its debt service out of net operating income.

Debt/Equity Ratio: The ratio between an enterprise's loan capital and its equity capital. The ratio between the amount owed lenders and the capital account of shareholders or partners.

Debt Service: The periodic payment for interest on and retirement of the mortgage loan principal.

Decreasing Annuity: Net operating income that progressively and systematically declines over the income projection period.

Deed: A document which conveys title or some ownership interest in real property, effective when executed and delivered.

Deed Description: The statement of the legal boundaries of a parcel of land contained in a deed of conveyance.

Deed of Trust: A security device by which the owner (trustor) conveys "bare legal title" to a trustee, to hold in trust for the benefit of the lender (beneficiary), as security for a debt or obligation. Places a lien on the real property.

Deed Restrictions: Private limitations established in a deed and which run with the land, regardless of owner.

Defeasible Title: A title or estate which can be nullified upon the violation of a condition. The opposite of an absolute title.

Deferred Maintenance: Items which are in need of immediate repair or replacement as a result of neglect.

Deficiency Judgment: A judgment that in some situations may be granted by a court when the value of a property sold in foreclosure is inadequate to satisfy secured debt.

Demand: The desire or need for goods or services. The quantities of goods or services that are or will be bought by purchasers at a corresponding series of prices.

Demographics: The vital statistics of a population. In appraisal, a study of population changes (density, age distribution, income levels, etc.) in an area.

Depreciation: A loss in property value from any cause.

Depth: The distance between front and rear property lines.

Depth Tables: Tables showing estimated percentage changes in value as the depths of lots vary from standard depths.

Deterioration: Impairment of condition; a cause of depreciation that reflects the loss in value due to wear and tear, disintegration, use in service, and the action of the elements.

Development Cost: The cost to create a property and bring it to an efficient operating state, as distinguished from the cost to construct the improvements.

Development Procedure: A procedure for valuing undeveloped acreage that involves discounting the cost of development and the probable proceeds from the sale of developed sites.

Development Right: The right to build on or beneath a property, subject to local zoning, building codes, etc.

Diminished Utility: The difference between the reproduction cost new or the replacement cost new of the improvements and their present worth as of the date of the appraisal; also referred to as accrued depreciation.

Diminishing Assets: Assets that are periodically reduced by exhaustion, lapse of time, etc., so that their value must also be reduced; include mineral deposits, copyrights, franchises for limited terms, and similar wasting properties in which value loss cannot be arrested by expenditures, e.g., maintenance of tangible fixed property.

Diminishing Returns, Principle of: The principle that states that when successive amounts of one or more factors are added to a fixed amount of other factors, the resulting benefit, in dollars or amenities, first increases at an increasing rate, then increases at a decreasing rate, and finally decreases completely.

Direct Capitalization: Capitalization of a single year's net operating income with a single overall capitalization rate.

Direct Costs: The costs for labor and material devoted to a specific unit of work; direct costs include labor, materials, equipment and subcontractors' fees and charges.

Direct Sales Comparison Approach: That approach used in appraisal analysis which is based on the premise that an informed buyer would not pay more for a property than it would cost to acquire an existing property with the same utility.

Discount Point: One percent of the face value of a note, charged as prepaid interest.

Discount Rate: The rate of return on a real estate investment; the annual percentage rate that reflects the competitive rate of return on an investment; also known as the risk rate. (Do not confuse with the Federal Reserve Bank's "discount rate"—the interest rate charged to commercial banks.)

Discounted Loan: The amount advanced by a lender is less than the amount the borrower has contracted to repay.

Downzoning: A change in the zoning characteristics of a property which places greater limitations on allowable uses.

Due-on-Sale Clause: A clause in a mortgage instrument that authorizes a lender to call the loan upon sale of the property. Prohibits "assumption" or "subject to" sales without the lender's consent.

Easement: Nonownership interest held by one person in the land of another, allowing the first person partial use of the land for a specific purpose.

Easement Appurtenant: An easement which is appurtenant to (runs with) the dominant tenement, and which might significantly affect value.

Easement in Gross: An easement which is not appurtenant to any parcel, but which might affect the value of the servient tenement.

Economic Base: The economic activity of a community that attracts income from outside the community.

Economic Base Analysis: An analytical technique which uses the relationship between basic and nonbasic employment as a means of predicting population and income as they affect land uses and real estate values.

Economic Impact Statement: A statement of a project's potential impact on the local economy, e.g., business, occupational, and tax effects.

Economic Life: The period during which the improvements to land add value to the property.

Economic Obsolescence: The adverse effect on value resulting from environmental influences external to the property itself; also referred to as locational obsolescence.

Economic Rent: Market rent. Compare with contract rent.

Effective Age: The age of a similar and typical structure of equivalent usefulness, condition, and remaining life expectancy. The age indicated by the condition and utility of a structure.

Effective Area: The actual buildable area on a site as determined by setback requirements imposed by public and private restrictions.

Effective Demand: The desire to buy coupled with the ability to pay.

Effective Gross Income: The estimated potential gross income less an allowance for vacancy and income loss plus other income.

Effective Gross Income Multiplier: (EGIM) The ratio of sale price or value to effective gross income; used to convert a single year's expected or average effective gross income into an indication of property value.

Effective Rate: The actual rate paid on a loan or produced by an investment; it is derived by dividing the amount of the actual annual payments by the actual investment or loan outstanding.

Effective Tax Rate: The ratio between property tax and its market value; the tax rate times the assessed value divided by the market value.

Elements of Comparison: The characteristics of properties and transactions that cause prices to vary: financing terms, conditions of sale, market conditions (time), location, and physical characteristics.

Eminent Domain: The right of government to take private property for the public good with just compensation.

Encroachment: Unauthorized use of owner's property.

Encumbrance: Anything which affects or limits the fee simple title to or value of property, e.g., liens and/or restrictions.

Engineering Breakdown Method: A method of estimating accrued depreciation under which separate estimates are made for the individual components and then totaled.

Environmental Impact Study: (EIS) A study projecting the long-range environmental effects of a proposed land use.

Environmental Protection Agency (EPA): An agency of the federal government established to control and prevent water, are, and noise pollution and to protect the environment in general.

Equitable Title: The beneficial ownership of a property, held by the vendee in a land contract or by the trustor who has given a deed of trust.

Equity: The net value owned by the owner of a property, calculated by subtracting all liens or charges against the property from its total value.

Equity Buildup: The increase in the equity investor's share of total property value that results from gradual repayment of a mortgage loan, increase in total property value, or both.

Equity Capitalization Rate: The relationship between a single year's pre-tax cash flow (actual, projected, or average) and the equity investment; used to convert pre-tax cash flow into an equity value indication.

Equity Dividend Rate: The annual cash throw-off to the equity investment divided by the original amount of equity investment.

Equity Fund: A limited partnership or real estate investment trust (REIT) formed to purchase equities in real estate; typically formed to develop projects and purchase equity in existing projects.

Equity Participation: The right of the lender to receive a share of the gross profit, net profit, or cash flow from a property on which it has made a loan; an additional return to the lender to compensate for unusual risk or the effect of inflation on the real value of the return on capital.

Equity Ratio: The ratio of downpayment to total price; the fraction of an investment that is unencumbered by debt.

Equity Yield Rate: The investor's internal rate of return (IRR).

Escheat: Title to the property reverts to the state if the owner dies without leaving a will or heirs.

Escrow: The deposit of instruments and/or funds with instructions with a third neutral party to carry out the provisions of an agreement or contract.

Estate: In real property, a possessory interest.

Estate for Years: A leasehold interest for a fixed period of time.

Estate of Inheritance: A fee estate.

Evaluation: A study of the nature and characteristics of an investment in real property in which a value estimate is not necessarily required. A systematic procedure for the answering a client's question about the nature, quality, or utility of an investment in real estate.

Excess Land: The amount by which a parcel exceeds the standard size parcel in the market.

Excess Rent: The amount by which contract rent exceeds market rent at the time of an appraisal. It may require special treatment in the income capitalization approach.

Exchange: Equities in certain types of properties may be traded, often to defer the capital gains tax liability incurred in a sale.

Exclusionary Zoning: The effect of intentionally or unintentionally excluding racial minorities and low-income persons from a community.

External Obsolescence: An element of accrued depreciation; an incurable defect caused by negative influences outside the property itself.

Extraction Method: Estimating land value by estimating the contribution of the improvements to the improved property and deducting this amount from the total sale price.

Extrapolation: Projecting beyond the range of the date on which the calculation or estimate is based: projections into the future that presume a continuation of observed trends, patterns, or relationships.

Facade Easement: A voluntary restriction that prohibits an owner from altering the facade of an existing building, generally for preservation of historical structures.

Factor: One of the elements that contributes to a particular result; e.g., land is a factor in the value of an improved property, or location is a factor affecting property value.

Fair Housing Laws: Federal, state, and local laws that prohibit discrimination on the basis of race, color, religion, gender, sexual preference, or national origin in the sale, rental, etc., of real property.

Farmland: Land devoted to or suitable for agricultural production.

Feasibility Study: A study to determine the likelihood that a particular project will meet the economic objectives of the investor.

Federal Housing Administration: (FHA) The government agency established to promote homeownership and the renovation of residences by means of government-guaranteed loans to buyers and homeowners.

Federal National Mortgage Association (FNMA): A private corporation, originally a governmental agency, which purchases loans from primary lenders. The major secondary money market. Nicknamed "Fannie Mae."

Federal Reserve Board: The governing body of the Federal Reserve System; sets U.S. money and credit policy.

Federal Reserve System: The central banking system of the U.S., consisting of 12 Federal Reserve Banks, their 24 branches, and the national and state banks that are members.

Fee: An estate of inheritance in real property.

Fee Simple Estate: The greatest interest that one can have in real property. An estate that is unqualified, of indefinite duration, freely transferable and inheritable.

Fiduciary: A person in a position of trust and confidence, as between principal and broker. An agent, as a fiduciary, owes a duty of loyalty and faithfulness to his or her principal.

Field Appraiser: An appraiser who conducts research and inspections, analyzes data, forms value opinions, and prepares appraisal reports. Contrast to review appraiser.

Fill: Soil added in order to level land; can create severe construction problems without adequate compaction.

Final Value Estimate: The range of values or a single dollar amount that the appraiser states in the appraisal report, based on reconciliation of the various value indications.

Financial Statement: A statement that reflects the net worth (assets and liabilities) of an individual or business.

Fixed Expenses: Those expenses which tend not to vary with occupancy and that have to be paid whether the property is occupied or vacant.

Fixed-Rate Mortgage: A mortgage in which the interest rate does not vary over the life of the loan.

Fixture: An item which was once personal property, affixed to real property so as to become real property.

Flat: (1) A floor or story in a building. (2) An apartment on one floor. (3) A multifamily, residential structure containing a limited number of units, each with a separate, outside entrance.

Floor Area Ratio: The ratio between the total floor area of a building and the area of the lot on which it stands; a ratio of 2.0 indicates that the floor area of a building is twice the total land area. This could be a two-story building covering the entire lot, a 10-story building covering only ⅕ of the lot, etc.

Forced Sale: An involuntary sale, such as by a court order or by a trustee. Not an acceptable comparable in the market data approach.

Forecasting: Predicting future economic and market trends.

Foreclosure: Procedure whereby property pledged as security for a debt is sold to pay the debt in event of default in payments or terms.

Form Report: An appraisal report made on a standard form, such as the FNMA/FHLMC standard form.

Free and Clear: Unencumbered by mortgages or other liens.

Freehold: An estate of unlimited or uncertain time; a fee or life estate.

Front Foot: Property measurement for sale or valuation purposes, measured by the front linear foot on its street line—each front foot extending the depth of the lot.

Front Foot Cost: The cost of a parcel of real estate stated per front foot.

Frontage: The length of the boundary along the public thoroughfare that the property abuts.

Functional Obsolescence: The inability of a structure to perform efficiently the function for which it is currently employed.

Functional Utility: The ability of a structure to perform the function for which it is intended, according to current market tastes and standards; relates to architectural style, design and layout, traffic patterns, and the size and type of rooms.

Garden Apartments: Two or three-story, walk-up apartments built in a garden-like setting.

General Contractor: A person or business that supervises the erection of buildings.

Gentrification: Middle- and upper-income people purchasing properties in a lower-income neighborhood.

Goodwill: Expectation of continued public patronage, a salable asset of a business.

Government National Mortgage Association (GNMA, Ginnie Mae): A federally owned and financed corporation under the Department of Housing and Urban Development that subsidizes mortgages through its secondary mortgage market operations and issues mortgage-backed, federally insured securities. See also Federal

National Mortgage Association (FNMA).

Government Survey System: A system of writing legal descriptions of parcels based on U.S. government surveys.

Grant Deed: The basic transfer instrument used in California in the sale of real property.

Grantee: The person to whom property is transferred by deed.

Grantor: The person who transfers property by deed.

Grid System: The rectangular subdivision of property used in many American cities; designed to make a minimum amount of road surface accessible to a maximum number of individual parcels.

Gross Income: In the capitalization process, the total projected annual gross income without provision for vacancy or losses.

Gross Income Multiplier: The relationship between sales price and income, expressed as ratio.

Gross Leasable Area (GLA): The total floor area designed for the occupancy and exclusive use of tenants, expressed in square feet.

Gross Lease: A lease in which the lessor pays all or most of the property expenses such as taxes, insurance, and repairs.

Gross Living Area: A measurement of residential space. Local custom determines how and whether areas such as attics, basements, and garages are included in the calculation.

Ground Coverage: The percentage of a lot covered by ground floor building improvements. Compare floor area ratio.

Ground Rent: That portion of total rent attributed to the land.

Heavy Industry: Industries that are physically extensive or complex and usually require large tracts of land; e.g., steel mills, refineries, foundries, packing plants; also, industrial operations that produce hazards or nuisances, e.g., objectionable fumes, pollution, noise, vibration.

Height Density: A zoning regulation that limits the maximum height of structures within a given area.

Hereditaments: Property which can be inherited.

Highest and Best Use: The most probable, reasonable use which will support the highest present value as of the effective date of the appraisal; that use which provides the greatest net return on the investment over a given period; that use, from among the reasonably probable and legal alternative uses, found to be physically possible, appropriately supported, and financially feasible which results in the highest land value; that use which fully develops the site's potential; or the most profitable use to which a property can be put.

Highest and Best Use, Principle of: The principle that states that real estate tends to be put to its highest and best use in a competitive market over the long term.

Historic District: An area designated by local or state authorities to preserve its historic quality. May involve demolition controls, design review, tax incentives, etc.

Historical Cost: The cost of a property when originally constructed. The present owner almost certainly purchased at a price greater or less than historical cost. Historical cost may be relevant to tax basis, but rarely to appraisal.

Household: All persons who occupy one housing unit, whether house, group of rooms or a single room.

Housing Starts: New housing units, both single-family and multiple, begun within a designated period of time.

Housing Stock: Total inventory of dwelling units in an area, both owned and rented.

Hundred Percent Location: Location of commercial property that produces the highest land value or highest rent; the best location available.

Impounds: A trust account in which funds are held, usually by a lender, for the payment of property taxes and insurance when due.

Improved Land: Land that has been developed for use by some type of construction. Improvements may be buildings, or the land may simply be improved by grading, draining, utilities, etc., as distinguished from raw land.

Improvements: Buildings or other more or less permanent structures located upon or attached to land.

Incentive Zoning: A desirable public improvement or open-space objective is established by government officials and developers are offered an incentive, greater building bulk, to provide the desired amenity. Planned unit developments and cluster developments are forms of incentive zoning.

Income: Money or other benefits received periodically.

Income Approach: The procedure in appraisal analysis which converts anticipated benefits to be derived from the ownership of property into a value estimate.

Income Capitalization: The process of applying the appropriate annual rate of capitalization to the annual forecast net income for the subject property to derive an estimate of present worth or value.

Increasing Annuity: Net operating income that progressively and systematically increases over the income projection period.

Incurable Functional Obsolescence: Functional obsolescence resulting from structural deficiencies or superadequacies that the purchaser would not be justified in replacing, adding or removing because the cost to cure would be greater than the increase in utility resulting from the correction.

Incurable Physical Deterioration: Items which are not feasible or economically justified to correct, in terms of market conditions as of the date of the appraisal.

Indirect Cost: A property development cost usually figured as a lump sum percentage which is added to the direct cost of material, labor, and subcontracts. Examples include legal fees, administrative expenses of the owner during construction, etc.

Industrial Park: A controlled, park-like development designed to accommodate specific types of industrial uses in a setting, with utilities, streets, railroad sidings, water and sewage facilities, etc., provided.

Industrial Property: Land or buildings suitable for industrial use; includes factories, warehouses, etc.

Infrastructure: Services and facilities that are basic to urban functioning, such as utilities and transportation.

Inside Lot: A lot that is not located at a street intersection, and unaffected by corner influence.

Installment Note: A promissory note that provides for the repayment of the principal of a debt in installments.

Installment Sale: For income tax purposes, a sale in which a seller extends credit, and defers payment of all or part of the capital gains tax.

Institutional Property: Property owned and operated by the government or by non-profit organizations, such as, hospitals, schools, civic buildings, or museums; also properties of private institutions such as banks or insurance companies.

Insurable Value: The value of the destructible portions of a property, which determines the amount of insurance that should be carried.

Insured Mortgage: A party other than the borrower charges a premium to insure payment in case of default by the mortgagor. FHA-insured mortgages and private mortgage insurance (PMI).

Intangible Assets: Intangible personal property which would be considered in the appraisal of a business opportunity.

Interest Rate: The rate of charge for borrowing money. Also a rate of return on invested capital.

Interim Use: A temporary use of a site or improved property, in contrast to its highest and best use.

Interior Lot: *See* inside lot.

Internal Rate of Return: The equity yield rate on invested capital, based on discounted future returns from the investment, including the reversion from sale of the property at a selected date.

Inverse Condemnation: An owner's right to claim damages and receive compensation for loss in property value caused by government action when actual condemnation action has not been taken by the governing body.

Invested Capital: The original capital, invested in an enterprise plus any profits that have not been withdrawn, but allowed to remain and add the equity.

Investment Analysis: systemic examination of a prospective investment in comparison to other investment opportunities.

Investment Builder: A company primarily engaged in the construction of residential, commercial, and industrial property to be retained as investments.

Investment Value: The value of an investment to a particular investor, as distinguished from market value.

Involuntary Conversion: Property is converted into money through insurance proceeds or condemnation, when the property is destroyed in whole or in part, seized, condemned, or threatened by condemnation.

Inwood Annuity Capitalization: The use of compound interest tables to discount a level income stream to a present value.

Joint Tenancy: A type of ownership of property by two or more people with the right of survivorship.

Judgment Lien: A money claim against property, established by recording an abstract of judgment.

Judicial Sale: A forced sale of property through court action.

Just Compensation: In condemnation, the amount of loss for which an owner must be compensated. May or may not be the same as market value of the condemned property.

Land: The surface of the earth plus subsurface and suprasurface areas.

Land Contract: A contract for sale of real estate in which possession is delivered to the buyer, with title remaining vested in the seller until all conditions of the contract have been fulfilled.

Land Patent: A document by which government conveys title to public lands to an individual.

Land Residual Technique: A valuation technique which presumes that the improvements represent the highest and best use of the site; the building is usually valued separately from the land, and the annual return on the building value (return on and return of investment) is deducted from the anticipated net operating income of the entire property. The residual amount is said to be attributable to the land and is capitalized at the appropriate discount rate to indicate the land value.

Land Use Regulation: Legal restrictions, such as, a zoning ordinances, that control the use to which land may be put. Controls may be established by restrictive covenants, contained in redevelopment or urban renewal plans.

Land Use Study: An inventory of the parcels in a given area, and their patterns of use.

Land Utilization and Marketability Study (LUMS): An analysis of the potential uses of a parcel of land that is to be acquired in an urban renewal project; considers the entire market to be served by an area and the effect of the project on the area; used to determine what the highest and best use of the land will be when the development project is completed.

Land Value Map: An assessment or appraisal map that shows the value of land by location, expressed as value per square foot, per acre, etc.

Landlocked Parcel: A parcel of land that has no access to a road or highway.

Large-Lot Zoning: The practice of zoning large lots for single-family residence only; used mainly in rural and suburban areas to restrict the local environment and protect existing real estate values.

Lease: A contract which transfers the rights of use and occupancy of real estate from the owner to another person for a specified period of time at a stated consideration.

Lease Interest: The leased fee estate or the leasehold. A real property interests that results from the separation of the bundle of rights by a lease.

Legal Description: Identification of a parcel of land according to a recognized system established by law, e.g., assessor's parcels or recorded tracts, blocks, and lots.

Legal Nonconforming Use: A use that was lawfully established in the past, but no longer conforms to the regulations of the zone in which it is located.

Letter Report: A brief appraisal report that contains only a summary of the conclusions derived in a formal appraisal.

Leverage: The use of borrowed funds at a profit.

Liens: Money charges against property whereby the property is used to secure debts.

Liquidation Value: The price that an owner is compelled to accept when a property must be sold without reasonable market exposure, e.g., in a bankruptcy or condemnation proceeding.

Lis Pendens: A recorded notice that litigation (a lawsuit) is pending which may affect the title of the real estate involved.

Loan Maturity: The period of time over which the loan is to be repaid.

Loan-to-Value Ratio: The ratio of mortgage to property value, usually expressed as a percentage.

Locational Obsolescence: The adverse effect on value resulting from environmental influences external to the property itself; also referred to as economic obsolescence.

Loft Building: A multistory building with an open floor plan that is typically used for light manufacturing, warehousing, and sometimes offices studios, or residences.

Maintenance: Keeping a property in condition to function efficiently; expenditures made for this purpose. Not considered to extend the useful life of the property or increase its book value.

Market: A system which brings buyers and sellers together through the price mechanism.

Market Area: A geographic or political area in which properties effectively compete with the subject property in the minds purchasers.

Market Data Approach: Same as Direct Sales Comparison Approach.

Market Rent: The rental income that a property would probably bring in the open market, based on market data.

Market Share: The portion of a trade area's potential, e.g., retail sales to be generated, office space to be absorbed, that can be attributed to a proposed facility; based on known market strength and the property's position relative to comparable facilities.

Market Study: Analysis of the general market conditions affecting a property to be marketed, including levels of supply and demand.

Market Value: (1) The most probable selling price for the property, given a willing and able buyer and a willing seller.

(2) As defined by the California Supreme Court, market value is the "highest price, estimated in terms of money, that a property will bring if exposed for sale in the open market allowing a reasonable length of time to find a buyer who buys with full knowledge of all the uses to which the property is adapted and for which it is capable of being used, neither buyer nor seller being compelled to act."

(3) The highest price in terms of money which a property will bring in a competitive and open market under all conditions requisite to a fair sale, the buyer and seller each acting prudently, knowledgeably, and assuming the price is not affected by undue stimulus.

Marketable Title: Title to property that is free of objectionable encumbrances and liens.

Mass Appraising: Valuing a large number of properties in uniform order, using standard methodology, common reference data, and statistical testing.

Master Plan: The comprehensive, long-range plan and regulations that guide physical growth and development of a community. Also called city plan, general plan, or comprehensive community plan.

Mechanic's Lien: A statutory lien on a specific property for labor or materials contributed to a work of improvement.

Mobile Ownership: A building is not affixed to the land, but remains personal property that may be moved by the building owner.

Mobilehome: As defined in the B&P Code, "a structure transportable in one or more sections, designed and equipped to contain not more than two dwelling units to be used with or without a foundation system."

Modernization: Worn or outdated elements are replaced with their current counterparts.

Modular Construction: Entire rooms are constructed in three dimensions and shipped to site location, requiring very little on-site labor.

Mortgage: A legal document which conveys an interest in real property pledged as security for the payment of a debt.

Mortgage Banker: A person or company that makes loans with its own funds, usually to be sold in the secondary money market, and usually to be serviced by the mortgage banker.

Mortgage Broker: A person or company who, for a fee, brings mortgage borrowers and lenders together.

Mortgage Constant: The total annual payments of principal and interest on a level payment amortized mortgage, expressed as a percentage of the initial principal amount of the loan.

Mortgage Correspondent: One who acts as an agent for a mortgage lender, negotiating and servicing their loans.

Mortgagee: The one who advances the funds for a mortgage loan and in whose favor the property serving as security is mortgaged; the lender.

Mortgagor: The borrower; one who gives a mortgage as security for a loan.

Most Appropriate Use: The land use that is considered to be in the best interest of the community as a whole. May or may not be the same as the highest and best use.

Most Probable Selling Price: The price at which a property would most probably sell if exposed on the market for a reasonable time, under the market conditions prevailing on the date of the appraisal.

Multiple Listing: A listing taken by a member of a group of brokers organized so that each member of the group shares his or her listings with fellow members. Listings can be for sale or lease of property.

Narrative Appraisal Report: Full discussion of the appraisal problem, the property,

the market data, and how the analysis of that data leads to a given conclusion of value.

National Register of Historic Places: An official listing of national historic and cultural resources that are considered worthy of preservation. Established by the National Historic Preservation Act of 1966.

Natural Resource Property: A property with natural resources that can be exploited commercially, such as, rock, sand, gravel, clay, oil, gas, coal, metals.

Negative Easement: An easement that prohibits the owner of the servient tenement from doing certain things.

Neighborhood: A community or part of a community in which the inhabitants, buildings or business enterprises exhibit a certain degree of homogeneity.

Net In-Migration: The number of persons moving into a given area is greater than the number of persons moving out of that area over a specified period of time.

Net Operating Income: Effective gross income less the annualized operating expense equals NOI. The annual net income remaining after subtracting all fixed and operating expenses but before deducting financial charges such as debt service or recapture.

Net Present Value (NPV): The difference, between the present value of expected benefits, and the present value of capital outlays.

Nominal Rate: The contract rate on a mortgage or the apparent rate on an investment. It is derived by dividing the annual interest payment or income by the original amount of the loan or investment.

Nonapparent Easement: An easement that is not obvious on inspection of the premises.

Nonbasic Industry: An industry which produces goods or services for local consumption only.

Nonconforming Building: A building that was lawfully constructed, but no longer conforms to the regulations of the zone where it is located, because of a subsequent change in zoning.

Noncontributory Costs: Those excessive expenditures made to prepare the site for its intended use.

Observed Condition Method: A method of estimating accrued depreciation which considers and separately estimates the deductions for physical deterioration, functional obsolescence, and economic obsolescence; these estimates are then totalled and deducted from reproduction cost new.

Obsolescence: Loss in value due to reduced desirability and usefulness. Features may be functionally or economically obsolete.

Offsite Costs: Costs such as streets, sidewalks, curbing, traffic signals, water and sewer mains, excluding actual construction costs of the buildings. Also called common costs or offsite improvement costs.

Offsite Improvements: Improvements which add to the usefulness (utility) of the site but are not located directly on it. Examples: streets, curbs, drainage, sidewalks, lighting, etc.

Open Space: May be private open space adjacent to dwellings owned by individual residents, public open space owned by a government, or common open space owned by a community association and set aside for the use of residents.

Open Space Ratio: The ratio of open space to the total site or building area.

Operating Expenses: For appraisal purposes, those expenses necessary to a property and which continue the production of the effective gross income.

Operating Income: Income derived from the operation of a business.

Oral Report: An unwritten appraisal report.

Overall Rate: The forecast annual net operating income divided by value or sales price.

Overhead Easement: The right to use space at above the surface of the land for power lines, avigation, air rights, etc.

Overimprovement: An improvement to a site that is too large or too costly for the highest and best use of the land.

Partial Interest: Divided or undivided rights in real estate that are less than the whole.

Perpetuity: The state of being everlasting; without termination. In appraisal, the income projected for land is considered a perpetuity.

Personalty: Personal property. Any property which is not real property.

Physical Deterioration: The actual wearing out of a structure through age and use, resulting in a loss of utility.

Physical Life: The period over which the structure may be expected to remain in existence as a functioning entity.

Planned Unit Development (PUD): A development in which buildings are clustered or set on lots that are smaller than usual, and large open spaces provided. Individual properties are owned in fee, with joint (or sometimes public) ownership of open areas.

Plottage: Increase in value of several parcels of land when brought under one ownership, making possible a higher utility as a whole. Also known as plottage increment. *See* Assemblage.

Point: One percent of the contract or face amount of the loan.

Police Power: The right of the state to regulate the use of private property for the protection of the health, safety, morals, or general welfare of the public.

Potential Gross Income: The total amount of rental income, assuming 100% occupancy. It is usually determined by multiplying the rent per unit by the number of units.

Power of Attorney: Instrument used to appoint an attorney-in-fact.

Prescriptive Easement: Continuous open and unauthorized use of owner's property which may place limitations on owner's title.

Present Value: The present value of a payment or series of payments to be received in the future.

Preservation Easement: An easement in gross which prohibits changes in natural or historic properties.

Pro Forma Statement: A projected financial statement for real estate, based on certain specified assumptions.

Progression, Principle of: The principle which states that property tends to increase in value when surrounded by properties of greater value.

Property: Anything of which there may be ownership. Bundle of rights.

Property Residual Technique: A capitalization technique in which the total annual net income is capitalized at an overall capitalization rate to determine a value for property, both land and building.

Proprietary Lease: A lease coupled with an ownership interest such as in a stock cooperative apartment.

Purchase Money Mortgage: A mortgage given by a purchaser of real property to the seller or to a lender in part payment of the purchase price.

Quantity Survey Method: A method of estimating construction costs which involves computation of the quantity and quality of all materials used and of all categories of labor hours required, to which unit cost figures are applied to arrive at a total cost estimate for materials and labor. To this are added estimates for other contractor's costs such as permits, insurance, equipment rental, field office expenses, supervision, other overhead and a margin for profit.

Rate: A ratio expressed as a percentage on an annual basis.

Rate of Interest: The rate of charge for borrowing money.

Real Property: Land, all improvements on and to the land, and all appurtenances to the land.

Realtor®: An exclusive registered designation of members of the National Association of Realtors®, its State Associations and Local Boards. Some jurisdictions make a distinction between Realtors® (who must be licensed as real estate brokers) and Realtor-Associates® (who hold a salesperson's license). Other jurisdictions designate their members as Realtors® regardless of their license designation.

Recapture Rate: The annual rate of return of an investment.

Reciprocal: A number divided into 1. The reciprocal of 4 is 1/4 or .25.

Reconciliation: The process by which the appraiser evaluates preliminary indications of value and from them selects a range of final values or a single final estimate of value.

Regression, Principle of: The principle which states that property tends to decrease in value when surrounded by properties of lesser value.

Remaining Economic Life: The number of years remaining in the economic life of the structure or the structural component, as of the date of the appraisal.

Rent: Consideration paid for the use and possession of a property for a certain length of time.

Replacement Cost New: The cost to construct, at current prices, a building having the same utility as the subject building, but built with current materials, standards, design, and layout. Replacement cost new presumably eliminates all functional obsolescence and, therefore, the only depreciation to be measured is physical deterioration and economic obsolescence.

Reproduction Cost New: The cost to construct, at current prices, an exact duplicate of the improvement, using the same materials, construction standards, quality of workmanship, design and layout, embodying all the deficiencies, superadequacies, and obsolescence of the subject improvement. It is the estimated cost of a structure which has all the functional and locational obsolescence of the existing building, if any, but none of the physical deterioration.

Reversion: The lump sum return to the investor at the end of the holding period; the return of rights in real estate to the grantor or to the lessor.

Review Appraiser: An appraiser in a financial institution, government agency, etc., who examines the reports of other (field) appraisers for accuracy and quality.

Sales Comparison Approach: The market data approach to appraisal, also called direct sales comparison approach.

Secondary Mortgage Market: Market for the sale and purchase of existing trust deeds and mortgages.

Security Agreement: The financing device which creates or provides for a security interest in the personal property that is being used to secure the loan.

Segregated Cost Method: A method of estimating construction costs which uses the major functional components of the structure as the unit basis; also known as the trade breakdown or builder's method.

Service Industry: An industry which produces goods or services for local consumption only; a nonbasic industry.

Setback: The distance a building must be set back from the front property line, often established by zoning regulations.

Simple Interest: Interest paid on the remaining principal.

Sinking Fund: A fund set aside from the income of property which, with accrued interest, will pay for the replacement of improvements.

Site: A parcel of land which is improved to the extent that it is ready for its intended use.

Square Foot Cost: The cost of one square foot of an improvement. Used to estimate the reproduction or replacement cost new of a building.

Stratification: The division of the real estate market into many submarkets.

Substitution, Principle of: The principle which states that the value of property tends to be set by the cost of acquiring an equally desirable substitute property.

Superadequacy: Those elements, in terms of cost, quality or capacity, which are in excess of that necessary to perform the intended function.

Supply: The quantities of goods or services which sellers offer or will offer to sell at a corresponding series of prices.

Supply and Demand, Principle of: The principle which states that value will increase as demand rises and decrease as supply expands.

Surplus Productivity: After all other factors of production have been paid a competitive market return, the remaining income is attributed to the land.

Tender: The offer of performance, not performance itself; when unjustifiably refused, places another party in default and permits party making the tender to exercise remedies for breach of contract. An offer of money.

Title Insurance: Insurance to protect the property owner against loss if title is imperfect.

Topography: The surface features of an area such as hills, rivers, etc.

Townhouse: A single-family, attached dwelling unit, sometimes with party walls. A building design common in large cities.

Total Living Area: The width of a residential dwelling multiplied by its length multiplied by the number of stories.

Trade Breakdown Method: A method of estimating construction costs useing the major functional components of the structure as the unit basis. Also known as builder's or segregated cost method.

Trade Fixtures: Articles of personal property annexed to real property but necessary to carry on a business and are removable by the owner of the fixtures.

Trust Deed: A deed which establishes a trust; generally an instrument which conveys legal title to property to a trustee and states the authority and the conditions binding upon the trustee in dealing with the property held in trust. A trust deed is similar to a mortgage in that it may be used to secure a lender against loss.

Underimprovement: An improvement on a site that fails to develop the land to its highest and best use.

Undivided Interest: A fractional interest in the entire property.

Unit-in-Place Method: A method of estimating construction costs which involves estimating the installed unit cost of materials or component sections of the structure. It accounts for the cost of both materials and the labor to put them in place, on a per unit basis.

Useful Life: The period over which the improvement may reasonably be expected to perform the function for which it was intended.

Vacancy Rate: The relationship between the present or projected number of vacant units and the total number of units available.

Valuation: The process of estimating value.

Value: Measure of worth or desirability of a thing, usually expressed in monetary terms. See also market value.

Variable Annuity: Income which varies from one period to the next, over the income projection period.

Warranty Deed: A deed which contains express warranties of title, specifically that the title conveyed is a good title, free of all encumbrances except those specifically set forth in the document.

Zoning: Governmental regulations relating to the use of land. An aspect of the police power.